No Gods
and Precious Few
Heroes

Twentieth-Century Scotland

New History of Scotland series

No Gods
and Precious Few
Heroes

Twentieth-Century Scotland

Christopher Harvie

Edinburgh University Press

To Virginia

© Christopher Harvie, 1981, 1993, 1998

First edition 1981 in *The New History of Scotland* series
by Edward Arnold (Publishers) Ltd
and reprinted with corrections and additions 1987.

Second edition 1993 by Edinburgh University Press.

Third edition 1998 by Edinburgh University Press.

Reprinted with corrections and additions 2000

Transferred to Digital Printing 2007

Edinburgh University Press
22 George Square, Edinburgh

Typeset in New Baskerville, and
Printed and bound by CPI Antony Rowe, Eastbourne

A CIP record for this book is available
from the British Library

ISBN-10: 0 7486 0999 7
ISBN-13: 978 0 7486 0999 4

Contents

Introduction

On 11 September 1997, the Scottish people endorsed the creation of their first parliament in nearly 300 years. Europe's most pacific national movement would reach its goal on Hogmanay 1999, at the end of a century unparalleled in its bestiality, in which perhaps a third of a billion were slaughtered for 'reasons of state'. Scotland's world-openness impressed, but some echoes were less reassuring. In 1996 in Hollywood's version of the career of William Wallace, *Braveheart*, an American-turned-Australian actor of far right views conjured up the sort of martyr all too salient in postcommunist East Europe; Toronto trams bore adverts showing the shivering Edinburgh junkies of Irvine Welsh's *Trainspotting*.

A remarkable cultural renaissance marked the last two decades of twentieth-century Scotland, and earlier editions of this book were a minor part of it, insofar as getting history into order is basic to any cultural revival. Nevertheless it was written as a textbook, and the writer of a textbook must of course exercise selectivity: principles for this are necessarily subjective ones. Yet the book ought not to be an exercise in intellectual autobiography; personality and opinions must not obtrude, concealing or distorting evidence to further a case. The reader must gain a picture that corresponds in its general contours as much as possible to the reality of 'life as lived', in which the features are noted and discussed commensurately with their importance. 'Reality' may be a question-begging phrase, but statistics of agricultural production, and sequences of political events are not. If the index does not yield a basic range of factual information about such matters, the book is not serving its proper purpose.

Yet any landscape is seen from a point of view, and subjectivity accentuates particular features. My standpoint in 1981 was sombre and critical, and informed the structure of the book. In my chapter-divisions – the largely chronological treatment of World War 1, and then four parallel chapters on economy, society, politics, and culture, covering 1922–64, ending with a further two chronological treatments of 1964–79 and 1979–97 – I have foregrounded the theme of Scotland's industrial stagnation and eventual decline: from being by any standards a substantial world industrial power in 1914 to its present status as a highly-specialised part of global capitalism, as uncertain and afraid as any cognate region as this particularly tormented century expires. But ought I, perhaps, to have stressed the advance in living standards of the mass of Scots people that has, apparently paradoxically, accompanied this process?

I believe not. This advance has been common to all West European nations, and in most of them has been much more rapid than in Scotland, where until the late 1950s similarities to the pre-1914 era were probably greater than to Sweden or Switzerland. The expansion in well-being has been recent, and looks like being short-lived, while the industrial base remains in decay. It has, moreover, benefited only 77 per cent of those born in Scotland since 1911, the rest having emigrated. In 1911 Sweden's population was only 16 per cent greater than Scotland's; by 1970 this margin had widened to 55 per cent. Swedish gross domestic product per head was barely half that of Scotland in 1911: about £32 against about £62. By 1970 it was £1,812 against £709.

By such standards, Scotland's twentieth-century performance has been grim. If those excluded from the beanfeast of nineteenth-century capitalism – the working class, for example, and women – have been let into the restaurant at last, they have found a cleared table and a decrepit kitchen, and have lacked the organizational experience or cohesive ability to do much about this.

In 1981 I was deeply affected by the grand pessimism of Lampedusa's *The Leopard* (1957). I wasn't alone, given its influence on Allan Massie and on David Gilmour's superb biography *The Last Leopard* (1985). Lampedusa's Sicily eyed the challenge of Italian nationalism, but shifted in its sleep only sufficiently to breed a predatory elite. With a 1997 cabinet almost half composed of Scots – how predatory remains to be seen – this side of the equation is in place. But Scotland, in the rapids of successive industrial revolutions, seems remote from Sicily's rural *anomie*. We have experienced the life-cycles of three huge capital goods sectors – heavy engineering, oil, and most recently electronics – the pressures to adapt to wartime demands, the creation of one of Europe's most sophisticated financial centres, and in golf, field-sports and whisky, we have provided the internationally privileged with their recreations. In the 1980s it seemed that the experience had exhausted the country; in fact it had changed the agenda in such a way that the future of the union state was called into question.

So, if I am to admit to a point of view – largely acquired during writing, not a previous conviction – it is this: that the strength of the nationalist case and the weakness of nationalist politics are facets of the same issue. Nationalists have, I think, been less wrong about the Scottish economy than anyone else; on the other hand their gloomy diagnosis of its problems has to include the failure of Scottish society to sustain credible alternatives to restrictive class-loyalties and mediocre personnel, and to a secretive bureaucracy. A structure of distinctive Scots corporations – church, education, law, local and devolved administration – has effectively transformed organic discontent into a sequence of manageable complaints. By contrast, nationalist political organization, without an identifiable 'foreign' presence to react against, and usually milked of its talent by UK institutions, has always proved inherently unstable. MacDiarmid's words:

> To prove my saul is Scots I mann begin
> Wi' what's still deemed Scots and the folk expect,
> And spire up syne by visible degrees
> To heichts whereo' the fules ha'e never recked

suggest incipient lack of control as well as enlightenment — something evident in the history of nationalist politics as well as in his own remarkable career. There is much here that resembles the condition of *anomie* diagnosed by Emile Durkheim – self-destructive violence which follows the collapse of accepted social norms – and it is all the more intense because the norms that are collapsing are those, not of pre-industrial society, as in Durkheim's day, but of industrial society itself.

European nationalism, at least of the liberal sort on which Scottish nationalism has modelled itself, was seen as an instrument that assisted economic development while preserving social cohesion. Scottish nationalists have attempted, almost uniquely, to use their politics and community-centred ideals as a means of mitigating economic decline. If they have so far failed in this task, they can at least console themselves with the fact that the institutions of the UK have been no more successful.

I may have offered my nationalist friends a backhanded compliment, but that is simply a necessary personal statement. As an historian, my business is not to prescribe political solutions, nor to convey reassurance about the past, but to 'tell it like it happened', and not flinch from Thomas Hardy's injunction: 'If way to the better there be, it exacts a full look at the worse'.

Introduction to the Edinburgh Edition

As with the new edition of 1993, while constrained by the need to retain the original plates, I have been able to revise the tables, correct errors and alter some interpretations, and have remodelled the bibliography, chronology and index. The fact that the rubric 'place of publication is London except where otherwise stated' has vanished from the bibliography is a tribute to my historian colleagues and to the renaissance in Scottish publishing. Among others who have helped as hosts and informants over the last decade, I'd like to thank in particular Kenneth Morgan, Tom Gallagher, Graham Walker, William Storrar, Jay Brown, Hamish Fraser, James Mitchell and Jim Treble. And not least those friends in Scotland, writers and artists, whose verve and originality has diffused much of the miasmatic pessimism which enveloped my original introduction. We may not have reached our Indies – yet – but there are absorbing places *en route*, and we now have the energy to see them.

Christopher Harvie
Tübingen, September 1997

Acknowledgements

I would like to thank the staff of Edinburgh University Library, the Open University Library, the Mitchell Library, Glasgow, and the National Library of Scotland, the Public Record Office, Kew, and the Scottish Record Office, Edinburgh, for their aid in securing access to papers in their custody, and the *Scotsman*, in which sections of Chapter 1 originally appeared. My former colleagues David Englander and Angus Calder at the Open University, and Hans-Werner Ludwig of Tübingen commented on parts of the draft. Jenny Wormald and Christopher Smout read through all of it. For their comments, encouragement, and advice I am most grateful. Much of the research for the book was done while I was Visiting Fellow at the School of Advanced Studies, Edinburgh University, during the winter of 1978–9, and I am greatly indebted to Professor William Beattie and Margaret Jardine for their hospitality. Tom Nairn, Neal Ascherson, Gordon Brown, and Stephen Maxwell helped me kick ideas about, in the interstices of the devolution campaign and Ian MacDougall's splendid *Labour Records in Scotland* could not have been more timely. My parents not only sustained me beyond the call of duty but had to undergo frequent interrogations about their experience of recent Scottish history; so too did my friends Chris and Bob MacWhirter. My debt to their daughter, Julie Brotherstone, for her friendship and enthusiasm, cannot now be repaid. Her death early in 1981, after a brave struggle with a crippling illness, leaves all who knew her the poorer. Ethel Kriger and Birte Graper of the University of Tübingen typed much of the manuscript. My wife Virginia, besides making a home for me in three countries, cast a helpful eye over the proofs and organized the index. My gratitude to everyone. I hope the result justifies their efforts.

Christopher Harvie
Tübingen, 1981

The title of this book, No Gods and Precious Few Heroes, *is taken from Hamish Henderson's 'First Elegy', and is used by his kind permission.*

1

'When the Lamps Went Out' 1911 – 1922

I

In the summer of 1911 Glasgow hosted its third great exhibition. Elaborate Scottish vernacular buildings, in Kelvingrove Gardens, emphasized its 'patriotic and educational' aim of endowing a Chair of Scottish History at the University of Glasgow. Its predecessors of 1888 and 1901 had been cosmopolitan. Nationalism was now in the air. The Liberals, confirmed in power largely by the Scots in 1910, were about to legislate on Irish Home Rule; their Scottish Federation was committed to Scottish devolution. The 60-year schism in the Church was on the point of being healed; the land system was being reformed; Gaelic culture had been popularized by William Sharp, Marjory Kennedy Fraser, and Hugh Roberton's Orpheus Choir. Art and architecture, in the age of Rennie Mackintosh, John Burnet, the Glasgow Boys, and the Scottish Colourists, were both distinctive and internationally respected.

But was there a spectre at the feast? Between 1906 and 1908 the Clyde's output of ships slumped to 50 per cent of its 1905 tonnage. In 1910 and 1911 American competition cut the dividends of the North British Locomotive Company to 5 per cent instead of an anticipated 10 per cent. By 1913 German steel was being unloaded on the Clyde at under the Scottish cost of production. Such developments were ominous for an economy in which eight staple industries — in order of numbers employed: agriculture, coal-mining, shipbuilding and engineering, textiles, building, steel and fishing — produced about 60 per cent of its output.

Yet the Scottish economy was more than a specialized sector of the UK economy. It was disproportionately large for a start. With 10.5 per cent of the UK population, it produced 12.5 per cent of UK output. Its consumer goods industries still made distinctive furniture, pottery, and footwear; English mass-production and food processing still had to contend with the factories of the Co-operative movement. Scottish housing, whether two-roomed stone-built tenement flats, farm steadings, or miners' rows, was quite different from the two-storey brick cottages of England and was (as a Royal Commission was shortly to find out) much, much worse.

Yet Scots workers were, on the whole, better off. Only 1.8 per cent of those insured in 1913 were unemployed, against 8.7 per cent in London. More of them were skilled; possibly 80 per cent in Glasgow, mainly in the metal trades, and large groups in the printing, brewing, and papermaking trades of Edinburgh. Craft pride was reflected in an 'independence of mind', shared also by 150,000 miners and a like number of farmworkers. New tendencies, however, were appearing. In Aberdeen socialism had grown since the 1890s. In Dundee, virtually a single-industry town, whose huge jute-mills were facing increased Indian competition, there had been a Labour MP since 1910. In 1909 the miners' unions had affiliated to the Labour Party, and in 1911 and 1912 severe strikes in the docks, the mines, and on the railways seemed to indicate growing social polarization.

Agriculture and Fisheries

In 1910 agriculture, the fulcrum of modernization of Scottish society in the eighteenth century, contributed 17.2 per cent of UK output. Highly-capitalized mixed farms on the east coast contrasted with subsistence crofting in the Highlands. Rents had fallen by 30 per cent since the 1870s, but by diversifying into cattle and livestock, feedstuffs and pasture — in 1910 they grazed 15 per cent of Britain's cattle and 30 per cent of her sheep — Scottish farmers had fared well. However neither landowners nor substantial tenant farmers felt happy about the Agriculture (Scotland) Act, passed, after five years of struggle, in 1911. Although it set up a Board of Agriculture, it exemplified the Liberal party's commitment to the ideal of a free peasantry, by extending the rights of security of tenure and rent control enjoyed by 27,000 Highland crofters to a further 28,000 Lowland small farmers, permitting the creation of new holdings and the consolidation of existing ones.

Scottish fisheries had likewise been transformed into a major food-producing industry. In 1905 Scottish landings were valued at £2.7m., or 25.5 per cent of the UK total (over 33 per cent if Scottish landings in England are included). In 1911 fishing employed 34,390 men and boys, 25 per cent down on 1893. Productivity, though, had grown as steam trawlers and drifters had replaced sailing boats, and new rail-heads on the west coast enabled more efficient marketing. Besides the men, up to 50,000 women were also seasonally employed onshore, or followed the herring fleet round the coast in its annual migration to the East Anglian fisheries. Of its catch, 85 per cent went for export.

Textiles

Textiles, the motor of early industrialization, had coped with market changes and relative decline. In 1905 cotton was only 1.4 per cent of UK production, and woollens only 8.7. Linen, at 14 per cent, was established in small towns along the east coast, centred on Dundee and Dunfermline, while Dundee had an almost complete monopoly of British jute manufacture − and indeed consumed about a third of the jute imported into Europe. Its greatest days had been in the 1870s, but its magnates often owned and managed its Calcutta rivals. Foreign competition in other textiles was met by a variety of responses. In Paisley J.&P. Coats and J.&J. Clark amalgamated in 1896, to create a monopoly in thread-spinning. Other firms drew on this technology to expand the machine-weaving of lace in North Ayrshire. Woollens − chiefly based in the Borders and the Hillfoots area − tackled Yorkshire competition by concentrating on high-quality products, and carpet manufacturing, in Glasgow, Bonnyrigg, and Kilmarnock, proved an important development. All the textile industries were dominated by exports, chiefly to Europe and North America.

Heavy Industry

Exports also underwrote heavy industry − coal, iron and steel, ship-building, mechanical and structural engineering − concentrated in the Clyde basin and the Lanarkshire and Ayrshire coalfields. But the rich mineral endowment of these fields − nearly two-thirds of Scottish coal production in 1913 − was now within sight of exhaustion. Growth was switching to the large new mines of Fife and the Lothians, dominated by Sir Adam Nimmo's equally large Fife and Lothian coal companies, and to the fast growing trade − 10m. out of 14m. tons exported − with east Europe. This caused big port developments at Leith in 1903, Grangemouth in 1906, and Methil in 1907. The Scottish miner was efficient, producing an eighth more than the UK average, partly because of the electric coal cutter, pioneered by Anderson, Boyes of Motherwell. By 1913 this accounted for 21.9 per cent of output.

Coal exports — a reversal to primary production — were a dis-turbing sign, particularly as iron-smelting, a major market, was declining along with reserves of Lanarkshire 'blackband' ironstone. In 1913 this met only 25 per cent of Scottish demand, and, with obsolete plant, pig-iron output fell. Steel-makers had to use imported pig and scrap and, badly undercapitalized, lacked the modern equipment of Cleveland and South Wales, where 'hot metal' flowed from blast to steel furnace. In 1884 they produced 50 per cent of UK output; by 1913 only 33 per cent.

Shipbuilding, however, was at its zenith. The slump of 1906–8 shaken off, Clyde yards set a record of 757,000 tons and 1,111,000 horse-power of marine engines in 1913 (respectively 33.4 per cent and 49 per cent of the UK total), when all Germany produced only 646,000 tons and 776,000 horse-power.

Although the naval race had increased warship production, this still accounted for only about 10 per cent of total output. More worrying was the Clyde's lag in adopting the new technology of turbines, diesel engines, and welding, and its dependence on orders from Scottish shipowners, who then controlled 4.5m. tons, 27 per cent of the UK fleet.

Engineering, with an output valued in 1913 at £16m. and a work-force of 78,000, involved a wide range of industries — locomotives and rolling stock (where Glasgow had about a third of total British capacity), hydraulic equipment, steam engines, cranes, pumps, pre-fabricated buildings, and all sorts of structural work. The huge Singer plant at Clydebank, employing over 10,000, the Acme wringer fac-tory, and Barr and Stroud optical instrument factory were evidence that it included more than heavy industry, but the latter firms set the tone: their capital was low, their individual orders small, they relied on a skilled workforce rather than on rationalized production. Innovation wasn't lacking — with Pilcher and Denny's work on aeronautics, Burt's invention of the sleeve-valve engine, and Anderson's electric coal-cutter — but Scottish companies depended heavily on exports. The North British Locomotive Company, sending 48 per cent of its engines to the colonies, and 16 per cent to foreign markets, was probably fairly typical. Increased foreign competition and glutted markets (partly owing to improved engineering efficiency which lessened replacement orders) caused problems. The 'NB Loco's' sagging dividends were one aspect, Beardmore's were another. The greatest engineering conglomerate on Clydeside, it had to be bailed out in 1903 by Vickers, yet its dynamic managing director, William Beardmore, continually broke free of Sheffield tutelage, with attempts at diversification that were imaginative and innovative, but rarely profitable, even after the boost offered by the naval race after 1906. And financial and legal troubles bedevilled and ultimately ended Scotland's pioneer venture into volume car production, the Argyll Motor Company, which went into liquidation in 1912.

Money and Power·

The free market was crucial to pre-war industry. Shipbuilders still haggled with their workers, suppliers, and customers; Glasgow iron dealers still established world prices. Clydeside, and after it the whole Scottish economy, reacted sensitively to fluctuations in world trade and in the shipping freight market. Its great firms were family concerns; their values usually artificially low. Weir's of Cathcart, pump manufacturers, were worth only £60,000 in 1913; Colvilles, the Lanarkshire steel giant, only £280,000 in 1918. Amalgamation and joint-stock companies were still fairly rare − railways accounted for almost three-quarters of the money invested in Scottish industrial joint-stock companies in 1908 − although the North British Locomotive Company, created as a public company by the fusing of the three family firms of Neilson Reid, Sharp Stewart, and Dubs in 1903, with a capital of £2m., a workforce of 10,000, and the second largest locomotive building capacity in the world, was a portent.

In terms of power there seemed to be three Scotlands: the countryside where the gentry held sway; Edinburgh; and Glasgow, culturally further apart from one another than either was from London. Edinburgh was still dominated by an upper caste of the 'old professions' − law, religion, and finance − parasitical on the gentry and to an increasing extent on business, yet keeping the latter at arm's length. (As late as the 1960s the Glasgow Croesus Hugh Fraser was regarded by members of the New Club as 'a mere draper'.) More realistic, though badly flawed, were the plutocrats of the West and Dundee. Energetic, imaginative, and a bit vulgar, they had Corots hanging alongside Faeds in their lobbies, and steam yachts on the Clyde. The fathers had sacrificed everything to technical and economic success; their sons were more ambivalent. They might stick on in the business and marry into other industrial dynasties, like the Bilslands, Colvilles, Weirs, and Lithgows. Or shift from industry into finance, as did many a Dundee jute baron. Or sell out and move into genteel society, like the Tennants or the Clarks. Campbell-Bannerman was one of the few to choose parliamentary politics, for which the mid-nineteenth-century Scottish bourgeoisie had little time — although industralists seem to have absorbed themselves more and more in civic affairs, often to the detriment of their enterprises. Was the 'Westminster carpet-bagger' a response to this abstention? Or was the real inhibiting factor in political life the rigidity of the Edinburgh governing caste? Yet such a union of finance and industry was necessary if the autonomy of Scottish capitalism was to be preserved.

Uncertainty was not confined to the wealthy. Skilled craftsmen, the backbone of the heavy industrial workforce, felt increasingly threatened by new machinery and an expanding labour supply. More women were working, and more boys, who could be sacked on reaching adulthood. For many small-scale industries, facing foreign competition, this was a desperate remedy, but even in the shipyards and engineering shops, pneumatic and self-acting tools were being advocated by employers who had seen their competitors' works in Germany and America, while miners faced competition from immigrant labour, after 1900 from Poland and Lithuania rather than from Ireland.

II Pre-war Politics

Political Scotland existed on two distinct levels: parliamentary and civic. In nineteenth-century England parliamentary elections had supplied the citizenry, in John Vincent's words, with 'the circuses of their lives'. The Scotland of Gladstone's Midlothian Campaign was more serious, but the idea of politics as social drama was even more deeply entrenched. Parliamentary politics were about status, citizenship, religious equality, and, less sublimely, patronage. 'Constructive' legislation played a small part, but the cast was a high-grade one, and Scottish connections abounded. In 1910 nearly a third of the Liberal cabinet were Scots or sat for Scots seats. The prime minister, Asquith, sat for East Fife and had married into the Tennant family of Scots chemical magnates. Balfour and Campbell-Bannerman, his predecessors, had both been Scots; so were the Unionist and Labour leaders Bonar Law and Keir Hardie, and Labour's ambitious secretary Ramsay MacDonald.

Yet there seemed little organic connection between Scottish affairs and Westminster politics. 'Lads o'pairts', moving south to politics and the civil service, passed front-benchers moving north to comfortable

and undemanding Scots constituencies – Liberal front-benchers, that is.
Although the split over Irish home rule in 1886 had weakened the post-1832 Liberal hegemony in Scotland, it was restored in 1906, and extended at both elections of 1910, even though these saw English Liberal seats fall from 309 to 189.

In 1910 there were 779,000 electors and seventy-two constituencies, plus three University seats. Voting was by ratepayers, so sons living

Table 1.1: Scotland: Numbers employed in main occupations, 1907–1995 (in thousands)

	1907	1924	1935	1951	1976	1995
Agric. and Fisheries (incl. farmers)	237 (1901)	220	203	167	84	39
Mining	132	150	94	120	35	4(38*)
Manufacturing total:	622	485	420	767	608	319
Iron and Steel	{231}	61	52	66	39	5
Engineering		130	98	293	258	135
Textiles	141	122	114	123	57	35
Food and Drink	71	59	66	96	91	{56}
Other Manuf.	179	113	90	189	163	
Construction	81	64	44	136	171	122
Remaining occupied pop. (mainly in service indust.)		c.402	c.609	1,011	1,208	1,480
Total occupied pop.	(1,982 in 1901)	1,321 (1923)	1,370 (1936)	2,201	2,106	1,998
Unemployment rate (as % of insured employees)	(3.7 UK)	14.3	21.3	3.1	6.9	8.1
UK unemployment rate		(11.6) 1923	(15.3) 1950	(1.5)	(5 7)	(8.2)

* Including all energy industries.
Notes: Estimated figures in italics.
Sources: 1907–35 from Census of Production; on agriculture and fisheries from *Scotland's Industrial Future* (1939); 1951 from Cairncross, ed., *The Scottish Economy* (1953) and 1976 from Department of Employment statistics. The total for 1901 is taken from the census returns, and is not comparable with the other totals.

at home and most lodgers were effectively excluded, while busi-nessmen had two votes. Such inequalities may have accounted for the conservatism of Scottish politics; they probably allowed Scottish Unionism to survive. It was only really healthy in the south-west and in a few city suburbs. The ascendancy it had briefly gained in the central belt, by recruiting the Orange vote, and (in 1900) the Catholics as well, was curbed by the end of disestablishment as a political issue (which neutralized the Church of Scotland) and the unpopularity of Tariff Reform in an exporting area.

The Liberals could draw on a solid tradition of support in east-coast burghs and counties and in the Highlands, where what the young Tory candidate John Buchan called their 'tribal incantations' of free trade, religious equality, and land reform still resounded. Provosts and local solicitors were still the power-brokers, the 'New Liberalism' seemed distant, and, unlike England, there had been no concordat between Liberals and Labour in 1906. What, then, caused Liberalism's con-tinued success? Hostility to the aristocracy seems a plausible explana-tion in the counties, and the 'causes' of the People's Budget, the Parliament Act, and the Pentland Land Act are consonant with this. But in the towns? Old sectarian loyalties remained powerful, but waters were moving disturbingly under the ice. The Miners' Federation affiliated to the Labour Party in 1909. Labour gained three seats – West Fife, Dundee, and Glasgow Blackfriars – in 1910. A lot of the idealism which, in England, went into the New Liberalism, was passing into heterodox but interlinked radical groupings, from the home-rulers of the Young Scots to the 10,000-odd readers (mainly Independent Labour Party) of Tom Johnston's *Forward*, while the government attempted to conciliate trade union-ism by reforming its legal status, and setting up Royal Commissions into housing and railways. By 1914, in response to union and woman suffragist pressure, a further reform bill was in prospect, yet neither the home rule bills moved in 1913 and 1914, nor the attempts to co-ordinate socialist activity, made much impact. Socialism and Liberalism were on the defensive; the Unionists won 4 out of 15 by-elections, 1910–14. Under pressure of the Ulster crisis, a revival of Unionism seemed imminent.

Perhaps this upheaval reflected a more fundamental institutional shift. Until 1906 the politics which actually affected Scots people's everyday lives had been civic ones: the affairs of the great cities (37 per cent of the population), of the burghs, and 900-odd parishes. These traditional units had, during the nineteenth century, continually acquired new powers. The process of rationalization had yet to begin. The parishes, not Poor Law Unions, controlled poor relief; and, unlike in England after 1902, remained the unit of education. The result was that the dominance of local élite groups was maintained: landowners, farmers, ministers, and schoolmasters in the parishes; businessmen, rentiers, and shopkeepers in the burghs. After the 1860s this élite had extended the interventionist powers of local government to cope with the social pressures of industrialization and to contain the urban working class, until a 'civic consciousness' had been created which endorsed, both in the theory of such as Edward Caird and Patrick Geddes, and in the practice of bodies like the City of Glasgow Improvement Trust, extensive measures of 'municipal socialism'. Much of this ideology was also common to the 'labour aristocracy' and even to the socialist movement, although it stopped short of any intervention which seriously affected the distribution of wealth and power. Yet it was under stress — from the lack of civic power to tackle housing, the most obdurate city problem, from the growing insecurity of skilled labour, and from the developing power of the state.

III Scottish Government

The suture between parliamentary and civic politics was the Scottish administration. Scarcely 'Dublin Castle' — with no Viceroy or separate exchequer — this operated from offices at Dover House in Whitehall and in Edinburgh. Through the Scottish Office, the Secretary for Scotland, a somewhat lowly member of most cabinets since 1885, dealt with political organization, patronage, and a range of Home Office affairs; he was also president of the Scotch Education Department, answered for the Boards (supposedly representing Scottish interests) of Agriculture and Fisheries, and Local Government, and, more tentatively, for the Lord Advocate's Department, which covered Scots Law.

The Secretary had usually been a peer, but Lord Pentland's Agriculture Act meant that his successors virtually had to sit in the Commons to handle questions and interventions, over a third of which were on agriculture, and about 10–12 per cent each on fisheries, housing, and public health. Otherwise his portfolio was limited; his control was strong in education but weak in local government and in industrial affairs, liaison with the Board of Trade being minimal. Much routine private bill legislation had been devolved to Commissioners in Edinburgh, and the Lord Advocate maintained a jealous control over such legal business: the Secretary only gained official precedence over him in 1912. He was still politically rather than administratively important: he reassured Scottish MPs — organized since 1907 in their own Grand Committee for non-controversial legislation — that the Cabinet was aware of Scottish issues, and after 1906 he kept the Scottish Liberal majority loyal to the premier. Pentland was Campbell-Bannerman's confidant, MacKinnon Wood a loyal Asquithian, and H.J. Tennant Asquith's brother-in-law. Most of the Secretary's year was spent in the south, with a trip around the Highland coast in the summer on a fishery cruiser. The 1914 trip did not take place.

IV Business as Usual?

War broke out on 4 August. The state assumed control of the railways, enemy ships were impounded and aliens interned. The Territorials — of whose 14 divisions Scotland supplied 2 — were mobilized. John Reith (later Viscount Reith), one of their officers, recalled that, for the first time, they were cheered instead of catcalled in the Glasgow streets. Not all wanted to be mobilized: the north-east was strong territorial country, but the war coincided with the harvest and the height of the fishing, and — so Joe Duncan reported in *Forward* — there was more enthusiasm for home defence than for avenging the wrongs of Belgium. Even Reith's battalion would only serve abroad as a unit. Fears of invasion abounded — troops guarded strategic viaducts; east coast towns put up barricades; the Shetland police force arrested all the staff of Lerwick Post Office — not without reason: Rosyth dockyard was still not completed; there was no boom on the Forth, nor on the entries to Scapa Flow. On 22 September German submarines sank three old cruisers off East Anglia and Admiral Jellicoe, First Sea Lord, ordered the Grand Fleet from the Nore to Scapa — then south-west to Lough Swilly. On 27 October the new dreadnought *Audacious* hit a mine and sank. Although the attack did not come, the Admiralty, in order to tighten its blockade of Germany, commandeered most of the larger ports on the east coast.

Meanwhile, after a disorganized start, the recruiting of the volunteer army — Ian Hay's *First Hundred Thousand* — began. Industrial districts and the Highlands alike responded enthusiastically, most employers promising to make up wages to peacetime levels. The percentage per head taking the colours in the new 'pals' battalions' was the highest in Britain. In Glasgow James Dalrymple, the autocratic manager of the Corporation Tramways, made his system a giant recruiting office and furnished a Highland Light Infantry battalion from Tramway staff alone. The army waived height restrictions and accepted 'bantam battalions' of tiny, tough Glaswegians. Of the 157 battalions which comprised the Regular Army, from which the British Expeditionary Force was formed, Scottish regiments accounted for 22. They made up a seventh of the Territorial Army, and almost a sixth of the 'first two hundred thousand'. About 9 of the 70 divisions which would be created by the end of the war comprised Scottish regiments, although by then — their usual two battalions swollen to 15 or 16 — their local identity had ceased to count for much.

The 'pals' could not foresee their slaughter by the thousand on the Somme in mid 1916 and at Ypres in 1917, but spent an idyllic autum training in southern England, strange and wonderful to boys from Glasgow machine shops or, like the famous 'Spud Tamson', from the 'barras'. The Scots battalions were the more distinctive for the relative absence of caste differences between officers and men; in England commissions were almost entirely confined to public school boys.

The wartime threat to an exporting economy soon came to the fore. The *Scotsman* reported panic in Border tweed and Highland tourism, and redundancies in the paper mills. Unions protested that ladies knitting socks for soldiers would drive even more out of work. The Berwickshire Hunt philanthropically decided to carry on hunting, 'to account for foxes, to have the young hounds properly entered, and above all, by keeping on the establishment, to avoid adding to the ranks of the unemployed'. By mid August the Local Government Board had met to propose relief schemes of public works, while a fund for the unemployed had raised £20,000 from Edinburgh and £12,000 from Glasgow, whose former provost, Sir Daniel Stevenson, urged employers to fill up vacancies caused by recruits, and the corporation to accelerate public expenditure programmes.

This panic soon abated. The Germans were turned back on the Marne; the stalemate of the trenches began. 'Business as usual' was now to reign until the carnage of the mid-1915 offensives. At Hogmanay its tone was accurately caught by the Unionist MP Sir William Raeburn in the *Glasgow Herald*:

> The war has falsified almost every prophecy. Food was to be an enormous price, unemployment rife . . . revolution was to be feared. What are the facts? The freight market . . . is now active

> and prosperous . . . . Prices of food have risen very little, and the difficulty at present is to get sufficient labour, skilled and unskilled. We have not only maintained our own trades, but have been busy capturing our enemies'.

War brought its own equilibrium. On the debit side, some raw materials and markets were cut off; enlistment reduced the labour force; government borrowing and purchasing increased inflation, insurance premiums escalated. Investment was switched to war *materiel*; the government controlled ports, railways, and ships; enemy attacks began to take their toll. But, on the other hand, imports of manufactured goods from enemy countries were cut off, and they were eliminated as competitors in other markets. Substitutes for imports were demanded, along with war contracts; there was less unemployment but also more opportunity for dilution and rationalization, and a substantial rise in profits. The 'impact of total war' was to be long in coming and the traumas it caused when it came were partly attributable to this equilibrium, and the need to change it.

Few protested against the war. Once Belgium was invaded, the Liberal pacifist movement, so nearly led by Lloyd George himself, was dispersed; the old Scottish radical and jurist James Bryce, one of its potential leaders, was to chair the committee that publicized 'German atrocities'. The newspapers, the Unionist and the vast mass of the Liberal party, and the churches, were totally pro-war; opposition was confined to the socialist left (although *Forward*, its main organ, reflected the division of opinion in the Labour Party), to one or two ministers in the United Free Church, and to a few Liberals, notably Sir Daniel Stevenson, who supported efforts in December 1914 to found the Union of Democratic Control, subsequently a meeting point for dissident radicals and anti-war socialists.

V Disruption

'Business as usual' complacency, which Raeburn exemplified, was understandable. The new army battalions did not see action until Loos in October 1915; casualties, though severe, were still only a fraction of what was to come. A sense of unreality pervaded the process of adapting to war production. The first problems — affecting the main institutions of Scottish finance, and some though not all industrial sectors — were mainly caused by disruptions to imports and exports and the financial system. The most obvious result, oddly, was an assimilation to Scottish banking practice. On 6 August 1914 pound notes, which had always circulated in the north, supplemented gold sovereigns in England. Otherwise the City of London rapidly took over control. The eight banks — the Bank of Scotland, the Royal Bank, the British Linen, the National, the Commercial, the Union, the Clydesdale, and the North of Scotland — were still Scottish-owned. Their ruling 'conference of general managers' got them to subscribe generously to the War Loans, and, in response to the Bank of England's fear of the High Seas Fleet staging a 'gold raid', shifted their bullion south. The investment trusts used their huge stakes in American railroads, mining companies, farms, and real estate as security for government loans in the US, or sold them to buy government stocks.

Textiles were hit immediately by the rise of 30–40 per cent in freight and insurance charges, and by the invasion of Belgium. The first town to fall was Verviers, the main source of yarn for the Border tweed industry. Substituted Yorkshire yarn wasn't good enough. Border machinery found it difficult to handle khaki (which was 50 per cent shoddy). Trade slumped and stayed down. The closure of the Baltic was likewise disastrous for linen, pushing the price of flax up by 65–75 per cent. The jute situation was more complex. The demand for sandbags was huge, while German commerce raiding checked the supply of jute and the products of Calcutta. Dundee was hit by a profiteering wave: spinners charged the inflated market price for yarn, but used jute bought at pre-war prices. Their profits soared to 56 per cent, while those of the weavers — subject to government price control — stayed at around 10 per cent. The only way of ensuring equity was for the War Office to organize the whole process, which it did after 1 June 1915. Since by 1918 a thousand million sandbags were to be shipped to the fronts, this early experiment had far-reaching consequences in the development of state control.

War affected the coalfields instantaneously. The German market — 2.9m. tons — was lost, and took the Baltic market with it. Substitute markets, hitherto served from Belgium and northern France, might have been found, but a second disruption supervened. Because of Rosyth's unavailability — until May 1916 — the Admiralty requisitioned the Forth coal ports. By 1918 exports had fallen away to under 2.5m. tons. Although, boosted by the demand for steel for munitions, production in the western coalfield was kept up, the troubles of the eastern field were rapidly reflected by the recruitment of miners into the forces. Scotland had the highest percentages in Britain: 26.5 per cent compared with 22.9 per cent in England and 22.5 per cent in Wales. But over 36.5 per cent of East Lothian miners were in uniform by August 1915, compared with barely 20 per cent in Ayrshire. With the coalowners guaranteeing (at least initially) to make up the difference between army and civilian earnings, there was obviously a strong incentive to enlist — where the alternative was parish relief.

Enlistment resulted in a serious decline in efficiency, as the remaining miners were less skilled, older, or less fit. By November 1915 the Government effectively shut off recruiting and in February 1916 its Coke and Coal Supplies Committee was set up to make the Scottish coalfields self-sufficient. This was not ultimately achieved until September 1917, when zoning of markets was introduced, and railway wagons were pooled and regulated. Government attempts to control prices were less successful. The limitation of home prices in July 1915 simply meant a switch to exports, and although regulation by local committees was ultimately achieved this was not effective until late 1917. Fundamental disruption had been caused to the industry. Manpower was depleted, the more productive eastern coalfield starved of capital and transport, and vital markets lost — as matters turned out, for good.

For fishing the war was from the start disastrous. The herring industry saw two-thirds of its market, in Germany and Russia, vanish. Exports had reached Russia through Germany, and efforts to export via Archangel largely failed. So, few fishermen refused direction into the Royal Naval Reserve, and by 1918 about 25,000 fishermen out of nearly 40,000 were thus employed, with 302 steam trawlers, 838 steam drifters, and 100 motor drifters.

The Highlands, a neglected backwater for so long, suddenly became the scene of frenzied activity. The anchorages of Scapa Flow and Invergordon had been designated in 1912 as out-stations to Rosyth; they became fully protected bases late in 1914. Their importance increased with the Northern Barrage project of 1917 for a continuous mine-field between the Shetlands and Norway. Over the metals of the single-track Highland Railway north of Perth thousands of special trains carried coal, sailors, mines, and ammunition; they returned south with the trees of Highland plantations, chopped down by the Canadian Forestry Corps. In mid 1916 the whole land-mass north and west of the Great Glen became a 'restricted area', which the traveller needed a pass to enter (Richard Hannay fell foul of this in John Buchan's *Mr Standfast*). Behind this new frontier places like Invergordon (population 1,110 in 1911) grew sevenfold. The aluminium works at Kinlochleven and Foyers underwent rapid expansion; in Raasay low-grade iron-ore was mined, railways and blast furnaces built, later to remain for decades as bizarre ruins.

Thus, leaving recruiting and armaments production aside, 'business as usual' was an illusion, bred of military complacency and the supineness of the Asquith government. A rational adjustment to war production was equally impossible. The machinery simply didn't exist, and its ethos was utterly remote from Scottish *laissez-faire* — a situation dramatized by the Jacks case, of June 1915. Partners of a Glasgow iron firm run by Andrew Bonar Law's brother were found guilty of supplying ironstone to (*inter alia*) Krupps in the early weeks of the war. The case was complex but it seems that the Lord Advocate may have been persuaded to drop charges against John Law, whose brother joined the government on 23 May. The relevant papers are still kept as confidential in the Scottish Record Office, but Bonar Law subsequently wrote that the firm's action would have been repeated by 99 out of 100 businessmen.

To the far-sighted, and notably to Lloyd George, Chancellor of the Exchequer in 1914, the drastic use of state power both in the industrial and social field was essential. In 1915 this was to result in accessions of power both to the Scottish Office and to the business classes, via the new Ministry of Munitions, and this challenged many of the institutions of Scottish politics.

VI 'The Red Clyde'

By 1917 some 250,000 men and women were producing munitions in Scotland. The government had invested over £11m., mainly in the vast explosives works at Gretna, but the Clyde Valley had the biggest concentration of production in the United Kingdom. Here 'munitions' — meaning all war *materiel*, from boots and blankets to tanks and battleships — inevitably expanded the heavy industries above all else, rapidly dispelling August 1914's fears of mass-unemployment. As the *Glasgow Herald* reported in December, when over a seventh of the workforce of the shipyards had enlisted: 'Now their greatest difficulties are those of obtaining sufficient labour, even at the high wages now ruling, and sufficient materials even at the equally high prices which are charged'. The Admiralty, which assumed overall control of the shipyards, experienced few problems. Production (an average of 520,000 tons) was never as high as in the pre-war peak of 1913, but warships required powerful engines and horsepower output rose by 58 per cent between then and 1918. Along with gun and shell demands, this multiplied problems for the engineering industry, which was losing skilled labour both to the front and to the shipyards. Management became determined on a drastic programme of modernization and rationalization.

The scene was thus set for the legendary episode of the Red Clyde. Left-wingers came to equate events in wartime Glasgow with Russian Bolshevism and the French army mutinies — both 1917 — and the German revolution of 1918, as part of a Europe-wide communist *démarche*. The problem was: why had it not been successful on the Clyde? Its leading figures, particularly that of the Glasgow schoolmaster Marxist John Maclean (1879—1923), briefly Soviet consul in Glasgow in 1918, have come to be venerated. Fifty years later, nuclear disarmers and nationalists alike would sing Hamish Henderson's 'Freedom Come All Ye' (1949):

> When Maclean meets wi' freens in Springburn
> Aa the roses an geans will turn tae bloom,
> An a black boy frae yont Nyanga
> Dings the fell gallows o' the burghers doon.

The Second Coming apart, there was a serious issue of Marxist politics here. Clydeside, 1914—18, showed an apparent convergence of Marxist political theory with industrial fact. A crisis-ridden capitalism's attack on the identity of the skilled workers — their 'actual humanity' — had coincided with their consciousness of their power and position: the classic situation of 'praxis'. Clydeside, a key arms production district where skilled workers were in a majority, should have provided a powerful lever for revolution. As such, its problems have never lacked committed historians, who see in it either useful morals for contemporary industrial struggles or else a terrible wrong turning — a socialist and nationalist revolution betrayed by orthodox Labourism.

But — was there ever actually or potentially a revolutionary situation? This would have needed (1) capitalists determined to use the war situation to solve peacetime industrial problems by 'dilution' — mechanizing work and reducing the element of skill; (2) militant and class-conscious activists consistently mobilizing support among a widening labour force; (3) government losing control both over public morale and public order. There was certainly evidence — at times — of all three. There was a serious industrial problem. Government, latterly,

became badly rattled. Selective quotation can produce a scarlet fer-
ment. During the Forty Hours' strike in February 1919 the Scottish
Secretary Robert Munro, for example, informed the Cabinet that 'in
his opinion it was more clear than ever that it was a misnomer to call
the situation in Glasgow a strike — it was a Bolshevist rising'. Even
more blood-curdling reports found their way south from the military
intelligence outfit of Sir Basil Thompson. The treatment of John
Maclean bears out a sense of panic. What is lacking, however, is a
consistent and developing pattern of working-class resistance and
leadership. In fact, beneath the rhetoric of both sides, actual conflicts
were episodic and widely separated in time, occupying in all only a few
months in the space of eight years. They consisted of:

1. The 'tuppence an hour' Engineers' strike of February 1915.
2. The Fairfield Strike of August 1915.
3. The rent strike of October –November 1915.
4. The imposition of dilution in Glasgow engineering shops,
   January–April 1916, culminating with the deportation of the
   shop stewards.
5. Then (after a gap of nearly three years, when the Clyde was
   practically free of industrial trouble) the Forty Hours' strike of
   January–February 1919.
6. The election of November 1922, at which 10 Labour MPs were
   returned in the 15 Glasgow constituencies, of whom James
   Maxton and John Muir had been prominent in the industrial
   and anti-war campaigns. These subsequently represented a
   fundamentalist socialist group in the Labour ranks.

However, when such episodes of conflict are examined, even this
limited consistency gives way. The situation becomes complex, individual crises and personalities become important. And the key figure
was not from labour but management: William Weir (Viscount Weir,
1877–1959), the managing director of G. & J. Weir Pumps of
Cathcart, who became munitions controller in Scotland on 13 July
1915. He was young and innovative, but was he the most appropriate
appointment? Responding to engineering's problems, Weir was
already familiar with new American labour-saving machinery and
'Taylorist' scientific management. He wanted wholesale industrial
reconstruction, and saw the war facilitating this:

The shortage of men now, and still more after peace, is giving

their chance to working women, and even to boys and girls. In
regard to our workers, whatever the unions may do, and not-
withstanding any guarantee given, employment can and never
will be the same again.

If this, in the *Scots Law Courts Record*, wasn't by Weir, it certainly
reflects his attitude. It wasn't shared by the rest of Clydeside management — with the possible exception of Beardmore — which treated
its periodic clashes with its workforce as a fact of life. But the war gave
the innovators their chance. It also injected into their attitudes an
aggressive, and genuine, element of moral fervour — Weir gave all
his firm's war profits to charity — of the same sort that took Reith into
the trenches. So when, in January 1915, the engineers threatened to
strike for tuppence an hour, his response, in a pamphlet *Responsibility
and Duty* of 30 January 1915, was scarcely tactful:

Every hour lost by a workman COULD HAVE been worked,
HAS been worked by a German workman, who in that time has
produced, say, an additional shell . . . to kill the British workman's brother in arms.

The engineers had been in dispute before the war but action was now
provoked by a rise of over 50 per cent in the cost of living. Co-op
members to a man, they saw inflation, correctly, as caused by the
profiteering of wholesalers, shippers, and insurers. Weir himself,
bringing in American workers at well above the Clydeside rates,
triggered off the strike on 15 February.

A fortnight later on 4 March it was settled by a compromise. On
17–19 March government and most of the unions signed the 'Treasury
Agreements' on wartime industrial relations, and on 30 April the
government set up the Clyde Armaments Output Committee, with
equal management and labour representation. Weir continued his
fulminations. He was given more ammunition by a report of 1 May
alleging poor productivity through absenteeism and drink. This was a
piece of temperance propaganda, which failed to take account of the
impact of enlistment and the resulting less-skilled labour force, as
Bonar Law pointed out in the Commons. Yet by 15 May Weir was calling for martial law in the munitions districts. Such scaremongering
served a political purpose. By 1 May Lloyd George was Minister of
Munitions, determined to dynamize production, and on 7 July the
great Jacobin appointed Weir munitions controller in Scotland with

an office that was 'in fact a miniature ministry of munitions'. On 30
August Weir abolished the Committee and replaced it with a nominal
board dominated by management. As the unpublished *History of the
Ministry of Munitions* comments:

> Just at the moment when these novel conditions called for free
> interchange of opinion between employers and workmen, rapid
> exploration of grievances, full explanation of the difficulties to
> be faced on either side, mutual goodwill and readiness to adjust
> habits and prejudices, the round table was broken up.

Weir had to set up a production plant which would be in operation
before the big offensives scheduled for mid 1916; thus he had to spend
and build before he had secured the full agreement of capital or
labour. By August, however, he had set up a co-operative shell production scheme for 28,500 shells a week. The individual firms drove
hard bargains: David Rowan took until mid October to agree 'owing
in the main to the firm's determination to protect themselves at all
costs against possible loss'.

He was — not surprisingly — less tactful with the labour force. He
had to secure dilution before the factories came into production, but
the Amalgamated Society of Engineers, sensitive to its members' privileged status and to ham-fisted attempts to enforce the Munitions Act
regulations, was slow to negotiate; management, too, wanted a quiet
life. Conflicts over the Act bubbled away: in August Fairfields struck
work, over leaving certificates, and some shop stewards were jailed.
Lord Balfour of Burleigh, the Conservative ex-Secretary whom the
government appointed as conciliator, found the strikers to be otherwise exemplary citizens, pillars of the Kirk with sons at the Front,
driven to revolt by what they regarded as arbitrary interference with
their liberties. The tact of Burleigh and Bonar Law contrasted with
the ineptness of MacKinnon Wood, who insisted on the strikers being
kept in prison, and the strike — the only major one in the shipyards — was settled equitably. It was swiftly followed by the Rent
Strike. This was less an aspect of industrial militancy than the
culmination of a pre-war Labour campaign against the rigorous terms
of Scottish house-letting and in favour of subsidized public housing.
Engineering management, eager to keep wages down, heartily con-
curred with it, while government, expecting to have to legislate on
Scottish housing anyway, ended it by promising a Rent Restrictions
Act, which was passed in May 1916.

Dilution, however, remained a battlefield. On one side were Weir, Lloyd George, and — playing an increasingly influential rôle — the Munitions Directorate in London under William Beveridge. On the other was the A.S.E., London-based but traditionally very decentralized, whose leaders had never faced a situation like this before, and manufacturers more concerned with remuneration than with productivity. Somewhere between the two were the workers, torn between alarm at the threat to their status and solidarity with their colleagues at the front, and all the time more dependent on their local union representatives, the shop stewards, a minority of whom were radical socialists of one sort or another. The attitudes of these, too, were ambiguous. Some welcomed dilution on theoretical grounds, as destroying internal barriers to working-class consciousness; others took a revolutionary anti-war stance. Some of the non-socialist shop stewards were the most bitterly obdurate of the lot, resenting deeply the inroads being made by women, and the Irish, into the preserve of the skilled male worker.

The main organization of the shop stewards was the Clyde Workers' Committee, founded during the 'tuppence an hour' strike. While purporting to speak for the mass of munitions workers, it was scarcely representative. Evidence to a Labour Party enquiry submitted that 'it was a heterogeneous crowd which had practically no constitution . . . you could represent a minority in the shop just the same as a majority, even though the minority was one'. This gave the far left its opportunity, and brought on to the scene such as John MacLean, who attended its meetings, though a schoolteacher, and others of Glasgow's rich collection of radical agitators from Christian pacifists to anarcho-syndicalists. This played into the munitions directorate's hands: to the industrial imperative they could add the tempting themes of sedition and revolution, and there was no shortage of volunteer martyrs.

The conflict came to a climax between December 1915 and April 1916. In December Lloyd George came to Glasgow, to win over the workers with his eloquence. He met the leaders of the shop stewards, to no avail; the great rally was a disaster. The Lord Advocate was obliged to seize an issue of *Forward*, which carried a report. But the Clyde had now nominated itself as a test case, and Beveridge and Weir moved rapidly to enforce dilution and thus break the A.S.E.'s resistance. On 28 January 1916 they appointed dilution commissioners, who rapidly drafted agreements covering most of the Clyde's engineering shops. A rearguard action, a strike at Beardmore's at the end of March, was broken by Weir arresting an assortment of shop stewards – including David Kirkwood and William Gallacher – and deporting them to Edinburgh.

Dilution was already going smoothly in most works before the Commissioners were appointed, so the March crackdown was helpful but by no means essential. The shell-forging and turning works opened by May, when the apparent defeat of Jutland (31 May–1 June) gave a new urgency, and reached full production by November, their products bound for the Battle of the Somme. By then Weir was in London, eventually as Air Minister, and the government munitions works were employing equal numbers of men and women; at the end of the war this ran at 30,000 women to 27,000 men. They caused little trouble, even when severe strikes reached the English munitions areas in May 1917. By late 1917 shop-floor co-operation – now led by men like Gallacher and Kirkwood – became such that the *Glasgow Herald*, earlier stridently anti-worker in tone, concluded in December 1917 that:

> The arrangements regarding the recognition of shop stewards are also significant as a sign of the times. They may portend syndicalism or they may not, but they certainly mean that the actual workers will be in closer touch with the machinery of their unions, and also with their employers, and familiarity is more likely to breed friendship than enmity.

By then, of course, the Bolshevik Revolution was a fact. In August the radicals had formed a Glasgow Soviet, greatly worrying Secretary Munro, and other members of the Cabinet, but it folded up when the Corporation would not provide it with a school classroom to meet in. Stories of vast meetings of revolutionary militants must likewise be treated with scepticism: Nan Milton, his daughter, tells us that, to demand John Maclean's release from prison in May 1917 '70,000 or 80,000 marched in the procession, while 250,000 lined the streets', but this was in fact the Glasgow May Day, and most of the demonstrators were protesting against the Munitions Act and discrimination against the Co-ops.

For the remainder of the war the Clyde was quiet, the Clyde Workers' Committee moribund. It was to be three years before there was any more trouble, in the Forty Hours' strike of January–February 1919. This strike was more a portent of the future disunity of the left than a climax to wartime discontent. On 14 March 1918 the Scottish Trades Union Congress (STUC) had called for a post-war 40-hour week, to prevent mass unemployment among demobilized men. After the 1918 election — in which the Unionists won 10 out of 15 Glasgow seats — this demand was echoed by a special conference in Glasgow on 27–8 December. The CWC revived itself to demand a 30-hour week. The strike actually took place in co-ordination with the Orange workers of Belfast, and on 27 January 40,000 came out, rising to 70,000 on the 28th, but, on the 30th, the Carters' Union settled for a 48-hour week. The government called a conference on this basis but, under pressure from Munro despatched 12,000 troops, 100 lorries, and six tanks to Glasgow. The climax came when a huge crowd — not wholly composed of strikers or even the unemployed — assembled in George Square on Friday 31 January to hear the government's decision on the conference. Suddenly the police (whose own relations with the government were edgy) staged what could only be described as a riot and charged the crowd: the response of the leaders, Gallacher and Shinwell, was to get the strikers out of the square and calm the situation down, in which by and large they succeeded, although at the cost of their own freedom. For a couple of days afterwards Glasgow was alive with troops, but the strike fizzled out at the news of a conference and continuance of the statutory regulation of wages and rents. The 'ringleaders' were subsequently tried and, incriminated by rather hypothetical plans for sabotage, given short prison sentences. In this way the 'revolution' ended, with less violence than 1848, when six had been killed in Chartist riots, and less destruction than the pre-war suffragettes had carried out. Although Sinn Feiners chipped in with sabotage and gun-running later that year, this had no connection with the industrial unrest. Pending the 1922 election, the Red Clyde was over.

Initially, the post-war situation seemed a draw between management and labour. Weir's notions of industrial reconstruction were not followed up by action; the practices of the skilled trade unions were restored. Peace, and the promise of widespread social and economic reconstruction, made even labour unrest seem an indication of vitality. Had not Lord Leverhulme, on the verge of his ambitious Scottish projects, declared in the *Glasgow Herald* in 1917 that it was 'the healthiest sign we have got today?' He — and those who confirmed the coalition in power in December 1918 — expected that the enormous investment in war production, and reparations from Germany, could be channelled into diversification of Scottish industry. The expansion of munitions production had depended greatly on electricity; so new schemes to tap hydro power were canvassed. The

capacity to make tanks, motor lorries, and aircraft on a large scale
seemed to promise a fresh start for the motor industry, and
Beardmore's announced an impressive investment programme —
'The firm's enormous resources will enable them to put "mass production" into practice'. Yet left-wing distrust was not fanciful. Allegations
of profiteering were well-founded. For all Weir's high-mindedness,
the *History of the Ministry of Munitions* admits that profits on completed shells ran at 'a somewhat high rate' throughout the war, and in
1916 profits on completed shell forgings rose as high as 40 per cent.
Little of this money was reinvested in industry. The Scottish banks in
1919 were glutted with huge capital balances, while the fashionable
artist Sir James Gunn remembered that *annus mirabilis*, 40 years
later:

> painters . . . benefited from the desire of war profiteers to trans-
> late their gains, pictures and prints providing a ready means.
> The one-man show at Cassells or Davidson's might sell out in a
> day . . . There was a boom in etchings: these were easy to store
> and prints soared to fantastic prices on a sellers' market: if I
> remember aright one of MacBey's reached the peak at 500
> guineas.

But where else could the money have gone? Much war investment
could only serve war purposes — like the vast development of engine
works for powerful naval vessels. With inflation out of control until
1921, industrial investment carried penal interest charges, as Beardmore's found to its cost. It was simpler, many Scottish capitalists
found, to sell out their shareholdings, buy land or invest abroad or in
the south. The revolution myth obscures the real change, and the real
loss, on the Clyde: co-operative decision-making over innovation had
been a genuine possibility. The shop stewards, who represented the
'Labour aristocracy', could be reverent as well as critical of their
bosses. But the tactlessness of Weir and the munitions directorate, and
the post-war slump, effectively threw this chance away. The workers'
distrust both of management and of new technology was confirmed,
but it was also plain that their own power was waning. The heroics of
the Red Clyde, faithfully retailed by further generations of activists,
masked a fundamental defeat.

VII 'A Land Fit for Heroes'?

For the Scots, the supreme sacrifice had also been a disproportionate one. Although the parliamentary return of 1921 simply divided 745,000 British dead by 10 to produce a Scottish toll of 74,000, most Scots probably agreed with the National War Memorial White Paper of 1920, which estimated 100,000 or over 13 per cent of Britain's dead. Scots territorials, at 5 per cent of the male population, nearly double the British average, suffered particularly badly in the mauling of their battalions in 1915.

Although men were retained by war industry and mining, casualties in urban areas still reached the British average — Glasgow's 18,000 dead tallies roughly with the British proportion of 1 in 54 — and the impact in the country areas could be twice as severe. The dead were overwhelmingly infantry privates; one officer died for every 13 men. Few Scottish working-class families escaped; still fewer lacked ex-soldiers who emigrated rather than face the dislocation and depression of the post-war years.

During and after the war both wages and prices escalated but, between 1914 and 1920, wages kept ahead in real terms by something like 25 per cent. The gains, however, were redistributed within the working class in a way that probably penalized Scotland. From a 1914 index of 100, a skilled shipbuilder's wage only rose to 223 in 1920, while an engineer's labourer's wage rose to 309. Women's wages seem to have risen to about 250. Welfare changes made notable additions to real wages: in particular, the extension of national insurance in 1920 to cover practically all manual occupations, and the retention of rent control. Although they were the prelude to an unprecedented depression, such changes meant that poverty would never again be as widespread as in the 1900s.

Even in the euphoria of early 1919 Scottish businessmen felt themselves in a new world. The control of much of their economy had moved southward through English takeovers or government intervention. Banking had shifted south from the start; the Ministry of Munitions ended dealing in iron on the Glasgow exchange on 31 May 1916. In 1918 Barclays and the Midland 'affiliated' the British Linen and Clydesdale banks. After the Midland took over the North of Scotland in 1923, three out of the seven banks were under English control, while the others had switched much of their investment, either into government stocks or the south's more profitable commercial concerns. Even the *Glasgow Herald*, usually no friend to nationalism, feared 'that ere long the commercial community will be sighing for a banking William Wallace to free them from Southern oppression'.

Because the Scottish economy was more complex, government intervention struck deeper than in north-east England or Wales. No major industry escaped. Besides coal and jute, heavy linen (another Dundee speciality), wool purchases, hides, leather, and meat, all important Scottish agriculture-based industries, were controlled through *ad hoc* mixtures of local supervision, compulsory purchase, and price-fixing. In agriculture and fisheries control went even further, using existing Scottish machinery. In response to soaring shipping losses, government in 1917 both introduced a measure of food rationing and demanded the conversion of grassland (which had a low calorie-yield per acre) into arable. An expanded Board of Agriculture carried this out through county agricultural production committees with paid executives and in 1918 expanded Scots arable acreage by over 30 per cent. As elsewhere, recruitment and later conscription forced wages up fast, and while the War Office plucked labourers from the farms, the Board sought to bring them back for ploughing and harvest. The Corn Production Act of 1917 established minimum wages, on a somewhat lower scale than in England, to be fixed by joint negotiating committees. Joe Duncan, the farm workers' leader, saw this as confirming his idea of the worker as a skilled highly-paid expert, rather than the Liberal idea of the peasant small-holder. But the promise of land for crofter soldiers remained, and was to prove troublesome.

Although the Board of Agriculture enthused over its new system, the Geddes Axe cut it down at the end of 1921, along with guaranteed prices and minimum wages. Scottish agriculture reverted to livestock, and initially declined less than the wheat-producing south. The case was worse in fishing.

With boats absorbed in Admiralty service, as minesweepers, patrol boats, and tenders, the loss of markets was not immediately noticeable. Indeed, the fishing fleet modernized its operations in the parts of the North Sea not covered by naval operations. Eight hundred sailing vessels were fitted out with motors during the war and a total of some 4,614 boats (just over 50 per cent of the fleet in 1914) managed to make 1918 'the most lucrative season ever experienced', in the opinion of the Fisheries Board. The Board had co-ordinated wartime purchasing and saw canning and increased fresh fish consumption as post-war options, but its main hopes still rested on the resumption of herring exports. In vain, because of the impact of the Russian civil war, Britain's hostility to Bolshevism, the collapse of the German economy in 1923, and the competition of the neutral and efficient Norwegian fleet. Although the industry's money income was £4.1m. in 1922, against £3.3m. in 1918 and £4.0m. in 1913, its real income had fallen by 53 per cent. Burdened with old equipment and decaying boats, the fishermen were faced with a future which promised no more than bare subsistence, derived largely from dumping herring at fish-meal factories.

To the Highlands the war brought a new desolation. The forests were felled, fishing boats rotted on the crofts where their owners had left them in 1914 — often never to return. Deaths and emigration ended several industries, such as slate quarrying in Lorne and Caithness; prohibition and liquor control closed down distilleries. The government, in a report of 1919, promised 250 miles of new railways (to be built with equipment salvaged from the western front), roads, bridges and piers, and an extensive forestry programme under the new Forestry Commissioners. Lord Leverhulme, who had bought Lewis in 1917, planned the industrialization of the islands on the Scandinavian pattern, around tweed and deep-sea fisheries. But all these schemes depended on continuing British economic prosperity. The returning servicemen were sceptical of this hypothetical new world and demanded their own land. The resulting friction hamstrung Leverhulme's plans; the depression swept both these and the promises of the government away. Population had held up in the 1911–21 decade, because the war inhibited emigration and the peace promised prosperity. In the 1920s it declined by 10 per cent.

Support grew during the war for collectivist 'reconstruction', but with Lloyd George the hostage of the Conservatives, the retreat was rapid. In Scotland, however, positive state policy was essential to remedy state-induced wartime distortions of economy and society. Without this, the Scots tended to surrender economic responsibility.

The instance of railway reorganization is of critical importance. In 1919 Sir Eric Geddes, the newly-created Minister of Transport, suggested nationalization, with an autonomous Scottish region. Under pressure from the Conservatives this became, in the White Paper of February 1921, the 'grouping' of lines into five private companies, substantially regional monopolies. The project for a separate Scottish company was maintained. The reaction of the business community, burghs, MPs, and trade unions in Scotland was alike furious. National control during the war had upgraded hitherto low levels of maintenance and wages on Scottish railways, whose costs had risen 291 per cent on 1913, compared with 227 per cent for the largest English companies. A separate Scottish company would be forced to maintain these standards, while carrying only 45,000 tons of traffic per annum per route mile, compared with 82,000 in England. The compromise between state and private enterprise would thus make the Scottish system uneconomic, jeopardize lines in rural areas, and reduce wage levels.

The result was a campaign, headed by Conservative, Liberal, and Labour MPs, in which the rhetoric of nationalism was used to secure the amalgamation of the five Scottish companies 'longitudinally' with the London Midland and Scottish (Caledonian, Highland, and Glasgow and South Western) and London and North Eastern Railways (North British and Great North of Scotland). This took effect in 1923.

VIII Reconstruction

This situation demonstrated the challenge to, and failure of, traditional Scottish government. There was certainly, in the law, the Church, and the educational system, a will to reform. The collectivist-inclined report of the Church of Scotland's Commission on the social and moral issues of the war (1919), admitted that 'in its teaching [the Church] has not explained either to the few or to the masses the urgency of social justice and Christian brotherhood'. The United Free Church, too, shifted from the Charity Organization Society-style liberal individualism of its 1911 conference on social welfare to a similar approach. School boards and teachers pressed for a comprehensive educational settlement. The whole reform movement was given enormous impetus by the Report of the Royal Commission on Scottish Housing, in October 1917 (after being adjourned from February 1915 to October 1916). Its indictment of landlords, local government, and the Scottish Office was as pungent as its descriptions of the state of Scottish dwellings:

> unspeakably filthy privy-middens in many of the mining areas, badly constructed, incurably damp labourers' cottages on farms, whole townships unfit for human occupation in the crofting counties and islands . . . gross overcrowding and huddling of the sexes together in the congested industrial villages and towns, occupation of one-room houses by large families, groups of

lightless and unventilated houses in the older burghs, clotted masses of slums in the great cities.

Its demand that a reconstructed Local Government Board for Scotland ensure minimal standards presaged a revolution in the powers of the Scottish Office. Yet, although this responsibility, and the new Board of Health, were enacted in 1919, it took until 1939 for the Scottish Office to integrate fully its social, agricultural, and industrial responsibilities. And even the 1919 act had been piloted through, not by the Scottish ministers, but by Dr Christopher Addison, the English Minister of Housing.

Much of the responsibility for the failure must rest with the Scottish Secretaries. MacKinnon Wood and Tennant made little mark on the Commons. When Tennant departed with Asquith in December 1916, Bonar Law, with an eye on the Clyde, stressed policy enforcement and a strong Lord Advocate, and appointed James Clyde (shifting his predecessor, the Liberal Robert Munro, to the Secretaryship). 'Parliament House rule',which the creation of the Scottish Office in 1885 was supposed to replace, was restored and at a critical legislative period. Disastrously. Munro's actions apropos the Forty Hours' strike have already been quoted. He frustrated Leverhulme's aims in the Hebrides; his Education Act lasted only 10 years. As Tom Johnston was to show in World War II, personality was critical in exercising the Secretary's powers. It was Scotland's tragedy that at this important period the Office fell to the dim representative of a failing political party.

IX The Political Reaction

In Britain the war and its aftermath saw the destruction of the Liberals and the rise of Labour. From 42 seats in 1910, Labour became the governing party, with 191 seats, in 1923. By 1922 Scotland took a leading rôle, returning 29 MPs (plus a Prohibitionist and a Communist) out of Labour's 142; and the Clydesiders helped elect Ramsay MacDonald, whom they respected for his anti-war stance, leader. But was war the motor of change? Arthur Marwick and Jay Winter have argued that it stimulated trade unionism and collectivist ideas, discredited New Liberalism and forced the Labour Party, in its 1918 constitution, to bid for mass support. The war gave this a distinctive dynamic – Arthur Henderson's admission into the war cabinet (1915) legitimated Labour as an interest, while subsequent conflict with the coalition over conscription, Russia, and a negotiated peace gained it support from disillusioned radicals. In the 1920s it became, in MacDonald's words, 'a party of the people', not of a class.

Against this Dr Ross McKibbin has argued that pre-war tendencies would anyway have led to the rise of a trade unionist, collectivist Labour – but not socialist – party. The expanding unions were already imposing their will on Labour. The factor, which 'transformed the conditions under which Labour grew', was the Reform Act of 1918, which expanded the electorate from 7.7m. in 1910 to 21.4m. in 1918, not only adding women over 30 but greatly expanding the male working-class electorate. This would have happened anyway, war or no war. While the war destroyed the Liberals' ability to control the situation, it did not change the tendency towards a working-class party. They would have had to cope with this in any case. The post-1918 Labour Party was not, however, socialist but a premature development of one wing of the Liberals. From that stemmed the tensions of the 1920s, which destroyed much of the ideological and constitutional liveliness of both radicals and socialists.

Scotland's wartime politics resembled the rest of Britain. Opinion at by-elections (only 4 out of 11 were contested) was overwhelmingly pro-government. On two occasions, in fact (Glasgow Central, 28 May 1915 and Aberdeen S., 3 April 1917) the main opposition candidate was more bellicose than the successful government candidate. A 'negotiated peace' candidate gained only 15 per cent on 10 October 1916 at the North Ayrshire by-election, against the local laird, Aylmer Hunter-Weston, despite three months' slaughter on the Somme, where Hunter-Weston was a general. Edward Scrymgeour, Churchill's prohibitionist and pacifist opponent, gained only 21.8 per cent against him on 30 July 1917 at Dundee.

The Unionists continued their pre-war recovery in the election of 14 December 1918. Although the Liberals won 43 seats, half of them were 'Lloyd Georgeites', and this, with 22 Tory gains, mainly in the west, aggravated chronic divisions and organizational weaknesses. Of the seven Labour MPs, two had gained mining seats, South Ayrshire and Hamilton, and the other three gains were in Aberdeen, Govan, and Edinburgh Central. Dundee and West Fife were retained. The Clyde failed to show Red, and the 'collaborator' Coalition–Labour Cabinet Minister George Barnes was returned for Tradeston. Polls were low, as many servicemen had yet to be demobilized, although high in mining areas, where many had already been brought home. But neither the war nor the 1918 Act seemed to have caused a major shift. In 1910 the average Labour constituency vote was 4,926; in 1918 it rose 28 per cent to 6,813, but the electorate had, over this period, risen 183 per cent from 779,000 to 2,205,000.

However, some loyalties had changed – notably in the Co-operative movement. The creation of the labour aristocracy between 1860 and 1914, this was still at its strongest in textile areas, like Angus and the Scottish borders, and in the coalfields. In Clackmannan in 1911 practically every family in the weaving and mining county must have had more than one member. Scots membership was about 10 per cent of the population; the UK figure was 7 per cent. It began the war jingoistically, the 1915 Congress refusing to aid German and Austrian co-operators interned in Britain. It also grew rapidly, because of its low prices and absence of profiteering, and by 1918 its membership was about 30 per cent up on 1911. In Lanarkshire, for example, it grew from 7.61 per cent to 11.46 per cent, in Edinburgh from 12.89 per cent to 17.39 per cent. But its societies were hit by the advantages that Lloyd George's policies of food control gave to its old enemies, the private wholesalers and retailers, and in 1917, led by Sir William Maxwell, the chairman of St Cuthbert's Co-operative Society, the Congress decided to organize as part of the Labour movement. In demonstrations in Glasgow in 1917 the problems of the Co-op came second only to the iniquities of the Munitions Act, and in December 1918 three Co-op candidates polled, collectively, over 19,000 votes and two came very close to being elected; elsewhere the shift of Co-op support to Labour gave the party a major boost. Such collaboration had been envisaged in pre-war negotiations, but it was not in fact to be formalized until 1926.

Left to itself then, the war would certainly have caused an improvement in Labour representation: eventually some 18 – 20 MPs might have been elected, mainly in the coalfields, with a few more in the cities. But economic circumstances were changed. In mid 1919 there were already danger signs; by 1920 definite alarm. Shipbuilding on the Clyde had gone above 650,000 tons in 1919 and 1920; in 1921 it dropped to 510,000 and in 1922 to under 400,000. With few orders in hand, the prospects for 1923 were dismal (less than 170,000 tons was actually completed). The fate of the shipyards was shared by the other heavy industries. North British Locomotive Company production dropped by two-thirds between 1920 and 1921. On top of this, promises were frustrated; the government's 'homes fit for heroes' programme, following a year after the report of the Royal Commission, and after a large pre-war building back-log, failed. Scarcely 2,000 houses were built in 1920, compared with 48,000 in England; in 1921 this was still only, 6,000 against 120,000. Costs were inflated, labour was scarce and expensive, and Scottish local authorities (in which landlords, already battered by the Rent Restrictions Act, were still trying to keep ahead of a Labour Party that was shrewdly exploiting the housing issue), dragged their feet.

This was evident to the Scottish Office. A report to the Board of Health on 'Industrial Unemployment and Distress' compiled in 1921 observed: 'it is difficult to pick out any industrial occupation as being principally affected by unemployment; almost all are in bad condition . . . those engaged in export trade and the means of export are worse than those engaged in the home trade', and urged a radical extension of relief measures, fearing that 'very inflammable elements which, while subjected during ordinary times to damping down by the saner and much larger section of the community, will not improbably be fanned into activity as the endurance of that more sober section is broken by the continued tightening of waistbelts around empty bellies'. Four years earlier the Royal Commission on housing had positively welcomed social discontent; now government feared it, with some reason. Extremist agitation − after the spring of 1920 directed by the Moscow-organized Communist Party − was giving new focus to the discontents of slum-dwellers and the unemployed, while Sinn Fein was active in support of the campaign against the British. The Labour Party − ably organized in the west of Scotland by Patrick Dollan − incorporated as much of this agitation as it could by a positive policy on rents and housing, and the Catholic Church and *ci-devant* Irish Nationalist organization switched its support. Although Labour won Bothwell and Kirkcaldy at by-elections, this came only just in time, as the slump struck severely at its working-class base.

The 1922 election, held on 15 November, set a qualified seal on this shift. The *Scotsman* found its pattern 'vague and confused', as well it might, since Lloyd George's forces acted in unison with the Unionists who had flung him from office three months before. There were 4 four-cornered and 19 three-cornered contests, but in another 43 the 24 'National Liberals' and 18 Unionists acted together. Away from west central Scotland there was, in fact, little change from 1918. Labour maintained an 'armed neutrality' with the Asquithian Liberals, and found itself hard put to maintain itself outside the 11 coalfield constituencies, where 9 of the MPs returned were miners' agents. It − or the left in general − scored a remarkable victory in

Dundee, where the pacifist E.D. Morel and the local prohibitionist Eddie Scrymgeour beat Winston Churchill, but it gained no more seats in Edinburgh and Aberdeen. The mobilization of a rural socialist vote, apparent in 1918, was not repeated — probably a consequence of the setback to Joe Duncan's Farm Servant's Union.

But it was in the Glasgow area that the real turn-round occured. Labour captured 10 of the 15 city seats, and Dumbarton, East and West Renfrew, and Rutherglen, while a Communist (Walton Newbold) got in for Motherwell. Many of those elected had played a prominent part in the labour unrest and anti-war movement on the Clyde, but their success probably owed less to this than to the post-war depression, the housing problem, and the alienation of the Catholic vote from the coalition government because of the Irish troubles. The right-wing press blamed the socialist exploitation — directed at working-class women — of a recent House of Lords decision that, due to a technical formality, all rent increases since 1916 were illegal: 'The technical right of the tenant to recall money which has been illegally taken from him has been worked upon by base appeals and has been used to the utmost to stimulate the virus of Socialism in the community', and observed of the Catholic voters, some 75,000 in Glasgow, who on 10 November had been instructed by the *Glasgow Observer* to vote Labour: 'Their vote, as it always is, has been organised from the top, and they have recorded the dictates of their leaders with the authority of automata'.

Such calculations were, however, far from the minds of the 8,000 who crowded into the St Andrew's Halls to send the new MPs south. With a religious service that had all the fervour of the signing of the Covenant nearly 300 years earlier or of Gladstone in Midlothian some 40 years before, the new MPs pledged themselves to a range of lofty generalities, at few of which would any Victorian radical have baulked, then left by train for the south. When David Kirkwood arrived at Westminster he remarked to John Wheatley 'John, we'll soon change all this', yet the Clydesiders were themselves the proof that parliamentarianism and political organization could tame revolutionary fervour, and emasculate the reactions to the changes which had so brutally altered the expectations of industrial Scotland.

By 1922 Scottish capitalism had changed profoundly. Markets were no longer expanding, nor was the free market any longer the principal mechanism of industrial co-operation. In significant areas near-monopolies had been set up — as in shipbuilding, steel, and coal — or mergers with English concerns, as with the banks and railways. The whisky industry was consolidated by the Distillers' Company. The majority of Scottish shipowners sold their fleets to the 'big four' (Ellerman, Furness Withy, Peninsular and Oriental, and the Royal Mail Line). Imperial Chemical Industries and Anglo-Iranian Oils took over the petroleum and petroleum-based chemical industries. The remaining Scots-based firms faced a difficult future: distilling, its profits low through wartime liquor control, faced prohibition in America; shipbuilding faced a dwindling freight market, and jute even stronger competition from an increasingly autonomous India. Many magnates got out while the going was good, vaulting on the post-war boom to the head of a British consortium. Was there an age-factor behind this? Were the sons of entrepreneurs born and based in Scotland less loyal to their country because of southern education, and possibly less confident of their ability to cope with the Scottish future?

During the war collectivism expanded in two areas: economic co-ordination and social policy. Scottish entrepreneurs, providing expertise unknown to the traditional civil service, helped to co-ordinate business and government – besides Weir, these included the shipping controllers Joseph (Lord) Maclay. Lord Inverforth, and Lord Inchcape, the remarkable Geddes family, Eric, Auckland, and Mona, who between them virtually took over ancillary military services, Sir Andrew Duncan and Sir James Lithgow. None of these were collectivists in any socialist sense, but they recognized the difference that the state could make to the economic health of their class. Their fathers had done without a state. After 1916 such entrepreneurs realized they needed one – to control the terms of trade, regulate supplies, and keep the workers in order – but they realized that this state was directed from the south. What had developed in Scotland was a 'welfarism' that restricted business autonomy. The emigrés to the south used their wartime experience to develop a modified capitalism, based on cartels, understandings with government, and the stimulus of consumer demand, while the autonomy of Scottish capitalism, already weakened by these defections, was further encroached upon at the margin by rent control, public housing, and the effective civic emancipation of the Catholics, traditionally the lowest-status segment.

And who lost? Old Liberalism was mortally wounded, not simply because of its election setbacks, but because the challenge of Labour's municipal success led rapidly to coalitions with the Unionists. The basis of 'civic reform' politics had been destroyed, crushed by economic decline on one side and by increasing working-class organization on the other. Yet the working-class itself had been hit. The hierarchy of the 'skilled men' was never to be the same again. The miners and fishermen had over two decades of economic depression before them. Agricultural affairs improved somewhat, but at the cost of the Liberal dream of a peasantry on Danish lines. More had died than simply the peasants whom Lewis Grassic Gibbon would commemorate, in the last lines of *Sunset Song*, 14 years later:

> They died for a world that is past, these men, but they did not die for this that we seem to inherit.

2

A Troubled Economy 1922 – 1964

There was a mighty paradox about the Scottish economy after World War I, and particularly in the years 1960-76. On one hand accelerated growth, and a fairer distribution of its dividends, was the work of the later period; on the other, these two decades have also seen the collapse of traditional industries, the general weakening of manufacture in both relative and absolute terms, mounting unemployment, continuing emigration, and what seems to be endemic social and political instability.

Table 2.1, based on the censuses of production and other official statistics, attempts to sketch some long-term trends. The real output of the Scottish economy, expressed in an index which takes inflation into account, grew by only 60 points, 1907 – 60, but by 101 points, 1960 – 76. The average male manual worker's real wage rose by 108 points in the first period, and by 101 points in the second. Yet unemployment rose from 3.6 per cent in 1960 to 6.4 per cent in 1976 and emigration (see table 3.1) – a reasonable commentary on people's economic expectations – was actually 15 per cent higher, 1951 – 78, compared with 1921 – 51, against a rate of natural population increase steadily falling in the 1970s. Scotland's recent gains must, moreover, be seen against much higher gains elsewhere. Real wages, for example, rose between 1960 and 1976 in West Germany by 174 points. This returns us to the gloomy spectacle of the industrial structure and its problems. How much was its fundamentally parlous condition after 1960 the result of previous events and decisions? And why was its dissolution accompanied not by poverty but by apparent affluence?

Whatever else this affluence did, it deferred consideration of problems of industrial structure which had seemed fundamental before 1939. It has required a lot of research – happily now being carried

Table 2.1: Scottish gross output, in million £s (at current prices)

	1907	1924	1935	1951	1960	1976	1995
Agric./Fisheries	26	54	42	97	113	480	1,646
Mining	25	34	21	50	62	177	1,187
Manufacturing	159	275	220	437	708	2,649	10,173
Iron and Steel		34	26	52	70	170	838
Engineering	62	52	41	157	281	952	3,930
Textiles	29	60	39	54	67	171	767
Food and Drink	31	75	65	67	125	605	1,975
Other	37	54	49	107	165	751	2,663
Construction	13	21	15	64	125	902	3,310
Service Sector	*42*	*101*	*133*	590	956	5,652	34,397
Scottish GDP	*263*	485	*431*	1,238	1,964	9,863	50,713
estimated % of UK output	*11.8%*	*10.5%*	*8.8%*	9.3%	8.7%	9.1%	8.5%
UK GNP (GDP after 1951)	2,230	4,615	4,902	13,287	22,560	108,384	596,623
Index of Scottish Production (1907=100)	100	99	107	126	160	261	385
Index of UK Production (1907 = 100)	100	111	147	160	218	340	535
Value of £(1900 = 100p)	93p	50p	61p	25p	20p	6.5p	2p

Note: Estimated figures in italics.

Sources: The data for 1907–35 were gathered from the censuses of production: the agriculture and fisheries figures for 1924 and 1935 from the *Reports* of the relevant Boards and Departments. The (very rough) estimates of (1) total Scottish GDP, 1907–35, and of (2) the Service Sector, 1907–35, were arrived at by assuming that the ratio of Scottish GDP to UK GNP was the same as Scottish industrial production to UK industrial production. The resulting figures give a notion of magnitude, nothing more. Data for 1951 and 1960 from G. McCrone, *Scotland's Economic Progress* (1965), and for 1976 from the *Scottish Abstract of Statistics* (Edinburgh, 1980). Value of £ from David Butler, ed., *British Political Facts* (1980 ed.).

out — to determine what these were, and it is still difficult to assess the effectiveness of the responses of the 1930s as possible strategies, as they were superseded by a London-imposed approach of 'demand-management' and 'planning'. Here, of course, the temptation to project back strategies which have contemporary attractiveness is alluring and dangerous. It is no use comparing Scotland with Finland or Sweden if no one in the 1930s was actually thinking in those terms. Professor R.H. Campbell has, as a result of wide reading in the archives of the Scottish economic establishment, argued that its fatalism — in face of the constraints of international demand and Scottish resources — was inevitable.

The problem, however, is broader than this. Post-1945 international demand was a different story from 1922–39, and so was the ostensible degree of planning in the economy. Scottish failures arose increasingly from missed opportunities instead of over-commitment, and from the absence of effective Scottish planning mechanisms. How much was this a legacy from the 1930s? There was then a general conviction among the establishment that diversification was necessary, a conviction also shared by nationalists and socialists. The government's own interventions, in the form of the Commissioner for the Scottish Special Area, his disbursements (amounting to more than £4m. between 1935 and 1938), and the plans propounded by the Scottish Economic Committee, favoured economic planning, explicit in the SEC's *The Case for Planned Development* (1938) and its evidence to the Barlow Commission. But its scheme for a Development Agency was never carried out and while the goals of planning and diversification were ostensibly pursued after the war, the means of attaining them was absent. The heavy industries were either disrupted by contradictory policies from central government, or allowed an independence that amounted, in the long run, to self-destruction. Diversification, divorced from a co-ordinated policy on heavy industry, underlay the 'planning' of the Toothill Report in 1961. In the 13 years between Toothill and the Scottish Economic Planning Enquiry of 1974, which recommended the setting-up of the Scottish Development Agency, the heavy industries dwindled to the extent that they were scarcely capable of supplying 10 per cent of the engineering requirements of the North Sea oil industry.

What influence did Scotland have on the UK economy? In the 1960s, H.W. Richardson and D. Aldcroft argued that the UK economy actually grew faster between 1922 and 1938 than before 1914. New industries — motor vehicles, electrical goods, chemicals, artificial fibres – along with building, expanded rapidly in southern England. Investment shifted from capital goods to serve the domestic market, and this shift was accelerated by the National government after 1931, which safeguarded the domestic market by tariffs, and through reducing unemployment benefit directed funds from the unemployed to the employed. The 'regional problem' was the price to be paid – but in UK terms not an unbearable one. Such historical interpretations have been used recently to argue that post-war regional policies were essentially a misconceived attempt to reverse the inevitable, and have simply resulted in an added incubus on the growing areas of the UK economy. But was the drift south inevitable? Were the new industries optimally-sited, highly productive, well-managed? Or had lack of planning meant that the underused resources of the north were paralleled by congestion and duplication of facilities in the south? Were service industries and white-collar occupations – with no great degree of, or criteria for, productivity – simply absorbing money and management skills needed for proper industrial construction?

II The Structure of Industry

As a percentage of total output, the traditional staples suffered a steep decline between 1907 and 1935, which then levelled off. In 1960 they still accounted for about a third, but by 1976 this had fallen to under a fifth.

Table 2.2: Trends in major sectors of output, in percentage

	1907	1924	1935	1951	1960	1976	1995
Staples: agriculture, fisheries, mining, steel, engineering, and textiles:	*53*	*48*	*39*	33	30	20	28
Other manufactures:	26	27	27	14	15	14	
Construction:	5	4	3	5	6	9	7
Service Sector:	16	21	31	48	49	57	65

Note Estimates in italic.

More serious was the rapid decline after the 1930s of other manufacturing industries – clothing, food and drink, paper, chemicals, timber, and leather goods – frequently as a result of competition from the expanding industries of the south. Although the expansion of services acted as a compensating factor, the result was a narrowing of the industrial base by the 1950s.

The economy remained, however, largely Scots-owned and dominated by small- to medium-sized concerns. Large factories (very common in the new industries of the south) were almost wholly confined to the heavy industries:

Table 2.3: Scottish factories, 1938

	Number of employees	
	1,500 +	250 – 1,500
1. Scotland outside Central Lowlands	2	44
2. Central Lowlands outside Glasgow Area	12	187
3. Glasgow Area (Lanark, Renfrew, Dunbarton)	35	143

Large factories (1,500 + employees)		(Scots-owned in brackets)	
Engineering	12 (7)	Shipbuilding	7 (7)
Textiles and derivatives	11 (10)	Co-operative Works	3 (3)
Metallurgy	8 (7)	Miscellaneous	8 (6)

III The Heavy Industries

Shipbuilding

The health of the Scottish economy depended intimately on international trade. Any fall in this meant overcapacity in shipping and a fall in owners' profits. Fewer ships were ordered and depression spread from the shipyards to the heavy industries. In 1921 not only did the naval market vanish, but the post-war boom collapsed. Shipping was glutted by the products of American shipyards, the confiscation of enemy ships, and the selling-off of the government's own merchant fleet, while trade remained sluggish and the British share of it decreased.

The Clyde's strength in passenger cargo-liners and specialized ships, for which high grades of craftmanship and finish were required, provided partial compensation. But the yards were constrained by old equipment and the restoration of pre-war working practices, while modernization was inhibited by the post-war inflation. Beardmore's, whose reconstruction ruined them, were appalled when their old machinery was eagerly bought up by their Clydeside rivals.

But rivalry was not the rule: shipowners reserved berths or bought shares in shipbuilding firms, which had coped with wartime shortages by buying up steelworks. A tight system of vertical cartelization ensued. For a time in the early 1920s Lord Pirrie presided over an effective amalgamation between Royal Mail Lines, Harland and Wolffs, Lithgows, and Colvilles, which dominated the Clyde. Such cartels were probably inevitable, but checked innovation and diversification, and the trade slump caused the whole edifice to collapse.

Until 1929 a booming American economy sustained transatlantic passenger travel by *nouveau riche* and immigrant alike and kept up demand for passenger liners. In 1930 Cunard-White Star laid down a £4.8m. 81,000-ton super-liner. But the consequences of the Wall Street crash ended work on 'No.534' (the *Queen Mary*) at Clydebank. Elsewhere, orders dried up; by 1933 Scottish output, at 74,000 tons, was lower than in the 1850s. In February 1930 Sir James Lithgow and the Bank of England set up the National Shipbuilders' Security Corporation to 'rationalize' the industry by buying up and 'sterilizing' under-used yards. It had cut capacity 15−20 per cent by 1935 − at the cost of great unpopularity − but by then work was resumed on the *Queen Mary* (completed 1936), Cunard laid down a sister ship, and the government started to subsidize cargo steamer construction. Overshadowing everything, rearmament brought, between 1935 and 1939, £80m. worth of arms orders. But the underlying problems of the industry remained as far from solution as ever.

Heavy Engineering

Heavy engineering, the other main export staple, was hit even harder. The fall in raw material prices cheapened imports but meant that underdeveloped countries had less to spend. UK exports to India, for example, fell by nine-tenths between 1913 and 1935 and exports through Scottish ports fell 42 per cent between 1913 and 1937. The market for railway rolling stock, mineral handling gear, sugar-cane crushers, and so on declined. The North British Locomotive Company had produced about 400 engines a year, mainly for overseas, between 1904 and 1914; between 1921 and 1931 this fell to an average of 150. Although the individual size and value of engines had increased, annual income fell by over 50 per cent. In 1932 the market collapsed completely, and never recovered. Much the same could be said of other heavy engineering works: boiler exports also dropped by 50 per cent between 1913 and 1935, and heavy machine tools, dependent on such industries, experienced a similar decline.

Coal

The problems of the coal industry were even more complex. In 1913 it had produced a record 42.5m. tons; between the wars its average

output was 30m., with much-reduced exports: the 1935 figure was
20 per cent down on 1913. Oil-firing at sea and electrification in
Ireland and Europe both contributed to this. Moreover, the great
Lanarkshire coalfield was now declining. In 1913 it produced 17.5m.
tons, by 1937 only 9m. tons. But the labour force fell faster than production, from 139,500 in 1913 to 86,500 in 1937. Large collieries (20
out of 400) now produced 75 per cent of the coal, output per man
increased, and coal cut by machine rose from 22 per cent in 1913 to 80
per cent by 1938. Such were the fruits of victory in 1926. Scottish production per man *vis à vis* Britain had already been 112:100 in 1913; by
1938 it was 141:118. This despite the problems of exploiting the
growing Fife coalfield — chiefly a shortage of houses. In the 1930s a
tight partnership between the state and owners was created. Labour's
Mines Act of 1930 had set up regional production quotas; an international agreement followed, cutting exports but boosting profits.
Although mining royalties were nationalized in 1938, shares in coal
companies had by then risen by 300 per cent. The losers were the
miners. Although they got pithead baths and welfare institutions,
their real wages fell by 4.5 per cent, 1913–38, and unionization
declined until in Fife in 1934 it was less than 30 per cent. Despite the
Fife miners' election of a Communist MP in 1935, demoralization
rather than radicalism was the result. In 1942 a Ministry of
Information report found the sentiment 'we would be as well off under
Hitler' disturbingly widespread in the Scottish coalfields.

Steel

Sixty per cent of Scottish steel (itself about 11 per cent of UK production in 1935) was usually destined for shipyards and the heavy
industries, so it was a perilous business. Dwindling local ore, under-
capitalization and foreign competition had been followed by arbitrary
wartime expansion and shipyard control. This no longer worked, but
was the industry to be reorganized as a Scottish monopoly, or allied
with English concerns? There was no decision during the 1920s,
because of the rivalry of management and firms, and the unhelp-
fulness of the banks. In 1929 the American consultants, Brasserts,
recommended concentration on a single large works using imported
ore at Erskine on the Clyde, but it was 1934 before amalgamations
produced Colvilles, with about 95 per cent of Scottish capacity.
During this period Stewarts and Lloyds followed another Brassert suggestion and moved their works and workforce south to Corby, in the

Northants ironstone fields, in 1932, taking with them most of Scottish tube-making. Rearmament brought vastly increased profits, aided by a 100 per cent rise in productivity 1924–37, but it also meant that the fundamental resiting of the industry was not proceeded with.

Textiles

Textiles scarcely fared better than the heavy industries, the number of employees falling from 137,000 in 1924 to 113,600 in 1935. In wool, changing fashion (a flapper consumed about a quarter of the cloth required for an Edwardian lady) and an extra, mid-twenties slump after the UK's return to the gold standard, drove many producers out of business. However, in the 1930s there was some recovery, notably in the semi-mechanized production of Harris Tweed after 1934, through catering for an enhanced leisure market. This probably also aided the expansion of knitwear in the Hillfoots and Border areas, while Shetland hand-knitting left an indelible mark on the fashion of the period. In carpets, too, Scotland, with a third of the UK industry, profited from the English building boom, not to speak of the invention of the vacuum cleaner. This came as a boost to the hard-pressed jute industry, increasingly subject to Indian competition. In 1938 it was on the edge of a precipice as the English economy faltered. 'Happy as a sandbag' had real meaning for Dundee in 1939.

Aircraft and Motor Vehicles

Scotland had developed substantial aircraft and vehicle industries during World War I, but in the 1920s, when complex passenger planes were a relative rarity, and military orders subject to government defence and purchasing policy, aircraft production vanished. Beardmore's experimented with heavy bombers and Weir's with autogiros. To no avail. Only when defence expenditure went up by 25 per cent after 1937 did production start to come north. Rolls Royce established their 'Merlin' engine plant at Hillington, and Blackburn's an airframe works at Dumbarton.

The failure to develop motor manufacture was more complex and more tragic. Before 1914 more than 40 firms had applied Scots engineering, coach- and bicycle-building skills to the problem. With a big landed and sporting clientele, the Scots 'heavy car' — the Argyll or Arrol-Johnston — up to three tons and 30 horsepower, was famous for finish and reliability. Albion did the logical thing, changed it into a lorry, and survived. Argyll's attempt to take the UK lead in volume production with a very advanced design hit technical and legal problems which ruined the firm in 1912. Reconstructed as a specialist producer, with several other firms, it lasted into the 1920s. Why did the industry then founder? Was it distance from southern markets and the west midlands smallware industry? Possibly failure might have been averted by earlier development of motor-cycles, as popular as cars until the early thirties, and anticipating the small car in terms of market, technology, and maintenance. A large and autonomous American plant might also have turned the tide. But the choice of Dagenham and Luton by Ford and General Motors in the late twenties, the impact of their output, and the 1929 slump, wrote finis to the local industry. In 1935 Scotland contributed only 1.5 per cent of UK production.

Chemicals

Scots chemical output was worth £19m. in 1924, £15m. in 1935; it had fallen from 10.2 per cent of UK output to 7.7 per cent. The reason was a combination of obsolescence and wholesale reorganization in new and gigantic corporations like ICI and Unilever. The Scottish dye-stuffs and bleaching industries crumbled rapidly under the new technologies of Cheshire and Teeside, while compensating developments by the great firms were restricted to petroleum products at Grangemouth and explosives at Ardeer. In the absence of state involvement, this specialization frustrated applied science in general. Pharmaceuticals, for example, remained despite Scotland's medical tradition a tiny sector until World War II.

Food and Drink

The decline of the industrial sector inevitably affected consumer goods, although Edinburgh, as a food-processing and brewing centre, remained an oasis of almost southern prosperity. But British drinkers swilled a third less beer and two-thirds less whisky between the wars, and American drinkers didn't legally exist — until 1933. Amalgamations dominated both industries: the Distillers' Company dates from 1923, McEwan Younger from 1931. Prohibition wasn't an unmitigated disaster for Scotland; it hit Bourbon, after all, harder than Scotch, and when the temperance movement in Scotland made itself felt in veto polls after 1913 there was a compensating movement towards the ambiguous pleasures of cigarettes, soft drinks, and confectionery — all of which showed substantial inter-war increases. Several large factories for canning and biscuit-making were opened at this time; as a result of the modern techniques they used, however, greater production was achieved with a smaller workforce.

Furniture and Fittings

High family expenditure on food was not repeated in consumer durables. There was no attempt to create a mass-production furniture industry, and the cartels that dominated the booming electrical goods industries had no desire to move their factories north. In 1935 only 2 per cent of electrical goods output came from Scotland, largely in the heavy machinery sector. Weir and Lithgow's attempt to set up British National Electric's household goods factory at Carfin met with little success. Small houses made for a small market, and one already saturated from the south.

Agriculture and Fisheries

Agriculture was still Scotland's major industry, but its labour force declined, 1921−38, from 126,900 to 105,300, and its output fell from £48m. to £40m., in UK terms from 17.2 per cent to 14.4 per cent. This stemmed partly from a growth in English productivity, partly from structural changes, and partly from government policy. Lorries and tractors cut demand for horses by a quarter; whisky decline pulled barley production down. More seriously, government's first subsidies — for beet (1925) and wheat (1932) — designed to safeguard English arable farming, penalized Scottish mixed farms (although these were inherently much more profitable). In fact of total subsidies of £68.25m. paid by 1935−6, only £4.2m. (6.1 per cent) went to Scotland. With the introduction of cattle subsidies in 1934 things started to change, but by then many Scots 'marginal' farmers had hit the trail for the richer lands of the south, like those whom Ronald Blythe recorded in *Akenfield*:

> News about East Anglia got around fast. It was the land of Goshen compared with Scotland. A better climate, easier working soil, with no damn great lumps of granite pushing out of it. It was, 'Come on, Wully! Come doon here!' It was 'Send home for brother Angus and for sister Mary and her man!'

The situation was so bad in fishing that even the Cabinet referred to it in 1934 as a tragedy. The East European market never recovered and Norwegian competition increased. Catches held up, with more efficient motor boats, but the rise in fishermen's real income, 1913–37, was barely 3 per cent. Louis MacNeice's comment was apposite:

> His brother caught three hundred cran when the seas were lavish,
> Threw the bleeders back in the sea and went upon the parish.

Only in 1935 was the Herring Industry Board established by the government to maintain minimum prices and assist re-equipment, but shortly afterwards overfishing brought the white-fish industry, centred in Granton and Aberdeen, into peril. By the time legislation had been prepared to aid it, its elderly fleet had largely been drafted for war service.

Transport

Economic decline meant contraction on the railways, intensified by 'rationalization' like the southward transfer of locomotive building. Staff fell by over 18 per cent, 1924–35. Since less than 8 per cent of mileage was closed down, gains in productivity were considerable, but modernization was delayed until the financial structure of the railways had been safeguarded by the transport act of 1933. Both the LMS and the LNER then introduced fast services to the south and powerful passenger and freight engines, but resentment continued because few orders for these came to Scotland, and government-subsidized electrification schemes were restricted to the English conurbations. Grievances over high freight rates were authoritatively endorsed by the Scottish Economic Committee in 1939.

Ramifying bus services slowed the drift from the countryside, and opened it to coach tourists. Started in the early 1920s, often by ex-servicemen converting old army lorries, these services quickly became dominated by Sir William Thompson's Scottish Motor Traction Company (1906). The railways took a 25 per cent interest in 1928 and increased this to 50 per cent by 1939. Although the tram remained the great symbol of urbanism the bus companies took over and closed down the smaller systems. The lorry and delivery van became familiar in the villages, but commercial road haulage was restricted by the sluggish development of light industry, and the rise of the private car by the small size of the middle class. In 1935 there was 1 car to every 25 people in England, but only 1 to 36 in Scotland.

The railways, along with Coast Lines of Liverpool (who took over Burns and Laird's Irish steamers in 1921), also over-saw the reconstruction in 1925 of David MacBrayne's. In return for a government subsidy of £40,000 per annum, freight and passenger rates were controlled, the elderly steamer fleet modernized and linked to new bus services. Coastal shipping was still important, with regular passenger and freight services to many smallish Scottish ports from England, as well as Leith and Glasgow. After 1932 it faced new competition. The S.M.T. started Scotland's first internal air service. In 1933 Highland Airways began flying from Aberdeen and Inverness to Wick and the Orkneys. Small companies proliferated over the next couple of years, but by 1936, as with the buses, two regional monopolies had taken over. Railway Air Services (a consortium of the 'big four') flew Anson monoplanes to Liverpool and Belfast; while Scottish Airways (incorporating two companies) flew Rapide biplanes to the west coast and Highlands. By 1939 the enduring pattern of Scottish internal services had been created.

Electricity

The provision of adequate electricity by Glasgow Corporation had been crucial to munitions production, and William Weir himself took a leading part in the creation of the State–private enterprise partnership of the national grid. An act was passed in 1926; construction started in 1927, and the Central Scottish Grid, stretching from Aberdeenshire to Carlisle, was complete by 1931. It cost, at £3m.–4m., about 20 per cent of the UK total, and was thus effectively a subsidy to Scottish industry, yet only 18.5 per cent of the work went to Scottish manufacturers. Between 1924 and 1929 the British Aluminium Company spent a further £5m. on a huge hydroelectric scheme to produce aluminium at Fort William, and in the 1930s three further schemes, purely for power supply, were built – in the Tummel area, at the Falls of Clyde, and in Galloway. Yet by 1935 Scottish electricity consumption was only 8 per cent of the British figure – much boosted by new industries in the south-east.

Electricity charges were higher than in the south, and few electrical goods factories moved north. Scottish developments essentially pumped electricity into the English grid, or produced semi-finished materials, and anger at this underlay the parliamentary defeat of the Caledonian power bills of 1936–8 — the only Scottish issue in the inter-war period to absorb the full attentions of the Cabinet.

IV The Problem Defined

The multifaceted nature of Scotland's crisis marked it off from the other 'depressed areas'. Although unemployment (25 per cent in 1932) was less than in Wales (40 per cent) or the north-east (33 per cent), it was also accompanied, as we have seen, by structural upheavals in practically every industrial sector, and in the long term aggravated by the policy changes of firms, financial institutions, and governments. Reduced demand for Scots capital goods coincided with foreign tariffs against Scots luxury goods. Declining landed wealth, and (until 1936) inappropriate government subsidies, hit the rural economy. Foreign unrest, autarkic policies, and loosening imperial ties menaced traditional markets. If revaluation in 1925 was bad, welfare cuts and protection after 1931, which aided southern 'home market' industries at the expense of exporting areas, were worse. To all of this the relief offered to coal by government aid, to steel by protection and rearmament after 1935, while magical for harried entrepreneurs (who suddenly saw an escalation in share values), could only be a palliative.

Scottish unemployment averaged 14 per cent, 1923–30. against the UK's 11.4 per cent. But in 1931–8 this percentage ratio rose to 21.9:16.4. Numbers on poor relief, 1929–36, climbed from 192,000 to 341,000, an increase of 76 per cent against a UK increase of 13 per cent. The contrast with London was even starker. There unemployment was at its worst at 13 per cent in 1932, and was running at 6.3 per cent by 1936, when even prosperous Edinburgh still had 12.3 per cent, Greenock had 20 per cent, and Airdrie 30 per cent. Only in 1930 did J.H. Thomas, for the Labour government (see p.96), commission the first regional surveys, when Professor W.R. Scott and his Glasgow University economists identified some 100,000 men in west central Scotland alone as 'permanently surplus'. Traditionally, the 'surplus' had migrated; an average of 147,000 had left Scotland each decade between 1861 and 1911. Between then and 1930 this more than doubled, but between 1931 and 1939 fell to under 100,000. Emigration had swelled the proportions of the old and very young in the 1920s; in the next decade those in employment became victims themselves.

Unemployment was not a function of industrial decadence. In

certain 'traditional' sectors it actually resulted from industrial advance. Between 1931 and 1935, for example, Scots productivity increased by 8 per cent, against 5.6 per cent in the UK. Unemployment hit family incomes and cut demand for consumer goods. Female labour in such industries fell, making matters worse. The middle class did not do so badly; rarely were more than 5.5 per cent of them unemployed. They suffered pay cuts, but their employment actually grew faster than in England between 1921 and 1931, by 20 per cent against 14 per cent — although there, too, emigration continued to operate as a safety valve. Scotland's demography aggravated unemployment, as the table below shows.

Table 2.4: Demographic trends

	1911–15		1936–40	
	Scotland	England and Wales	Scotland	England and Wales
Birth Rate per 1,000	25.4	23.6	17.6	14.7
Death Rate per 1,000	15.7	14.3	13.6	12.2
Natural increase	9.7	9.3	4.0	2.5

A rate of natural increase about 30 per cent greater than that of England meant that a larger working population was entering a comparatively stagnant job market. In Scotland in 1923 the labour force was 22 per cent and by 1938 24 per cent of the population. In England, however, the equivalent percentages were 26 and 33, a divergence largely made up by the growth of women's jobs and the service industries. As a result of this, there was 20 per cent less earning capacity in a Scottish family compared to the UK average, and this increased the period at which families were at risk from poverty (chiefly when they had children under earning age).

V Planning a Way Out

Government was not inactive, but scarcely helpful. Faced with over-extended heavy industries (which might yet prove to be of strategic importance) and a labour surplus, Lloyd George and later the Unionists handed the former over to the Bank of England, and tackled the latter by assisted migration schemes, enacted in 1920 and 1928. By 1939 these had shifted 250,000 men and women, largely to the south of England. Labour was more positive; continuing Lloyd George's Trade Facilities Act of 1921, which gave low-interest loans to foreign buyers

of heavy engineering products (bringing about £5m. before its abolition by Churchill in 1926), and in 1929–31 instituting a public works
programme, mainly involving roadbuilding. Neither Labour nor the
Unionists questioned the 'balanced budget' – and defended it
against Keynes's and Lloyd George's *Yellow Book* plan for reflation
through deficit financing. This involved roadbuilding and electrification, paid for in the long term by an increase in the general tax-
paying capacity of the country by its 'multiplier' effect on economic
growth. However negative such reactions, the problem remained:
could such schemes have revitalized a Scottish economy so deficient in
the 'new' industries it proposed to stimulate?

In such situations the banking system played in Europe a critical
rôle. Not in Scotland, where the strength and sophistication of its
financial institutions – a virtue during industrialization – now
channelled investment away from the country. The habit of investing
in England was also strengthened by the sheer need to sustain the debts
of heavy industry. Although innovative financiers like J. Gibson
Jarvie – the founder of hire purchase – struggled to set up a
Scottish industrial investment trust, the banks were unwilling to take
the risk, and only in 1938 did such a scheme get off the ground. The
existing Scots-American trusts had taken a hammering in 1929; where
they survived, they were much less adventurous. In fact, most interest
in Scottish affairs was taken by the Clydesdale, whose owner, the Midland Bank, was a lone proponent of unorthodoxy in the financial
world. The banks continued to cater for the middle-class, not only as
clients but by providing a wealth of 'white-collar' jobs in their con-
stantly multiplying branches.

Self-help

The Labour government, in a purely cosmetic move, had encouraged
regional groups for industrial development. Partly stimulated by this,
on 7 May 1930 the Convention of Royal Burghs set up the Scottish
National Development Council, the main resolutions being moved by
Sir Alexander McEwen of Inverness and the Duke of Montrose, both
later of the Scottish Party. Despite its nationalist origins, by late 1931
it had the support of Sir James Lithgow, and of William Elger of the
Scottish Trade Union Congress, and in 1932 it even got a grudging
measure of government funding. It took on a full time staff and two
years later had produced several reports on economic problems, and a
glossy quarterly magazine, *Scotland*.

Lithgow was the SNDC's key figure. He shared many of Weir's strengths and weaknesses: talented, hardworking but undiplomatic, he had a logical case for backing it. Only by drastic reductions in capacity and manpower did he see the heavy industries surviving; other industries were needed to absorb the surplus. At the same time he had no expertise in the consumer goods sector. As the SNDC gathered momentum, so did factory closures. Between 1932 and 1934 58 factories opened in Scotland, 88 closed.

Government Action

Only now did government begin to move. In 1932 and 1933 Walter Elliot, as Minister of Agriculture, stimulated enquiries into health and nutrition in areas of high unemployment, on the advice of his friend John Boyd Orr of the Rowett Research Institute, Aberdeen. As a result the Cabinet on 28 March 1934 agreed to 'informal' investigation of central Scotland, south Wales, north-east England, parts of Cumberland and Lancashire, partly in order to smooth the path of the new Unemployment Assistance Act (see p.77).

As a result, on 24 October the Cabinet suggested a 'Special Areas' Commissioner, with four regional agents. But Sir Godfrey Collins, Scottish Secretary, gained a separate appointment – probably because of pressure from Lithgow and the Unionists for administrative devolution. The original investigator, Sir Hugh Rose, an Edinburgh paint manufacturer and head of the Organization for the Maintenance of Supplies during the General Strike, became the first (unpaid) Scottish Commissioner.

His 'Special Area' covered the counties of Lanark, Renfrew, Dumbarton, Fife, and West Lothian, and parts of Ayr and Stirling. Not Glasgow: to declare the 'Second City' a 'distressed area' was too much. Between 1934 and 1939 Rose and his successors Sir David Allan Hay and Lord Nigel Douglas-Hamilton, spent some £4m. Initially they could only aid public works, but after 1937 they assisted small firms through the Special Areas Reconstruction Association. There were failures: some doomed, eccentric smallholding experiments; several ailing firms, bailed out, going to the wall; but the Commissioners did co-operate imaginatively with the SNDC. Rose recommended in his first report, November 1935. 'An authoritative Scots body . . . financed by the government to explore industrial conditions, and in general aim at introducing into our economic structure . . . [an] element of orderly and planned development'. These proposals went far beyond his local remit, but Collins backed them against the inter-departmental Special Areas Committee and in March 1936 authorized the Scottish Economic Committee, only six months before his sudden death.

The Scottish Economic Committee

The Economic Committee under Sir William Goodchild was formally a sub-committee of the SNDC but the Commissioner paid for it and it co-operated with Elliot, now Secretary of State. It was a timely move, as in March 1937 Baldwin announced the Barlow Commission into the Distribution of the Industrial Population. The SEC reported on the Highlands, light industries, and rearmament policy. It gave evidence to Barlow, published as *Scotland's Economic Future*. It helped promote the Empire Exhibition, Scottish Industrial Estates, Films of Scotland, and the Scottish Special Housing Association, but, on the outbreak of war, it was suspended. Whitehall regarded it with suspicion, and its advocacy of autonomy was, during the war, replaced by the policy of centralized allocation of industry advocated by the Labour Party's 1937 committee of enquiry, under Hugh Dalton, which underlay his 1945 Distribution of Industry Act. But it had, for a few years, focussed Scottish 'middle opinion' approaches to economic and social reconstruction.

It drew on Boyd Orr, whose Rowett Research Station extended its influence from agriculture into welfare, science policy, and propaganda, involving Sir Stephen Tallents, John Grierson, and E.M.H. Lloyd, as well as Elliot, its former research fellow. It rejected the somewhat abstract neo-classicist economics of Sir William Scott in Glasgow and Sir Alexander Gray in Edinburgh in favour of the Keynesian ideas of James Bowie, director since 1931 of the new Dundee School of Economics. Finally, it linked up with the planning movement. Inaugurated by Sir Patrick Geddes, this had been strengthened by the creation of the National Trust for Scotland in 1931 and of the Saltire Society in 1936 by William Power, Boyd Orr, Bowie, and Thomas Johnston, and transformed into an influential advocate of economic and physical planning.

Elliot made the Empire Exhibition of 1938 in Bellahouston Park, Glasgow, the climax of these developments. Costing £11m., it drew on all his connections in science, publicity, and the arts. Architecturally ultra-modernist in design – its architect, Thomas S. Tait, brought in the young Basil Spence and Jack Coia – it was to draw, besides 13m.

visitors, light industries to the new industrial estates. The summer of 1938 was the summer of Munich — and it rained — but it demonstrated that there had been a real advance in analysing the Scottish problem. The SEC, the Clydesdale Bank's report, and Bowie's *The Future of Scotland* (1939) gave the problem a new social dimension. When Bowie, for instance, calculated the investment in a moderate-sized town at £10m., he questioned the sort of accounting which could close its local industry as unprofitable. But such analyses were of an economy distorted by rearmament, while factors seen as under-lying — stagnant international trade and an English population decline — proved temporary. The maxims, and many of the personalities, of the 1930s were to prove important after the war. But were they still relevant?

VI World War II

Between 1939 and 1945, in contrast to 1914–18, war production was subject to centralized control. An embryo organization had existed since 1924, and in December 1933, after Hitler had come to power, a small, and mainly Scottish, advisory group of industrialists — Weir, Lithgow, and Sir Arthur Balfour — assessed potential wartime demand. Detailed planning began in 1936 but until 1939 most organi-zation and expenditure was still geared not to total war, but to the finance and facilities that were available in peacetime: only the expenditure of the RAF was placed on a potential war footing. After World War I armaments production had been cut back to a minimum — the Royal Dockyards and Ordnance Factories and a few outside firms. It had also changed in nature. Army and air force demand was for the internal combustion engine and its derivatives; when Lithgow tried to interest Scottish industrialists in these he met with little success. Scottish industry was anyway ill-suited to supply them. Yet, as the most suitable factories lay in the south of England, skilled labour moved south to fill them. Only in Admiralty orders — to the shipyards and Beardmore's — did Scotland do well. When war broke out again Beardmore's again acted as the nucleus of gun and armour production, expanding into factories at Dalmuir, Germiston, and Linwood, and Clyde shipyards turned out an average of 400,000 tons of shipping a year — five ships a week by 1943 — not much under their 1914–18 levels.

At the outbreak of the war, which this time involved conscription from the start, unemployment fell to 20,000 (1.6 per cent) and stayed there. But other effects were serious: 'concentration' of non-munitions production meant that many Scottish factories were simply closed down, often permanently ('other manufacturing industry' fell from 26 per cent of output in 1935 to 14 per cent in 1951), and until late 1941 90 per cent of requisitioned factory space was used for storage. Thirteen thousand girls were drafted to the midlands, causing some political unrest. By July 1942, under pressure both from Scottish MPs, Tom Johnston at the Scottish Office, and the Scottish Council on Industry, storage had fallen to 57 per cent, and by 1945 some 7,000 war-connected projects — 13.5 per cent of the UK total — had been set up, including 119 complete plants: a total investment of £12m. Of these the 26 under the Ministry of Aircraft Production were the largest, employing 100,000 workers by 1945. Scotland became the main staging post both for convoys and for aircraft; Prestwick in 1944 was the busiest international airport in the world.

The workforce changed radically; from 80 per cent male in 1939 to only 60 per cent in 1944. Agriculture expanded: arable acreage increasing 15 per cent to its 1918 level through revived agricultural executives, 75 per cent subsidies, guaranteed prices, and a state holding of 227,000 acres. Wheat and barley acreage doubled, potatoes increased by 75 per cent. Yields — doubtless because of well-fertilized soil — exceeded England and Wales in practically every crop, sometimes by over 30 per cent. The number of tractors more than doubled, from 6,250 to more than 16,000. The fishing fleet was reduced from 5,000 to only 936 boats but, as fishing in English waters was effectively banned, it did creditably, although much of it remained obsolescent.

However, the apparent unity of 'the people's war' masked disturbing trends. Although Johnston could claim several economic gains, such as the creation of the North of Scotland Hydro-Electric Board, and could boast of the absence of a 'Red Clyde', citing a strike record of only 0.7 per cent of working days lost, productivity was persistently poor in munitions factories and very bad in the mines, and Ministry of Information reports cited an undercurrent of discontent, which expressed itself in volatile politics (see p.103). Although the fighting itself claimed only 40 per cent of the casualties of World War I, deaths in the RAF were twelve times and in the Merchant Navy almost two-and-a-half times greater. As the proportion of casualties among officers and warrant officers doubled, Scotland, with 15 per cent of UK secondary pupils, sacrificed too many from a generation in whom even more hope had been invested than in the men of Flanders. Their losses were to echo in subsequent inadequacies of management and innovation.

World War II drastically changed economic and social policy. Labour's 1945 victory made this explicit, but the 'managed' economy, achieved through monetary and especially fiscal policy, really dates from May 1940, when Chamberlain left office and Keynes moved to the Treasury. Chamberlain was not hostile to economic planning — witness the Barlow enquiry — but the new power of 'middle opinion' exemplified by the Beveridge Report (December 1942) integrated the new economics with the 'right' to full employment and health care, and was reinforced by the growing power of Labour in the coalition — personified by Ernest Bevin at the Labour Ministry. The Attlee government's policies were essentially a continuation of wartime practice. Hugh Dalton's Distribution of Industry Act, 1945, actually carried by Churchill's brief caretaker ministry, applied this consensus to regional policy. But, though it drew on the Barlow Report, it rejected the autonomous development authority proposed by the SEC in favour of a centralized system of permits and advanced factories built by the Board of Trade. Although the Council on Industry became the Scottish Council: Development and Industry in 1946, with representation from local authorities, unions, and industry (or at least parts of it), and joint bodies were set up between the Scottish Office and other ministries concerned with industry, the valuable semi-autonomy of the SEC was lost — tragically at a time when increasing numbers of decisions ended up in the hands of less-than-expert Whitehall mandarins.

VII Indian Summer

Was 1940−1951 an economic watershed, as Labour claimed — at least until the late 1960s? Had nationalization of 'the commanding heights', centralized allocation of factory space, investment incentives, and physical planning combated the drift south and promoted diversification? Or did the managed economy, by masking fundamental industrial continuities, increase the problem of readjustment?

For a start financial assistance was limited, even by the standards of the 1930s — in real terms government assistance was only about 56 per cent over the resources allocated to the pre-war Commissioner. The main weapon was compulsion. Yet there was little need to compel plants to the north, because of the lack of factory space and housing accommodation in southern England. Moreover, American companies feared losing European markets through possible tariff increases and shipping shortages, and were anxious to open factories wherever the British government allowed them. Even so, expansion was severely curbed by the financial crisis of 1947, and the prevailing export drive actually restricted diversification, while in the heavy industries the export drive, controls on investment and profits, and the absence of state assistance deferred large-scale re-equipment. After 1947 regional assistance dropped by a third; during the 1950s it was actually less, in real terms, than in the 1930s, and all but nominal.

Although industrial building in Scotland had run at 12.2 per cent of the UK figure between 1945 and 1951 it fell to 6.5 per cent in 1958. Regional policy may have been an article of Labour faith, but in 1951 the Scottish Council's Committee on Local Development concluded that 'the disappearance of large-scale unemployment has by no means been due entirely, or even principally, to the new policy'. The wartime decline in the range of Scottish manufacturing was never made good, and by 1953 Cairncross reported that 'dependence on the heavy industries has grown rather than diminished'.

Shipbuilding

The need to restore wartime destruction — allied losses *alone* came to 23,351,000 tons, compared with total losses during World War I of 15,053,786 tons — and the bombing of enemy ships and shipyards, brought an Indian summer to the Clyde. But Cairncross noted the 'comparative indifference' of the heavy industries 'to new equipment, new knowledge, and new opportunities for development'. They had merely been granted a stay of execution. They did not attempt to reverse the sentence.

The slump of 1957–8 in the Scottish heavy industries, which turned out terminal, started with a drop in demand. But the underlying trend was in fact a quite unprecedented demand for ships and engineering. In 1954 world shipping totalled 97m. tons, freighters averaged 6,000 tons, and the world's largest ship was the *Queen Elizabeth* at 83,000 tons. By 1973 world tonnage was 289 million, largest ship, the tanker *Globtik Tokyo*, grossed 239,000 tons, and the combination of containers and 'inter-modal' transport had completely transformed freight handling. The closure of the Suez Canal in 1956 focussed attention both on oil consumption (Britain's grew 200 per cent, 1950–60) and on its transport. The Cape of Good Hope route both demanded and permitted huge ships, and their pattern influenced other cargos and dock design. Scots had experimented with the new technology for years — Brassert's plan for a waterside steelworks in 1929, Dennys' construction of the first modern car ferry in 1939, the Finnart oil-discharging port in 1952. But these innovations were not capitalized on. Why?

It is difficult to find any simple reason. Development failures for instance, beset car ferries. Scotland's early lead was hit by the 1939−55 decline in motoring, and by the sinking of the roll-on, roll-off *Princess Victoria* off Stranraer in 1953. Several years were to pass before another attempt was made, but by 1964 the Germans and Swedes had cornered the market. As the airlines took their toll, vehicle ferries were the only way that the 'hotel-ship' yards would survive, yet Dennys, the major short-sea builders, were one of the first casualties in 1961. They were soon followed by other specialist firms, like Simons-Lobnitz of Renfrew and the Grangemouth Dockyard Company.

The tragedy was that these yards reached Scandinavian standards of craftmanship and tranquil labour relations. By contrast, the great Clydeside concerns were a mess. Their family managerial dynasties were suicidally conservative, in design, marketing, research, and labour relations. Their equipment was depreciating by £9m. per annum, while only half that sum was being re-invested. Research and development ran at a paltry £250,000. Rationalization was badly needed — in Japan 5 engineering works served 18 main shipyards, on the Clyde 9 works served 16 yards — but it was seldom even discussed, management rivalries and union bloody-mindedness ruling even joint consultation out of court.

Engineering

Heavy engineering initially benefited from its semi-monopoly position. Until 1950 railway orders were almost at the 1920 level, and in 1947 Pressed Steel Fisher established a huge waggon plant at Linwood, near Paisley. Yet diesel and electric locomotives were taking over, and the North British Locomotive Company was unable to supply them successfully. Although reprieved by the £1,050m. British Railways re-equipment programme, which also brought orders for 34,000 out of 46,000 new waggons to Scottish works, and Glasgow electric 'Blue Trains' orders to Pressed Steel, it closed in 1961. Shortly afterwards Linwood was turned over to the motor industry.

It was not all loss, however. Many of the techniques of heavy industry were equally applicable to construction, which grew rapidly in the 1960s, and the reservoir of skilled manpower was indispensable for installing and maintaining the first generation of light engineering 'transplants' — Westclox, IBM, Hoover — and after 1962 the motor plants of Linwood and Bathgate. What had been lost, however, was the link between skill and innovation: something which not even the establishment of the National Engineering Laboratory at East Kilbride in 1947 could remedy.

Steel

Scottish steel largely provided plates and castings for heavy industry: in 1950 15 per cent of its output went to mechanical engineering, 15 per cent to constructional engineering, and 20 per cent to shipbuilding. Only 0.3 per cent went to the vehicle industry (12 per cent in the UK). Although a 'hot-metal' works was built at Clydebridge in 1938, Motherwell, Hallside, Glengarnock, and Parkhead still used Siemens open-hearth furnaces to reduce a mixture of scrap and imported pig-iron. After 1945 scrap and coking coal were scarce, and steel imports grew. But political uncertainty inhibited planning: Labour announced nationalization in 1945, but did not table a bill until 1948. Delayed by the Lords, the takeover only came in January 1951, 10 months before the return of the Unionists, who in 1953 returned the industry to private hands, subject to overall control by a state board. The nationalized board favoured reviving Brassert's scheme, but its successor in 1954 let Colvilles build a new integrated iron-and-steel works at Ravenscraig, near Motherwell, served by an ore-discharging plant at Glasgow's General Terminus Quay. This opened in 1960, and alongside it in 1962 the company started a steel strip mill to serve the motor industry. Economists had favoured a shore site in south Wales, but mounting government unpopularity in Scotland prompted Harold Macmillan to split the scheme and loan Colvilles £50m. In 1967, when Labour renationalized the industry, Scotland's output of strip steel had risen six-fold, but overall production continued to decline. Twenty per cent of UK output in 1920, it had fallen to 12 per cent in 1960. The industry was badly sited, technically conservative, and its large product range was dictated by its predominately local market: all aspects that the corporate planning of the new British Steel Corporation announced itself ready to remedy.

Energy

Labour nationalized the mines in 1948, and shortly announced plans for major expansion intended to double output to 30.6m. tons by 1965. This involved exploitation of the Fife coalfield and centralization of production in 13 large mines, of which the greatest, Rothes, was to cost £15m. But, partly because of the expenses of mine-sinking, and partly because of the numbers still working in old pits, productivity remained low, and the Scottish region of the National Coal Board slid into deficit. The complete failure of the huge Rothes venture in 1960 sanctioned a rapid contraction of the industry. By 1970 production was down to 12.7m. tons and the labour force to 29,700. Its situation had not been helped by the Hydro Board. By 1961 the Board's construction programme was virtually complete and it supplied over a third of Scottish electricity. Before the war socialist and environmentalist critics of Highland water power had stressed this consequence. Johnston had sold it successfully as an agency for regenerating the Highlands, a national investment, and a triumph for Scots autonomy – and it was subsequently rarely criticized. But it was none of these things; without it, coal might not have hit the trough of the early 1960s. By the middle of that decade the Hydro Board's contribution was plainly inadequate, and a programme of large steam generators – coal, oil, and nuclear – was announced. Power generated, about 1,900 Megawatt Hours in 1939, rose to 2,208 MW in 1950, 3,017 MW in 1961, and 10,378 MW in 1978.

Agriculture

War and Labour government completed the reconstruction of agriculture. After 1947 the state guaranteed prices for farm produce, injecting 20 per cent of UK agricultural expenditure into Scottish farming, against 6 per cent in 1939. Scotland had only 11 per cent of UK output but, as livestock received higher subsidies than arable produce, her dependence on it increased. By 1964 she produced 15.2 per cent of UK livestock, compared with only 9.5 per cent of livestock produce (milk, eggs, etc.) and 7.5 per cent of arable crops. Farms were consolidated and sophisticated equipment bought, as rural electrification was extended. Land workers, 120,000 in 1945, tumbled to under 40,000 in 1964. Although they were better off and could now afford a car, freezer, and television, the differential between their income and that of the farmers widened. It now made sense for landowners to farm their own land, so the 'gentleman farmers', whom the sociologist James Littlejohn had noticed filtering into *Westrigg*, proliferated.

Agricultural-based industry also flourished. Meat- and fruit-canning expanded in Fraserburgh, Dundee, and Fochabers, and was supplemented by freezing and vacuum-packing. Brewing and distilling grew spectacularly. Breweries, increasingly English-controlled, pushed up output from 1.2m. barrels in 1939 to over 2m. barrels in 1960, subsequently soaring to over 5m. barrels in 1980, although enthusiasts regretted the abandonment of traditional ales in favour of lager-type beers for the English market. Distilling's post-prohibition upswing was checked by the war, but it subsequently became Scotland's leading export industry. In 1975 its output was valued at £312m. Shipbuilding brought in only £215m.

The Service Sector

After World War II the service sector rose to dominate the economy. In 1936 its components – transport and distribution, business and commerce, and public service – made up about 32 per cent of output, against 36 per cent in the UK. By 1958 Scotland had almost reached the UK level of 49 per cent; in the 1960s she went ahead. Given the extent of the country, transport and distribution were always important; likewise the public services. But business and commerce lagged: in 1958 income from these was still 28 per cent below the UK level, while in 1961 Scotland had only 7 per cent of UK administrators and managers. The activity of retailing was checked by low expenditure per head, which actually fell from 92 to 90 per cent of the UK level 1953–62. It remained fairly distinctive until the mid sixties: few public markets, a strong but rather stagnant Co-op movement, and enough future in department stores to stimulate the activities of tycoons like Isaac Wolfson and Hugh Fraser. Self-service came late, around 1960, and only in the 1960s did growing consumer expenditure attract the English multiples. By 1978 Scottish consumer expenditure was actually slightly over the UK level, but the incomers had changed the face of the Scottish high streets completely.

Transport

Transport changed slowly in the 1950s. Tramcars dwindled, and finally vanished from Glasgow in 1962. Cars were still relatively rare outside country districts, because of dense and cheap bus services, and the sheer difficulty of accommodating them in the narrow tenemented streets of the big towns. The railways had changed little. Only five trains a day ran from Glasgow to London in 1957; the fastest one took 7 hours 40 minutes, 70 minutes longer than 1939. There were still 3,208 miles of track. New roads were few, save in new towns and housing schemes, but by 1960 even the most local routes had been surfaced, although in the Highlands single-tracked roads were still the rule. MacBrayne's steamers still loaded goods, cattle, and cars 'over the side'; puffers still chugged through the Forth and Clyde and Crinan Canals, out to the beaches of the Western Isles.

Change began in 1955, with the start of the Forth Road Bridge. By the time it opened in 1964, a Tay Road Bridge was also under construction (opened 1966) and road expenditure had risen from £2.6m. to £34m., or in real terms by 1,000 per cent. This was at the expense of the railways, which were drastically rationalized, both by Conservative and Labour governments. This process benefited some areas — intercity passenger, container, and bulk traffic, but the division of responsibility between the Ministry of Transport (railways) and the Scottish Development Department (roads, ferries, and buses) frustrated coordination. The fruit of the vast expenditure of 1960–75 was a railway system reduced by 42 per cent and a fall of 50 per cent in bus passengers.

Tourism

Tourism was equally impeded by poor planning. Boosted by holidays with pay after 1938, it roughly doubled in size between then and 1958, to earn about £50m. a year. But it remained unsure of its aim: a mass market or a wealthy one? Although the government set up a Scottish Tourist Board in 1946, it gave it only £20,000 in 1958, and by then the mass market was going: the Clyde was losing out to the Costa Brava. When the state did intervene, stimulated by the Irish example, in the 1960s, it perpetrated some horrid developments — the Aviemore centre — and squandered assets like the Clyde steamers. Business had doubled again by 1970, but grew only a third as fast as the rest of Britain. The Highlands and Islands Development Board, however, served its area well, and also boosted the quality of crafts and souvenirs. In the 1950s families toured the Highlands in Morris Oxfords and complained about Japanese knick-knacks. In the 1970s they could buy quality pottery and handweaves to take home in their Datsuns.

VIII Planning Redux

Scotland's economic problems in the late 1950s were difficult to unravel. Structural changes in the heavy industries were fundamental, but government actions aggravated them. Deflation in late 1957 – the consequence of an overambitious defence programme – coincided with the phasing-out of National Service. Civilian jobs were shed, while the potential labour force was swelled. The government stopped subsidizing shale and jute and cut back the coal industry's plans. As a result, unemployment in Scotland doubled between 1958 and 1959 from 58,000 to 116,000, while the outlook in the heavy industries and mines, and on the railways, seemed even worse. The general election of October 1959 made Scottish apprehension explicit.

'The spectre of the 1930s' or the result of labour fractiousness? There were grounds for both views. Productivity was poor: in the mines scarcely higher than 30 years earlier. Incoming American firms placed Scotland, with Italy, at the bottom of their productivity scale. The memory of what productivity had meant in the 1930s went deep. 'Hostile suspicion', Cairncross noted in 1952, 'often flares up in reaction to proposals in which there is any hint of labour redundancy'. With some reason. Agriculture saw a rise in productivity of 300 per cent, 1939–60, but this benefited the farmer or the consumer, not the weakly-organized farm workers or the local community. Other unions were more grimly defensive.

But management was often no better. As Tom Burns showed in *The Management of Innovation* (1961), the 'mechanical' relationships between departments in Scottish firms lacked the strength of the 'organic' corporate identity of American firms. Scottish managers found relief from difficult organizational problems either by blaming others or by assuming 'irreconcileable differences of attitudes and codes of rational conduct'. Scottish inventiveness could still produce the marine stabilizer and fibreglass, but long-term planning, state or private, was missing. Too much responsibility had drifted south, and too much ability had followed it. The successors of flawed giants like Lithgow or Weir were, as advocates of 'planning', more diplomatic, but also less original and less energetic. Consensus was preferred to abrasiveness, even if the resulting cosiness made it difficult to ascertain success or failure.

The planners, the Scottish Council and the trade unions had been kept out in the cold by the Unionists. The Council had attracted many

American firms, but could foresee stiffer opposition — both from the EEC (1957) and from Eire after the Whitaker Report of 1958. The grandiose regional plans of Mears, Payne, and Abercrombie had lain in pigeonholes for a decade; as the backlog of war-delayed building was completed in the mid 1950s, the architects and planners feared a repetition of the hard times of the 1920s; they were echoed by property men, the construction industry, and, increasingly, the road transport lobby. The STUC, too, had helped attract American firms by conceding union privileges. It was now worried that militancy would grow with unemployment.

But the spectre of economic decline was not the only motive for 'planning'. British attitudes changed sharply in the mid 1950s; a quite unprecedented hedonism propelled the country out of the 'Victorian straitjacket'. As usual this reached Scotland a bit late, but by 1959 Scots were lumping grumbles about smaller houses, fewer cars, worse food, and more restrictions alongside concern about mounting unemployment. When Gavin McCrone's detailed survey *Scotland's Economic Progress* came out in 1965 it showed a growth rate (9 per cent, 1954–60) running at half the UK level, and income per head 13 per cent lower than the UK average — political factors as (if not more) important than industrial reconstruction.

In 1960 Macmillan, through the Local Employment Act, resumed an active regional policy, and the Scottish Office, acting through the Scottish Council, began 'An Inquiry into the Scottish Economy'. The resulting 'Toothill Report' (November 1961) was politically important: it revived the concept of planning and gained it consensus support. As an economic diagnosis it was much more suspect. The central problem remained that of the heavy industries. Before 1939 their productivity grew but their market stagnated; after 1950 the opposite was the case. Yet was their decline inevitable? Cheap labour and raw material might have gone, but skills, adaptiveness, and a valuable range of ancillary industries remained. Could specialized types of production be maintained, or should heavy industry gradually be phased out in such a way that its ancillary industries became self-standing and its skills were preserved? Toothill ignored heavy industry almost completely, in favour of 'new industry' growth-points, infrastructural improvement, and industrial incentives. By dismissing further measures of economic devolution, it also removed the possibility of a planned adaption from old industries to new. In comparison to the Scottish Economic Committee's realism in 1938, Toothill, despite its similar vocabulary, was a sad decline.

The Scottish Development Department (1962) and the Central Scottish plan (1963) stemmed directly from Toothill, and Labour was quick to use it as a stick to belabour 'stop – go' Unionist policies. But Labour after 1964 dropped Toothill's positive insistance on 'growth points' in favour of a broad Scottish Development Area, only to find itself giving first-aid to the rapidly declining heavy industries. The Scottish Council itself subsequently rejected the Toothill formula: in 1970 it proposed *Oceanspan*, which intended to revive heavy industry by using the Clyde as a transhipment port for western Europe. It seemed a sensible option, but 'to lose traditional industries with comparative international advantages', as the economist Peter Jay told the Council in 1974, was to court 'a perpetual dynamic of decay'. By then, heavy industrial decline had gone too far.

3

The Pillars of Society 1922 – 1964

I

'A separate society', according to Tom Bottomore, in *Sociology*, implies 'political independence along with distinct economic, religious, and familiar institutions'. Plainly, Scotland fails to meet such criteria. Its politics and its economy are clearly those of the United Kingdom, albeit with important variations. Yet Bottomore's more detailed list of 'functional prerequisites of society', in the same book, suggests a more complicated picture. These include, besides economy and politics, systems of communication: 'arrangements (including the family and education) for the socialization of new generations and . . . systems of ritual, serving to maintain or increase social cohesion'. Communications and culture — certainly distinctive — will form much of chapter 5. This chapter will deal with socialization, ritual, and social stratification. Such categories are not, of course, mutually exclusive; they overlap. Different interpretations have seen inherent structure and system as crucial or, in the case of Marxism, have seen the central motive of human action inhering in one part of the system — the economy — which fundamentally influences all other parts.

In Scotland education, religion, and law have functions that are political as well as social. They both legitimate Scottish distinctiveness and require the systematic adaptation of British legislation. Moreover, in the absence of a Scottish legislature, they have a political life of their own, concerned to maintain their status — and that of their members — in a society on the whole more pluralistic than that of the south. This causes problems for the historian. The history of Scots institutions, written 'from the inside', has stressed their distinctiveness over their actual function, while, conversely, studies of British society more rooted in a class-analysis have tended either to exclude Scotland, or to subsume its experience by aggregating its data into

British patterns which it then treats as norms. This co-existence of parochial complacency and metropolitan insensitivity has meant that no real attempt has been made to relate Scottish distinctiveness to class structure.

If Scotland substantially originated the study of 'man in society' in the eighteenth century, and produced Sir J.G. Frazer and Sir Patrick Geddes in the nineteenth, twentieth century Scottish sociology has had an unhappy history. In contrast to inter-war European states, where sociology was an essential ingredient of liberal or social-democratic social planning, the Scots produced only a handful of research papers, and the *Third Statistical Account of Scotland* (commenced in 1943) was a sad declension from Sinclair's *Accounts* of the 1790s and 1830s, — a failure reflected palpably by the planning mistakes of the 1960s. Can this be attributed to the plight of the Scottish universities in the inter-war years, and their lack of investment in research (see p.78)? Possibly, but the country produced some good social scientists, and some of them taught in the universities. If there was little inclination, or external pressure, towards the study of Scottish society this was reinforced by the power of the Scottish institutions themselves. The result necessarily complicates the writings of chapters like this. What follows can only be a sketch, with impressionistic data, and a guide to where further research is necessary, with some hunches and generalizations, pending that massive task.

II The People

Between 1921 and 1961 Scotland's population grew by only 6 per cent. Despite consistently lower rates of natural increase — 5.9 against 7.2 per cent in the 1920s, 4.4 against 6.7 per cent in the 1950s — the population of England and Wales grew by 21 per cent.

Out-migration was the main reason, but this was not simply a function of economic deterioration. It was higher in the Edwardian period and in the Indian summer of the 1950s than in the stricken 1930s, when absence of opportunities elsewhere seems to have checked it by at least 50 per cent, thus contributing to Scotland's persistent unemployment. A positive 'emigration ideology' was certainly present — especially in the post-war period when overseas emigration prevailed over 'drifting south'. As *Scotland* reported in 1956, 90 per cent of emigrants were under 45, and most were 'drawn from the most important industrial groups'. Family ambitions, rather than personal economic circumstances, prevailed as a motive. In the 1960s losses came to

94 per cent of natural increase; in the 1970s they were 163 per cent.

Regional population distribution changed relatively little after the late 1800s. The Scots who lived in the central Lowlands certainly increased from 61 per cent of the total population in 1871 to 76 per cent in 1961, but the proportion dwelling in the 4 cities and 20 large burghs – 51 per cent in 1901 – scarcely changed. The drift from the countries north of the central belt – 8 per cent between 1911 and 1931 – had dropped to 2 per cent by 1951. Some industrial growth and better communications (especially cars, buses, and delivery vans) certainly helped combat farm mechanization and fishing decline, until electrification, oil, and the activities of the Highlands and Islands Development Board came to the rescue. Between 1951 and 1974 population rose by 15 per cent. Lacking such inputs, the southern uplands, where population held stable until 1951, dropped by 6 per cent in the same years.

Buses, council housing, and lack of long-term planning also preserved, in the central belt, many old industrial settlements that ought to have been evacuated and demolished. As a result an unlovely 'third Scotland' sprawled from South Ayrshire to Fife, merging with outlying city housing schemes, speculative developments, and new towns. The 'third Scotland' was neither much liked nor at all well known. Somewhat isolated, ignored, lacking city facilities or country traditions – even lacking the attentions of sociologists – yet, as the

Table 3.1: Population, 1911 – 1998 (in thousands)

		Natural	Net Migration	
	Scotland (% of UK)	*Increase*	*to rest of UK*	*Overseas*
1911	4,760 (10.5)			
1911–21		360.2	–238.6	
1921	4,882 (10.4)			
1921–31		352.4	–330	–60
1931	4,842 (10.5)			
1931–51		502.3	–210	–10
1951	5,096 (10.1)			
1951–61		339.3	–140	–142
1961	5,179 (9.8)			
1961–71		346.3	–169	–157.5
1971	5,228 (9.4)			
1971–81		55.9	–54.1	–92.1
1981	5,180 (9.2)			
1981–90		21.0	–99.0	
1990	5,102 (8.9)			
1998	5,120 (8.6)			

UK included all Ireland

Table 3.2: The New Towns

	Population 1975	
	Actual	*Planned*
East Kilbride (1947)	70,000	95,000
Glenrothes (1948)	32,000	70,000
Cumbernauld (1956)	31,000	70,000
Livingston (1962)	21,000	100,000
Irvine (1969)	46,000	120,000

population of Glasgow plunged 25 per cent, 1951–80, it steadily grew, and showed a fair amount of political volatility in the 1960s, as though nationalism provided some sort of substitute for the community identity it lacked.

One ingredient of 1960s politics absent in Scotland was racial tension. The post-war labour surplus meant little inward migration. As the Irish inflow slackened after the 1920s, most incomers were English (5 per cent of the population by the 1960s) usually in somewhat temporary armed service or management rôles. They found Scottish education and housing sufficiently strange to make major office transfers a tricky business. Hence Toothill's attempts to reassure them. The tension that the Irish had earlier aroused in Scotland, and that coloured immigration provoked in England in the 1950s and the 1960s, was absent. New Commonwealth immigrants were only 0.2 per cent of the 1966 population, compared with 1.1 per cent in the UK, no more noticeable than the communities of Jews, Italians, Poles, and foreign students in the larger towns. As the immigrants either integrated well, or were unobtrusive, working class racialism was absent. Were the Scots more tolerant? Possibly. Despite much anti-Irish propaganda in the 1920s, the Catholic community had become well integrated, and there were few reverberations from events in Ulster. But immigrant numbers were never sufficient to put this to the test.

III Family and Household

Scottish families, in common with the rest of the UK, fell in size in the twentieth century; but they still remained larger than the British norm, even in 1961: something that increased the non-earning section of the population — and thus the poverty figures — in the 1930s. More children survived than previously. Due largely to antisepsis, infant mortality fell from 1 in 6 in the 1890s to 1 in 8 by 1911 (under the UK figure of 1 in 7); this rate of improvement was not sustained. In 1938 it was 1 in 11, but England had improved to 1 in 16, and Holland stood at 1 in 30. This was largely due to Scotland's industrial depression and poor housing, although possibly aggravated by later marriage and inferior antenatal facilities. In the 1930s government and local authorities started to shift confinements to maternity homes, a process continued under the National Health Service. Angus, for example, got its first maternity hospital in 1939; by 1948 60 per cent of births were in such hospitals, and by 1966 97.8 per cent. By then infant mortality had fallen to 1 in 66.

Large families were also due in part to a large Catholic population: 15 per cent in 1961, against 10 per cent in the UK. But among the Protestant middle classes attitudes were changing. In 1918 Dr Marie Stopes, the product of an Edinburgh liberal background, published *Married Love*, her famous plea for the acceptance of sexual pleasure in marriage and, logically, of contraception. This was attacked by all the churches — the Kirk only grudgingly changed its mind in the 1940s — but family planning clinics were opened in the cities, and in the 1930s Aberdeen formulated one of the most advanced family planning and maternity services in Europe, under its Medical Officer of Health, Sir Dugald Baird. 'Artificial' contraception was less important than *coitus interruptus* until the 1950s, but family size dropped from around five to two children. Reduced drinking must have helped this, and doubtless, too, a growing if grudging valuation of the wife's rôle as wage-earner and housekeeper.

In its turn, this exposed marriage to greater stress. Divorces, while more available than in pre-1914 England, were prohibitively expensive, and reform was delayed until 1938. Thereafter the number increased considerably, to 2,000 in 1951 and nearby 3,700 in 1966. Divorce reflected both growing instability and male irresponsibility; the number of single-parent families, 4,000 in 1947, grew to over 25,000 in 1972 — although this also testified to a welcome disinclination among Scotswomen to tolerate the semi-servitude that marriage had often entailed.

Before World War I, and for a long time afterwards in heavy industry areas, women acted as housekeeper: usually to more than one worker per household. But they had become 25 per cent of the labour force in 1921, 35 per cent in 1961. Wages were still poor, and rose from under 40 per cent of male wages in 1921 only to 50 per cent in 1961. But women were arguably more socially mobile than men; they voted with their feet. Littlejohn, in *Westrigg*, noticed that a farmworker's daughter could marry a farmer without the latter losing caste, and otherwise would often move into towns in search of eligible partners.

The same applied to miners' daughters, reluctant to housekeep in male-dominated pit villages. Even before post-1945 light industries set out to attract women, they were in the majority in Scottish towns. This was true of textile communities, but as women usually outlived their menfolk and then moved near to relatives this meant that in the 1950s (when the overall ratio was 101 men to 109 women) a large Scottish town would show only 88 single men to 124 widows, while a country district would show 110 single men to only 81 widows.

Surveys, like Willmott and Young's of East London, stressed the shift from 'extended' to 'nuclear' families. The Scottish case was less straightforward. Scottish farm-workers had moved around almost like nomads although minimum wage and national insurance (1935) was bringing this to an end. The extended family — with its 'hive' of relatives living close to one another — was really an urban phenomenon, and a relatively recent one.

A 1960s survey of Edinburgh housing estates found that in Wardieburn, a 1930s slum clearance scheme, 83 per cent of families had relatives in the city, in 27 per cent of the cases no more than a mile away. By contrast, only 35 per cent of families in owner-occupied Silverknowes had Edinburgh relatives. As grannies and aunts helped bring up children and run the household — an unthinkable activity for men — the working-class 'hive' of interlocking activities (contrasted with the middle class 'network' of optional acquaintances) was relatively female dominated. It was also menaced, both by the growing numbers of working women, and by the impact of rehousing. The Edinburgh survey found three responses to this: 'escalators' aimed at an affluent nuclear family, buying more consumer goods — though not housing or private education. Fathers played a greater part in looking after the family and decorating the house: 'Ubiquitous is the cherry moquette suite, the contrasting wallpaper, the television set in one corner, and the budgie in another'. If the 'escalators' resembled the 'affluent workers' of Goldthorpe's Luton survey, the second group were more characteristically Scots: often composed of people, originally from the same area, who tried to recreate the same interdependent working-class community. Success tended to depend on the 'stair-heid' politics of a dominant working-class woman, such as the one who organized a fry-up on Granton foreshore. Where such were lacking, in the slum clearance estates like Wardieburn, the older residents regretted the 'paradise lost' of their old communities, and were seemingly incapable of integrating either unruly youngsters or the 'problem families' that increasingly were dumped there.

The initial poverty of Wardieburn families diminished their resilience. Working-class community required some degree of affluence: it was no substitute for it. Ultimately, affluence even gave the extended family a new lease of life. Car ownership rose from 1:7 people in 1961 to 1:5 in 1978 and 1:3 in 1990. Telephone ownership rose even faster, from 1:7 in 1961 to 1:2 in 1978. With 81 per cent of homes connected in 1990, families could remain 'extended' even after rehousing.

Family life preserved accents, although broadcasting, 'talkies', and the hostility of the schools to the 'speech of the street' emasculated the old dialects. 'Speaking broad' was a badge of working-class identity, and the English of working-class leaders, who could either be inarticulate (like William Adamson) or else of an almost artificial 'cut glass' or 'plum in the mooth' precision, bore out some of Edwin Muir's suppositions about the consequences of having to be literate in a foreign language. In London, however, Scots was less socially crippling than provincial English. Sean Connery's Edinburgh accent — referred to by one critic as 'Martian' — established him as a very potent 'James Bond': a part that could never have been played by a Brummie.

IV Housing

Family life was limited, above all, by poor housing. In 1911 less than 8 per cent of the population of England and Wales lived in one- and two-roomed houses: in Scotland 50 per cent. High land values, legal peculiarities, rapid urbanization, a tradition of multi-storey living and relatively low rents had led to an acceptance of lower standards.

Despite the Royal Commission's report, after 1918 the situation became, if anything, worse. Those living in one or two rooms had dropped by about 3 per cent per decade, 1871–1911, to 50 per cent of families. But the fall between then and 1931 was only to 44 per cent. The Commission had talked of a target of 250,000 new homes (rather over a quarter of the existing housing stock). Between 1919 and 1939 300,000 were in fact built, but in 1935–6 the first survey to supply equal criteria north and south of the border found that 22.5 per cent of Scottish homes were overcrowded, compared with 3.8 per cent in England. The best Scottish case — Edinburgh with 17 per cent - was almost equal to the worst English one — Sunderland with 20.6 per cent. Clyde valley towns commonly reached over 40 per cent and even council houses (by then, about 12 per cent) were as overcrowded as the national average. In all, almost 50 per cent of Scottish housing stock was now deemed inadequate.

A further inhibiting factor was the tenants' success in winning rent control. As private renting was now inherently uneconomical, landlords had no motive to alter, enlarge, or repair properties.

Even after 1918, the rate of new building per head of population was only 60 per cent that of England, there being no equivalent to the building boom of the 1930s. The conditions which led to it — growing industries, cheap mortgages (building societies were almost non-existent in Scotland) and raw materials, the inward migration of labour, and potential customers — were all lacking.

Finally, local authorities and the state were both inexperienced. Local authorities had, before 1914, rehoused fewer than 1 per cent of Scottish families, but the Housing (Scotland) Act (1919) made them the main instruments of housing construction. This inexperience, coupled with the absence of a proper advisory staff or effective cost controls, meant that the first generation of council houses were over-priced, and the 'Addison Act' was a virtual dead letter by the time of the Geddes cuts. Between 1919 and 1923 only 25,000 houses had been built. The Chamberlain Act of 1923 subsidized privately-built houses for rent by £4 per annum, and built over 50,000. The Act of 1924, however, was largely Scottish in conception and execution, the work of John Wheatley, the ablest of the Clydesiders. By this an annual subsidy of £9 per house per year was paid to the local authority by the state. When passed to the tenant, this meant a cut of between a third and quarter of his weekly rent, or an extra room. The number of houses built 1925-9 went up by 140 per cent on 1920-4.

The theory behind these Housing Acts was that council houses would cater for the better-off tenant, whose relatively tolerable accommodation would then be available to the less well-off. At the bottom of the ladder, slums would thus steadily be cleared. However, this 'stepladder' needed some affluence to work, otherwise it simply subsidized the better-off while the slum-dwellers stayed put. In 1930 Labour shifted the stress to wholesale slum clearance and rehousing on new estates, built to higher densities, while the later Act of 1935 concentrated on more selective remedying of the overcrowding revealed by the report of that year. Walter Elliot placed particular stress on housing, attained an inter-war maximum of nearly 20,000 completions in 1918, and formed the Scottish Special Areas Housing Association, a government building organization using new construction systems. This was to play a remarkable rôle in the post-war period.

The slum clearance schemes of the 1930s were cheap housing and looked it. Wardieburn and Craigmillar in Edinburgh and Blackhill in Glasgow, with their monotonous rows of three- and four-storey tenements, gave their tenants more rooms and a bathroom, but deprived them of easy access to pubs and shops. They separated 'extended families' whose small but closely-grouped rooms and kitchens were often a sort of extended house. They were already acknowledged as centres of social dislocation by the 1940s.

Housing remained an acute problem after 1945. Although 'prefabs', mass-produced in former aircraft factories, were an imaginative innovation, exports took priority over housing, while town planning schemes provoked tension between the planners and the municipalities, particularly Glasgow. Anxious about green belt constraints and the drift to new towns and overspill schemes, the towns turned to technology. Glasgow's first multi-storey scheme, in Partick, was completed in 1952. The Unionists, inspired by Harold Macmillan, boosted the rate of housing completions by over a third. In 1954 they built over 38,000 houses, 12.5 per cent of the UK total. The best pre-war year, 1938, saw only 26,000 completions, 8 per cent of the UK figure. The cost, however, was measured in size and quality: the tradition of the slum-clearance schemes persisted.

The Unionists remained faithful to Elliot's pre-war concentration on public housing. Although private householding trebled, to 20 per cent of completions, between 1954 and 1964, this compared with an English rate of 62 per cent of completions. A comparison between 1921 and 1961 shows a fall in private renting common to both countries, from over 80 per cent of households to under 25 per cent. But in Scotland the main change was to council tenancy (42 per cent compared with under 24 per cent in England), while owner-occupancy lagged badly, because of rent control, low council rents, and the absence of the building-boom. Under 25 per cent of Scots households were owner-occupiers, compared with over 42 per cent in England. Thus, in contrast to other areas of social policy, state intervention actually increased the differentiation between Scottish and English society, and in an area which impinged closely on political behaviour.

V Food

Reports on Scots eating habits and nutrition are plentiful for the pre-1914 period but less so for the period between the wars, despite the fact that it was the research of the Scottish agriculturalist John (Lord)

Boyd Orr that, in his *Food, Health and Income* of 1936, concentrated attention on the effect of malnutrition on between a third and half of the population. On the whole, pre-1914 reports alleged an apparent paradox: diet deteriorated as the population got wealthier and more urbanized. The oatmeal and milk diet of the agricultural labourers, though unvaried, was high in protein and roughage, and thus superior to the growing tendency to consume tea, white bread, and strong liquor. In 1938 a Ministry of Labour enquiry disclosed that, with long-term reductions in the cost of imported foodstuffs, the variety of food increased, with a greater amount of meat, poultry products, and fruit, but its unbalanced and unhealthy aspects continued. Sugar, which produced short-term increases in energy, but at the cost of tooth decay, constituted a disproportionate part of the Scots diet (5.4 per cent against 4.9 per cent in an English family's food budget); the Scots were also deficient in fresh vegetables (11.8 per cent against 12.8 per cent). For those in industries and areas afflicted with unemployment and low wages, standards may even have deteriorated since the nineteenth century. To this end, in the 1930s, the programme of free milk in schools and of domestic science classes was an attempt to cope with the 'secondary' malnutrition of about 20 per cent of the population; but for the lowest 30 per cent nothing short of a guaranteed increase in income could ensure an adequate standard. World War II seems to have brought this about: D.J. Robertson, in 1953, calculated that the index of Scots expenditure on food had risen from 110 in 1939 to 244 in 1951, while the UK figures had only gone up to 228 from 109. Yet peculiarities persisted: more was still spent on cereals and sugar and less on fruit. In general terms, Robertson concluded, Scottish household expenditure was 'more definitely urban and determinedly in the tradition of the working class' than elsewhere.

Scotland remained an austere place in the 1950s. The high alcohol consumption of the pre-1914 period had fallen away. In 1953 the Scots spent 18.4 per cent less than the UK average on drink, and relatively little on eating out. Strict licensing laws and a dearth of good restaurants (one of the main problems faced in its early years by the Edinburgh Festival) were at least a partial explanation. They made up for this by smoking like no one else in Britain, spending 11 per cent more than the UK average on tobacco. 'Can there be life after dark?' was a question asked by others besides Arthur Marwick in the early 1960s, but matters were soon to change.

VI Health

Twentieth-century Scots were eating well, if not too wisely. They were also growing taller and living longer. A Glasgow boy born in 1910 would on average be 4 ft 7 in. tall at 13 and weigh 75 lb.; a 13-year-old in 1954 would be nearly 4 in. taller and 15 lb. heavier. To what extent were these improvements the result of the institution of a national health service in 1948, of incremental increases in general health care, of growing affluence? Again, the detailed research has yet to be done, but a preliminary view suggests that the National Health Service improved rather than revolutionized health care – as with maternal provision. The conquest of tuberculosis and infectious disease in general was another major success. Before World War I the mortality rate from TB was 20.8 per 10,000. Isolation of cases, better public health, inspection of milk products, X-rays, cut this to 10.8 per 10,000, even before the invention of antibiotics – itself a much advertised triumph of Scots medicine, in the person of Sir Alexander Fleming – ended the menace of 'Bluidy Jack' forever. Fever cases also subsided between the wars, for similar reasons. The county of Angus had 231 per annum in 1908, 81 by 1965. The concomitant of a decrease in such 'young people's diseases' was an increase in the death-rate from heart disease and cancer, which struck after the age of 60.

There was a steady increase in hospital provision and treatment, aided by the National Insurance Acts of 1911 and 1920. Hospitals were divided both by type and organization: the disproportionately large number of voluntary hospitals, staffed by consultants and residents in the larger towns, and those provided by the local authorities, sometimes consultant-staffed, more often cottage or isolation hospitals attended by the local GP. The two types were gradually coming to resemble one another: many voluntary hospitals were heavily subsidized by trade unions, while local voluntary organizations, like the county nursing associations set up after World War I, removed the 'poor law' stigma from the local authority hospitals and made them part of an increasingly effective local health service. On the eve of World War II this was further enhanced by the construction of four large 'Emergency Medical Service' hospitals in the rural areas – Law and Strathyre, Peel and Stracathro – designed to cope with bombing raids on the main cities. When these did not materialize, Tom Johnston used them as the basis of improved civilian medical services, a factor that made the transition in 1947 to the five regional hospital boards of the NHS particularly easy. Again, the administrative momentum of the Scottish Office ensured that it would control the new system.

Under the boards were 65 management committees, while a parallel system of Health Executive Councils governed the GP services. The county councils and larger burghs constituted the third segment — the local health authorities covering infectious diseases, school medical and dental services, midwifery, and public health. The new service was not long in making an impact on some of the worst problems. An integrated maternity service helped reduce infant mortality. In Glasgow it fell from 1 in 13 in 1947 to 1 in 28 in 1953. There were much needed improvements in eye treatment and dentistry, and in preventive medicine insofar as it affected the school system. But, despite the fact that the reform was carried through by Aneurin Bevan, the doyen of the left, socialist hopes of a salaried medical service, concentrating on occupational health services and preventive medicine, and otherwise organized in health centres, foundered on the rock of the British Medical Association. With the experience of the Highlands and Islands Medical Service (1913) and the memory of the depression, Scots doctors were more committed to the service than their English counterparts, but by the 1960s inadequate capital expenditure, and the emergence of new problems associated with an ageing population were making their mark, while the gap between the health conditions of the well-off and the poor remained as wide as ever.

VII Unemployment and Poverty

Many of the traditional institutions of Scottish life managed to preempt their own reform, or impress their character upon it to render the result distinctive. In the case of the poor law, however, the process of elimination of such regional differentials was wholesale. Few, certainly, could be found to shed tears for the old system, which before 1914 denied a guarantee of outdoor relief to the able-bodied workman. In practice, this qualification was rarely observed: nine-tenths of relief granted was outdoor, and even Beatrice Webb commended the Scottish poor law on the professional approach of the parochial relieving officers, usually the local schoolmaster. But after the war it was all too evident that the principles of the old poor law were incapable of coping with a situation of endemic industrial depression. In 1921 the unemployed were granted statutory entitlement to outdoor relief. But, while the poor remained a parochial responsibility, rates of relief varied, and depression-struck parishes found themselves imposing crippling burdens on local industries simply to meet relief payments, a factor which tended to accelerate industrial closures. In 1929, therefore, the Local Government Act transferred relief to the counties, and funded it substantially out of block grants from central government.

Compulsory national unemployment insurance, funded by stamps paid by workers and employers alike, had been introduced in 1911 and after 1919 was extended to cover most workers (except those in agriculture or with salaries of more than £250 per annum). As unemployment spiralled after 1929 the fund, administered by the Scottish insurance commissioners, went into deficit, and cuts in benefit were a condition of the loan from foreign bankers in 1931 which split the Labour cabinet and brought about the National Government. These cuts were promptly introduced. They discriminated heavily against women, the long-term unemployed (who could now only claim benefit for 26 weeks), and those who had only paid in a few months' contributions. Those from whom benefit was withdrawn were now paid a transitional benefit from the state, on a scale of hardship assessed by a means test. This was conducted by local Public Assistance Committees, and took into account all family circumstances, like working sons and daughters, savings etc. National insurance had always been regarded as a right honourably worked and paid for. Transitional benefit, and the poor law to which it was an overture, were regarded as stigmas, accepted only in extreme circumstances and rendered all the more unwelcome by the inquisition into family circumstances involved. The bitterness about the 'means test' has lasted to the present day. Government policy, however, had its effect. By 1932 about 50 per cent of benefits were means-tested, and as a last resort, the poor law was by 1935 relieving 59,000 workpeople and 101,000 dependents, where in 1930 it had relieved 15,900 and 34,000. Scales of relief still varied widely from place to place and Scotland was particularly badly penalized by the fact that the block grant was not commensurately increased. Between 1930–1 and 1934–5 Scotland's expenditure increased by £1,800,000 (19 per cent), while the block grant only increased by £100,000 (4.7 per cent); as a result, Scotland's rates were over 6 per cent higher than England's, an additional discouragement to industrial development. Even after the Unemployment Act of 1934 made relief a national responsibility, under the Unemployment Assistance Board, Scottish local authorities still had to raise £800,000 (28.5 per cent) of the £2,800,000 (or 5 per cent of total unemployment relief) not covered by the Board, an anomaly not removed until 1937. The intention of the new Board had been to fix national standards of relief and combat the anomalies of the awards made by the local Public Assistance Committees: in practice it found itself sanctioning such variations, and also expressing more generalized disquiet about working and living conditions in Scotland. Left-wing agitation alleged that the UAB was an instrument for policing the working class, and cited the grim work camps that it operated in Argyllshire, but its rates were not ungenerous and in many ways its reports helped awake government to the need for further expenditure on relief works and housing.

Before the Unemployment Assistance Board came into action, those dependent on the dole in Scotland, in 1935, totalled a staggering 1.16 million, or nearly 250 in every 1,000. After World War II, and the adoption of a full employment policy, the UAB's successor, the National Assistance Board (1948), had to deal with about a tenth of that number, who had fallen through the pensions and insurance 'net'. The NAB's first chairman was George Buchanan, 20 years earlier one of Clydeside's unruliest MPs. He exemplified a shift in the left's attitude to Westminster. Twenty years earlier he and his colleagues had argued that Scotland's comparative poverty constituted part of the case for home rule. James Maxton had said in 1923: 'We mean to tell them they can do what they like about English children but that they are not going to suffer Scottish children to die'. Now, with Scotland still relatively poorer than England, the fact of equal entitlement to benefit was quoted as a clinching argument for the Union.

The welfare state diminished poverty, it did not eradicate it. Gradually, the numbers requiring assistance increased, from 20 per 1,000 in 1947 to 38 per 1,000 in 1961 and 62 per 1,000 in 1972. This was partly the result of unemployment, but also attributable to the growing number of old people, and the casualties of an increasingly unstable society, such as unmarried mothers and deserted wives. Moreover, those entitled to benefit frequently either did not claim it, or mis-spent it, and the results were readily apparent in family break-down and juvenile crime. This provided the background to the enquiry, chaired by Lord Kilbrandon, into children's courts (1964) which led in due course to the children's panel system and, in 1968, to the Social Work (Scotland) Act, which integrated child care, home helps, mental health, probation, and, later on, prison welfare and hospital social services. The Act was not only an advance on previous practice, but radically different from English arrangements. Thus, even in an otherwise integrated area, a measure of Scottish distinctiveness had been restored.

VIII Education

If Scotland showed the gulf between groups that characterized an upwardly-mobile society, then education was largely responsible. The Scots had always prided themselves on the accessibility of their educational system to the bright but badly-off. So far this has not been subject to much statistical verification, but it seems that, while valid for the mid nineteenth century, recruitment patterns narrowed before World War I, and the universities had become steadily more middle-class oriented. But all such relationships were altered by the war, and the Act of 1918 was intended to remedy the effects of four years of disruption. Subsequent retrenchment frustrated its main intentions. Its envisaged leaving age of 15, for instance, was not enacted until 1939, just in time to be postponed 'for the duration'. Although Scotland continued to receive about 14 per cent of British educational expenditure, her relative performance declined. She had 18 per cent of secondary pupils in 1913, 15.3 per cent in 1938. Moreover, the day of the all-ability local school was ending. Anticipating the recommendations of the English Hadow Report, the new secondary schools were after 1923 divided into 'junior' and 'senior secondaries', only the latter being academic. Although this made little difference in many county districts, it created a serious social gulf in the larger towns, and also increased the propensity of the gifted to move out once they had their qualifications. Jenny Lee, who left a Fife mining community for university and politics, regretted the fact that most of those who used this stepladder then broke off all connection with the community that had originally given them their chance.

Higher education fared badly between the wars. The number of full-time students at the four universities fell from 10,400 in 1924 to 9,900 in 1937, while the English universities registered a rise of nearly 19 per cent. The decline was worse among women (26 per cent) than among men students, although even here the lack of job opportunities in areas in which the Scottish universities had traditionally excelled — such as engineering, metallurgy, and naval architecture — meant that the development of research and the modernization of facilities was severely curtailed. Although English university expenditure rose by over 90 per cent during this period, the equivalent

Scottish figure was scarcely a third of this. As a result, the best Scottish students tended to move south for postgraduate work, and there was little development of new subject areas. Worst of all was the stagnation of vocational and further education, the development of which had been stressed by the 1918 Act. As late as 1955 only eight local authorities had technical colleges, and barely a tenth of school leavers attended them full-time. Day-release certainly grew rapidly after the war. There had been only 900 students in 1939; there were 24,000 in 1955. But this was only a fraction of the potential. If *Scotland* condemned the 'sheer ignorance' of 18-year-olds in 1961 as 'a bleak omen for the future', it was scarcely the fault of the youngsters themselves.

Discussion of future policy was not made easy by three major reorganizations in as many decades. The elected Local Education Authorities of the 1918 Act lasted barely a decade before being swept away by the Local Government (Scotland) Act. Neither they nor the school management committees which replaced the old School Boards had been particularly successful; perhaps they had simply not been given enough time. The professional organizations tended to fight a series of defensive battles over redundancies, wage cuts, and threatened status. The result of both was an intensely 'political' spirit which militated against real discussion of the nature and goals of education. Radicals, like A.S. Neill, were forced out; where there was innovation it tended more and more to come from the Scottish Education Department, since 1921 situated in Edinburgh, and its inspectorate.

The 1944 Act was anticipated by the re-establishment of the Advisory Council on Education, an achievement of the wartime Council of State, and after 1945 there were some notable innovations in curricula and methods, aided by more determined central direction from the inspectorate and increased expenditure on school building. The main beneficiaries, however, were the academically inclined; as Scotland lacked the English 'O' level system, until 1961 the vast majority — 93.4 per cent — of pupils left school at 15 without any qualification. By 1978 58.3 per cent of pupils gained at least one 'O' level, and 17.2 per cent gained three or more Higher-level passes. As only 3.7 per cent reached this stage in 1951, the wastage of talent was palpable.

IX Law and Order

So far as criminal statistics can be compared — and the means of keeping them varied radically between police forces, let alone between Scotland and England — the Scots were ceasing to be appreciably more criminally inclined than the English. In 1938 crimes known to the police ran at 11 per 1,000 of the total population; the English proportion was 7 per 1,000. By 1951 both countries had increased to 14 per 1,000. Even the 1938 figure was an improvement on the situation before World War I, with a reduction of almost two-thirds in drink-connected offences, which fell further to only one-fifth of the 1913 level. Did types of crime vary with levels of affluence? Some criminologists have argued that periods of economic recession see a rise in crimes against property while periods of affluence see a rise in crimes against persons. Yet violent crime in late 1930s Scotland was running at a level six times that of the south, and subsequently declined. Nor was the impact of the two world wars uniform: crime slumped in World War I, stayed down during the inter-war period, but rose during World War II.

Crime is an area of Scottish society that has been badly neglected, yet that surely offers huge rewards to the Scottish Richard Cobb who can use the plentiful evidence of the courts to explore the pathology of Scottish society. For this period we can at least say that crime was urban, masculine, and relatively unorganized — at least in a commercial sense. For Glasgow gangs devoted to fighting and drinking, petty theft and protection rackets were simply a means to this end. Drinking had certainly much to do with violence in the cities, with two major waves of gang warfare sweeping over Glasgow in the 1930s and 1960s. Yet the Western Isles, statistically awash with booze, were virtually crime-free. The connections between crime and religious communities need exploring, too. In nineteenth century Scotland two-thirds of the Scottish jail population was Catholic, disproportionate for the whole of society, if not for its poorest part. How much was this the result of poverty, how much of discrimination by a Protestant magistracy? It had fallen to 25 per cent by the 1920s, when the Catholic minority had legitimized its position. Irish political violence was not imported, save on Clydeside just after World War I, as Irish nationalists in Glasgow attempted to aid the struggle against the British Army in Ireland. But this was far less conspicuous than the suffragette campaign before the war, when middle-class ladies carried out acts of violence and destruction at which the leaders of the Red

Clyde would have blenched. As a rule, though, the women of
Scotland — truly the country's most oppressed group — were consistently law-abiding, and became even more so. The ratio of male to
female crime was 4:1 in 1913, 12:1 in 1951.

Violent crime was working class; murder a family affair. Fraud, tax
evasion, and embezzlement were traditional middle-class wicked-
nesses, but corruption was relatively new, occurring where business
met the local government system, from the 1930s increasingly run by
inexperienced men, handling huge budgets on small personal
incomes. It came to play an important if tragic rôle in city corporations, quasi-governmental bodies, the trade unions and the
co-operative movement, swelling with the complexity of business
organization and the drive to attract investment. To the old grandees
of local government it resulted from the extinction of civic politics and
the rise of Labour, but it was surely also the result of a governmental
system peculiarly remote and secretive.

Scottish police forces, like those of England but unlike the
Metropolitan Police or the Royal Ulster Constabulary, were local
concerns. There were in 1920 32 'joint-county' or 'county-burgh'
authorities — of which Glasgow was the largest in Britain. Archaic in
equipment and organization, they found it difficult to cope with political disturbances — as 1919 in Glasgow showed — urban violence,
and growing traffic problems. Sir Percy Sillitoe, coming to Glasgow in
1933, found elderly officers, a decrepit CID, and (it later turned out)
corrupt political leadership. His reforms, soon copied in other cities,
ranged from policemen's checked cap-bands to police boxes and
radio-controlled cars.

It is more difficult to talk of innovation in the prison service. For the
first half-century Scottish prison admissions consistently declined,
from 50,000 to under 9,000. There was thus little pressure to modern-
ize the prisons, which dated mainly from the mid nineteenth century.
On the other hand, as crime rose during the 1950s, these became
increasingly overcrowded. Admissions were over 12,000 in 1961, and
peaked at 18,773 in 1975. While readers of the *Sunday Post* were
alternately reassured to see enemies of society behind bars and
scandalized at the privileges they were alleged to enjoy, it is doubtful
whether incarceration in ancient and crowded buildings diminished
the anti-social tendencies of the inmates.

Law had, of course, civic and economic as well as criminal
functions. It was a central part of the Edinburgh caste-system and the
world of the investment trusts, and before 1914 was judiciously

assimilating to the south. When assimilation accelerated, after 1918, there were two responses. Lord Macmillan (Unionist Lord Advocate in the 1924 Labour government) personified one, moving south to the English bar and becoming legal handyman to successive governments. Andrew Dewar Gibb, also a Unionist and Professor of Scots Law at Glasgow, personified another, shifting, through a defence of his subject, to the chairmanship of the SNP. In the 1940s another Unionist, Lord Cooper, played a major part in the revival of Scots legal studies, and under his disciple, Professor T.B. Smith, Scots lawyers claimed an almost Savigny-like identification between Scots law and the national *geist*. Lawyers were still over-influenced by the chances of party patronage, but after 1945 they took a prouder line, stressing their law's closeness to the codes of the European nations. Solicitors, with academic qualifications absent in England, took on a more active business rôle, acting as estate agents as well as conveyancers in house sales. The new legislation of the 1960s thus strengthened the internal pressure for reform. The creation of the Scots Law Commission under a leading innovator, Lord Kilbrandon, in 1965, appeared to confirm this, and the difficulty of transferring its recommendations to the statute book subsequently became a major argument for devolution.

X Religion

The disestablishment of the Church of Wales was carried by parliament in 1913. Because of the war, it did not become law until 1920. In the following year, however, the Church of Scotland Act permitted an established presbyterian Church to remain north of the border. This effectively brought to an end the savage sectarian rivalries of the nineteenth century. Eight years later the main dissenting group, the United Free Church, fused with the Church of Scotland. The way had been clear for unity since the early 1900s. When the United Presbyterians and Free Church had merged in 1900, the wrangling and litigation had been such that the dissenting leaders seem simply to have become fed up with their traditional aim of disestablishing the Church of Scotland. There were some differences of view, but not many, over World War I, and complicated negotiations over teinds or tithes, but the upshot was a presbyterian Church more united than it had been for over a century, although no longer reaching the 36 per cent of the population the three churches had reached in 1886.

Formally, Scotland was still a religious country, although its actual religious balance was changing. In 1930 the Church of Scotland claimed 1,271,095 members, 26.2 per cent of the population; the Catholic Church claimed 560,000, or 11.2 per cent (9 per cent in 1886). The Church of England, by contrast, had only 11.0 per cent. By 1960 the rate of decline seemed to have been halted. The Kirk claimed 25 per cent of the population, but the Catholic percentage had risen to 14.9. In the next 14 years the Kirk's percentage was, however, to drop to 20.4. While some of this can be attributed to a more scrupulous weeding out of nominal members, who had hitherto inflated the figures artificially, the evidence of ministers' reports in the *Third Statistical Account* is of a steady drift from regular religious participation from World War I on.

The Kirk was affected by the withering away of its secular rôle — for instance by the end of the parish councils in 1929, on which ministers tended to sit as if of right — by the challenge of slum clearance and rehousing, and by secular alternatives in education and entertainment. The Catholic Church, on the other hand, reinforced its position largely through the 1918 Education Act's provisions for its schools to become part of the state system while retaining their religious distinctiveness, and through a further influx from the Free State and Ulster in the 1920s. This caused a strong racialist reaction both among conservative presbyterians and some nationalists and had some influence in the rise of the Protestant Action in the 1930s (see p.100).

In the united Kirk two tendencies, Catholic and Evangelical, competed. The Iona Community, founded in 1930 by the socialist and pacifist George MacLeod, sought a more mystical and ritualistic religion, as well as a stronger social commitment. Funded substantially by James Lithgow, it devoted itself to work in the slums of Clydeside as well as to the reconstruction of the medieval abbey of Iona. A decade later, after 1947, the Rev. Tom Allan's 'Tell Scotland' movement, which culminated with the Rev. Billy Graham's 1954–5 Glasgow Crusade, reinstated the Evangelical tradition. The two clashed violently in 1961, when a committee of the General Assembly, including MacLeod, recommended the reintroduction of bishops in the Kirk, only to have its report rejected by the Assembly in session, after an energetic campaign by Beaverbrook's *Scottish Daily Express*. The Church remained a paradox. Middle-class in recruitment and leadership, and on the whole evangelical in theology, it nevertheless adopted, largely at the behest of the clergy, a range of liberal policies on race, the arts, sexual morality, and home rule. Until the 1960s it was, effectively, the last redoubt of old-fashioned Scottish liberalism. But its appeal to the progressive young was dangerously limited, and in due course a generation of intellectuals, who could sympathize with the Church's radicals, like MacLeod or Kenneth MacKenzie, personally and on political issues, simply slipped away from formal belief. With an ultramontane dogmatism not far behind that of Eire, on the other hand, the Scottish Catholic hierarchy could observe growing numbers of communicants until the mid 1960s, with a number of distinguished converts, and a high reputation in literature and the arts.

When religious identification expressed itself in politics, however, there was a paradox. While the political choice of Protestants broadly followed class lines, Catholics, including middle-class Catholics, voted overwhelmingly for Labour. This was partly to do with traditional Irish resentment of Unionism, and partly because Scottish Labour was careful to protect the Catholic Church's educational privileges. This had its bizarre side. In 1931 the Catholic *Glasgow Observer* simultaneously anathematized socialism and advised the faithful to vote for Jimmie Maxton! But, given the general weakness of Labour organization in the west of Scotland, the well-organized Catholic lobby consistently exercised a conservative influence on the party. On the Protestant side the links between the Established Church, the Orange Order, and the Unionists seem to have lapsed during the 1920s, prior to the amalgamation with the predominantly Liberal U.F. Church, but as its membership fell in the 1960s, the politics of the Church — as far as one can judge from its monthly, *Life and Work* — seemed to settle to the right.

XI Class

Taken as functional systems, the main institutions of Scottish social life showed variable and sometimes contradictory degrees of assimilation to UK norms. An absence of coloured immigrants, larger families, the prevalence of rented public-sector housing, different eating and drinking patterns, more pervasive religion — all of these provided considerable areas of distinctiveness in everyday life. The economy had, of course, steadily been assimilated to the south, carrying with it the system of social welfare, but in other important areas of public intervention such as law, education, and housing, Scotland radically diverged from England. This complexity is scarcely illuminated by generalizations such as that by Professor Peter Hall, alleging assimilation on the grounds that 'We get the same morning papers, we see the same television programmes, we buy the same goods in identical supermarkets, lured by the same advertising'. Yet a treatment of institutions remains a distorting one if it does not attempt to relate them to the economic structure by dealing with class relationships and their connections with the distribution of economic power. Socialists who attacked Scottish nationalism during the 1960s argued that the real division lay along class lines, and that working-class consciousness was the common property of British working people. Bearing in mind the subsequent fate of Scottish nationalism, that argument still has to be met.

This approach is not, however, proved by saying that Scotland is a more working-class country than England. This can be a mark of divergence, not congruence. Mark Abrams' calculations of income distribution for *The Home Market* show a Scottish upper class, largely based in Edinburgh, actually strengthening its position over the period 1934–49 period, while there is also a growth in the percentage with 'working class' incomes. Both extremes of the social scale grow in numbers, while the middle class actually declines from 21.8 per cent to 18.9 per cent, its English counterpart growing at the same time from 21.3 per cent to 26 per cent.

Table 3.3: Percentages in income categories, 1934 and 1949

| | 1934 | | | | | 1949 | |
	Eng.	Scot.	Edin.	Glas.		Eng.	Scot.
Grade A					Grade A		
(£520 +)	5.3	3.4	7.0	2.0	(£1,000 +)	4.0	4.1
Grade B	21.3	21.8	29.0	27.0	B (£650–1,000)	8.0	6.4
(£208–520)					C (£400–650)	18.0	12.5
Grade C	73.4	74.8	64.0	71.0	D (£225–400)	61.9	64.9
(£0–208)					E (£0–225)	8.1	12.1

(Over this period the value of the pound was roughly halved, so the income divisions are broadly comparable.)

Even allowing for distortions, this shows a more proletarian country, and one likely to show strong evidence of class-consciousness. Even if we accept — especially if we accept — that the educational system promoted social mobility, the corollary of this is usually an increase in tension between classes. From what little sociological research was carried out in Scotland in this period — and I am heavily in the debt of James Littlejohn's lucid and perceptive *Westrigg*, a book that goes far beyond the bounds of the 'Cheviot Parish' it surveys — we seem to see class-consciousness developed to an almost pathological degree. In

Westrigg Littlejohn found working people deeply conscious of being, in Marx's phrase, 'of a class, but not for a class'. This penetrated social and recreational life as well as work relationships, and was closely related to the masculine dominance of rural working-class life. Women were more mobile, and in the upper social classes exercised a greater degree of responsibility, but this went along with a greater use of 'managerial' or 'problem-solving' skills by the upper classes as a whole. As a result, 'on any issue the working class is sharply divided while the middle classes are more unanimous, though with a difference of emphasis between property owners and professionals'. This was evident within working-class organizations — where the move of a working-class person to a leadership rôle was itself resented as a breach of class solidarity.

The application of this perception to Scottish politics shows, I think, an analogous development, with the leadership of Scottish working-class organizations increasingly recruited from the middle class, or deferring to middle-class ideologies. How had this come about? Again, in the absence of detailed research, we can only speculate. By destroying the Lowland peasantry, eighteenth-century 'improvement' had, arguably, also removed the local relationships of kin and community, out of which a localized 'organic' society, with its demotic political and leadership structures, had emerged on the continent and in Ireland. The Scottish alternative was the consciousness of the skilled industrial worker, but this was something that lacked both realistic political expression, and was greatly dependent on industrial changes that the working class could not control. Although the aftermath of World War I saw the rise of the Labour Party, it also saw the frustration of this class's bid for political leadership, and the beginning of its decline.

Socialists welcomed the broader working-class solidarity that they expected to emerge from this. As its president, William Leonard MP told the STUC in 1925:

> There can be no denial that the gulf which at one time divided the skilled from the unskilled is fast disappearing, and, as a craftsman, I welcome the change. It is not that we are less capable than our forefathers, but that their dexterity and fine points of craftsmanship are no longer needed by our present methods, and the same tendency is bringing up to our level those who at one time were dubbed 'only labourers'. Unemployment is with us until we dismiss Capitalism. I care not what type of government

we have, if it tries to work this lack of system – the problem will remain.

This was a view sanguine to the point of self-deception. A decade later the Unemployment Assistance Board was more grimly realistic:

> One unfortunate feature is the number of skilled workmen of various kinds who cannot be absorbed into their own industries and who are gradually drifting into the general labouring class. a section which is already over-crowded and which is likely to occupy the Board's attention for many years to come.

The skilled working class had supplied the labour and co-operative movement with most of its leadership, yet its own identity was ambiguous. Its culture, for instance, was almost wholly derived from the middle class. Thus, as it broke up, the more intelligent of its younger generation tended to shift into the middle class, through the educational system, or emigrate, rather than attempt to politicize the unskilled. The two sons of Willie Gallacher both went to university, and were both killed flying for the RAF in World War II. Mrs Gallacher mourned her 'poor, clever bairns'. It would never have occurred to her or her husband to deny them the chance to leave their class.

Thus, although economic change seems to have increased class ploarization, the institutions of Scottish society actually inhibited the development of a positive political class-consciousness. They provided means of 'spiralling' out of the working class, and they also created, through the expansion of public intervention, a range of middle-class organizational and leadership rôles – schoolteachers, local officials, councillors and MPs, social workers – what Stephen Maxwell has called 'a state-sector middle class'. With the dwindling-away of indigenous capitalism, and the relative isolation of Unionism as an agricultural interest group, this class exercised effective dominance over much of Scottish society in the 1960s.

4

Politics and Government
1922 – 1964

I

There was an Irish Question in British politics throughout the nine-teenth century. It became obsessive after 1880, and refused to dis-appear even after the setting-up of the Free State in 1921. There was no Scottish Question. Between 1922 and 1964 few specifically Scottish issues preoccupied the Commons for more than a few hours, or Cabinet for as many minutes, even at the pit of the depression. The only one that did, the Caledonian Power Bill of 1936 – 8, had impli-cations for national defence. This may give a clue to Scotland's unobtrusiveness. Before 1945 high politics in Britain meant the Empire and foreign policy. The Irish took constitutional issues away with them; the subtraction of their 70-odd anti-Tory votes helped account for Conservative hegemony until 1945 and, by implication, for Parliament's restricted preoccupations. The Government of India Bill, not the slump, took up 84 per cent of legislative time in 1934 – 5. Things had changed by 1964: in real terms government expenditure was 300 per cent more than in 1914: from 28 per cent of a pre-war budget of £207m. it had risen to 77 per cent out of £6,727m. Plainly, only when government became preoccupied with social policy, after 1945, could Scottish issues intrude themselves — unless they were constitutional issues. But the nationalist movement was never strong enough to create these.

Scottish politics had, however, patently changed after World War I and the 1918 Reform Act. What, then, were they about? Old Liber-alism viewed the new electorate and new politicians with vast distrust. To Asquith the Paisley voters in 1920 were 'for the most part hopelessly ignorant of politics, credulous to the last degree, and flickering with gusts of sentiment like a candle in the wind'. Did they want, or even know very much about, socialism? Margot Asquith fairly accurately nailed Rosslyn Mitchell, who beat Asquith in 1924, and who had drafted the Clydeside Labour members' dramatic pledge in 1922, as 'highly educated and no more Labour than you'. Nineteen thirty-one was to show that Scottish loyalties to Labour were thin, and its inter-war career was scarcely consistent or imaginative. Labour may have replaced Liberalism on the left of a continuing two-party system, but the latter's collapse, sudden and still not fully explained, left a vacuum not filled until 1945.

What filled it? A class-based loyalty to Labour's welfare programme? This may have fitted the 1950s, but the 1960s and 1970s have suggested greater complexity: class-politics were skewed by the distinctive nature of Scottish local government and its close relationships with a largely Scots-based administration. If Scots made 'secular' political choices, they did so in an increasingly Scottish context, but there was nothing determinate about this evolution. It was as much the work of Unionists as of Labour, and of the momentum within Scottish administration itself.

II Labour contained 1922–1935

Unionists and Liberals

November 1922 inaugurated a brief period of three-party politics, but by December 1924 the Unionists were dominant. Their breach with Lloyd George had preserved their independence. They had 335 seats in 1918, 345 after November 1922. In Scotland, however, they lost 17 seats in 1922 and gained only one in 1923. Only in 1924 did the party sweep forward to 38 seats – although in 1935 it still held 37; not until 1964 did its representation drop below 30.

The reasons for this success were the result of organizational rather than social change; its total vote changed little from 1924 to 1955. The formation of the Scottish Unionist Party in 1911 united rural conservatism with right-wing urban liberalism. The SUP had five regional councils, but remained firmly under the control of the parliamentary leadership and of Conservative Central Office, a relationship strengthened by the virtually unbroken line of the Scots who chaired the party: Sir Arthur Steel-Maitland from 1911 to 1917, George Younger from 1917 to 1923, J.C.C. Davidson from 1926 to 1930, and John Baird from 1931 to 1940. Steel-Maitland and Davidson, in particular, modernized local party organization, with regular subscriptions and (at least nominally) elective committees, provided an efficient agency service, and greatly increased income from business sources – aided greatly by the rightward shift of former Liberals. This was reflected in a rise in membership: in Glasgow it increased from 7,000 in

Table 4.1: MPs elected for Scottish constituencies 1900–1997 (showing number of MPs and % of vote)

	Unionist		LU/NL[1]		Lib.		Lab.		Others	
	MPs	%	MPs	%	MPs	%	MPs	%	MPs	%
1900	21	+	17	(49.0)	34	(50.2)				
1906	8	+	4	(38.2)	58	(56.4)	2	(2.3)		(3.1)
1910 (Jan.)	8	+	3	(39.6)	59	(54.2)	2	(5.1)		(1.1)
1910 (Dec.)	7	+	4	(42.6)	58	(53.6)	3	(3.6)		(0.2)
1918	32	(30.8)	19	(19.1)	15	(15.0)	7	(22.9)	1	(12.2)
1922	15	(25.1)	12	(17.7)	16	(21.5)	29	(32.2)	2	(3.5)
1923	16	(31.6)			23	(28.4)	34	(35.9)	1	(4.1)
1924	38	(40.8)			9	(16.5)	26	(41.1)	1	(1.6)
1929	22	(35.9)			14	(18.1)	36	(42.4)	1	(3.6)
1931	50	(49.5)	8	(4.8)	8	(8.6)	7	(32.6)		(4.5)
1935	37	(42.2)	7 + 1	(7.6)	3	(6.7)	20+4	(41.8)	2	(1.7)
1945	25	(37.4)	5	(3.7)		(5.0)	37+3	(49.4)	4	(4.5)
1950	26	(37.2)	5	(7.6)	2	(6.6)	37	(46.2)	1	(2.4)
1951	29	(39.9)	6	(8.7)	1	(2.7)	35	(47.9)	1	(0.8)
1955	30	(41.5)	6	(8.6)	1	(1.9)	34	(46.7)		(1.3)
1959	25	(39.7)	6	(7.5)	1	(4.1)	38	(46.7)		(2.0)
1964	24	(37.3)		(3.3)	4	(7.6)	43	(48.7)		(3.1)
1966	20	(37.7)		–	5	(6.8)	46	(49.9)		(5.6)
1970	23	(38.0)			3	(5.5)	44	(44.5)	1	(12.0)
1974 (Feb.)	21	(32.9)			3	(8.0)	40	(36.6)	7	(22.5)
1974 (Oct.)	16	(24.7)			3	(8.3)	41	(36.3)	11	(30.7)
1979	22	(30)			3	(10)	44	(42)	2	(18)
1983	21	(28.4)			8	(24.5)	41	(35.1)	2	(12.1)
1987	10	(24)			9	(19.2)	50	(42.4)	3	(14.3)
1992	11	(25.7)			9	(13.1)	49	(39)	3	(22.2)
1997	–	(17.5)			10	(13.0)	56	(45.6)	6	(24)

[1]Liberal Unionist to 1912; 'Coalition Liberal' 1918–22; 'National Liberal' 1931–64.
Note: The totals of MPs include two university MPs 1900–18 and three 1918–45. These seats were abolished in 1948. As they polled by proportional representation, party percentages cannot be established.

1913 to 20,000 in 1922 and 32,000 in 1929, a figure almost double the individual membership of the Labour Party *and* the ILP for the whole of Scotland.

Unionist cohesiveness triumphed over Liberal disorder. Traditionally the nominal independence of the Scottish Liberal Federation had been countered by the combination of front-bench MPs and reliable local managers – usually solicitors. The wartime split was fatal to this. Even the rallying-call of 'free trade in danger', which unified Asquithians and Lloyd-Georgites in 1923 – not to speak of the mysterious Lloyd George fund – brought no recovery, and in 1924 organization collapsed. Only one candidate had been nominated for a Glasgow seat on the eve of the October election, and only eight MPs survived it, mainly in rural areas. When Lloyd George at last succeeded Asquith as leader in 1926, he found all but one of them –

Table 4.2: The backgrounds of Scottish Members of Parliament at selected elections, 1910 (December) – 1997

	1910			1922			1945			1964			1979				1997			Totals
	U	Lab.	L	U	Lab.	L	U	Lab.	Other	U	Lab.	L	C	Lab.	L	SNP	Lab.	L	SNP	
Business	1	–	24	3	3	5	14	1	–	3	4	–	7	2	–	1	2	1	2	73
Landowning/farming	4	–	5	1	–	2	6	–	–	9	–	2	3	1	–	–	1	1	–	35
Law	3	–	17	6	–	7	1	2	–	4	1	1	7	2	1	1	5	5	1	64
Education	1	–	–	–	4	1	1	5	–	–	7	1	2	8	1	–	19	–	2	52
Other professions	2	–	11	5	5	12	9	7	1	6	7	–	3	9	1	–	11	3	1	93
White collar	–	–	–	–	1	–	–	4	–	–	9	–	–	9	–	–	1	–	–	24
Trade union and labour organisers	–	3	–	–	16	–	–	6	–	–	4	–	–	7	–	–	8	–	–	44
Skilled workers	–	–	–	–	2	–	–	14	1	–	10	–	–	6	–	–	9	–	–	42
Others/unidentified	–	–	1	–	–	–	1	1	–	2	1	–	–	–	–	–	–	–	–	7
Totals	11	3	58	15	31	28	32	40	2	24	43	4	22	44	3	2	56	10	6	434

Archie Sinclair in remote Caithness — intractably Asquithian. In 1929 it was farmers' discontent about falling prices, not Lloyd George's imaginative 'Yellow Book' programme (see p.49) that brought five gains. But Liberal performance in Scotland was almost 30 per cent worse than in the UK as a whole, largely because the rise of urban Labour had led, even more swiftly than in England, to 'anti-socialist' mergers with the Unionists. Nineteen twenty-nine proved to be the last rally. Party discipline collapsed, Lloyd George fell sick; in 1931 Scottish Liberals were to support the National Government overwhelmingly.

Labour

But the greatest blow to the Liberals was the first Labour government. In December 1923 Ramsay MacDonald formed a minority administration. Scots made up a quarter of the cabinet, and provided its major successes, with MacDonald's conciliatory foreign policy and John Wheatley's Housing Act (see p.71). Otherwise little could be achieved — save proof that Labour could govern and that the Liberals were devoid of strategic alternatives. The electorate condemned them in October 1924. But in Scotland Labour lost eight seats, and by the time of its next victory in 1929 inadequacies of organization and the setback of the General Strike had taken their toll.

As an organization, Labour occupied a median position between Unionist integration and Liberal autonomy. But its structure after 1918 was an awkward compromise between federation and mass organization. The executive of its Scottish Council had six union representatives, four from constituency parties and trades councils (often more or less the same thing), four from women's sections, two from the ILP, and one apiece from the moribund SDF and the Fabians. Less than half of the 80-odd unions affiliated to the STUC sent delegates to Scottish Conference — only 31, for example, in 1930. These represented just 42 per cent of engineers, 39.5 per cent of textile workers, 45.5 per cent in the distributive trades. Strongly affiliated unions, like the miners (89 per cent) and railwaymen (83 per cent) had been hard hit by the depression, and only five of the 36 Scots-based unions sent delegates. Were they represented through the trades councils, or simply uninterested in politics? Labour was less nationalist than the STUC, and also weaker at the grass-roots; individual membership per head of population was only a third of that in London in 1929. This was partly due to the strength of the ILP, and partly to trades council representation – although this opened them to Communist influence.

If in 1922 the Clydesiders had acted as kingmakers for MacDonald, they faced competition. In the same year the Cambridge-educated former conscientious-objector Clifford Allen became ILP chairman and moved the party to a left-liberal position, appealing to middle-class reformers as the intellectual power-house of the left. With success: membership increased from 25,000 in 1922 to 60,000 in 1926. But Allen's aims conflicted with the Glasgow MPs' desperate concern with unemployment and, to a lesser extent, with their nationalist inclinations.

At the industrial grass-roots, moreover, the ILP had to face the British section of the Communist International or Comintern. The Communist Party of Great Britain (CPGB), founded in July 1920, included some Clydeside revolutionaries, but its structure implied obedience to Russian directives. Leaders who survived tended to be former Scots Catholics, accustomed to ultramontane control; less docile radicals followed the example of John Maclean and retreated into obscure and uncompromising sects. The CPGB had some electoral success before 1924, while its relationship with Labour remained undefined. Walton Newbold held Motherwell from 1922 to 1923; James Geddes came second in both years at Greenock. But, although its housing agitation helped increase Labour support, its attempts to affiliate were rebuffed in 1924. Thereafter it attempted to penetrate the unions through the Moscow-funded National Minority Movement which helped to raise the political temperature in the months before the General Strike of 4 – 12 May 1926.

The General Strike

The strike – MacDiarmid's 'Camsteerie Rose' – arose from the declining economic position of the coal industry, and the attempts of the mineowners to force wage reductions. The vacillations of the General Council of the TUC, pledged to support the miners, were reflected by the leaders of the STUC and the 'first-line' unions – in transport, mining, docks, and printing. Preparations were sketchy, save in some coalfield areas where the Minority Movement organized 'Councils of Action' to enforce picketing and control food supplies. The government, by contrast, had been preparing since 1919. The Lord Advocate had organized an emergency administration, with Scotland divided into five regions; their officials could call on the forces and the Organization for the Maintenance of Supplies, a private body of volunteers — some from the extreme right.

The initial impact was most dramatic in transport. Trains stopped, even on the remotest branch lines. But the government machine got supplies moved by car and lorry, while student-manned trams (which were fairly easy to drive) provided a skeletal public transport service in the cities. There were many acute confrontations: the working-class solidarity demonstrated by the strike extended far beyond the limits of union membership. Even Orange flute bands joined the picket lines, although the Grand Masters were as hostile as the Catholic hierarchy. On 11 May the 'second line' unions downed tools, but that evening the General Council in London backed down:

> The thistle like a rocket soared,
> An' cam' doon like the stick.

'Demoralized by the utter and absolute capitulation' — in the words of a young participant, Jennie Lee — the strikers went back to work. Many were sacked, demoted, or otherwise victimized. The miners stayed out until November when, driven by hunger and the approach of winter, they surrendered. For a former élite, it was a terrible defeat, with wages and status reduced to a level little above that of the unemployed. In other respects, however, political Labour benefited. The strike destroyed such working-class loyalty to Liberalism as remained: Simon and Asquith had condemned it as fiercely as the ex-Liberal Churchill. Municipal Liberals had acted with Unionists to assist the government and penalize strikers. Although the Communists gained support during the miners' lockout, they lost most of it when it ended, but the Labour Party moved forward strongly in municipal politics — in Edinburgh after the November elections its seats rose from 6 to 14. The strike cut at the roots of revolutionary millenarianism; it also enhanced the notion of 'British' class politics, and so diminished the nationalist element in Scottish Labour, while the subsequent victories on the councils made local power a real possibility — especially in the eyes of astute managers like Patrick Dollan.

Unionist Reform

Baldwin remained in power until 1929. Because of Winston Churchill's orthodoxy as Chancellor (see p.49) his government only aggravated Scotland's economic plight, a situation, one suspects, not fully appreciated because of the drift of front-benchers away from

Scottish seats (with only one exception, no premier, chancellor, or foreign secretary sat for a Scottish seat between 1922 and 1963, although five had done so between 1900 and 1922). Scotland's relative political instability (the Unionists kept a consistent hold on only 45 per cent of Scottish seats, 1918–39, compared with 65 per cent in the English Midlands) was probably a factor here, though Scottish businessmen were equally reluctant to go into parliament. Unionist MPs were not distinguished, and the majority of them tended to be drawn from groups – like advocates and landowners – remote from Scotland's economic and social problems. But there were a few exceptions, and fortunately one of them played a key rôle in the Scottish Office for many of the inter-war years: Walter Elliot.

Elliot, the son of a wealthy auctioneer, and the only 'professional' Fellow of the Royal Society ever to become a Cabinet minister, had been a Fabian while at Glasgow University (one of a brilliant generation which had included James Maxton, Tom Johnston, and James Bridie). He entered parliament in 1918 – 'Will stand, which party?' had been his (apocryphal) response to nomination – and while in office became associated with collectivist, if somewhat paternalist, social reform. He was no nationalist but, as Under-Secretary for Scotland, 1923–9, was largely instrumental in securing two major changes in Scottish administration: the reorganization of Scottish central administration and the Local Government Act of 1929.

The first measure, carried through in 1928, converted the system of nominated boards, only indirectly responsible to parliament, into orthodox civil service departments on the lines of the Scottish Education Department. This was criticized by William Adamson, the former Secretary under Labour, for subordinating Scottish administration to Whitehall 'to a far greater extent than has ever been the case', but in fact it coincided with a physical decentralization of government from Whitehall. By 1936 1,333 out of 1,416 civil servants working for the Scottish departments were based in St Andrew's House, the new government headquarters in Edinburgh, planned in 1929 and built, to the design of T.S. Tait, between 1932 and 1936. But the departments of agriculture, education, and health, and the Scottish Office, were only linked by their responsibility to the Secretary of State. Effective co-ordination still had to be achieved.

Much more drastic was the Local Government Act of 1929, from which stemmed much of the nationalist agitation of the 1930s. Without the usual preliminary of a royal commission, and going far beyond the changes carried out by Neville Chamberlain in England, it swept away the parish councils, the Local Education Authorities, and many of the powers of the smaller burghs. The new system consisted of 4 counties of cities, 20 'large burghs' (over 20,000 inhabitants), and 31 county councils which divided between them the responsibility for most local authority services; 171 'small burghs' retained limited public health and housing powers, and in the 'landward areas' of counties somewhat nominal 'district councils' got what was left. The historic Scottish parish was now a religious and registration area: nothing more.

The Nemesis of Labour

The act attracted vociferous opposition from Scottish local authorities, from the infant National Party, and from Labour, which pledged itself to repeal it. MacDonald's failure to do so, after he formed his 1929 administration, was the first pratfall in a troubled and ultimately disastrous ministry. Labour had gained strength after the General Strike, but not unity. In the ILP Maxton had supplanted Allen and attempted to win the party to an alliance with industrial militants; but this caused a divergence with the Glasgow grass-roots which Dollan cultivated so zealously. Some of the party's more convinced home-rulers, like R.E. Muirhead and C.M. Grieve, moved to the Nationalists. Wheatley, its one real statesman, who might have brought unity, was out of action, in the toils of an expensive and embarrassing lawsuit. MacDonald excluded him from his government. Ill, embittered, and extreme, he flayed Jimmy Thomas's inept attempts to cope with unemployment. Then, worn out, he died in May 1930.

The alternative policies were by now coming not from Clydeside but from Birmingham, where the Scotsman Allan Young was Sir Oswald Mosley's economic adviser. Would Wheatley have supported them, had he lived? Tom Johnston, who succeeded Thomas in March 1930, was certainly sympathetic to many of Mosley's Keynesian ideas, but, echoing Scottish Labour's rejection of Lloyd George's 'Yellow Book' proposals, swung *Forward* against the old enemies − bankers and tariff reformers.

Among the moderates, whose moralistic socialism co-existed, increasingly unhappily, with classical economics, this had logic, when expounded by the Chancellor Philip Snowden's articulate Scots lieutenant, Willie Graham: in exporting areas, tariffs meant retaliation and further unemployment. Until October 1929 MacDonald's policy of tariff reduction and disarmament made sense to most Scots Labour

MPs, but after the Crash, they could only demand the preservation of welfare benefits. Adamson, the Secretary of State, and Graham, resolute as Snowden against MacDonald's stumbling approaches to protectionism, were all found, in Labour's last Cabinet division on 23 August 1931, in the minority of nine voting against expenditure cuts. *Forward* went into the November election urging 'Shot and Shell against Bread Taxes', but it turned out to be 1906 in reverse. In Scotland only seven Labour MPs survived.

The National Government

MacDonald's appeal seems to have had some influence in swinging Scotland round to supporting the National Government. Whereas in Wales Labour still held a majority of seats, in Scotland the party collapsed. The effective co-ordination of Liberal and Unionist voting meant that a 2:1 majority in votes was transformed into a 6:1 majority in seats. Their huge majority did not benefit the National parties much. In September 1932, when the government negotiated the Ottawa agreements, and broke with the tradition of free trade, its Liberal supporters split. Sinclair, who had been Secretary of State, went into opposition with four of his colleagues. His successor, Sir Godfrey Collins, commanded the National Liberal remainder in Scotland. Wrangles continued in the Scottish Liberal Federation until 1935, when the 'Nationals' were expelled — henceforth becoming virtually indistinguishable from the Unionists. As for the latter, the unexpected size of the victory actually made their MPs even less representative of Scottish business than they had been in the 1920s.

This, however, was a disadvantage to Scotland rather than a benefit to Labour, which made no headway in by-elections and only a qualified recovery to 20 seats in 1935, and was plagued by a bitter feud with its old component, the ILP. Although when it disaffiliated from the Labour Party in 1932, the ILP claimed four of the seven surviving MPs, most of its Scottish members remained loyal to the idea of affiliation, and later that year set up the Scottish Socialist Party. Dollan was its effective leader and it took with it most of the ILP's 127 Scottish branches. ILP membership fell by 75 per cent, and far-left infiltration rapidly destroyed its organization in all but a few seats.

The Communist Party succeeded it as the representative of the far left — but not without difficulty. On instructions from Moscow, it had changed its line in 1928, turned on the Labour Party, and supported breakaway trade unions. On the whole this led to its increasing isolation, save in a few areas like the 'Little Moscows' of the Vale of Leven and Clydebank. Only in Fife, where William Gallacher engineered a breakaway from the Mineworkers' Union called the United Mineworkers of Scotland, was it successful. Gallacher beat the lacklustre William Adamson, Labour's former Secretary of State, in the 1935 election, but by that time, under the threat of fascism, the Communist line had changed once again.

The events of 1931, and the subsequent splits, did great damage to the left. In the 1920s Scots Labour MPs wielded strong influence in the parliamentary party; between 1931 and 1935 this momentum was lost. Successful policy initiatives thereafter tended to come from the south, particularly after Labour won the London County Council in 1934 and established a socialist laboratory on parliament's doorstep. The Scottish Socialist Party was dogged by legal battles over who should control the property of the ILP branches that affiliated to it, and expired in 1940, probably to the relief of Transport House, which did not like the left-wing company it kept. The Peace Pledge Union and the Left Book Club thrived, but not among Labour's economically parched grass roots, where the Co-operatives steadily declined. Returning to Fife in 1936, Jennie Lee, now married to Aneurin Bevan, found herself asking, 'Why were all the finest people I knew in the grip of a kind of spiritual paralysis? Where was all the vigour, the belligerancy, the robust certainties that had characterized the labour movement as I remembered it in my teens and early twenties?'

III Consensus Nationalism 1935 – 1950

NPS to SNP

Nineteen thirty-five confirmed the Unionists in power. Labour had been checked; the Liberals were disintegrating, the Communists a tiny minority, and the Nationalists marginal if picturesque. But nationalism went on to provide a unifying theme. The condition of Scotland had got relatively worse, raising problems for government and opportunities for the opposition. This issue didn't upset the dominance of the two parties, but their manipulation of it gave a distinctive tone to Scottish politics.

Political nationalism was garrulous — we know more about it than about the parties for which 90 per cent of Scots actually voted — but more significant than its low membership and few votes would imply. The National Party of Scotland, founded on 23 June 1928, largely by intellectuals of the Scottish Renaissance (see p.131) and former ILP activists, gained some 5,000 members by 1929 – about the same as the Scottish ILP. Its leaders, however, had to cope with a hostile environment and internal divisions over strategy. By 1929 voters had settled into a new two-party structure, and were reluctant to budge. Given events in Europe, nationalism was a dubious ideology. So, was the NPS to compete with Labour as a radical force, or try to enter the vacuum created by the collapse of Liberalism?

The NPS – largely run by the ex-ILP members John MacCormick and Roland Muirhead – struck out on radical lines. To little purpose. In 1929 it gained an average of less than 5 per cent in two contests. In 1931, this grew to 10 per cent in five contests, but in subsequent by-elections improved little. MacCormick, increasingly dominant, now switched tack, trying to attract dissident Unionists (at this stage much encouraged by the activities of Lord Beaverbrook and his new *Scottish Daily Express*) and former Liberals. Some of these had just launched, in September 1932, the Scottish Self-Government Party, when a disastrous by-election result in East Fife in February 1933 (Eric Linklater polled only 3.6 per cent among a menagerie of fringe candidates, partly conjured up by Beaverbrook at his most impish) moved MacCormick to purge the NPS of its fundamentalists (May 1933), and (November 1933) back the Scottish party leader Sir Alexander MacEwen (1875–1941) at the Kilmarnock by-election. MacEwen polled 16.9 per cent, and in April 1934 the parties amalgamated, largely on Scottish party terms, to form the Scottish National Party. Afterwards, however, membership fell steeply, to only 2,000 in 1939. There were some promising by-election results, but the 1935 vote showed no improvement on 1931.

The Right

National grievances were, however, present, even among the government parties, foreshadowed by the formation of the Scottish National Development Council in 1930. In 1932 MacDonald himself reverted to his earliest convictions by suggesting some measure of Scottish home rule. Scottish Unionist opinion quickly repudiated this in a series of meetings and manifestos in 1932-3, but pressed for administrative devolution and special economic measures, a demand which underlay the creation of the Scottish Special Area Commissioner (see p.50), the Scottish Economic Committee, and the Gilmour Committee on Scottish administration, together with the interventionist policy of

Walter Elliot, Secretary of State 1936–8.

Elliot was conscious of the need to legitimate the Unionists as a party of moderate, statist reform, one that could both incorporate the Liberal tradition and attract the working class. Despite 1931, there were still deficiencies in both areas. Many Unionists remained bitterly distrustful of the Liberals. As a future Secretary of State, James Stuart, wrote: 'I do not think I have ever suffered or enjoyed the friendship of a Liberal. I regard this as fortunate for they form a race apart, sitting on the fence and incapable of deciding whether to jump down on one side or the other'. A century's enmity could not easily be overcome.

One of its products had been the identification of the Unionist party with militant protestantism. Until the 1920s officials of the Orange Lodges had sat on the Scottish Council. Sometime before 1930 this link was dropped. Because the Liberals had to be courted instead? Because the Orangemen were less deferential than they ought to have been   witness the actions of some of them in supporting the General Strike? Certainly, it seems too easy to equate protestant militancy with Unionism, then or subsequently. One of the first things that the Lanarkshire migrants to Corby after 1932 set up was an Orange Lodge; by 1960 there were six, but Corby Council had yet to elect a single non-Labour member. Although in the 1950s Catholics voted disproportionately for Labour, the protestant vote still split roughly on the British average. Orangeism was probably more cultural than political.

That Unionism could not count automatically on protestant support was shown by the rise of a distinctively right-wing movement in the 1930s — the Scottish Protestant League in Glasgow, and Protestant Action in Edinburgh. The first had four councillors in Glasgow by 1934; and the second became in 1936 the second-largest party in Edinburgh, with 31 per cent of the vote, returning a maximum of nine councillors. This movement has been well documented by Dr Tom Gallagher. The rise in the poll it caused — of 50 per cent in Edinburgh in 1936 — has some similarities to the SNP's municipal impact in the 1960s (see p. 148). It had some vaguely fascist overtones — it directed propaganda equally against Unionist landlords and Catholic control of the Labour Party, and its Edinburgh leader, an ex-serviceman called Cormack, claimed to have a bodyguard and an armoured car — but it seems to have had no real connection with grievances stemming from economic hardship. It did better in prosperous Edinburgh than in Glasgow at the worst point of the depression, and in fact waned in the west as it grew in the east. Even in Edinburgh, it broke up in the late 1930s. Apart from it, the radical right was absent. Although several of Mosley's closest confidants were Scottish — Charles Raven Thompson, Dr Robert Forgan, and John Scanlon, all of whom had a left-wing background — and some Conservative MPs voiced pro-Hitler sentiments, the only time Mosleyite candidates stood, in 1937 municipal elections, they were humiliated.

In May 1938 Neville Chamberlain moved Elliot from the Scottish Office to the Ministry of Health. In October he reluctantly supported Chamberlain over the Munich agreements with Hitler, thus sealing his fate in 1940. Churchill dropped him, and he never held office again. The loss to Scotland of the only first-rank British statesman who identified himself with Scottish issues was a severe one, and it was particularly acute for the Unionists, who were just beginning to lose ground to Labour. In terms of Westminster performance Labour had scarcely deserved this, but they were making up a lot of ground in local government. They captured Glasgow in 1933, Motherwell and Clydebank in 1934, Dundee in 1936, and Falkirk in 1937, and made steady progress in the industrial counties. This was to create a new and powerful Labour interest, and one that Elliot at the Scottish Office had actually encouraged by increasing housing and educational programmes, which redounded to the credit of the local authorities.

The Popular Front

On the eve of war this was, however, somewhat masked by a revival of home-rule agitation on the left. Tom Johnston became in 1935 Labour's Scottish affairs spokesman and, while shifting politically to the centre and towards administrative rather than legislative devolution, he continued to encourage agitation for home rule, through groups like the London Scots' Self-Government Committee. This body, run by a couple of energetic journalists, had made the not surprising discovery that it was easier to influence Scottish affairs in London than in Edinburgh, and organized an imaginative range of meetings and pamphlets which at least gave the impression that the Labour leadership, up to and including Clement Attlee himself, favoured Scots self-government. Various things helped this, not least the Popular Front policy adopted by the Communist Party in 1935. Casting around for common causes with socialists and liberals, and worried at its own tiny Scottish membership (2,815 in December 1938) it adopted nationalism. Where it went, the stage army of the Popular Front followed; not only Ritchie Calder and J.B.S. Haldane but

Krishna Menon and Jawaharlal Nehru addressed meetings organized by self-government groups, while on May Day 1938 the Communists paraded in tartan, carrying banners of Bruce and Wallace, Burns, Calgacus and (rather oddly, in view of his high toryism) R.L. Stevenson.

Popular Front activities extended further, as the international situation worsened. Scots companies fought in Spain in the ranks of the International Brigade, sustaining heavy casualties, and in December 1938 one of the most important assaults on the policy of the Chamberlain government was mounted when the Duchess of Atholl resigned her Perthshire seat to contest it as an independent backed by the Popular Front. She lost, but only narrowly. Despite the seeming imminence of war, inter-party nationalism continued to bubble away, encouraged by MacCormick, who also tried to stifle neutralist and pacifist activity within the SNP. There was to be a great convention to launch an all-party campaign for home rule in September 1939. There was war instead: 'imperialist war' to such Communists as still remained in the party, and the fundamentalist nationalists who joined them in opposing it.

Labour policy-making proceeded, meanwhile, on two levels. We already know, from chapter 2, which was the more significant. The Dalton enquiry of 1937, and Dalton's translation to the Board of Trade in 1942, was to lay the foundation of the Direction of Industry Act of 1945, on which a generation of Labour prescriptions were based. This was, however, a success secured in the corridors of power. Overtly, Labour was to show a much more nationalist front in the Scotland of World War II.

World War II

The war both boosted Labour's political recovery and helped reinforce the apparent distinctiveness of Scottish planning and economic policies, in response to widely articulated and cross-party demands, and the surprising amount of success enjoyed by the SNP. After February 1941 the desire for change was personified by Tom Johnston, whom Churchill appointed Secretary of State.

In contrast to World War I, industrial relations were tranquil; Johnston considered the loss of only 0.07 per cent of work-days on Clydeside through strikes as adequately laying the ghost of 'the Red Clyde'. But Ministry of Information surveys showed a high level of dissatisfaction with the way the war was being run, verging even on disloyalty; these were moreover borne out by vociferous criticism by MPs both of left and right and by the success of the SNP towards the end of the war. In July 1943 Sir John Reith recorded a conversation with Johnston:

> He is very bothered by Bevin and other English ministers who do things affecting Scotland without consulting him. He thinks there is a great danger of Scottish nationalism coming up, and a sort of *Sinn Fein* movement as he called it. The Lord Justice Clerk [Lord Cooper] had said in a letter that if he left off being a judge and went back to politics, he would be a Nationalist.

In terms of its past performance, and its political history during the war, the SNP did well. It got 37 per cent of the vote at the Argyll by-election in April 1940, and although its home rule and independence wings split bitterly in June 1942, John MacCormick going off to form Scottish Convention, it went on to poll 41 per cent at Kirkcaldy in February 1944 and to win Motherwell in April 1945. It took on in Scotland many of the radicalizing functions of Common Wealth, although CW, whose Scottish representative was David Cleghorn Thomson (see p.128), had one of its first notable successes when Tom Wintringham nearly won North Midlothian in February 1943. He included home rule on his platform. So too did Sir John Boyd Orr, returned in April 1945 as an independent for the Scottish Universities. Such pressure was astutely managed by Johnston to get increased autonomy for the Scottish Office.

Johnston's *Memories* invest this process with rather more symmetry than it seems to have had. He wrote that he demanded from Churchill a Council of State, composed of all living ex-Secretaries, to vet all proposed Scottish legislation. If the council approved it, the Cabinet was to press parliament to legislate with minimum delay. It was to be advised by a body representative of Scottish business, trade union, and local authority opinion, and Scottish MPs were to meet regularly in Edinburgh. It was in fact over six months before the Council met, and then its remit was confined to post-war problems, while the Scottish Council on Industry, the larger body, was independently convened by Johnston on 2 February 1942. There were a couple of meetings of MPs in Edinburgh, which were not successful. That the Council of State shifted to concentrate on wartime administration was largely the result of a forcible intervention by Elliot in December 1941, arguing that post-war reconstruction could not be divorced from attracting wartime industry. Thereafter the Council met regularly until May 1943. The parallel Scottish Council on Industry was not the fully-fledged development commission for which James Bowie and the Scottish Economic Committee had pressed, but it countervailed the *laissez-faire* attitudes of the central office of the Board of Trade, strengthened its local representatives, and gave comprehensive backing to efforts to attract industry and plan the economy. Around it Johnston set up a proliferation of specialist committees – ultimately totalling 32 – investigating subjects as diverse as hill sheep farming and the teaching of citizenship in schools. Substantial practical gains were registered: Scotland received a full and varied quota of war industries; a committee under Lord Cooper cut through the Gordian knot of environmental and vested interests which had throttled the Caledonian Power Bill before the war, enabling Johnston to set up the publicly-owned North of Scotland Hydro-Electric Board; the public sector in medicine was extended; the Scottish Office gained planning powers; and planning groups for the major Scottish regions were set up well in advance of legislation.

Was all this a move towards formal devolution which Johnston's successors betrayed? Not really, Johnston disliked London government, but preferred efficient administration to 'partisan political strife'. His Scottish success, moreover, coincided with the capture of the 'commanding heights' of Whitehall by moderate collectivists – which Paul Addison has seen as a crucial component of Labour's 1945 victory – and didn't come long after Labour's own capture of major Scottish local authorities. The political system that resulted – a form of 'government by consultation' – both incorporated municipal Labour and guaranteed the key policies that sustained it: low-rent council housing, and denominational schools. It was confirmed by Labour's sweeping victory in the 1945 election, dispelling (for the time being) the nationalist apparition, and reducing the Unionists from 42 seats to 30.

Johnston left politics in 1945, subsequently becoming head of the Scottish Tourist Board, the Scottish Forestry Commissioners, and, in 1948, of the Hydro Board. In 1946 the Scottish labour movement lost, by death, two other major figures. One represented a body that, because of his activities, had steadily grown in influence; the other's political party virtually died with him.

The STUC

William Elger had become General Secretary of the Scottish Trades Union Congress in 1922. He found a small and rather decrepit body, dating back to 1897, which differed from the British TUC in including trades councils as well as unions. Many of these unions, however, were local craft associations, with a declining membership. If it were to survive it would have to establish its independent status. Elger's first survey of unionism revealed in 1942 that only about one-third of the Scottish workforce (*c*.500,000) was unionized, and of this number only 290,659 were affiliated to the STUC. In Elger's words, there was 'no Trade Union Movement as distinct from Unions'; the relatively non-militant east was actually better unionized than the 'wild red West'; and the traditional Scottish unions were atrophying in decaying industrial sectors. There were, for example, 11 independent Scottish unions in textiles, against 4 English ones, but in growing sectors like public employment English unions had a monopoly. Elger concentrated on building up a Scottish 'movement' by winning over sceptical English unions to affiliation, even at the cost of amalgamations between them and Scottish unions. By 1939 he could look back on a 33.8 per cent increase in affiliated membership while the labour force rose by only 10 per cent (the British TUC's affiliates rose over this period by only 7.5 per cent), and a position in which the STUC had become a respectable part of the government's consultation framework.

This was not achieved without opposition, particularly from the trades councils, in which Communists of the National Minority Movement were firmly entrenched and occasionally exercised control. Their initiatives to secure backing for the National Unemployed Workmen's Movement were sustained but unsuccessful, as were their attempts to dissuade the STUC from co-operating with its 'class enemies' like Lithgow and Bilsland by joining the Scottish Economic Committee in 1936. An executive member, C.W. Gallie of the National Union of Railwaymen, put the central option confronting the STUC succinctly: 'Were they to sit quietly by until they ushered in Socialism and found themselves the possessors of a bunch of derelict industries?

This was virtually to become a text for the STUC's subsequent policy. Although firmly in a minority in the SEC, on the creation of its successor, the Scottish Council in 1942, the STUC had its position further strengthened, and its consultative role was enhanced by the post-war Labour government.

The Post-war Left

The other death was that of Jimmie Maxton. For the House of Commons his lank, unkempt figure, wit and humanity symbolized the 'decency' and moral passion of the left, the spirit of the 'Red Clyde' glowering out of its mists in Lavery's famous portrait. Not surprisingly, the ILP had for a time that other thorny moralist, George Orwell, as a member. But as a party it had long since collapsed. In 1938 its MPs had negotiated to rejoin Labour, but Maxton's pacifism would not accept Labour's conversion to rearmament. When he died, its two remaining members soon took the Labour whip. Campbell Stephen died in 1948, and the Unionists won his seat. John McGovern, the ILP's most violent and undisciplined MP, moved sharply to the right and ended his career as an exhibit on Moral Rearmament platforms, testifying to the evils of Communism.

Paradoxically, the victory of 1945 seemed to end Labour's golden age. Its personalities were dead or had retreated to the fringes. The local party structure, with its newspapers, choirs, theatre groups, and cycling clubs, had largely collapsed. In the 1950s there were probably not more than 500 regular Labour activists in the whole of Glasgow. This was not unwelcome to local councillors who wanted a quiet life, and whose financial probity was not always above criticism — there was a particularly embarrassing sequence of corruption trials in Glasgow in the late 1930s and early 1940s which made Johnston threaten to rule the place with commissioners. Nor did it really disturb party organizers cast in the mould of Sir Patrick Dollan, Arthur Woodburn, and William Marshall, who concentrated on organization and discipline at the expense of participation and ideas. The time of the 'wee hard men' had come.

Electoral success compensated Labour for such afflictions. It was not so with the Liberals. Their decline continued inexorably. Sir Archibald Sinclair was an effective air minister in the wartime coalition, but took little interest in Scottish affairs, rarely attending the Council of State. He lost Caithness in 1945, and Dingle Foot lost the party's other Scottish seat at Dundee. 'The old fire of Liberalism, which had burned so ardently during the great days of the Midlothian campaign, was now almost extinct', noted Alison Readman after attending an Edinburgh meeting addressed by the party's most notable MP, William Beveridge. Despite an energetic campaign in 1950, there was little recovery. The party gained two seats — though one of these was Jo Grimond's in Orkney and Shetland — and lost 30 deposits. Need the collapse have been so great? Possibly not, as after the war liberalism of a sort had a remarkable revival.

The Covenant Movement

While secretary of the SNP before the war, John MacCormick had courted the Liberals. In 1937 he negotiated a pact with Lady Glen-Coats allowing his party a free run in 12 constituencies of its own choice, and after leaving the SNP he stood as a Liberal in Inverness in 1945. Meanwhile his 'Scottish Convention' — backed by some authoritative names from outside political nationalism such as Sir John Boyd Orr, Naomi Mitchison, and Professor John MacMurray, and expertly serviced in its economic intelligence by James Porteous, who had been Assistant Secretary of the Scottish Economic Committee — carried on steady pro-home-rule propaganda with a view to organizing a convention on the lines of the one aborted in 1939. In 1947 such a gathering took place, with 600 delegates, broadly representative of the churches, local government, the Co-operatives, and liberal opinion in general. The following year its second meeting approved a Covenant demanding home rule within a federal system, and at the third meeting, in October 1949, attended by 1,200 delegates, this was ceremonially signed. Subsequently it gained two million signatures. But the general elections of 1950 and 1951 supervened without any home-rule intervention. This was disastrous: by the time MacCormick had produced a continuing organization, the impetus had passed. The fact that many of its opponents gave aid to the Covenant movement prejudiced Labour against it from the beginning. In December 1947 MacCormick had stood against Labour at Paisley as a 'National' candidate. Paisley had a traditionally high Liberal vote, but by accepting Unionist support he alienated the Liberals. Ultimately he polled 20,668 against Labour's 25,000, and Labour never forgot it.

Labour's Response

Attlee's first choice as Secretary of State, Joe Westwood, who had been Johnston's Under-Secretary, proved a failure and was sacked in October 1947. Arthur Woodburn succeeded him. As Secretary of the Scottish Council of the party he had given guarded endorsement to home rule during the war. He now rejected it, but used the growing support for Scottish Convention — 'a kind of smouldering pile that might suddenly break through the party loyalties and become a formidable national movement' — to persuade the Cabinet to create a Scottish Economic Conference and to widen the scope of the Scottish Grand Committee. For over 40 years it had been restricted to the committee stages of non-controversial Scottish Bills; it could now consider them in principle at second reading — if the House as a whole approved — and debate the Scottish estimates. This still proved insufficient to halt the growth of Scottish Convention, or the intention of the Unionists to exploit what they saw as a protest against the centralization of the Labour government's nationalization policies. 'I should never adopt the view', Churchill told Edinburgh electors during the 1950 campaign, 'that Scotland should be forced into the serfdom of socialism as a result of a vote in the House of Commons'. After the election Attlee removed Woodburn and replaced him with Hector McNeil, a figure more in the Elliot mould who had done well as a junior minister at the Foreign Office. But he had little time to prove himself; on 26 October 1951 Labour went out of office.

Nineteen fifty was not to be the last time that a Unionist leader would play around with the rhetoric of nationalism, fairly unscrupulously. In fact the Unionists recovered little from the setback of 1945, although they were to do better in 1951. As a party they seemed increasingly remote from Scottish reality, their MPs increasingly drawn from the landed, agricultural, and professional classes, and they lacked Labour's connection to municipal politics, in which the right wing was still represented by local 'Progressive' or 'Moderate' parties. Yet possibly their reasons for being at Westminster were more rational than anyone else's. Wartime and post-war reform in agriculture had created a powerful interest which required this central representation. Labour took far longer to exploit its Westminster position.

IV A Part of the Whole? 1950–1964

The 1950s were tranquil. The romantic episode of the snatching of the Stone of Destiny from Westminster Abbey in 1950 — in which Mac-Cormick was involved — proved to be the swansong of the Covenant movement. On coming to power in 1951 the Conservatives set up the Balfour Commission into Scottish affairs, but removed home rule from its remit; the result was to be a modest increase in the powers of the Scottish Office, which took over responsibility for electricity in 1954 and roads in 1956. In the Indian summer of the heavy industries, the country was enjoying a stability otherwise absent for nearly half a century, and the Unionists did well, in 1955 getting an absolute majority of the Scottish vote, as well as Scottish MPs. This was partly through beating Labour at its own game. James Stuart, the aristocratic Secretary of State, got on well with Labour MPs, exceeded Labour's public housing programme by over a third, and at last secured substantial transport investment – with the Forth Road Bridge and Glasgow railway electrification. But this masked a failure to tackle the fundamental economic and social problems of the country.

During the icy years of 'Austerity' Labour had lost Glasgow and other big local authorities (a gradual process as only a third of councillors were elected each year). In the early 1950s it won them back, and then held them for 15 years, but its parliamentary presence was not effective. McNeil had moved to the right, and virtually left politics for business; his successor, Tom Fraser, though an able administrator, was unaggressive. Scottish political quiescence may have been deceptive, but it coincided with the development of 'behaviourist' political sociology, derived from American practice. This supposed a growing degree of British 'political homogeneity' – with voters increasingly conditioned by 'common' factors like social class, and 'consumerist' choices between the respective parties pushing out sectional and regional issues. Scotland seemed part of the whole.

In the later 1950s the economic situation worsened, and the labour movement got more aggressive, partly because of mighty upheavals in the Communist Party. Still subject to 'Cold War' proscriptions, the Communists had retained many of their wartime recruits and in the early 1950s had about 10,000 members in Scotland, a quarter of the party's UK total. Although electorally unsuccessful – Gallacher had lost West Fife in 1950 – its members were harder-working and better-briefed on the Scottish economy, and more corruption-resistant, than their Labour equivalents. Then, in 1955 and 1956 Kruschev's denunciation of Stalin and the Russian invasion of Hungary forced many intellectuals and activists to leave the party. One result was the New Left movement which grew up around the universities, contributing to developments as diverse as the folk-song revival and the Campaign for Nuclear Disarmament; another was Labour's acquisition of several hundred competent and radical activists. (In 1965, for example, the President, Secretary, and Vice-President of Edinburgh City Labour Party were all ex-Communists.) The result energized the left, although whether those who had followed the fiats of the Kremlin for decades could also provide imagination and open-mindedness was another matter.

This was also reflected in trade unionism. The STUC continued to grow faster than the TUC. Between 1939 and 1969 its affiliated membership increased by 128 per cent compared with 93 per cent. Elger's policy of collaboration with the Scottish Council and the Scottish Office had been continued by his successor, George Middleton, and the STUC, as 'honest broker' to incoming companies, ensured that non-union shops met union rates of pay and conditions. It, and many of the trades councils, were strongly anti-Communist until the mid 50s but ex-Communists steadily pushed it leftwards, and it developed links with unions in eastern Europe. This shift was accelerated by economic deterioration after 1958, but Middleton was able to turn it to the STUC's advantage by using it as a political bargaining counter. He built up close relations with Harold Macmillan, with him played a considerable part both in directing industries northwards and in creating a regional planning consensus. The increasing influence of the left also meant the return of home rule, traditionally backed by the Communists, to the STUC's programme in 1969, but the importance of this should not be exaggerated: union pressure had always been directed at equalizing Scottish and English wage-rates. The possibility of regional wage-bargaining, a central feature of German devolution, was always rejected. Whatever their declarations to the contrary, the unions were unionist.

Between 1958 and 1959 Scottish unemployment doubled. 'You've never had it so good' did not awake sympathetic echoes in the north that October, and Labour won four Unionist seats. Although Macmillan and his Scottish Secretary John Maclay subsequently exerted themselves to establish new industry, to introduce the concept of economic planning, and to reorganize the Scottish administrative machine to cope with these developments, they were frustrated by other aspects of their own government's programme, such as the drastic railway cuts of the Beeching programme and the run-down of the coal industry. Although it commanded widespread support in Scotland, the generalizations of the Toothill Report (1961) were not infallible, but scarcely had Maclay accepted its recommendations, and announced in March 1962 the creation of the Scottish Development Department (taking over planning and housing from the Department of Health, and roads, electricity, and local government from the Home Department) as its administrative embodiment, then he vanished in Macmillan's July purge. His inexperienced successor,

Michael Noble, had not only to face incessant attacks from the Labour benches, after March 1963 well co-ordinated by William Ross, but increasing indiscipline in his own ranks.

As rural Unionism had established itself more as an interest group than a political force, it was vulnerable to a rise in the political temperature. In the early 1960s the Liberal revival began to supply this. The party's fortunes had stayed low during the 1950s, although a popular candidate, like the broadcaster and former Rugby internationalist John M. Bannerman, could still produce the occasional good result. But under the charismatic, if somewhat olympian, leadership of Jo Grimond, after 1957, it began to show its teeth. As a result, indiscipline and individual protests on the Unionist back benches grew, until Scottish debates tended to become a sort of martyrdom for ministers. Labour, too, was pressed — in April 1961 Bannerman ran them very close at Paisley — but a series of by-election setbacks seemed to promise Unionist humiliation in the approaching general election. In this respect at least the 'evolution' of Sir Alec Douglas-Home in October 1963, after Macmillan's enforced retirement, served Unionism well. Under a somewhat antique exterior, Home had all the unsentimental realism of his class, and spoke the language of the agricultural interest. This language proved all but untranslatable to the political correspondents who followed his election campaign in Kinross and West Perth, but it helped secure him a triumph.

All things considered, the Unionists did not do too badly in 1964. Labour gained three seats from them (much less of a swing than in the north of England) and the Liberals gained three, also coming second in another eight. The Scottish National Party, an almost imperceptible presence in Scottish elections during the 1950s, but which had come second to Labour in the West Lothian by-election of February 1962, performed poorly, giving little indication of the trouble that it was subsequently to cause the main parties only a couple of years later. But a closer look at the SNP would show an accession of membership, money, and organizational ability, under the imaginative leadership of William Wolfe and Ian MacDonald, while on the Liberal side there was a growing divergence between its Scottish support and its British aims. The Liberal successes showed that a strong Scottish radicalism still subsisted beneath the two-party system, of which the idea of home rule was an important component. Yet Grimond, and his successors, still fundamentally looked to the south, and to the notion (apparently demonstrated at Orpington in March 1962) that they would prosper by ministering to the discontents of the English suburbs. Their failure to concentrate on a Scottish programme (a repetition of Sinclair's mistake in the 1930s) was subsequently to imperil them, just as Labour was to be hoist by the expectations of planning and social welfare it had created.

V *Dramatis Personae*

Twentieth-century Scottish politicians have not had a good press: observers have often contrasted the social irrelevance of the Unionist gentry and lawyers and the inarticulacy of Labour with the front-benchers of the pre-World War I period. But the latter's 'fortnight once a year' attentions were only possible when the role of government was limited. When this changed, and Scotland got more politically unstable, the front-benchers left. (In 1910 over half of Scottish MPs lived in England; by 1979 less than 10 per cent.) The Unionist response had some logic: their MPs represented first business and then, as economic autonomy declined, and they lost urban seats, the politically significant interest of agriculture. Labour's declining prestige was not due to the party becoming more proletarian, though it suffered from the southward shift of trade union authority. In 1922 its MPs were dominated by miners' agents; in 1964 by local councillors. More than a third of its MPs were 'middle class' in 1922, two-thirds in 1964. Its waning influence probably resulted from two factors. After 1945 the Labour party was centrally controlled by a small but very well-organized Oxford-educated élite, which (with a five times better chance of office than non-Oxford MPs) never made up less than a third of most Cabinets. Secondly, the growth of Scottish government both absorbed Scottish MPs, and created conventions which barred them from 'British' portfolios in areas devolved to the Secretary of State, such as education or housing.

The press also assaulted Scottish MPs for their silence in parliament. This was unfair. While they spoke less on non-Scottish subjects, they worked hard within the Scottish committees (further ones were added in 1957 and 1962) and on questions to ministers. Questions to the Secretary roughly quadrupled between 1924 and 1962. These not only reflected his increased powers but population distribution as well. In 1924 (when there were 34 Labour MPs) nearly two thirds of questions concerned the Highlands. Between 1960 and 1964 Labour made Scottish question-time, with every enquiry wired-up to supplementaries, a distinctive and deadly tactic.

The personnel of local authorities was similar, but their status was even lower. Until the mid 1970s the independent right survived, in 'Progressive' or 'Moderate' parties, while independents ran most county and district councils. After 1929 local hegemony shifted from gentry and minister to businessmen and retailers in the smaller towns, but this was outweighed by the increasing domination of permanent officials – medical officers, surveyors, directors of education. In the towns the representation of capital shifted from manufacturing to trade; and, after 1945, as housebuilding and redevelopment increased, to the construction industry. Labour representatives tended to be lower-middle rather than working class: small businessmen, union officials, and housewives. Both sides were inhibited by the fact that the 'state sector middle class' – teachers, civil servants, council employees – was banned from local office until 1974. The exclusion of a group which provided about 20 per cent of Labour MPs in the 1960s unquestionably harmed Labour in particular – as did the fact that many working-class councillors were employees of council contractors, who thus reinforced their interest.

Twenty per cent of Edinburgh councillors in 1960 were women. Their local government rôle grew, but their parliamentary rôle stagnated. At no time were there more than five women MPs (6 per cent) and after 1983 there were only two – although in terms of numbers elected (13.5 per cent of UK women MPs) and years served (11.7 compared with 11.1 UK average) Scotland's record was actually a little better than its machismo image, and the trade unions' persistent neglect of women's issues, would suggest. But Scandinavian countries had, by the 1960s, over 20 per cent of women MPs, and this example probably had some influence on the prominent rôle of women in the SNP, where they made up 3 out of 13 MPs, 1967–79.

By 1964 'St Andrew's House' had indeed become 'Dublin Castle', with 7,000 civil servants under its sway, and was the terminus of most enquiries and appeals, not only from MPs but from councillors. It developed a dynamic of its own, particularly in environmental, educational, and economic planning after 1960, culminating in the Toothill Report. John Mackintosh and others accused it of subservience to Whitehall, yet against Whitehall's secrecy and lack of professional specialism, St Andrew's House's more problem-orientated structure made it potentially more flexible and imaginative. Still, while not an Oxbridge fief – only about 20 per cent of its senior staff were from Oxbridge, compared with over 50 per cent in Whitehall – had it the planning and economic skills that its expanded

commitments demanded? Scottish administration has yet to be anato-
mized, but its heads tended to be directly drawn from the Scottish
universities, and hence to reflect both their deficiencies in the social
sciences and the constricting social solidarity of the Edinburgh professions. Only in the 1970s, for instance, did it receive an adequate
economic intelligence department, under Gavin McCrone.

Two biographies, moreover, provide a worrying insight into the
development of this secretive institution. John Highton became Permanent Under-Secretary under Elliot in 1936. Working class in background (his brother was Chairman of Glasgow Trades Council) he
organized unemployment investigations and adult education in his
spare time, and was well placed to give administrative shape to Elliot's
innovations. Tragically, he died after only a few months in office.
George Pottinger, a dynamic figure of the 1960s, whom many
expected to become Permanent Under-Secretary, cultivated an
impressive upper-class lifestyle. At his trial in 1975 it was found that,
for years, he had been in the pay of the corrupt Yorkshire architect
John Poulson, to the tune of £30,000, entanglements of which his
colleagues and superiors were unaware. Highton was the sort of
administrator the Scottish Office needed. Pottinger, perhaps, was led
to his downfall by his aspirations towards the Edinburgh upper-class
values that prevailed instead. Were such values relevant to a modern
administration?

As Scots MPs – especially the Labour members – were fairly
homogeneous, it seems surprising that a 'Scottish interest' took until
the 1960s to emerge. Lack of leadership seems critical. In Max
Weber's formulation 'imperative co-ordination' – the acceptance of
common goals and discipline – comes, pending an organized
bureaucracy, from a 'charismatic leader'. Parnell was such a figure in
Irish politics in 1880s, linking peasantry, local leaders, Church, exile
politicians, and MPs. The machinery he helped create survived his fall
in 1890. Tom Ellis and David Lloyd George, who might have done the
same for Wales, weakened Welsh nationalism by their co-option into
UK politics. There was no parallel to either in Scotland: the
Clydesiders did not attempt to lead Scottish MPs in the 1920s; there
was hardly anyone to lead in the 1930s, and although Johnston came
close to the Weberian pattern in 1941–5, he chose not to develop a
political movement.

What inhibited leadership? The constraints of Scottish working-
class consciousness (see p. 86)? A relatively open entry into the
southern élite, which drew the politically and administratively able

away — particularly between the wars? Certainly, for those who stayed, law, local government, education, and the Church offered secure and reasonably influential niches, while MPs who tried to build up a party following in Scotland as well as at Westminster ran risks. Elliot and Johnston lived beyond 65, but William Graham, Hector McNeil, and John Mackintosh died in their 40s; Wheatley, Maxton, Keir Hardie, Noel Skelton, and John MacCormick at around 60. Stress-based ailments terminated or damaged enough careers to suggest that the peripatetic life damaged party politics — particularly on the left — more than the other power-bases of Scottish society.

For the traditional institutions had their own élites, too. The reunited Church now eschewed party politics, but it still pronounced on political issues. Although two UF ministers — Campbell Stephen and James Barr — were prominent Labour MPs, they dissented from Church unity, and no ministers have followed them into parliament. The lawyers showed their solidarity in 1931, when the Lord Advocate, Craigie Aitchison, the Solicitor-General, and most of the Advocates Depute left Labour to join the National Government. Yet Labour still loved a lawyer; in 1936 another advocate, Robert Gibson, was chairman of its Scottish executive. Finally, after 1918, educational politics intensified to the point of impenetrability, with the incorporation of the Catholic schools, the shifting of the SED to Edinburgh, the education authority experiment, central salary negotiations, and the growing unionization of the teaching profession.

Did party majorities matter more than leaders? Probably not. Tom Johnston, leading the minority party in World War II, was a success; the Liberal Secretaries of World War I, with huge majorities, were flops. In our own day, Labour's 11-seat majority was not sufficient to counter Bruce Millan's distinctly anaesthetic effect on the devolution debate. The Secretary of State's position was surely critical. Until 1964, when his Welsh counterpart was created, he was unique in his control over a wide range of government functions and patronage. But was he party manager, administrative reformer, or national leader? The first rôle — the line of least resistance? — was taken by the weakest. The second, pioneered by Elliot as Under-Secretary in the 1920s, meant co-operating with local authorities and creating an administrative cadre. Elliot's precedent was followed *de facto* by Collins, Johnston, Woodburn, McNeil, and Maclay, and as a matter of principle by William Ross. The result was usually a consensus in favour of collectivist reform. But Johnston and Ross also encouraged a specifically Scottish will towards change: a difficult situation to master if, once expectations had been raised, the political machine failed to deliver the goods.

Finally, Labour in particular had to supply an ideological substitute for élite solidarity. Practically all the Unionist Secretaries were drawn from, or had married into, the Scottish landed and commercial establishment. They knew fairly well how to serve its needs. In the case of the best of them, Walter Elliot, there was also an intellectual input, the residue of pre-1914 'civic consciousness'. Hence the liveliness of his collaboration with its professional representatives, such as Boyd Orr or Grierson. Until 1941 Labour lacked a socialist concept of Scottish government (Adamson exemplified right-wing trade unionism at its dimmest) or an explicit power-base. Johnston, Dollan, and Elger created this base, but its essential pragmatism ruled out further ideological development, not only towards home rule, but virtually in any direction that might challenge the power-brokers in local government and the unions. This sterility meant that, when its plans turned sour in the late 1960s, Labour was peculiarly vulnerable to the challenge of the SNP.

5

Mass Media: High Culture
1922 – 1964

I

In the National Museum in Helsinki are three great stained-glass windows: Ethnography; Philology; History. These sum up the attempt of nineteenth-century Finnish liberals to give their nationalism an intellectual basis, by concentrating on the customs, language, and common experience of their people, on the whole still peasants. This implied, of course, a process of selection; the whole thing could pass for an exercise in intellectual hegemony. Different in aim, though not, possibly, in actual outcome, was the 'great tradition' of British intellectuals invoking 'culture' as 'the great hope in our present difficulties' -- the intention of Carlyle, Mill, Ruskin, Arnold, and so on being to combat tendencies towards materialistic, capitalist, and class-divided democracy by positing the goal of cultural excellence as a 'common pursuit'.

Scotland cannot quite be fitted into either tradition, although expatriate Scots largely formulated the second. It had long ceased to be a peasant society, but its popular culture was still quite distinct from that of England. Yet this culture, and the position of the intellectuals within it, was the result of the coincidence of a particularly dramatic industrial impact with an intellectual ambivalence towards cultural nationalism, and an effective transference of political nationality — not necessarily to Westminster. In the changed circumstances of the twentieth century the national model exerted its pull, but it was countered by this other experience. The result was to be an intellectual dialectic — the 'Scottish Renaissance' — of enormous quality and interest, although its linkage with politics and popular culture remained as complex and unsatisfactory as ever.

II Popular Culture and the Impact of War

Working-class culture, before 1914, was deeply divided: between rural and urban, between respectable and rough, between Catholic and Protestant, between men and women. In the country literary culture was limited: James Littlejohn found in *Westrigg* in the late 1940s that its staples were still the Bible and Burns. Long working hours meant that the same was probably the case elsewhere, though folk song survived in the 'bothies' of the north-east and among tinkers and fisher-folk. But this oral tradition had difficulties in the machine shop and the mine, leaving the male industrial worker with the choice between respectability and roughness, meaning drink. The first meant 'improvement', through the Churches, adult education, or the labour movement. Although sustained by philanthropy and local government, 'improvement' had to struggle against inimical living and working conditions.

Roughness underlined the sheer unpleasantness of working-class life. Football, the 'bevvy', the sluggish Sunday — these were emotional escapes rather than a form of socialization. There was no elaborate pub society, such as Brian Harrison has described in England. In Scotland the architectural magnificence of pubs was strictly proportionate to the drinkers' income. Instead, devoutness and drink were frequent doppelgangers, among Catholic and Free Churchman alike. Spirit drinking — as in Scandinavia — and 'wee haufs' helped overcome foul weather and draughts (for a majority of Scots workers probably spent most of their time in the open), and tiny crowded houses. If the result was a certain social inadequacy, then it would have been much worse but for the women. They created a home-life and a sort of community-politics, even if only through policing by gossip. They stayed away from drink and crime, saved, organized their families, read. They were a coiled spring.

War broke up many of these divisions. Although it breached religious sanctions, it also gained some of the objects of the temperance movement, as liquor control and stringent licensing cut heavy drinking. There had been 1 pub to every 424 Scots in 1900; by 1955 there would be only 1 to 806. In the same period drunkenness convictions declined tenfold to 2.6 to every 1,000 people. Both as cause and consequence of this more cash was spent on other recreations. Women's wartime gains meant that their exclusion from leisure was no longer possible, while along with the Liberal hegemony there departed much of the power of the churchgoing middle class to control the weekend. Catholics were notoriously flexible about the Sabbath, and so was the internal combustion engine. In 1910 only 21 Sunday trains had run on the Caledonian Railway, but buses operated regularly on Sunday, and motorists drove whenever they liked. Bus tours — for sport, sightseeing, or drinking — car trips to country tea-rooms, the growth of mountaineering and hiking, gave urban Scotland access to recreations previously confined to the well-off or determinedly secular.

III Outlets: Sport

If sport of various sorts dominated Scottish leisure time, there was good reason for this. With a large land area relative to population, Scotland had been, next to Switzerland, 'the playground of Europe' in the nineteenth century. A sportive ethos had been created, even if it was initially a socially restrictive one. It is worth looking at it in some detail.

We can begin by dividing it into three main areas: leisure-class activities, mainly field sports; spectator sports; and participant sports. The first were in theory participant sports, but they were much more important as economic activities, and as indicating social boundaries. A vast amount of rural Scotland was devoted to grouse-moors and deer forests. They were an important part of the Highland economy, an even more important hindrance to its development, and an essential ingredient of Scottish upper-class life. Yachting involved more of the middle classes, and was definitely of some benefit to the boatyards of the Clyde. If the middle classes fished a lot, they seem to have gone shooting infrequently, and hunted rarely if at all. But, to judge by *Scottish Biographies* (1938), participation in sport seems to have been, in Scotland much more than in England, a badge of social respect-ability. Thirty-seven per cent of a random sample of entries played golf, 17.5 per cent fished. Only 2 per cent and 1 per cent admitted to an interest in music or art. But then, only 1 per cent said they followed football.

For most Scotsmen, sport meant football. Watching and discussing it took up much of the weekend, and it filled a third of the popular press. Save in the Borders, Rugby Union was middle class. Cricket was less so, but mainly confined to the east coast. Shinty never took on outside the Highlands — unlike in Ireland, there was no nationalist attempt to promote 'Scottish' sports. Yet football was politically important: it defined class, gender, religion, and nationality, and ritualized and contained all of these. The period 1920–39, years of potential social upheaval, was its golden age. It was almost a paradigm of the Scottish situation: its skilled artisans were paid by little local oligarchies, or cleared off to richer fields in the south. The internationals with England, 12 out of 20 won by the Scottish David, were often the only time the best players represented their country, and all the more symbolic for that. Only with the onslaught of television did gates start to fall — by over 30 per cent, 1955–65. For George Blake in *The Shipbuilders* (1935) the crowd at 'ra gemme' — drink, swearing, and all — stood for the values of the skilled workers: decadence was represented by the new greyhound tracks, dedicated purely to the cause of easy money.

The politics of football between the wars are a curious business, anyway. The middle classes, the Churches, government encouraged football playing as an antidote to the demoralization caused by unemployment. But the same classes made social boundaries more rigid by imposing rugby on many senior secondary schools. They may have seen the enemy as commercialism — football pools became commonplace in working-class homes in the 1930s — and their goal may have been the 'democratic game' of the Borders, but the headmasters forgot that rugby needs grass if it is not to be murderous, while football simply needs a ball. So football tended to become an affirmation of working-class solidarity against 'improvement'. The aristocracy was little troubled by such scruples, and was appropriately rewarded. The fifth Earl of Rosebery was popular in Scotland despite his racehorses, his son because of them, although off-course gambling was not made legal until 1969.

Other participatory sports expanded, admitted women, but remained otherwise more class-bound, because of expense. Bowls and pigeon-racing remained symbols of artisan worth. Tennis, like curling in winter, spread from the upper to the middle class. With the help of municipal courses, golf filtered further down, although the golf club remained a major centre of middle-class socializing. Only in the 1960s did sailing and winter sports cease to be the preserve of the well-off, but rowing and amateur athletics, out of the same stable as the Boys' Brigade and YMCA, involved all classes. Aptly enough, Scotland's greatest runner of the inter-war years, Eric Liddell, forfeited an Olympic gold medal in 1924 by refusing to run on a Sunday. Swimming, in heated baths which were a by-product of the public health movement, was probably the most democratic participatory sport, and one in which Motherwell, in particular, did well.

IV Outlets: Indoor Entertainment

Enthusiasm for sport was a blow struck against a malign climate. Indoor entertainment, and the cinema in particular, had technology as well as unemployment on its side; it offered warm and reasonably harmless refuge from drink and overcrowding. Theatres and music halls either withered or blossomed into this new life. Glasgow's 14 fell to 9 in 1940, though some of her sentimental singers and alarmingly ethnic comedians put up a strong fight. The winter pantomimes of such as Tommy Lorne and Will Fyffe virtually merged into their summer seasons at holiday resorts. But by 1929, when talkies arrived, Glasgow had 127 cinemas. Large burghs had three or four apiece by the 1940s, and even the smallest towns would boast one, sometimes in bizarre conversions, like a former church in Melrose and a brewhouse in Kelso. Even the wilds were reached by the travelling projectors of the Highlands and Islands Film Service. To the Scots the movies were magic. In 1950 Glasgow people went on average 51 times a year, and Scots as a whole 36 times, while the English paid only 28 visits.

Reports on Scottish youth dwelt on the evils of 'corruption by Hollywood'. Certainly, Scottish cinemagoers were more likely to be corrupted from across the Atlantic than from England. They disliked British films save where these dealt with Scottish themes. On the other hand there seems to have been a positive commitment to film culture, with a film society showing continental films in Glasgow in 1929, and an 'art' cinema, the Cosmo, opening in 1939.

Almost more important, and like the cinema a 'mixed' activity, was 'The Dancing', which gripped Scotland in the 1920s and only died with the ballroom style in the 1960s. Young men in their 'paraffin' − three-piece suits and slicked-down hair − and girls would flock, up to six nights a week, to huge dance halls. Glasgow had 30; in some you could dance for six hours for sixpence. Liquor was banned and there wasn't much sex around; the stress was on skill and style − a classy evening out for the poor and unemployed. Some dance halls were the scene of clashes between Glasgow gangs, graphically described in MacArthur and Long's *No Mean City* (1934), but there's a curious innocence about the fact that the toughest gang leader would only dance with men. The halls were in the main fiercely respectable, and Glasgow dancing was by World War II the best in Britain.

V Outlets: Literacy and its Uses

At the time of the 1872 Education Act 14 per cent more Scots children than English children were at school. This factor still affected popular culture a couple of generations later. The Scots had accustomed themselves to literacy, endowed it, and organized for it. Public esteem was reflected in library provision, while popular spread was facilitated by a disproportionate number of booksellers and newsagents, and a thriving demotic literature.

Libraries had been a feature of town and country alike during industrialization, and they were rapidly expanded in the early twentieth century by donations and state action. Carnegie presented whole buildings and their contents to the larger towns in the 1890s and 1900s, while J. & P. Coats gave every school in the country a collection of classic works (religion carefully excluded). Finally the education act of 1918 made school libraries part of the county system, and enlarged them. Dunbartonshire, for example, started with a private endowment at Helensburgh, gained early in the century two Carnegie libraries at Dumbarton and Clydebank and a municipal one at Kirkintilloch, and after 1918 added 90 branches in schools and eventually a travelling van. Libraries were a prudent investment. Between the wars they were a refuge for the unemployed, leafing through papers (with the racing pages pasted over) in the relative warmth. Utilization figures must therefore be treated with caution as evidence of literary awareness. But Scots were certainly devoted readers by British standards; by 1960 Edinburgh held the record for books borrowed per head per annum: 13.

The Scots read newspapers avidly; despite a lower standard of living, and consequent reduction in advertising revenue, their purchases were comparable with the rest of Britain in 1936. Probably, in the central belt, they were actually higher: Glasgow was until 1957 the only city outside London with three evening papers. The rise of the Sundays was even more remarkable. There had been none in 1913, but by 1949 the *Sunday Post* claimed one of the most saturated markets in the world. Lack of advertising obviously hit magazines, but even here the Scots established an export ascendancy, with the products of Thomson and Leng, the 'Dundee Press'.

The newspapers that Scotland read were avowedly Scottish in tone, and became more so as the *Daily Herald* declined and the *Daily Mail* set up a Scottish edition. But the pattern of ownership had changed radically in the 1920s. English firms rapidly took over mass-circulation papers, although Outrams of Glasgow, Findlays of Edinburgh, and Thomson and Leng still survived. Only Outram's *Glasgow Herald* and Findlay's *Scotsman* were in any sense quality papers, with authoritative correspondents and reviewers and full political coverage; the others were dominated by local issues and sport. When Beaverbrook's Glasgow incursion of 1928 caused a circulation war, 'human interest', crime, and sport gained his *Scottish Daily Express* the upper hand, although Scotsmen — George Malcolm Thomson, John Gordon, John Junor — acted as senior counsellors at the Aitken court.

In 1900 T.W.H. Crosland assaulted Scots literary men in *The Unspeakable Scot* for reducing all literature to journalism. The remarkable research of Dr William Donaldson has indeed shown how central journalism was to Scots literature from the mid-nineteenth century on, with the weekly provincial press a conduit of radical politics and popular enlightenment. By 1990 however, there was some loss of publishing nerve. Although Scots firms — chiefly Collins, Blackie, and Nelson — produced a disproportionate number of British books, they tended to specialize in theology and reprints (which frequently ended up anyway as Sunday School prizes). The only firms with an interest in publishing contemporary Scots authors were the rather staid concerns of Oliver and Boyd and Blackwoods. A notable southward shift in the 1880s had coincided with the creation of the modern 'literary industry' of agents, publicity, and

Table 5.1: Scottish daily newspaper ownership, 1920-1992

	1920		1940		1992	
	number of papers	owners	number of papers	owners	number of papers	owners
Glasgow	5	all S	7	4S 3E	4	2S 2MN
Edinburgh	3	all S	4	2S 2E	2	2MN
Aberdeen	4	all S	2	2E	2	2MN
Dundee	4	all S	2	2S	2	2S
Paisley } Greenock }	2	all S	2	2S	2	1S 1MN
Sundays	2	all S	1	1S	4	1S 3 MN
total:	20	20 S	19	11S 8E	15	4S 2E 9MN

(S = Scottish-owned; E = English-owned; MN = Multinational)

Table 5.2: Scottish newspaper readership, 1935 and 1949

	1935		1949	
	Scotland	UK	Scotland	UK
No. of papers taken per family per day	1.5	1.5	0.66	0.70
No. of Sunday papers per family	1.1	1.7	2.26	1.9
No. of magazines per family per week			0.9	1.07

Source: M. Abrams, *The Home Market* (1950)

commercialism. And only one kind of Scottish literature was able to exploit this market.

They key figure was Sir William Robertson Nicoll, and the chosen instrument Hodder and Stoughton. Nicoll provided a bridge between the perfervid polemic of the mid-Victorian and the London literary industry with the British Weekly (1886) and the Bookman) (1891); he drew on the techniques of Scottish industry and the products of educa tion; he brought women in, with the significantly titled Woman at Home (also in 1891). Thirty years later, in *Hugh Selwyn Mauberly*, Ezra Pound would refer to him as 'Dr Dundas'. This was apt. Nicoll ran a new gravy train of patronage – literary, this time – to the south. His school of 'Kailyard' writers established the market for the 'Scottish story' and made aspirant authors only too aware of the riches it could provide.

The Kailyard developed beyond the Scottish parish. In the twentieth century it is better to define it as a literature whose content was established by market analysis. It was targeted not only on the Scots but on the emigrant community and a general middle-class readership which wanted to be reassured that, in an age of increasing social alienation and class-polarization, community identity was still possible. Poliitically it was midly reformist: Mrs Burnett Smith ('Annie S. Swan'), Nicoll's henchperson, was a prominent Scottish suffragist, the Liberal Party's first woman candidate, and a founder of the SNP. It may be unfair to endorse MacDiarmid's opinion that the anti-Kailyard novels of George Douglas Brown and James Macdougall Hay, *The House with the Green Shutters* (1900) and *Gillespie* (1913), were 'the same thing disguised as its opposite', but fairly soon even this genre had been swallowed by it, in the novels of Jane Duncan and A.J. Cronin. In the twentieth century the Kailyard strain changed and expanded into a somewhat disproportionate Scots presence in general readership light fiction, from adventure stories through historical novels to animal tales and hospital romances. Behind Alastair MacLean, Nigel Tranter, Mary Stewart, Dorothy Dunnett, Gavin Maxwell, James Herriot, and Lucilla Andrews might have been the shadowy lineaments of Stevenson, Scott, Dr John Brown, and Mrs Oliphant, but what mattered was the literary machinery that Nicoll and his friends had set up. As time went on, it drew on its more prole-tarian wing, the Dundee press, which sustained the same values but salted them with older and less respectable popular fictional tradi-tions. In *The Uses of Literacy* (1957) Richard Hoggart noticed how, along with detailed and faithful renderings of working-class life,

Dundee women's magazines specialized in serials in which the path of true love was splashed with quite a lot of blood, but James Cameron, a distinguished graduate of Thomson and Leng, recollected the strictness of the rules: drawings could show slit throats but not bare knees.

Patterns of Scottish leisure had thus changed to cope with increased income, changing relationships between the sexes, and increased (if not always intended) free time. They were both more individually-and more socially-oriented than those of England. Popular literature was at a premium in a country of small houses, where it at least offered a range of individual options. The alternative was organized social activity, provided municipally or commercially. The commercial structure was partly Scottish-owned, as in football, but was also, like many inter-war enterprises, increasingly dominated by large-scale English-run concerns.

Scotland was weak in family activities: gardening, for instance, increased, but not to the same extent as in England with her lower-density housing developments. Coarse fishing never became, as in the south, the most important participatory sport. Those who lived in the country, or could afford it, caught trout; the rivers and canals in the industrial areas were too polluted for roach or bream to survive. Hobbies requiring house-room, like model engineering, woodworking, motor car maintenance, and 'do-it-yourself' projects, were virtually ruled out. Educational reports commented on the inadequacy of Scottish girls as cooks and dressmakers, citing the same reasons. The growth of domestic science classes in the schools was a response. In the long run such factors probably had some part in the decline of skill within the Scottish working class. The state provided no countervailing resources, as technical education remained miserably inadequate, and voluntary working-class education – through the Workers' Educational Association in its early years and the Marxist National Council of Labour Colleges – was geared to political militancy and workshop organization rather than to acquiring new techniques or 'the full rich life'.

VI Uplift and Improvement

Although the expansion and diversification of popular entertainment certainly mitigated the tensions of the depression, it was not planned to do so. However, explicit attempts were made, by voluntary bodies and the state, to direct recreational activities in specific directions. These reflected the waning of traditional institutions of social co-operation, new technological possibilities, and new client groups.

The main diminution was of religious fervour. Although this had yet to register in terms of Church membership (see p.83), and the Churches still took a leading rôle in many of the developments to be surveyed, the primacy of 'controversial divinity' had vanished. Instead, the churches developed their social organizations, and some bodies traditionally connected with them provided paradigms for more secular developments.

The Freemason style, for instance, expanded significantly. Masonry had always been important in Scotland, with about 25 per cent of lodges in Britain and about 10 per cent of adult males as members. One of the few areas of interclass mixing, it was supplemented in the inter-war period by ex-servicemen's organizations, most notably the British Legion. Such bodies could have become — as in France or Germany — intensely political. Instead the Legion, founded under the headship of Earl Haig in 1921, provided a combination of social activities, quasi-masonic ritual, and religious involvement which made it a conservative and mildly nationalist presence. Analogous groups like Rotary — an American import which brought together the 'leaders' of local trade and industry, and established itself very strongly in Scotland from 1912 on — provided such 'non-political' (and by implication, conservative) bodies with a 'general staff'.

Unlike masonry, the British Legion and Rotary accommodated women — though at arm's length in separate and subordinate women's organizations. A similar logic had led to the creation in 1918 of the Scottish Women's Rural Institutes. The Board of Agriculture had set them up to increase participation in the war effort, and they expanded after the war until most parishes had branches. Like the Legion, their values were conservative and mildly nationalist. In fact they helped on its way a major Kailyard revival, the Community Drama movement, whose annual festival swelled from 35 competitors in 1926 to over 1,000 in 1936. The artistic standards of such groups were not high: their demand for 'kitchen comedies' ruined play-wrights, like the pacifist miner Joe Corrie, who had something serious to say, but until television arrived they remained an important element of Scottish popular culture.

In another area of activity the Churches were still successful. In Scotland there were no national youth organizations like the Czech Sokol or the Irish Fianna, although the socialist nationalist John Kinloch did persevere with Clan Scotland, and the Scottish Youth Hostel movement, formed after the German model in 1931, had much of nationalism about it in its early days. But the real growth was in the

Scouts and the Boys' Brigade. Both were founded before 1914 but only really expanded in the inter-war years, when they also added parallel girls' organizations. Of the two, the 'BBs' were the more urban and proletarian — all you needed was a white belt and a pillbox hat, instead of the Scouts' expensive bushveldt paraphernalia — and even more than the Scouts, they were tied to the Churches. BBs would be shocked to hear of Socialist Sunday Schools (in Glasgow, naturally) where Jesus didn't feature but humanist hymns by such as Edward Carpenter were sung. Not to much effect. Socialist Sunday Schools declined along with the ILP, and the Co-operative's Woodcraft Folk could never really compete with bugles and woggles. God had all the best tunes.

The failure of the political culture was also glaringly evident in the weakness of 'serious journalism' — this despite, or possibly because of, the important positions held by Scots in British political journalism, such as James Margach, Robert Carvel, or Alastair Hetherington. Scotland sustained no regular Unionist or Liberal magazines, and those of the left, once so promising, steadily declined, although *Forward* and *Plebs* of the National Council of Labour Colleges limped on until the 1960s. It took individualists — John Wheatley, James Leatham, Guy Aldred — to run socialist papers, and these usually died with them. By contrast, the nationalist *Scots Independent* has lasted since 1926.

As might be expected, 'institutional journals' flourished, but at the cost of parochialism. The Kirk had the monthly *Life and Work*, the Catholics the weekly *Glasgow Observer*, law the *Scots Law Times*, teachers the *Scottish Educational Journal*. In contrast to these, and to the situation in Wales and Ireland, attempts at a national critical review were usually failures, although there was usually a hopeful newcomer around to pick up the guttering torch. Between 1926 and 1934 William Power edited *The Scots Observer*, a well-meaning if clumsy vehicle for the literary revival; in 1934 the SNDC took over the fight with *Scotland*, which closed down during the war but performed respectably in the 1950s and 1960s. The left-wing Scottish Reconstruction Committee tried its hand with *New Scot* (1945–50), the Saltire Society with the *Saltire Review* and *New Saltire* (1954–64), but the formula was never found to raise circulation beyond a few thousand. Dundee's *Scots Magazine* (founded 1739) with a dependable mixture of anecdote, local coverage, and a huge exile sale, and Outram's somewhat classier *Scottish Field*, proved incomparably more successful.

Scottish cultural developments had depended on patronage, and a consequence of the depression and the southward migration of capital was that business patronage declined. Edinburgh University, for instance, received no endowments on the scale of the pre-war gifts of the Usher and MacEwan families. State grants were increased following the formation of the University Grants Committee in 1918 but, as noted earlier (see p.78), they simply ensured that the situation didn't deteriorate further. But State action did ensure a major improvement in research facilities. Following the 1918 Education Act a Scottish Central Library was set up in 1921 to co-ordinate local activities, and in the same year the creation of a National Library began. It got its act in 1925 and took over the 750,000 volumes of the Advocates' Library. In 1936 its building, to the design of Reginald Fairlie, was started on George IV Bridge, Edinburgh. Because of the war, it took 20 years to complete. After 1956 Scottish researchers had the most convenient and efficient copyright library in Britain, but its earlier absence was sadly missed.

If the state in this way encouraged a national cultural movement, its other major action was much more ambiguous. Radio began in Scotland in March 1923 under the private British Broadcasting Company. Three years later it was transformed into a public corporation. Ten years later it reached over 40 per cent of Scots homes. In charge of both was John Reith, apostle *par excellence* of uplift and improvement, yet at the same time the architect of an extremely centralized organization. Although the BBC set up a Scottish Region, its autonomy was limited; promising attempts to marry its aims to those of the literary renaissance by David Cleghorn Thomson and Moray MacLaren ended in frustration. Ultimately, under the regime of the Rev. Melville Dinwiddie (1933–57) the BBC in Scotland became a by-word for puritanical parochialism. Many of its early staff stayed in post much longer than Dinwiddie. No one would grudge those gentle Uncles and Aunties the right to become national institutions, but not at the expense of a broadcasting service that could have done so much more to cope with Scotland's social and cultural problems. The Scottish BBC was in fact a paradigm of the fate of regional organizations within otherwise highly-centralized UK bodies. The nominated Broadcasting Council was selected to represent the Scottish establishment, and it tended to concur with an equally conservative local executive. If talented radicals could be got rid of by promoting them to positions at the centre, who would complain, least of all at Broadcasting House?

VII The Scottish Renaissance

A provincial culture, distinct from that of England for various reasons, rather than superior to it. An acute awareness among Scottish intellectuals of the power of parochialism and the mediocrity of its cultural values; a sense of attraction to and revulsion against the metropolis. These factors appear to be constant throughout our period. But they were made explicit by the sudden efflorescence of the Scottish Renaissance in the 1920s and, despite its subsequent setbacks, this continued to sustain, and ultimately strengthen, a sense of a distinct national intellect.

World War I had not, in itself, stimulated Scottish literature, if the work of the two Anglo-Scottish front-line poets C.H. Sorley and E.A. Mackintosh be excepted, although a Scots-Canadian medical officer, John MacCrae, did create one unforgettable symbol, in the lines,

> In Flanders fields the poppies blow
> Among the crosses, row on row

while at Craiglockhart Sanatorium in Edinburgh an enlightened psychiatrist stimulated two battle-scarred officers to publish their poetry — Siegfried Sassoon and Wilfred Owen. Popular literature had done its bit, with the novels of 'Ian Hay' (*The First Hundred Thousand* and its sequels) and the saga of *Spud Tamson*, Glasgow 'ned' turned war hero proved (we have Harry McShane's word for it) a very effective recruiting tract. John Buchan, possibly the most energetic war reporter and propagandist, loaded Richard Hannay with symbolism and sent him off to the Red Clyde, among other places, in *Mr Standfast* (1918). The result was not very convincing. The tragic impact of the war had to wait for a decade and a half to be commemorated, in Grassic Gibbon's *Sunset Song* (1932).

But before society had readjusted itself, the upheavals, not merely of the war but of revolution and cultural radicalism, gained an articulate and aggressive voice. Christopher Murray Grieve, 'Hugh MacDiarmid', son of a Langholm postman, had been a socialist journalist in 1914. He saw service in Salonika and France, but the war, as such, scarcely registered on him. He used his time abroad to devour the literature and recent history of Europe and then turned on Scotland a mind grown international. As a literary editor his first anthology, *Northern Numbers* (1920), was respectful to older literati like Buchan and Neil Munro; his third series dropped them and adopted a radical tone, at once nationalist and revolutionary. Behind this lay the impact of the Irish war of independence (1919–21), the onset of the depression, and the influence of John Maclean. Although James Connolly, a Scot by birth, had been *Forward*'s Irish correspondent, the constitutional left had ignored the Irish Rising. Now, after his sacrifice, Connolly's aim seemed to have succeeded. Poets and socialists had together pulled their country away from the English connection. Yeats became a senator and was awarded the Nobel prize, and in 1922 James Joyce published *Ulysses*, assaulting the preconceived limits of the English language. To MacDiarmid, already associated with the radical *New Age* group, a centrifuge seemed to be at work; the hegemony of English, as well as of the Empire, was collapsing. The parochialism of Scottish literary life would have to be destroyed. 'Dunbar, not Burns!', 'Not Traditions – Precedents!' were the watchwords of his *Scottish Chapbook* (1922), and he went on to lay down to the teachers of Scotland, between 1925 and 1927, the standards that a new Scottish culture would have to achieve to gain international acceptance.

Thus far he resembled the great 'political' critics of nineteenth-century European literature – Carlyle, Belinsky, Brandes – but he also punched his message home with poetry of rare muscle and skill:

> O Scotland is
> The barren fig
> Up, carles, up
> And round it jig!
> A miracle's
> Oor only chance.
> Up, carles, up
> And let us dance!

By 1925 the French critic Denis Saurat was writing of the 'Scottish Renaissance', a term which MacDiarmid instantly appropriated. For his aims were not simply the achievement of a national literature akin to that of Norway or Ireland, but something consonant with Scotland's experience – an achievement on a world scale.

Controversy and contradiction governed MacDiarmid's philosophy. He would confront the debased vernacular with the abstracted rationality of the Scots forced abroad by the absence of a genuinely national culture. His aim was a perpetual unrest, 'a Caledonian antisyzygy' (a phrase borrowed from Professor Gregory Smith's

Scottish Literature of 1919). There were other nationalist patrons, like William Power or Ruari Erskine of Mar, who had nurtured any and every shoot of Scots literary ability. MacDiarmid was prepared to flay as well as encourage. Confessedly anti-English, he was also prepared to be equally anti-Scottish, where the enemy was smugness and complacency. This verse is cut into his tombstone:

> I'll hae nae hauf-way hoose, but aye be whaur
> Extremes meet — it's the only way I ken
> To dodge the curst conceit o' bein' right
> That damns the vast majority o' men.

MacDiarmid could still have been an isolated figure — there were plenty of gloomy precedents among nineteenth-century literary nationalists — but his self-confident initiative coincided with growing doubts among publicists, home rulers, and scholars not just about the Scottish economy but about the survival of nationality in face of the political centralization induced by the war, and also with a remarkable flowering of literary talent. The foundation of Scottish PEN (1926) and the National Party of Scotland (1928) were possibly the key literary–political events, but the decade 1924–34 also saw MacDiarmid's 'A Drunk Man Looks at the Thistle' and his first and second 'Hymns to Lenin', the first novels of Neil Gunn, George Blake, Eric Linklater, Fionn MacColla, and Naomi Mitchison, the critical writing of Edwin Muir and the early plays of James Bridie. And then, between 1932 and 1934, hammered straight on to a typewriter in a few weeks out of a short life, Lewis Grassic Gibbon's Mearns trilogy, later to be known as *A Scots Quair*.

What unified these, besides a degree of literary success which, if modest by British standards, was unprecedented in Scotland, and a general identification of literature with nationality? MacDiarmid wrote in 'The Kulturkampf: to William Power' (1935) that:

> No man can state the truth of Scotland,
> But he can establish some sort of relation
> Between his truth and the absolute. . . .

> Artists cannot be taken out of their own times and places
> To be shown around — just as the beauty of a tree
> Cannot be made visible by uprooting the tree;
> Here, they were shown together with their country.

The sense of finding a voice in Scotland, as well as for Scotland, was crucial. Besides the war and the wounds it had dealt, besides resentment at the failure of home rule and the failings of political parties, there was also a rebellion against parental authority, a discovery that sex could be talked about, even enjoyed, a sheer desire to write because no other means of communication and protest were available, much as women had used novel-writing to break their social isolation a century before. In this sense the achievement of the renaissance was personal rather than social or national. But an escape from the formula that had been Scotland did not necessarily mean a commitment to MacDiarmid's vision of a nation regenerated through the reconstruction of the old Scots tongue and political militancy. MacDiarmid had seen the recovery of Lallans as both democratic and nationalistic, but after the collapse of the General Strike in 1926 (see p.94) he moved to a position both more intransigent and more aristocratic, invoking scientific supermen just as Carlyle, his model in so many respects, had invoked Cromwell and Frederick the Great.

After 1930 MacDiarmid rarely wrote in Lallans, but the relevance of his work was shortly to be dramatized by the extraordinary achievement of Grassic Gibbon's trilogy. Like MacDiarmid, who was eight years older, Gibbon was an autodidact who had knocked around in journalism and the more boring parts of the services, all the time grasping for some great scientific world-view, and then fused his ideas, under intense pressure, onto the experience of Scotland. The result — *Sunset Song, Cloud Howe,* and *Grey Granite* — like MacDiarmid's 'Drunk Man' combines the sweep of historical change — the transition from rural to urban, the impact of the General Strike, the collapse of the Labour government — with the grip of individuals' struggles with one another, with society, or with the land itself, for their own identity.

Gibbon was ambiguous about nationalism, although his use of the Scots tongue amply proved its vitality. Yet the impact of the *Quair* seems ultimately ambiguous, even elegiac. Chris Guthrie, its central figure, returns to farm her father's Aberdeenshire croft, and dies. Her son, Ewan, leads a hunger march south to London. The old rural life ends, the industrial struggle begins. And yet in Gibbon it is the rural life that seems real, and the industrial episodes two-dimensional by contrast. Much the same can be said of MacDiarmid. The absorbing interest in nature, in character, demonstrated in the symbolism with which he invested his home landscape of Langholm, co-exists awkwardly with his 'scientific materialism' and dogmatic and sometimes inhumane politics. In 1936 Edwin Muir courted — and got — MacDiarmid's wrath by arguing, in *Scott and Scotland*, that the vernacular had no future. His premises were actually the same as MacDiarmid's: English was a foreign language, in which the Scots had never really been articulate. Muir's only remedy was a systematic linguistic assimilation. Given the achievements of MacDiarmid and Gibbon, this may seem tactless, but Muir had hit at a weak point. The greatest triumphs of the renaissance still failed to penetrate to the real matter of Scotland. The society that Gunn or MacColla or Mac-Diarmid or Gibbon celebrated was marginal to the urban life that the mass of the people now lived. Even the Kailyard had managed to make the transition which writers of much greater talent had failed to do.

The Scottish renaissance's failure to supply 'the great bourgeois novel' — anything comparable with the triumphs of Mann, Musil, Proust, and Joyce — was not its own fault. As Doris Lessing has pointed out, partly because Britain did not go through, or even seriously attempt, the centralizing process of state-formation in the nineteenth century, the essentially provincial attitudes of the gentry remained too strong for too long. Further, in Scotland, the tradition of the skilled craftsman, passing from the crofter to the weaver and the engineer, and safeguarded by the essentially 'planned' nature of the transition to industrialization, kept alive a range of attitudes that were never wholly of industrial mass-society. When, in *Grey Granite* (1934), Chris Guthrie rounds on an unemployed man: 'My class? It was digging its living in sweat while yours lay down with a whine in the dirt', she is speaking for more than the tradition of the Mearns peasants — for a series of now-vanishing skills which even when found in the engine-shops had more in common with those of the miller, blacksmith, and ploughman than with those of the assembly-line operative. Although MacDiarmid asked in his 'Second Hymn to Lenin'

> Are my poems spoken in the factories and fields
> In the streets o' town?
> Gin they're no, then I'm failin' to dae
> What I ocht to ha' dune

his ambition for his own poetry was rarely realized, and in fact was only intermittently held. The ordinary people still read the Dundee Press and went to Burns Suppers, while MacDiarmid's later poetry grew more cerebral and elitist: 'a sound like talking to God' was not something everyone could hear.

By 1936 the renaissance was over, and MacDiarmid an embittered exile in Shetland. Those whom it had stimulated to write continued to write — the best novels of Gunn, the Gaelic poetry of Sorley MacLean and George Campbell Hay, were still to come. But they were no longer part of a movement. Scottish *political* nationalism, as if in reaction to the word's increasingly unpleasant European connotations, was moderate, centrist, and not very effective, and, despite the founding of the Saltire Society in 1935 and some patronage from Elliot as Secretary of State, the revival did not move out of literature into other fields. It had been as paradoxical a development as MacDiarmid had wished for. It was about Scotland, yet would it have succeeded without the support of Anglo-Scots and London publishers and critics who took up its writers when they might have been ignored in the north? Without the advocacy of Ivor Brown, the Leavises, or T.S. Eliot? It was about politics, but these were infinitely varied. MacDiarmid wrote great socialist poetry — 'The Ballad of the General Strike' — in the same year that he prefaced *Albyn, or the Future of the Scots* with texts from Barres and Maurras, the pillars of the French right. Grassic Gibbon may have based the plot of *Sunset Song* on Frenssen's *Jorn Uhl* (1900), a German classic of the 'blood and soil' school favoured by the Third Reich — which also responded enthusiastically to the peasant society depicted by Eric Linklater and Neil Gunn. Both were blameless democrats, yet Linklater, Compton Mackenzie, and above all James Bridie represented an ironic, convivial Toryism, rather in the style of *Noctes Ambrosiana*, far removed from the Marxism of MacDiarmid and Gibbon. Oddest of all, it showed men — particularly Gunn and Gibbon — writing with sensitivity about women, while their pub society still kept women on the sidelines. The best women writers, Rebecca West and Naomi Mitchison, still went south. But, just as the one fully-aware person in 'The Drunk Man' is the poet's wife, the personnel of the renaissance frequently had to be kept together by the quiet civil servant Helen Cruikshank, poet and secretary of Scottish PEN. It was good sense for a later woman writer, Muriel Spark, to capture the spirit of 1930s Edinburgh in an opinionated Miss Jean Brodie, dabbling in authoritarian European politics, but at the time getting her 'set' to think for themselves.

Linked to the renaissance had come another characteristic activity of nineteenth-century nationalism — the compilation of a linguistic dictionary. Here, in fact, was a classic instance of transferred nationality, as the apotheosis of standard English, the *Oxford English Dictionary*, was the creation of one 'lad o' pairts', Sir James Murray, and was carried on by another, Sir William Craigie. In the 1920s Craigie returned to Scottish themes, and set about the creation of a *Dictionary of the Older Scottish Tongue*. MacDiarmid hailed this as a major reinforcement of the literary revival, a conviction confirmed by the fact that when Craigie circulated the imperial outposts of tartan nationalism, Burns Clubs and Caledonian Societies, he got only two replies to 500 letters, both refusing to help. The dictionary compilers divided into two. Craigie's first volume came out in 1931 and is still underway; the (post-1707) *Scottish National Dictionary* appeared between 1931 and 1975.

Yet a renaissance on a Florentine scale, which transforms an entire culture, requires patronage provided by economic growth, or political institutions that encourage the artists involved. Scotland's Medicis, if they had not moved south, were preoccupied with not going bankrupt. The money was not around to encourage the art forms that needed it. The literary renaissance came cheap; funds of an altogether different order were needed for theatre, music, or architecture.

VIII Architecture and Art

Architecture and design, what Ruskin called 'the greater arts of life', are crucial instances. In the 1890s Charles Rennie Mackintosh had laid down the principles of a modern Scottish architecture, combining the vernacular – 'as indigenous to our country as our wild flowers, our family names, our customs, or our political constitution' – and the functional. But his aims were confounded by the economic decline in building in Edwardian Scotland, and by 1914 many of the best Scottish architects had gone south or, like Mackintosh himself, given up. There was to be no recovery after the war, Major building was effectively restricted to council houses and schools, and most of this work went to the rather unimaginative architects' departments of the local authorities. There was a reaction. In 1932 the nationalist Robert Hurd restated Mackintosh's case, armed with examples of what architects could do in small nations like Finland and Czechoslovakia. One of this emerged the Saltire Society, and the movement for better town planning. Under Walter Elliot, the state also emerged as a major patron, with Thomas Tait's St Andrew's House (1935–9) and the £11m. project of the Empire Exhibition, which Tait supervised and which also involved the young Basil Spence and Jack Coia. The effects of this long innurition, however, were to be tragically apparent when large-scale building again took place in the 1960s, and a respectable number of good modern buildings were literally overshadowed by disasters like the destruction of Edinburgh's George Square and the multi-storey housing programme. In design the situation was, if anything, worse. As the Scottish Economic Committee's enquiry into light industry in 1937 found, there was a tradition of expensive hand-crafted work in textiles, furniture, and glass, but, below that, design standards were awful. The manufacturers who tried to remedy this were few, though the textile magnate Alastair Morton, patron of Picasso and Braque, deserves honourable mention. Conscious action over design education, of the sort that enabled Scandinavian countries to compensate for high prices through high-standard mass-produced goods, was almost totally lacking.

If Scottish architecture was disadvantaged by the absence of great patrons, Scottish art was constrained by already having adapted itself to a middle-class clientele. In contrast to mid-nineteenth-century painters like MacWhirter and Faed, engraved versions of whose sentimental studies of Scottish country life and scenes from Burns could be found on countless artisan walls beside samplers and family photographs, the 'Glasgow Boys' of the 1880s and their successors, the 'Scottish Colourists' — E.A. Peploe, F.C.B. Cadell, and Leslie Hunter — produced moderately-priced oils, water colours, and etchings for a middle-class public, represented by private buyers and the developing municipal collections. These collections, run by gifted connoisseurs like Sir James Caw and T.J. Honeyman, deserved their high reputation, but the indigenous art they patronized was domestic in scale and socially unadventurous. Scottish art may have avoided the worst ramps of the international 'art market', but public art like murals was non-existent and the innovators — Alan Davie, Robert Colquhoun and Robert MacBryde, Eduardo Paolozzi — got out. If Tretchikov's green ladies had taken over in living rooms from 'Burns's Meeting with Highland Mary', where was the improvement in that? Even photography, potentially the most radical art form and one that nineteenth-century Scotland had helped create, rarely escaped from the seductions of a photogenic landscape. Fine work was done in Scotland by the Londoner Jim Jarché and the American Paul Strand, but not by the Scots themselves.

IX Theatre and Music

As with art and architecture, so with theatre and music? In both the latter cases twentieth-century economic problems complicated a situation in which the Calvinist ethos had scarcely encouraged such art forms. That nineteenth-century Scotland had managed to sustain some dramatic activity and a modest musical revival was remarkable enough, given the puritanism of the Kirk and the total absence of the institutions of religious music-making which had sustained the great achievements in England of Parry, Stanford, Elgar, Vaughan Williams, and Holst. But just as touring repertory companies survived by sticking to tried formulas and the classics — the radicalism of Alfred Wareing's Glasgow Repertory Company, 1909–14, which premiered Chekhov in Britain, was late and short-lived — Scots music also played safe. The Scottish Orchestra had been founded in 1891. Until 1959 it never had a Scots conductor — although its direction included at various times Walter Susskind and Sir John Barbirolli — and its programmes included little music by Scots composers. MacDiarmid never hesitated to criticize this, though music was scarcely his strong suit, and to advocate the songs of his friend and collaborator Francis George Scott, and the sort of national musical revival associated with Bartók and Kodaly in Hungary. This involved the systematic recovery of the folk-song tradition, and its use in musical education as well as composition. The problem was that this activity had already been pre-empted by a variation on the Kailyard. Following on the rise of pipe-band music in the nineteenth century, Mrs Kennedy-Fraser and Hugh Roberton had made Gaelic song into an undemanding if attractive middlebrow taste.

Another model of national cultural sponsorship was provided by the Irish Free State, which in 1924 made the Abbey Theatre in Dublin the first subsidized theatre in the English-speaking world. The Scottish National Players (1922–34) were directly influenced by the Irish example, but hamstrung by lack of funds, although they gave the young Tyrone Guthrie his first chance as a director and produced in 1928 the first play of Osborne Henry Mavor or 'James Bridie'. Both men rapidly advanced to a British reputation, as did many of the actors from another Scottish independent venture, the left-wing Glasgow Unity Theatre (1938–47). During World War II, however, there were two important developments. Bridie and others set up the Glasgow Citizens' Theatre, and Bridie was nominated by the Scottish Council of State, on the recommendation of Elliot, his closest friend, to the Council for the Encouragement of Music and the Arts (CEMA), the forerunner of the Arts Council and of a programme of systematic state funding.

The result of this was something that no one could have foreseen:

the Edinburgh Festival. It was not secured by any Scottish initiative but by the owner and manager of Glyndebourne, John Christie and Rudolf Bing, who saw that after the ravages of the war there was no chance of Glyndebourne, Munich, or Salzburg mounting their festivals for several years. They lighted almost by chance on Edinburgh and on a sympathetic Lord Provost, Sir John Falconer, and Corporation, Arts Council, and a public appeal got £60,000 together. In 1947 Edinburgh found itself hosting Bruno Walter, Szigeti, Alec Guinness, Margot Fonteyn, Barbirolli, and Kathleen Ferrier. The Festival's artistic success was never in doubt. Whether the host would accept the transplant was another matter. But the romantic tartanry of the Military Tattoo on the Castle Esplanade attracted mass enthusiasm, while the rediscovery and presentation by Robert Kemp and Tyrone Guthrie of Sir David Lyndesay's renaissance morality, *The Thrie Estaites*, in the spectacular setting of the Church's Assembly Hall, showed that Scottish theatre had now the skill and talent to rise to this challenge.

The Festival took time to permeate Scottish life. Even in the 1960s, to defend it in the Edinburgh City Labour Party was like publicly kicking an old-age pensioner. But gradually it helped break up Scottish middle-class philistinism, and led directly to a great expansion in musical activity, which culminated in the launch of Scottish Opera in 1960, under the direction of the Scottish National Orchestra's first Scots-born conductor, Sir Alexander Gibson. If there was still little Scottish music in its repertoire, this was the result of the fashionable obscurity of modern Scottish composers, not of their absence. That the examples of Bartók and Kodaly were ignored by such as Thea Musgrave and Iain Hamilton was doubly unfortunate, as the post-war period saw, through the work of men like Norman Buchan and Hamish Henderson, the revifying of the folk-song tradition. Apart from the fact that interest in it tended to outcrop in the same radical milieu, it is difficult to explain why Edinburgh, and the Royal High School in particular, became the nursery of some of the best jazz talent in Britain, including Sandy Brown, Al Fairweather, and Stan Greig. But, in the late 1940s, it did.

X Bohemia or Utopia? Literature, Cinema, Television

Royal High was also, through its English master, Hector MacIver, one of the centres of a literary bohemia in which the spirit of the renaissance still fermented away. 'The view from Regent Road', MacIver's pupil Karl Miller has written, 'towards the planes and declivities of the sleeping Lothians, took in a landscape which was far from benighted, a hinterland where contributing poets and pamphleteers lay in their suburbs and country cottages'. MacDiarmid had written to Roland Muirhead in 1928 that it would be 20 years before his aims would be understood. He was accurate to within a few years. In the 1950s came international recognition, academic honours, and the republication of his poems in accessible editions. At the same time, Scotland also saw a rich poetic output: the ironic, contemplative voice of Norman MacCaig, the austere Orcadian threnodies of George Mackay Brown, the robust bar-room Lallans of Robert Garioch and Sydney Goodsir Smith; Edwin Morgan, the Glasgow Marinetti, actually applauding the planning earthquake that had hit the place, Derick Thomson and Iain Crichton Smith carrying on Sorley MacLean's revival of the Gaelic lyric. Scottish poetry was almost a surrogate politics, with parties and manifestos — a romantic world, maybe, but more interesting and possibly also more realistic than the self-conscious flat-footedness of the English 'Movement'.

Yet MacDiarmid's self-questioning 'Are my poems spoken . . .' was as much an epitome of the Scottish predicament in the 1960s, as Yeats's 'We had fed the heart with fantasies, The heart's grown brutal with the fare' was to prove relevant to Ireland. The renaissance had remained an intellectual preoccupation. In the 1920s it had wilfully distanced itself from the main developments in popular entertainment. In the 1950s there had been another revolution in the media, but its consequence was to be a continuation of this isolation.

A powerful prosecution case can surely be mounted against the renaissance. MacDiarmid aimed at national regeneration, but his methods were those of the nineteenth century, or even more antique forms of pamphlet literature and 'flyting'. He totally ignored the impact of film and broadcasting. Would matters have been different, one wonders, if Compton Mackenzie's attempt to make him edit a critical magazine on broadcasting — *Vox* — in 1929 had succeeded? If this had worked, could his influence have been swung beside that of the other great Scots cultural innovator of the period — John Grierson?

Like MacDiarmid, Grierson had had his outlook changed by the Russian revolution. He had a vision of a new society in which film — exemplified for him by the work of Eisenstein, Pudovkin, and Vertov — became the great public educator, the link between intellectual and people. Much of this was held in common with Reith, and indeed was drawn from that stock of Hegelian ideas of social improvement which floated about the Scottish universities before 1914. But Grierson viewed the media itself as a revolutionary force. 'The imaginative treatment of reality' — his definition of documentary — implied destroying the traditional boundary between culture and society.

Grierson's achievements in the 1920s and 1930s were protean. He travelled to Russia, and publicized the work of Russian directors, even impressing the arch-reactionary Rudyard Kipling. Walter Elliot got him to set up the Empire Marketing Board Films Department in 1927, which brought him to Scotland to film *Drifters*, the first classic of British documentary, in 1929. It was about the only film he made by himself: his main aim was to teach, and there were few British directors whom he did not influence. Before he left for Canada in 1939 to create the Film Board of Canada, probably that country's most distinguished cultural contribution this century, he had helped reorientate British films towards the realistic treatment of social issues.

His influence was not lost on Scotland. Walter Elliot got his help in setting up Films of Scotland in 1938, and a growing number of directors came to make films that, even when comedies or dramas, dealt realistically with the problems and attitudes of contemporary Scotland. Michael Powell's *The Edge of the World* was the first of a distinguished line of films — John Baxter's *The Shipbuilders* (1945) from George Blake's novel, Alexander MacKendrick's *Whisky Galore* (1945), Powell's *I know where I'm going* (1945), MacKendrick's *The Maggie* (1953), and Philip Leacock's *The Brave don't Cry* (1952). As evidence of intellectual attempts to grasp the 'condition of Scotland question' such films can bear comparison with the poems and novels that preceded them. *The Maggie* — the duel between puffer captain and American millionaire — can be analysed as a pessimistic parable of the establishment of American industry in Scotland, for example. But the problem was that films, like any new industry derived from electrics, were firmly based in the south. Like MacDiarmid, Grierson's training was Hegelian. He believed that a change of consciousness was the effective victory. But economics were even less favourable to a genuine Scottish film industry than they were to the renaissance.

Like MacDiarmid, Grierson was fundamentally a product of the Scottish artisan class, and required the sustenance of a national base. After his Canadian triumphs he returned to Scotland, and to frustration. The cinema itself was proving mortal. Television started in Scotland in 1952. In that year there were 41,000 sets; a decade later there were 1,119,000. The number of cinemas was halved, and visits dropped to 10 per person per annum. In 1953 'the box' got a big boost from the Coronation; in the following year the BBC was challenged by Independent Television. In Scotland Reithianism clung on hard, and the Canadian Roy Thomson, who had just taken over the *Scotsman*, had to battle hard to get support for Scottish Television. Two years after its foundation in 1955 he could describe it as 'a licence to print money'. It was certainly not a cultural ornament. It allowed Grierson to present documentaries, but not to make them, and its drama and current affairs work was poor. With only 5 million viewers to beam advertising at, STV was much worse off than, say, Granada in Manchester, and Granada it was that got the ablest Scots documentary makers for its *World in Action*, just as the BBC, in its successful counter-attack, was able to use many of the best Scottish producers and actors — again, all too often, in the south. Yet STV did establish a Scottish identity of a sort, with a great expansion of sports coverage and local news. Both of these were relatively inexpensive to produce, but they provided career opportunities for those ambitious to make a Scottish reputation, and they provided a fertile ground for nationalist publicity to grow in. Thus, although literary life in Scotland in the 1960s was unprecedentedly lively, and MacDiarmid was able to say, in retrospect, that 'one of the main aims of my *Contemporary Scottish Studies* has now been realized — the recognition that anything that purports to be a contribution to Scottish literature must be judged by the standards applied to literature in all other civilized countries', the renaissance's successors now had to cope with two Kailyards, one traditional and one electronic.

6

Future Deferred?
Scotland 1964–1979

I

Two contradictory themes inevitably affect this chapter: the waywardness of political nationalism, lurching in manic-depressive spasms from dramatic success to humiliating setback. Did the failure of devolution arise from misinterpreted politics? Was the 'Scottish dimension' itself unreal — only an opportunist revulsion from the deterioration of the British state? Did this only mask accelerated integration, producing a politics incapable of constructive constitutional action, no matter how much high-minded prompting it received?

The 1980s looked superficially like the 1920s, with high unemployment reinforcing unimaginative Labour loyalties. Yet beneath this were trends which were not volatile: support for independence steadily grew. It had been only 9 per cent when first polled in 1945, and stuck around 20 per cent in the 1970s. In the early 1990s it was vying with devolution as the favourite option, hovering around the 35 per cent mark, and much of this support was coming from the Labour ranks. Scottish intellectuals, moreover, no longer regarded a Scottish commitment as a turning away from the 'real world'. The problem of being Scots, like that of being Catalan or Czech, was now seen as being important in a Europe that was rejecting the established ideologies of capitalism or communism in favour of the protection of individual liberties, community participation, and the natural environment — although such enlightenment was still constrained by the strictures of the Scottish class system.

II 'The White Heat of Technology'

Volatility was scarcely apparent in 1964. Labour was confident that 'planning' and 'technology' would settle the fundamental problem of economic decline. This prescription in fact differed little from Macmillan's initiatives, but it was comfortably remote from Labour's bitter debates on nationalization in 1959–60 and, as presented by its

new leader, Harold Wilson, it appeared a dynamic alternative to the
'stop-go' cycles and Venetian intrigues of the Conservatives' last years.
Wilsonian 'technocracy' may have had even less to do with science
than with socialism, but in Scotland this was not immediately
apparent: the Toothill Report and STUC collaboration had already
given planning consensus backing. But the Unionists were penalized
by continuing threats to railways and collieries, and the leadership of
Sir Alec Douglas-Home, however welcome in the counties, seemed a
provocation in the housing schemes. For Scottish Labour MPs, on the
whole on the right of the party, 'planning' was magic. Labour's 15-seat
majority in Scotland clinched their shaky 7-seat grasp on office.

In *Signposts for Scotland* (1962) Labour had ignored home rule
but, besides increases in housing, health, and welfare programmes,
promised new development bodies. The chief of these was the Highlands and Islands Development Board, funded by block grant, which
William Ross, the new Secretary of State, carried in 1965. The
Unionists described it as 'undiluted Marxism'. Unwisely, as after the
1966 election most Highland constituencies were in Labour or Liberal
hands. Labour also set up, in Scotland as well as in the other British
regions, economic planning boards and councils which were supposed
to co-operate with the new Department of Economic Affairs in formu-
lating and executing the *National Plan*. This emerged in October
1965, forecasting a 3.8 per cent annual growth rate between then and
1970.

The *Plan* was never at any time a detailed strategy; after the
deflation of July 1966 it was not even a pious hope. The regional bodies
were failures. They started without trained staffs; by the time they got
them the policy had dissolved. But in Scotland the new Scottish
Development Department was to hand, and provided a Regional
Development Division. So the *Plan for Scotland* which Ross presented
in January 1966 was much more detailed and specific than any of the
English regional responses. It echoed Toothill's stress on new industries, but it also linked employment growth to social expenditure.
Housing, hospitals, roads, and schools — building these would both
improve the infrastructure and create more jobs than were being lost
in the old industries. The resulting spending power would attract the
service and consumer goods industries which Scotland lacked. So
enquiries began into Scotland's major social problems, while local
teams advised on physical planning not only in the main industrial
areas but in the north-east and borders, with their endemic problem of
depopulation.

For a time there was a near-euphoric atmosphere in higher education and the social sciences — among a minority, true, but one which was now growing, in the post-Robbins period, and was taking on the tasks for which it had pleaded 30 years earlier. Professionals were replacing the gentry and the businessmen on public boards and advisory committees; departments of geography, economics, town planning, and social work were expanding. So much are the social sciences in Scotland the product of the mid 1960s that for years it has been difficult to stand back, survey the period, and see how little was actually achieved.

The crucial problems were not intrinsically Scottish. Could planning be successful when the state lacked firm control of investment institutions and sterling remained an international reserve currency? And when, as yet, there was no cadre of senior civil servants committed to it? In Germany the success of the 'social market' economy had still depended on tight control of banking, and the devolution of detailed planning to Land governments; in France highly-centralized planning was carried out by the meritocracy produced by the Hautes Écoles in Paris. But in Britain the only effective instrument open to government was the management of demand, and as the Fulton Commission found in 1968, the administrative class of the civil service was still biased against professional and technical expertise.

Scotland faced the consequences of both dislocations. With an economy still disproportionately dependent on capital goods industries or, as far as new industries were concerned, on public expenditure, she was slow to respond to injections of cash into the British economy, while acutely sensitive to deflationary measures. Moreover Labour's enthusiasm for government-sponsored amalgamations within the private sector, as well as nationalization, further increased the external control of the Scots economy, without promising any more sympathetic understanding of its problems. Finally, the executants of planning were themselves inexperienced, finding a way over new and treacherous ground, and subject to the lures of well-heeled and unscrupulous pressure groups.

So, despite the fact that public expenditure per head in Scotland was 20 per cent over the British norm by the late 1960s, and that most of this excess was due to investment assistance, the fundamental problems of the economy still persisted. Some remarkable progress had been made in industrial attraction, notably the expansion of the electronics industry from 7,500 jobs in 1959 to 30,000 in 1969 — three times the growth foreseen by Toothill — yet the situation of the heavy industries continued to deteriorate. Shipbuilding and engineering took with them into the shadows, moreover, satellite industries — optics, hydraulics, control mechanisms — whose record as innovators had been high in the post-war period, when the marine stabilizer, fibreglass, and the steam catapult had originated in Scotland. Although publicity stressed that educational resources had induced American electronics concerns to move to Scotland, their record in utilizing these was bad. Although American firms as a whole employed 87,730 in 1973, they had taken on only 250 graduates between 1965 and 1969. Economic control, research, and development was concentrated, as never before, in England or overseas, and so far the government had made no attempt to create Scottish institutions that would countervail this drift.

This meant that detailed regional planning in Scotland was from the start distorted: stressing the areas that the Scottish Office itself could handle, such as roads and housing. The regional plans both lacked sociological depth and, following the Buchanan Report of 1963, were over-influenced by American land use/transportation planning techniques. In the context of using state expenditure to manage private consumption, these assumed that (1) the state, by building roads and public housing, injected resources directly into the economy, and (2) it regulated the economy by controlling private housing and motoring through mortgage and hire-purchase rates. A fashionable application of Keynesian principles, whether this was an appropriate solution to Scotland's industrial and social problems was another matter. Carried out, such plans disrupted existing industries and communities and undermined the public transport on which most people depended. In 1966 Glasgow had only 1 car to 11 people, compared with 1 to 4 in Surrey, yet the city's urban motorway plans were among the most ambitious in Britain. Even before the fuel crisis in 1973 official thinking had moved away from the Buchanan formula, but by then the damage done to Glasgow was past help. Road and urban renewal schemes had resulted in the closure or relocation away from the city of much local industry, and unprecedented numbers of people had been moved into the new and unproven experiment of high-rise housing. Always more conservative and subject to influence by environmentalist groups, Edinburgh had shelved a motorway scheme in 1969, but by the time such caution became the new orthodoxy, tens of millions which could have been used for environmental improvement or industrial investment had been squandered.

Many of these schemes were based on shaky political foundations. Local government was antique; the income and status of Scots councillors low even by British standards. Moreover, party control over council activities was sketchy, especially in the west and in Labour-controlled wards where councillors frequently regarded active local parties with an unfriendly eye. Corruption was a fact (see p.81); in the late 1960s it was serious enough; but the sheer failure to apply any political perspective to 'planning' went far beyond this, and was largely the responsibility of Labour, as the traditional Scots majority party. Labour responded badly to criticism. Although the natural party of the planners and social scientists, it was all too clearly subject to Michels' 'iron law of oligarchy' — centralized, authoritarian, equally suspicious of socialist 'theoreticians' and of the Scottish 'capitalist' press. If Ross and the party secretary William Marshall quarantined their more articulate critics like John Mackintosh — the leading authority on cabinet government — the local party hierarchies were scarcely more flexible, and such attitudes encouraged press and public alike to view the advance of the SNP with indulgence.

By 1968 'planning' was in disarray — and worse. Deflation checked regional assistance expenditure, while unemployment increased beyond 1961 levels. Investigations that had been commissioned into social problems, such as the 1967 report by Professor Barry Cullingworth, *Scotland's Older Housing*, were exposing conditions that the government could do little about — and thus making effective propaganda for its critics. Despite Labour's many worthwhile initiatives — the Scots Law Commission (1965), and the Social Work (Scotland) Act (1967), the new town of Irvine (1969), the appointment of the Wheatley Commission on local government (1965) — the central economic failure imposed a mounting penalty. Paradoxically, even Labour's successes accelerated its undoing: rehousing, the uprooting of old communities and old relationships, overspill, new industries and new towns were creating a less settled working class which was tempted to explore a new politics.

III The March of the Nats

Labour won the March 1966 election convincingly, returning 46 Scottish MPs. Then trouble started. A seamen's strike, causing much disruption in the Scottish islands, was ineptly handled. A run on the pound provoked a battle in the cabinet between the expansionism of the DEA and the orthodoxy of the Exchequer, which the latter won:

expenditure was cut, planning effectively killed. Unemployment started to increase. The right wing and Liberals made gains in the May municipal elections, then in July Gwynfor Evans struck the first blow for nationalism by winning Carmarthen for Plaid Cymru.

Within two years the government's Scottish political problem was to change to one of 'coping with the Nats'. Most of its supporters saw this as fudging the main issue: the growth of the Scottish National Party vote was simply a protest against the government's non-socialist economic policies. To a minority it was more complex: a reflection of the remoteness and inadequacy of Scottish politics, as well as of a persistent national consciousness. But there was no dodging the fact (or compelling fantasy) that the SNP had in eight years grown from 2,000 to perhaps 100,000 members.

This had not come out of the blue. The Scottish situation favoured third party growth, if not a repetition of the Convention movement of the 1940s. The Unionists were too deeply tied to agriculture (although they were beginning at last to become aware of this), and their re-adoption of the name 'Conservative' in 1965 scarcely helped them in the following year. But what of the Liberals? In 1965 David Steel added Roxburgh to the three constituencies captured in 1964, and in 1966 they took West Aberdeenshire.

The trouble was that, as in the West Country and Wales, this revival reflected the radical tradition as well as the problems of remote areas. For the leadership, these successes were overshadowed by the lure of the English centre, especially after 1962, when opinion polls briefly put the Liberals ahead of the 'big two'. Though a fickle fellow, 'Orpington Man' showed up often enough to divert the attention of Grimond, and after 1967 Jeremy Thorpe, from Scottish policies. The division was replicated in Scotland itself. In the major towns, outside Greenock and Paisley, activists tended to be disproportionately English, remote from the working class, and vague although sympathetic on Scottish issues. This was often more than could be said of Liberalism in the northern isles or the Borders, which was much more conscious of region than of nation. At any rate, after some fumbling negotiations in 1964 the Liberals kept their distance from the SNP, so the latter inherited many of the mainly liberal impulses which had gone into Scottish Convention, although it retained its Sinn Fein-like programme of full independence through a withdrawal from Westminster once it had captured a majority of seats. Unlike Convention, it was also determined to contest elections – and election results largely sustained, and ultimately betrayed it.

No government ever regarded by-elections with quite the awe of the Wilson administration of 1964–70. At first its life depended on them, but after 1966 their huge fluctuations rocked a premier whose sensitivity seemed to outweigh his grasp of strategy. And Scotland, with a gaggle of elderly Labour MPs, was particularly at risk. On 9 March 1967, at Glasgow Pollok, the SNP candidate got 28 per cent, and Labour lost the seat. In the May local elections the SNP poll rose from 4.4 to 18.4 per cent. In the same month Tom Fraser left his safe Hamilton seat for the chairmanship of the Hydro Board. In the course of a long campaign Labour demonstrated all its organizational failings, while the economic situation got worse and devaluation became inevitable. On 2 November the articulate SNP candidate, Mrs Winifred Ewing, turned a 16,000 Labour majority into an SNP one of 1,799. Next May the Nationalist vote at the local elections rose to 30 per cent.

Two main analyses quickly emerged in the Cabinet. The first saw the SNP as a protest which had either to be endured or combated (according to the left) with 'socialist policies'. The second saw the SNP, along with the huge fluctuations in British local elections, as evidence that the balance of central and local government had to be recast. Paradoxically, the 'territorial' ministers — Ross and the Welsh Secretary, George Thomas — took the first view, while English departmental ministers, notably Richard Crossman, took the second.

Studies of the SNP, its voters and activists — and before long there were many — could be made to back either interpretation. It was plainly drawing into politics, in both capacities, people whom the parties had hitherto failed to involve. Votes at municipal elections rose sharply in 1967 and 1968, and much SNP support, particularly in the big towns, seemed to come from previous non-voters within the working class, whose patriotism had rested at the football level until tapped by SNP propaganda. The new nationalist councillors likewise had little previous political experience. Only about 40 per cent of a representative sample had been members of the SNP for more than three years, and only 13.5 per cent had been members of other parties. All of this — and the subsequent inept performance of many of the SNP councillors — bore out the 'protest vote' interpretation. Yet the SNP vote showed a more consistent pattern in new towns, and in country areas of the east of Scotland, and the general demand for a greater measure of home rule was being echoed, not simply by the Church of Scotland and the STUC, but by bodies as diverse as the May Day Manifesto Group from the New Left, and, most disturbingly, the

Conservative party. The Scottish Unionist conference had called for devolution in 1967, and in the following May Edward Heath set up a Committee of respectable churchmen, constitutionalists, and ex-ministers, under Sir Alec Douglas-Home, which reported positively in March 1970. Heath's own subsequent record of inaction, and Home's well-timed repudiation of devolution just before the 1979 referendum, cast valid doubt on the party's actual commitment, but it probably played a key role in prompting Wilson to set up a Royal Commission on the Constitution in December 1968.

The Labour government's move from hostility to an apparent open mind about home rule helped to check its decline in Scotland, while the SNP ran into internal problems. It had acted as a focus for a range of discontents; it now found it difficult to formulate positive policies that would not lead to it being identified in conventional left − right terms. Its 1969 conference showed a division between a 'social-democrat' wing around Wolfe, and a more traditionalist 'independence first' wing around Arthur Donaldson, whom Wolfe defeated for the Chairmanship. The poor performance of its councillors was embarrassing, and its repeated claims that Scotland was being over-taxed were authoritatively combated by Dr Gavin McCrone who, in *Scotland's Future: The Economics of Nationalism* (1969), calculated that Scotland still remained indebted to England in the tune of £56m. − £93m. per annum. In October 1968 Labour did well in a by-election at Glasgow Gorbals, where the large Catholic vote refused to swing to the SNP; in May 1969 the SNP's municipal vote fell to 20 per cent, and in the South Ayrshire election they did no better against Labour's aggressively unionist candidate, Jim Sillars. Membership was falling, some of the activities of the 'heid-bangers' of fundamentalist nationalism proved worrying, given developments in Ulster. All things considered, the SNP did well to take 11.4 per cent of the vote and get one MP elected in June 1970. After this election the Conservatives had a UK majority of 30, but they had made only three gains in Scotland, only one from Labour. With only 38 per cent of the popular vote Heath's new Secretary of State, Gordon Campbell, was even more exposed than John Maclay had been in 1959.

IV Labour and Industry

Scotland's 'balance of payments' deficit reflected the rapid growth of public expenditure, especially on industry: in 1964 £15m. had been thus spent; by 1973 £192.3m. − in real terms a 900 per cent increase.

Scotland had by then absorbed about a third of the cash available under the Local Employment Act (1964), Regional Employment Premiums, and shipbuilding subsidies — 9.3 per cent of the British labour force got 15 per cent of government industrial expenditure and agricultural subsidies and 17 per cent of UK cash for roads. Only Edinburgh and Leith were left out of the 'Scottish development area'. Besides this, government also pushed major enterprises northward. The Unionists 'persuaded' a pulp and paper mill to locate at Fort William in 1964; in 1968 Labour got an aluminium smelter established at Invergordon. Not without protest from its employees, the Post Office (later National) Savings Bank was shifted to Glasgow in 1968, and, more amicably, the headquarters of the Forestry Commission (which did most of its business in Scotland anyway) was moved from Basingstoke to Edinburgh in 1978. After a troubled start, the Highlands and Islands Development Board, whose budget had grown to £4m. per annum by 1973, provided useful and flexible finance for local industry, tourism, and transport, and brought Scotland abreast of local development strategies in other countries with remote and underpopulated regions. Yet — was this strategy working? Manufacturing wages certainly improved: 91 per cent of the UK average in 1961, they were 96.6 per cent in 1971. Yet the labour force fell. Male workers fell by 6 per cent, and a 6 per cent rise in women workers still left an overall decline of 1.75 per cent. Unemployment rose from 3.1 to 5.8 per cent, its relationship to the UK figure changed only imperceptibly, and annual emigration in the 1960s actually increased by 16 per cent on the previous decade. In fact, although £641m. had been spent between 1966 and 1971 in creating 105,000 jobs, in the same five years 156,000 had been lost, mainly from heavy industry and agriculture. Mines and farms, traditionally labour-intensive, made up half this figure, yet, besides these 'structural' changes, technological innovation was inducing sweeping increases in productivity, the full consequences of which even union leaders were only dimly aware. The first container terminal in Britain, for instance, was opened at Grangemouth in 1968; within a decade general cargo handling had dwindled away; the main Glasgow docks had been filled in and the dock labour force decimated. By the 1970s, too, 65 per cent of the coal mined in Scotland's dozen or so remaining collieries was being conveyed by automatically loading and discharging bulk trains to the hoppers of four huge power stations. Over £150m. investment in BP's oil refinery and petro-chemical complex at Grangemouth had yielded less than 2,000 jobs. Even in industries where employment in the late

60s had seemingly stabilized – like steel and shipbuilding – rumours of rationalization and contraction were by 1970 becoming more insistent.

Behind this lay, moreover, far-reaching changes in company control. The Wilson government, as well as nationalizing iron and steel, sponsored extensive industrial amalgamation. Anthony Wedgwood Benn, the minister of technology, was particularly enthusiastic, seconded by businessmen and trade unionists seeking specific advantages – such as a monopoly position, or a national wages structure. As swiftly as in the early 1920s control shifted southward, or abroad. Scots ownership still prevailed among small firms, but external control increased with size, until by 1977 only 3 out of the top 10 Scottish industrial employers were Scots-controlled.

Even before Peugeot took over Chrysler in 1978 the Scottish-owned sector in manufacturing industry had dropped to 41 per cent of employment. Forty per cent was controlled from England, 15 per cent from North America, and 1.5 per cent from the EEC. Paradoxically, government money for job-creation – over £6,000 per job in the average case – often seen 1 to reduce employment, through new technology and rationalization. Moreover, as trade-union pressure had made up wage differentials, an important incentive to move north had been lost. Although Scottish financial institutions remained healthy, Scottish industrial capitalism was now of only marginal importance. Old-fashioned tycoons like Lithgow and Bilsland had retained a paternalist sense of obligation, which led to developments like the Scottish Council. This was unlikely to be replicated in the boardrooms of the City of London and Los Angeles.

The economics of some of the new transplants soon looked shaky. The vehicle factories at Linwood and Bathgate were, by 1970, operating at barely 50 per cent capacity. One reason was bad industrial relations, partly due to the difficulty of adapting a hitherto skilled workforce to the numbing discipline of the assembly line; another was the failure of ancillary trades to come north. If 20 per cent of the parts entering Linwood were Scottish this was a success, since the West Midlands' economies of scale kept the average cost of an English part down to £0.096, against £0.246 for the same part made in Scotland. But even when manufacturing was successfully transplanted, the 'generative' elements of the parent companies – research and development, organization, corporate planning, marketing – rarely shifted from the south. In 1972 Scotland came ninth out of 10 British regions in research and development expenditure, and government research allocated to Scotland, 1964–73, was only 5.1 per cent of the British total.

V Society and Culture

Labour's 'modernization' goals were only partly economic, however, and the limited progress made was partly masked by the social and cultural changes initiated or encouraged by the government, which altered traditional institutions and social life on a scale unparalleled since the nineteenth century, or even, in some cases, since the Reformation.

Education

Education was an important route to equality in social democratic theory, and a reinforcement of economic diversification. Encouraged by inspectors and some teachers, reform was under way before 1964. The institution of O-levels meant an increase in candidates from 17,175 in 1961 to 83,805 in 1967. Fifteen per cent more were staying on to 16, although the leaving age was not raised until 1973. Following Labour policy, Ross instructed local authorities to reorganize secondary education on comprehensive lines. In comparison to England the transition was fairly painless: by 1974 98 per cent of pupils were in comprehensives, against under 50 per cent in England. Overall, the size of schools increased, and their numbers fell. In 1947 171,193 secondary pupils attended 1,037 schools; in 1974 over 400,000 attended 439.

At the same time both the primary and secondary curricula were reformed, following a working party report of 1955 and the Brunton Report of 1963, which stressed vocationally-centred studies for non-academic pupils. Both reforms were contentious, but tended to be drowned out by the clamour of the profession itself, as it debated its reorganization after 1966 under a General Teaching Council for Scotland.

Partly to provide teachers, partly to supply the troops of the technological revolution, higher education expanded. Following the Robbins Report of 1963 the great technical colleges of Glasgow and Edinburgh received charters in 1964 and 1966, as did Queen's College, Dundee, in 1967. A new university at Stirling opened in 1968. Student numbers doubled to 33,000 between 1960 and 1969, although their percentage of the British total slightly decreased, from 16 to

15 per cent. The government also opened three education colleges, at Falkirk, Hamilton, and Ayr, in 1964−5 and, largely through the Industrial Training Act (a Conservative measure of 1964) dramatically expanded technical colleges, which had over 80,000 full-time, day, or block release students by 1970.

Yet was expansion enough or in time? Could the school really check Scottish social inadequacies? The Advisory Committee Report of 1947 had placed the school in the front line against 'a barely literate populace, debased by vulgarisms and corrupted by Hollywood'. The language was inapposite for the 1960s, yet the less didactic new curricula actually stressed parental involvement, at a time when television and working mothers were changing the structure of Scots families. Was such innovation not, therefore, more likely to benefit the middle class? Moreover, innovation spared two disquieting aspects of Scots education − religious schools and corporal punishment. If education was now to centre on the child in the community, why divide it into two communities? If education was to be a partnership, why retain this savage sanction? Catholic schools may have protected their position by a judicious scepticism about the new methods: this appealed to many non-Catholic teachers, but the political problem remained; although Labour preferred to ignore it. Corporal punishment answered the challenge of the bully, but it also preserved an esteem-system in which he and his values of 'toughness' survived. So, despite all the expenditure on them, many potential sixth-formers were by 1970 leaving the comprehensives to take qualifications in the more adult atmosphere of further education colleges.

The teaching profession, over 52,000-strong in 1973, had grown by 60 per cent in 20 years. Counting universities and further education, teachers now outnumbered all but three groups of manufacturing workers, yet despite strong unionization they were remote from the working class and internally divided. Graduates (mainly male) declined from 46 to 39 per cent, increasing tension with largely female non-graduates. A profession 66 per cent female remained as subject to male hegemony as skilled engineering had been before World War I.

There was, moreover, little unity between it and the anglicized staff of the universities, and tensions grew in the 1970s as it looked likely that 'British' universities would remain aloof from 'Scottish' education. These were aggravated by the fact that the first largish generation of Scots postgraduates confronted a less-than-inspiring, but tenured, university establishment, recruited in the fat years of the mid 60s.

Housing

Housing was an ostensible success story. Between 1960 and 1970 completions rose from 28,500 to 43,100, roughly double the rate of demolitions. Surviving smaller or older houses now tended to be occupied by young couples or single people. Yet Cullingworth pointed out in 1967 that a third of Scottish families were living in 'inadequate' accommodation, and much of this was steadily deteriorating into slums.

Rent control and low council rents meant that private landlords could never undertake renewal, and although Cullingworth suggested that private rents could be subsidized by grants to landlords, a Labour government would never wear this. Owner-occupation in large old tenements involved difficult modernization problems, let alone rising mortgage rates. That left co-operatives or associations, or council policies of renewal rather than demolition. By 1970 both were being pursued, but progress was slow.

As private tenants (21 per cent in 1977) dwindled, owner-occupiers (26 per cent) and council tenants (53 per cent) grew. In industrial burghs such as Motherwell over 80 per cent of households rented from councils. But St Andrew's House gained more central control over rents, which in 1967−8 moved to more realistic levels − and brought a bonus to the SNP in local elections. Problems of housing management, however, also increased, mainly involving 'anti-social families', slum-clearance schemes of the 1930s and 1950s which now required total renewal, and the future of many multi-storey blocks scarcely 10 years old. Leaving aside design problems, like the Glasgow blocks with lifts too small for coffins and stretchers, these had required sophisticated technology, regulated heating, and regular maintenance. They didn't always get it. If heating was switched off, because of rising charges or falling income, condensation and mould appeared; if lifts broke down, families and pensioners were stranded 200 feet up. By 1980 several ambitious projects, such as Edinburgh's 18-storey Martello Court, were actually uninhabitable.

Housing didn't show Labour at its most imaginative. Low-rent policies had narrowed its municipal constituency while the lack of alternatives to council housing tied improvements too closely to government expenditure, which deflationary policies were reducing. Wholesale clearance destroyed communities; building contract awards and house allocations led to periodic corruption charges. The losses of 1966−8 cut some of the dead wood out of the councils and enabled some improvement in the early 1970s. Not before time: a survey based on the 1971 census showed that Scotland had 77.5 per cent of Britain's 5 per cent of 'worst areas' for social deprivation. Ironically, the reformers were frequently Labour councillors who were neither tenants nor working class.

Religion, Sex, and Drink

In 1960 almost 70 per cent of Scots over 14 were claimed as church members, compared with around 23 per cent in England and over 90 per cent in Ireland. But that year was the Church of Scotland's peak, and after 1970 the Catholics, too, started to decline. Television and Sunday entertainment obviously took their toll of marginal Christians, but there was also a more fundamental lapse in belief among the 'serious' middle class — albeit a century after the same development in England. The attitude of, say, students and teachers to religion was not malignant: they simply transferred their commitment to other social or political organizations. Whether these provided adequate compensation was another question.

Among professions with a strong sense of local position — such as law or banking — church membership remained strong, but its grip on the lower middle and working classes, which had survived the 1950s largely due to church extension programmes, could not cope with the social changes and population movements of the 1960s. As it became more middle class its politics moved to the right, and in the 1970s it trod an uneasy path between a rather diffuse ecumenicalism and the revival of fundamentalism which had gripped Protestant America. As for the Catholic hierarchy, the election in 1979 of a conservative, populist pope came as a welcome reinforcement of its own position. Both Churches seemed to have halted their concessions to secularism, but it remained to be seen how effective a conservative restatement of dogma would prove.

Religious decline was bound up with upheavals in family and personal relationships. The marriage rate increased, but for many couples it was now a second attempt. Divorces rose by 400 per cent between 1961 and 1974, although subsequent simplification, by transfer from the Court of Session to the Sheriff Courts in 1977, did not lead to a further escalation. Family size fell to nearer the English norm, and numbers of single-parent families rose. People talked more about sex. In the case of the Churches they seemed sometimes to talk of nothing else. It certainly posed a challenge to their traditional puritanism, but not one which they came out of particularly well.

Rational concession certainly did not appear to pay dividends: the Church of Scotland accepted divorce reform, abortion, and state provision of contraception; its numbers fell faster than those of the Roman Catholics, whose leaders resolutely opposed all three. Whether rank and file Catholics did so is another matter: their attitude to contraception, for instance, seems to have been much the same as that of the Free Church to drink.

On drink, the puritan case was more straightforward. Scots spending per capita on alcohol, 89 per cent of the UK level in 1955, rose to 109 per cent by 1970. Why? Because of more affluence? More consumers? Fewer abstainers? Or a combination of all three? Licensing hours had been extended, women were accepted in most pubs, young people were no strangers to drink. Had the 'dour drinkers of Scotland' vanished? The Clayson Report of 1975 thought that drink could now become a civilized accompaniment to life, and opening times were extended to a Continental pattern in 1978. Scots alcoholism ran at five times the UK rate; and smoking levels were destructively high, but most pubs now offered cheap and good food; Scots football supporters sobered up and were even counted a droll attraction by the continentals; spending on drink fell back to 102 per cent of UK levels in 1990, when only 36 per cent of the male population smoked, compared with 51 per cent in 1980. A wholly healthy Scotland? Not quite. Drug addiction rose from 90 addicts notified in 1980 to 525 in 1990, and provided an environment for the spread of Aids.

The Arts

Intellectual life in the 1960s and 1970s was lively — for a minority. Although the commercial theatre was now all but extinct, experiment thrived at the Traverse and the Citizens and on the Festival Fringe. It even became less remote from the pubs and housing schemes, as John McGrath's 7:84 Company, the indescribable talents of Billy Connolly, and the work of such as James MacTaggart, Eddie Boyd, Roddy Macmillan, and Peter MacDougall for television gave it a greater demotic edge. Sir Alexander Gibson, appointed conductor of the Scottish National Orchestra in 1959, helped set up Scottish Opera in 1963, and by 1980 the country's musical life was richer — and internationally more respected — than it had ever been before. The annual pollination of the Edinburgh Festival had borne rich fruit, as had the help of local authorities and government. Scotland's share of the Arts Council budget had dropped from 8.4 per cent to 6.3 per cent between 1948 and 1963. Under Jennie Lee, now Wilson's arts minister, it climbed back to 11.4 per cent by 1970, extending subsidies to painting, literature, Gaelic culture, and folk music.

MacDiarmid lived on until 1978 as an honoured if wayward national institution, alternately courtly and infuriating. 'He'll charm old ladies on to the mantelpiece/And leave them there' as Norman MacCaig put it. He outlived most of the other writers of the Renaissance, but there was a talented succession. Poetry and the short story thrived in the quality papers and the little magazines, and the novels of the time, if not immediately appreciated, showed a determined effort to come to terms with the traumas wrought by Calvinism and industrialisation on the Scottish psyche. J.D. Scott's *The End of an Old Song* (1954) ended with his anti-hero burning his ancestral castle down. One retrospective image of Scotland was thus destroyed, but with it also the 'high road to England'. Writers like James Kennaway, Robin Jenkins and William MacIlvanney saw something moulding in the Scots experience – not necessarily positive, but not to be ignored. At the same time George Mackay Brown and Iain Crichton Smith were articulating the distinctive experiences of Norse and Gaelic Scotland, and Muriel Spark and (on stage) Cecil Taylor the continuing, fricative argument of Scot and Jew.

At the time this activity was underestimated, not least by the present writer. It took a determined increase in Scottish publishing activity, particularly in history writing, reviewing, and reprinting, in the 1970s and 1980s, to display the liveliness of the post-Renaissance literary output. Perhaps, in retrospect, bogeyman Knox loomed too darkly, and there was too enthusiastic a dash to the psychiatrist's couch. R.D. Laing and Aaron Esterson may have worked in London, but Karl Miller was not alone in connecting their perceptions about the social origins of schizophrenia with their native land, home of the Justified Sinner and Jekyll and Hyde. Miller himself, out of Hector MacIver's Royal High School by Leavis's Cambridge, contributed to the plethora of analyses that followed the rise of the SNP and was responsible for the Marxist philosopher Tom Nairn's first bout with nationalism. Within a few years Nairn's *The Break-Up of Britain* (1977) had become the central text of a new and unsentimental intellectual nationalism. Overall, the 'lads o'pairts' seemed, at least mentally, to be returning home, and there was a shift from the imaginative to the analytical; work by Scots and about Scotland, in history, politics, and economics, was as distinguished as anything since the eighteenth century.

In the 1970s everyone, seemingly, talked politics. A few, like Neal Ascherson, were worried that there didn't appear to have been the sort of literary movement that nationalism ought to gestate. Rather too many big publishing names closed down or moved south – Nelsons, Oliver and Boyd, Collins – and native literary and political reviews still tended to have short lives. *Scottish International* was good while it lasted (1966-74); Edinburgh students nurtured their valuable *New Edinburgh Review* and added *Cencrastus* at a timely moment, when many were overcome by post-Referendum *accidie*. *Radical Scotland* (1982-91) invented the 'Doomsday Scenario' and helped change the language of 'respectable' Scottish political discourse. By the 1980s the quality papers, edited now by the sons of 'renaissance' men – Arnold Kemp on the *Herald* and Magnus Linklater on the *Scotsman* – could hold their own with anything coming from London; and the BBC and 'independent' broadcasting were showing initiative and a European sense. 'Work as if you were in the early days of a better nation', was the injunction of Alasdair Gray, from whose *Lanark* (1982) there seemed to flood out the pent-up experience of the country from the Reformation onwards. Happily, his advice was taken.

VI Conservatives, Ships and Oil

After six years of Wilsonian ductility, the new Conservative government seemed to know where it was going. It took up the principles of the Wheatley Report of 1969 and in 1973 reorganized Scottish local government, creating nine regions with powers over planning, transport, social work, and education, and 53 districts, mainly dealing with housing. Joint bodies supervised the police, but health services were placed under separate nominated authorities in the following year. Such sweeping changes implied that Edward Heath had ceased to toy with devolution, and although the Scottish Office acquired an Economic Planning Department in 1973, its authority slipped back.

Energy was not however the same as effectiveness, and Heath, pledged to 'roll back' Labour's interventionism, soon ran into a crisis in shipbuilding. The rescue of Fairfield's in 1965 had shown that the industry badly required government investment. It received it somewhat haphazardly. After the Geddes Report of 1966 Labour reorganized Clyde shipbuilding in two groups: Scott Lithgow, based on Greenock and Port Glasgow, and Upper Clyde, based on Clydebank, Linthouse, and Govan. In the latter case management and unions vied with one another in exploiting the settlement, its economics became chaotic, and in late 1970s, as losses on pre-reorganization contracts mounted, some of Heath's most doctrinaire ministers demanded near-total closure. But, by the time UCS reeled into receivership in June 1971, the government's policy had already been changed, and it had nationalized the bankrupt Rolls-Royce. It now had to suffer a reverse on the Clyde, in the full glare of publicity.

The workers at the threatened John Brown's yard started a 'work-in' on 30 July. Led by two articulate Communist shop stewards, Jimmie Airlie and Jimmie Reid, they captured the attention of the media, and raised almost £250,000 and considerable public support. The government shifted its policy to retain and re-invest in two of the UCS yards, while Brown's was, after dramatic transatlantic negotiations, taken over by the Marathon Engineering Company of Texas for oil-rig building.

No one came out of the UCS affair with much credit. The 'work-in' was merely a publicity coup. There was no industrial reorganization. A sequel in 1975–6, when the new owners of the *Scottish Daily Express* shifted printing to Manchester, and its workers attempted, with government assistance, to produce the *Scottish Daily News*, was disastrous. But UCS highlighted one problem of industrial reconstruction. 'Old' nationalized industries, like railways, electricity, or coal, could draw on long traditions of state involvement or municipal enterprise. Could reorganization of manufacturing industry be achieved not only without this, but by remote control from London? Opinion – among civil servants and on the left – was beginning to shift away from centralized planning towards greater regional autonomy.

But there was a powerful counter-current, of which Marathon was a portent. By 1973 oil exploration had moved to the fore, and almost 90 per cent of the equipment for it had to be imported. To blame with hindsight is easy, but could the consequences of the Yom Kippur War of November 1973 – the Arabs' use of their economic muscle, the six-fold increase in the price of crude oil – not have been forecast? Well, to some extent yes. An oil famine was in prospect from 1967, when exploration off Scotland started; early in 1973, by suspending oil import quotas, the USA forecast substantial price increases. Government could have explored some preliminary options; instead, its reactions were hasty and brought Scotland little benefit.

North Sea oil exploration began off Holland in 1959. Gas was discovered off East Anglia and pumped ashore in 1965, and in 1970 the first commercial 'Scottish' field – the Forties – was located. This was to come on stream in 1977, the whole project yielding 13m. tons annually by 1980. Only in 1973, however, did government and business really take an interest. The southward shift of control, post-nationalist boredom with Scottish affairs, an apparent slackening in the Scottish Office, may all have played a part. Thereafter the hyper-activity of politicians simply concealed the fact that they could do little to control either the rate of oil extraction or the distribution of oil-related contracts. The sooner the fields were on stream, the better for the balance of payments — even if this meant surrendering to the Americans' command of the appropriate technology.

Apart from Marathon's products, exploration rigs were nearly all built abroad, as were supply vessels. The only important construction in Scotland was of production platforms, vast steel or concrete structures which had to be assembled near the fields. Heath quickly secured construction sites, bruising a few environmentalists. But although seven were prepared only five were used, and all but one of these were in areas remote from the job-starved upper Clyde. As a result they got an unstable workforce. Their Yukon-like atmosphere, or the garish and inflationary affluence that hit the north-east, was no compensation for the missed opportunities of industrial development.

As if anticipating such haphazard 'planning', the SNP launched in September 1972 its own well-articulated campaign: 'It's Scotland's Oil'. Besides the Middle East, several events thrust it into the foreground. The MP for Govan died, and Labour seemed determined to repeat the Hamilton scenario. The report of the Kilbrandon Commission on the Constitution appeared a week before polling day in early November. Labour found it 'at first glance totally unacceptable'. The SNP won.

VII To the Referendum

The weakness and opportunism of the major British political parties underlay the subsequent constitutional crisis, which lasted until the referendum and election of 1979. In the election of February 1974, called amid the chaos caused by the miner's strike and 30-hour week, Heath lost 16 seats and Labour gained 3, but the main swing was to third parties. In England the Liberals went up from 13.6 to 24.2 per cent; in Scotland the SNP from 11.4 to 21.9 per cent. Labour, which formed a minority government, had a manifesto rich in socialist rhetoric, but little chance (or even, in the Cabinet, inclination) to do much about it. But it was now challenged in 10 Scottish seats by the SNP, which had added six Conservative and one Labour seat to the one it held after 1970. Harold Wilson, expecting an election any week, had to act on Kilbrandon, both to conciliate centrist opinion and secure his Scottish flank. The rest of 1974 was to present the actors and the scenario of a complex and ultimately disastrous drama.

Devolution divided Labour in Scotland. Its Scottish executive, having voted in favour on 10 March, threw out the government's pro-devolution green paper on 22 June. The Cabinet and Transport House invoked the big unions which, at a special Scottish conference on 18 August, brought the Scots to heel. Just in time. Labour went into the 10 October election committed to a somewhat nebulous Scottish Assembly. Such manoeuvres probably encouraged rather than checked the SNP vote; in October, while Plaid Cymru's vote declined slightly, the SNP's rose to over 30 per cent. It captured another four seats, and now challenged Labour in 35 out of its 41 while, at the height of the oil excitement, its oil policy attracted enough attention to suggest that a Scottish breakaway would not disappoint international financial institutions – although on reflection the move of capital into Scotland probably increased external control rather than the opposite. In some areas like retailing and the press (see p. 123) the devolution clamour concealed the fact that not simply English but multinational firms had made important inroads.

Several factors dominated the subsequent scene. In Scotland some socialists enthused over devolution in publications like the *Red Paper* of May 1975. They were given some support by the creation in 1975 of the Scottish Development Agency, which reversed the Dalton approach (at least in principle) and restored much regional autonomy. But a reaction had already set in. In May 1974 the first elections for the new regional and district authorities had produced several huge Labour majorities in Strathclyde, Central, Lothian, and Fife, with a strong interest in establishing and upholding their power; and distaste for devolution still existed, not only at the Scottish grass-roots but among English MPs and the Cabinet itself. This struck directly at the drafting of the White Paper, and a battle – in contrast to 1967–8, now between pro-devolution territorial ministers and hostile English departmental ministers – delayed its appearance until late in 1975.

The White Paper was essentially a Whitehall creation and showed a successful resistance by ministers and civil servants to the concession of any significant degree of autonomy to the Assembly. In this way it cut across the historical evolution of the Scottish Office and prevented a logical division of its responsibilities. Housing was devolved, but mort-gages – and so private housing policy – withheld. Education went north, but not universities; infrastructure planning – including the new SDA — but not economic planning; transport, but not railways; law, but not courts or judges; local government, but not police. The Secretary of State still retained substantial powers: over agriculture, fisheries, most of law and order, electricity, large areas of economic policy. He stayed in the Cabinet, but also had quasi-Viceregal powers vis à vis the 142-seat Assembly. He would appoint its executive and adjudicate on whether its enactments were within its *'vires'* or not. Scotland would continue to send 71 MPs to Westminster.

Our Changing Democracy satisfied only such groups as had been forced into action: the Labour establishment, Whitehall, the unions. In Scotland it was generally condemned. Pro- and anti-devolutionists alike argued that its concessions could only be a first stage. Hostility among business groups, local authorities, and some unions increased, the spirits of the 'Antis' having received a fillip by the results of the EEC referendum of 5 June. In this a co-ordinated campaign by the pro-Europeans against a disunited and mutually-hostile anti side, dominated by Labour and the SNP, converted a January poll of 29 per cent pro-EEC and 45 per cent anti, to 58.4 per cent and 41.6 per cent. On a low poll (61.7 per cent) Labour and SNP could not mobilize their vote: an encouraging sign should there be a referendum on devolution.

In the shadow of the White Paper, the devolutionist left made the first tactical mistake. Early in 1976 Jim Sillars and various associates, mainly journalists, created the Scottish Labour Party. 'The Magic Party' — socialist and devolutionist — proved for a short time remarkably popular: it attracted about 900 members, comparable to about 25 per cent of regular Labour activists, but it also drew in left-wing sects, without gaining a 'bottom' in the trade unions. As a result, Sillars presided, ineffectively, over a party consumed by clashes between middle-class ideologues. The SLP episode was a disaster for devolution: it isolated its most eloquent left-winger, and gravely weakened the cause within Labour.

Nor was it aided by Harold Wilson's sudden resignation in April 1976. James Callaghan, his successor, replaced both Ross and Lord Crowther-Hunt, Wilson's constitutional expert, and Ross's successor, Bruce Millan, a competent administrator, fatally lacked his public personality. Difficulties soon mounted. The Scotland and Wales Bill, tabled on 13 December by Michael Foot, was literally incomprehensible, as it did not transfer sovereignty but abstracted powers from existing legislation. It was, morever, evident that the Conservatives, since February 1975 under Mrs Thatcher, were prepared to exploit to the full the divisions that existed between the Cabinet and the unenthusiastic Labour back-benchers and the discontent of the Liberals, who had ostentatiously not been squared by any offer of proportional representation. In committee the bill sank into a quagmire of 350 amendments, from which Foot's concession of a referendum could not extricate it. An attempt to force a 'guillotine' on 22 February 1977 failed by 29 votes.

There was little reaction in Scotland: no demonstrations, no riots. The SNP went ahead to 36 per cent in the opinion polls, but the hiatus pending a new bill being tabled, on 4 November, proved critical. The steam had gone out of the issue. Nationalism expressed itself in a notable coolness towards the Jubilee celebrations of June 1977, and became a fascinating topic for intellectuals, but it did not affect the Scots electorate like unemployment – the consequence of Labour's tight monetary policy – which advanced from 3.6 per cent in 1974 to 7.6 per cent in 1978. While John Smith, a Labour advocate, piloted the new bill through the House, Scottish MPs sat silent. Only the hostile were vociferous, although they were partly mollified by a clause which made the ultimate enactment of the bill depend on over 40 per cent of the Scots electorate voting 'Yes'. During this gap, on 13 July, John Mackintosh, one of its most convinced proponents, died, aged only 48. The Assembly might have given him the chance of high office that the Labour Party had continually denied him; his eloquence was certainly needed to save it.

In Scottish politics, the bill seemed, however, to have paid off. While English by-elections were disastrous for Labour, in Scotland it easily beat off the SNP challenge – even in Hamilton (1978 was not a good year for extremes of patriotism, being dominated by Scotland's appalling performance in the World Cup). But trouble was on its way, in the shape of the same trade-union power that had secured devolution in 1974. The unions, like Scottish nationalism, had their price, and in 1978 it came due. In October, perhaps encouraged by such election successes, Callaghan postponed a general election until after the referendum, and shortly afterwards announced a rigid pay policy. The result was catastrophic, for him, as well as for devolution.

In October 1978 the Whitehall élite seemed to have squared the union magnates and the nationalists – if each of these groups could command its forces. By February 1979 union discipline had collapsed. A tide of badly organized strikes coupled with the worst winter since 1947 aided the Conservatives while demonstrating working-class disunity. The intricate compromises Whitehall had written into the Devolution Bill offered no easy solutions, to this, or Scotland's growing economic problem. And Labour and the SNP again failed to mobilize their vote. Both had minorities who hoped that devolution would fail, and the imaginative ideas for deploying the devolved powers canvassed by the young and mainly middle-class supporters of the Assembly were almost drowned out by the well-heeled 'Scotland says No' campaign's constant harping on the themes of expense, bureaucracy, and disruption, echoed loudly by the *Scottish Daily Express*, whose new owner, Victor (Lord) Matthews, ditched Beaverbrook's cherished home rule in the interests of Conservative policy.

On 1 March, Referendum day, 63.63 per cent of the electorate turned out to vote. The highest poll was 67 per cent in the Borders, the most hostile mainland region; the lowest was 49.4 per cent in the SNP-held Western Isles, which voted 'Yes'. These two were almost an epitome of the whole. The Labour heartlands – Strathclyde, Central, and Fife – ensured a 'Yes' majority, but only Highland joined them. Lothian was only just 'Yes', Tayside only just 'No'. The main Liberal or Nationalist areas – Borders, Grampian, Orkney, and Shetland – were all hostile. The Assembly won, but only by 32.85 to 30.78 per cent, 7.15 per cent short of the 40 per cent hurdle.

Before the referendum, nationalist and radical socialist intellectuals had preached the doom of social democracy. Between January and May 1979 doom occurred: its devolution compromise was destroyed: by unions demanding an end to wages policy, by Scots local government magnates clinging on to their own authority, by an antique but incredibly tough landowning class – represented by the two Old Etonians who did more damage than anyone else to devolution, Tam Dalyell and Lord Home – and by the Nationalists themselves. It was the SNP MPs who ended a less than distinguished parliamentary presence by rejecting Callaghan's offer of all-party talks and tabling the vote of no-confidence that on 28 March brought his government down. In the election on 3 May Labour took its revenge and removed the threat to most of its seats, while the SNP saw its vote fall to 18 per cent and lost (albeit usually by narrow margins) 9 of its 11 seats, 8 to the Conservatives. But Labour's Scottish success was over-shadowed by its shattering defeat south of the border.

VIII 'We in Scotland'

'Instant post-industrialisation'

The 1980s was to be an extraordinary decade, but the Scots did not enter on it with hope. Nor, if the election of 1992 were its terminus, did they leave it with their expectations much altered. Throughout the world an economic neo-liberalism which claimed descent from the Scottish enlightenment was knocking over command economies and social democracies. Some expatriate Scots – Andrew Neil of the *Sunday Times,* Dr Madsen Pirie of the Adam Smith Institute, Professor Norman Stone – were implicated, at least in the publicity offensive that accompanied this. Yet the ideology itself found little echo in Scotland. When Mrs Thatcher travelled to Edinburgh to instruct the Kirk in morality in 1988 she was received no more than civilly. Two years later the extravagant use of the regal 'we in Scotland' in a hard-fought interview with Kirsty Wark seemed to indicate that *hubris* was imminent. On 22 November 1990 it struck.

Mrs Thatcher often came north. Why? Scots regarded her with dislike, occasionally with loathing; a Scottish Conservative memo in 1987 recommended a period of prime ministerial indifference. Yet Scotland figured in the ideology of this 'absolute bourgeois'. Thatcher's relationship with the English establishment was ambiguous: deferential to the crown, effectively neutral in religion, grinding out honours as no premier had done since the war. In Scotland, she perhaps believed, her values could come into their own. The poll tax was born of a Scot, Douglas Mason; and her most drastic (and in England, most unpopular) venture into institutional reform followed the appointment of a Highland Calvinist, Mackay of Clashfern, as Lord Chancellor.

Thatcher believed rational Scots ought to appreciate her classical economics, and was distressed (though not disarmed) when they didn't. But she had a further reason for observing Scotland; the country was keeping her in business. The fuel trade surplus, from North Sea oil, bankrolled her 'achievements', reaching a peak of £6 billion in 1985, or about 8 per cent of the balance of payments. Initially, this did Scotland little good. The high petro-pound, coupled with the 'sado-monetarism' of a tight money supply, helped induce one of the worst recessions ever, which carried away much of the industry expensively induced to settle in Scotland in the 1960s and 1970s, such as the Corpach pulp mill, the Invergordon aluminium smelter, and the motor vehicle plants at Linwood and Bathgate. Industrial closures and unemployment were implicitly deployed by government – along with measures curbing trade union autonomy – to discipline the labour force: with some success. The question of 'who runs the country' was settled in the government's favour: definitively by the long-drawn-out miners' strike of 1984–5.

By 1990 the heavy industries had dwindled to only three shipyards on the Clyde, collieries at Longannet and Monktonhall, and the threatened steelworks complex around Ravenscraig. Mechanical engineering output alone slumped by 28 per cent between 1979–85. The Silicon Glen phenomenon, instead of achieving the 'critical mass' which would generate high value-added concerns, obeyed the policies of the multi-nationals which controlled it and slowed up; textiles and whisky were in trouble; and manufacturing (including energy production) was down to less than 30 per cent of GNP, employment dropping from 605,000 in 1979 to 412,000 in 1986, and investment falling by two-fifths, from £561 to £339 million.

Government ministers spoke consolingly of the fact that Scottish workers exported more per capita than the Japanese, and to some economists the shift to services was inevitable. In the 1980s 'services' became an overloaded grab-bag, packing in everything from computer software to selling hamburgers. (In 1989 Ronald McDonald probably mattered more than Adam Smith in projecting Western values to Eastern Europe.) But while Baden-Württemberg still had manufacturing running at over 40 per cent of GNP in 1987, and 'microcapitalism', sponsored by powerful regional authorities, had revitalised the textile and clothing industries of central Italy, even oil could not prevent a reduced manufacturing sector putting the country increasingly in deficit with the rest of the UK, whose own balance of payments plunged ever deeper into the red. Attempts to check this by raising interest rates could only make a bad situation worse.

The stock-market crash of October 1987 was followed not by a slump but by an extraordinary consumption and property boom, fed by the government. But by mid-1988 a trade deficit, stemming directly from the shrinkage of manufacturing, forced a drastic correction and, soon, a long-drawn-out recession. In this Scotland – for the first time – suffered proportionately less than the south of England. Unemployment peaked at 15.6 per cent in 1985 (UK: 11.8 per cent); it fell to 8.1 per cent in 1990 (UK: 5.8 per cent) but in recession rose to only 9.2 per cent in December 1991. The UK figure was 9.0 per cent. Scotland's wages fell further below UK levels (from 99 per cent in 1980 to 93.5 per cent in 1990) but Wales was more successful in using this differential to attract new investment.

'There is no such thing ...'

This mitigation wasn't due to the oil business, in the doldrums with a collapse in world prices – from $40 a barrel in 1980 to $14.50 in 1986, ironically the year of maximum North Sea production. The downside to a neo-liberal economic policy which transferred resources to the wealthy (which the latter promptly invested abroad!) was infrastructural deterioration. Unplanned, unregulated London had become an expensive, inconvenient and unreliable business centre; its house prices were exorbitant; travel to work a torture. To one sympathetic commentator, Anthony Hilton of the *Evening Standard*, the circumstances surrounding the takeover of Distillers by Guinness in 1986 could only suggest that, in the City, 'dishonesty has become institutionalised'. Against this, infrastructural investment in Scotland – in transport, communications, banking – seemed to have paid off. Comparisons by Walter Henderson showed the highest output of graduates *per capita* in Europe. Edinburgh and Glasgow – the European Culture Capital in 1990 – were consistently rated among the top European cities, and a growing agglomeration of high-grade and science-based service industries were attracted north, not to speak of 'white settlers' who exchanged expensive south-eastern property for its cheaper Scottish equivalent, and lived in part on the proceeds. This in-migration even caused an upward blip in the population figures towards the end of the decade.

There seemed, however, little acceptance within the Scottish bourgeoisie of the Conservative ideal of a privatised, acquisitive 'lifestyle'. This existed, certainly – in the boutiques and posh restaurants of Edinburgh and the 'merchant city' of Glasgow – but it was combated by doctrines of social 'fairness' and frustrated nationalism, which meant that doctors, bankers and lawyers espoused principles unthinkable among equivalent groups in the south. Were these Michael Frayn's 'herbivores ... with eyes full of sorrow for less fortunate creatures, though not usually ceasing to eat the grass'? Possibly. Not only unemployment – in some places affecting the third generation – but a deliberate government policy, modelled on Reagan's America, of forcing down wages and substituting part-time for full-time work, seemed aimed at that third of the population which struggled to survive on or below the poverty line. Although the state sector in housing fell from 54 per cent of tenancies in 1979 to 40 per cent in 1990, thanks to concessionary sales to tenants, the limits of privatisation were reached when tenants simply could not afford to become owners. The grim system-built suburbs of East German towns in 1990, after the Wall fell, still seemed somewhat better endowed – with piped central heating, fast, subsidised trams, cheap grocery stores, community centres and kindergartens – than Castlemilk or Craigmillar.

7

The Start of a New Song?
1979–1997

Piper Alpha, 6 July 1988; Lockerbie, 21 December 1988; Dunblane, 13 March 1996: if Europe and the rest of the world encountered Scotland it was through these catastrophes and not through economic adaptation, the autonomy movement or cultural revival. The three disasters were not, however, acts of God. The Piper Alpha platform, as Lord Cullen's inquiry established in 1990, was overloaded and ill-maintained, through pressure to maximise oil and gas output. Those responsible for the Lockerbie bombing are still shadowy: Arab terrorists, drug dealers, secret service spooks? The killing of the Dunblane children exposed both the availability of lethal handguns and the way in which other 'close-knit communities' had trusted their children to a disturbed and dangerous misfit, rather than undertake voluntary activities themselves.

No-one was an island, and globally there was much to be pessimistic about. A warmer climate aided Scots tourism, but the thinning of the ozone layer doubled skin cancer cases, 1981–91; caesium from the Chernobyl reactor polluted the hills in May 1986 and effluent from salmon-farming and oil polluted the seas. Euphoria over the fall of Communist Europe in 1989–90 soon gave way to worries about hyperinflation, ungovernability and civil conflict if the 'new democracies' failed, and low-wage competition if they succeeded. Market utopia seemed as deceptive as its socialist predecessor, and doomed to be much shorter-lived. Had the time for the Scots to decide on their nationality simply come too late, when the dreams both of European union and of small nations were falling apart? But what was the alternative?

The Conservatives sought to replace social democracy's concept of welfare citizenship with their ideal of the shareholding consumer. Mrs Thatcher's dictum 'there is no such thing as society, only individuals and families' reflected ideological vagueness as much as primitivism lurking behind her political *nous*. Her marketism didn't help solve the problems crowding in on the world, and found few takers in Scotland. In a decade which saw the monarchy, banks, City and media undermined by folly where not by downright criminality, the losers were the traditions of Tom Nairn's 'enchanted glass' of Britishness rather than Scottish institutions.

II Industry

The decline of traditional industry accelerated in the 1980s. Scottish industrial capitalism was literally halved in the takeover boom of 1985–6, when £2.4 billion out of £4.7 billion of Scottish manufacturing capital was transferred to London control. By 1986 less than 30 per cent of GNP, employment in it dropped from 605,000 in 1979 to 412,000 in 1986, with investment falling from £561 million to £339 million. Between 1984 and 1994, GDP at current prices rose by 219 per cent, but manufacturing rose by only 85 per cent and the numbers it employed fell by 23 per cent between 1985 and 1994. The Scottish steel industry died. Despite its workers' defiance of the miners' strike in 1984–5, Ravenscraig's intrinsic viability was not enough to save it from the rationalisation programme of a privatised British Steel. Strip manufacture was centralised in South Wales and the works, scarcely thirty years old, closed in 1992 and was demolished in 1996. By 1996, too, the shipyards seemed close to the article of death. Govan, now run by the Norwegian firm Kvaerner, had only one order; GEC's Yarrow yard lost out on naval work to VSEL at Barrow-in-Furness. This left only the small Ferguson yard at Port Glasgow and the UIE yard at Clydebank, now French-owned. In the east, the former Royal Dockyard at Rosyth lost the contract to refit Trident submarines and was effectively mothballed. The QE 2 was re-engined with diesel engines in 1987; it was little consolation that the German Bremer Vulkan yard, which did the job, was now every bit as imperilled.

Oil production, down from 127 million tonnes in 1986 to 91.3 million in 1991, started to rise again until in 1996 it passed its 1986 peak. But in contrast to Norway, where the Statoil regime secured an income of £5 billion a year, UK income was in 1996 less than £2 billion, in an industry controlled by multinationals. The Cullen report was supposed to secure better safety, determined bilaterally by management and unions, but, after a surge in union activity in the early 1990s, management's concentration was on CRINE (Cost Reduction in the New Era) and labour felt itself even more disadvantaged. Although the North Sea had enabled remarkable breakthroughs in technology – which predicated the fully-automated hi-tech factory – these had little to offer the Scots: a new-style floating production platform for West of Shetland could as easily be built in Cadiz or Singapore. Similar global networks would supply the electronics, and of these the Scottish micro-chip would be only a humble part. After the Brent Spar crisis of 1994, governments realized that efforts to establish national control might bring only the problem of coping with the millions of tons of equipment now lying on the seabed.

Trade unionism declined, from 1,053,908 unionists affiliated to the STUC in 1979 to 913,186 in 1987 and 659,871 in 1997. The bulk of these was in the public sector. In Silicon Glen, 'sweetheart deals' – union recognition in exchange for no-strike clauses – seemed the best that could be got. Attempts at employee ownership on the buses were short-lived; the Monktonhall colliery, a gallant attempt by miners to run their own show, closed in 1997, leaving only the Longannet complex, though opencast extraction gouged coal out of Lanarkshire, Ayrshire and Lothian. Aluminium survived in Burntisland, Fort William and Kinlochleven, and paper manufacture continued at a few sites, while a new Finnish-owned pulp mill opened at Irvine. Menaced by cheap competition from the Far East and East Europe, and by high value-added fashion fabrics from Italy and France, the textile industries continued to contract, with only a dozen or so factories in operation in the Borders, the Sidlaws and Western Isles. Economic historians were gloomy about the overall picture. According to Peter Payne:

> In future, it is possible that the Scottish economy will be forced to shed entire fields or sections of activity; only those in which Scotland possesses some degree of comparative advantage will survive. One of these might be tourism; another, the provision of higher education; and a third, if Silicon Glen does prove able to move into software, electronics.

Transforming a capacity for 'getting by' into the competitive culture of Thatcherism was by definition difficult, not least because regional preferential assistance fell 34 per cent between 1986 and 1990. Malcolm Rifkind also carried through the poll tax and the two electricity boards were privatised (although Scottish Nuclear, which supplied most of the power, remained with the state until 1996; its forcible amalgamation with the British Nuclear concern further eroded Conservative support).

Did this create a viable Scottish capitalism? Scottish Electric proved predatory and took over the Lancashire and Wales MANWEB concern; Stagecoach became an aggressive international bus operator. But all of this depended on close links with finance. A couple of takeovers could change the entire scene.

In 1992, a Fraser of Allander Institute report noted that between 1985 and 1989 seventeen of Scotland's seventy-nine PLCs were taken over, representing 38 per cent of their turnover and 55 per cent of their capital. This could be neutral, even beneficial, as regards employment. It was one way of inducing inward investment. But high value-added functions – marketing, research and development, and specialist supply – went south. Although Scottish manufacturing recovered (in real terms it was in 1996 10 per cent up on 1990), this was almost wholly to do with electronics. Silicon Glen provided the motor: 35 per cent of Europe's personal computers, 25 per cent of the world's auto-tellers and 12 per cent of semi-conductors were built in Scotland. After 1983 there were around 43,000 jobs (13 per cent of the workforce) in the electronics industry. The value of production went up fourfold by 1991, yet there were obvious signs of crisis, and the prospect of a switch in investment to East Europe and other even-lower wage locations. Payne gloomily predicted only 17,500 jobs being left by 1997, but these in fact grew to 55,000 in 1996. Long-established firms such as IBM and Motorola were joined by increasing numbers of plants, not just from the United States (which had 80 per cent of electronics investment in 1992) but also from Japan and 'little tiger' economies, eager to settle in the European Union before the barriers went up. Yet even the successful Compaq operation had its headquarters in America, its European centre of manufacturing, research and development in Munich, and its plant at South Queensferry, whose great advantage, according to its management, was the speed at which part-time labour could be found, and as easily dispensed with.

In contrast to the dogmas of government, and the apparent abandonment of regional economic policy, it was evident that action to promote inward investment was being taken across party lines, and was determined to make an impact. Locate in Scotland, a subsidiary of Scottish Enterprise, secured £853 million of inward investment in 1989–90 (68 per cent of it from the USA). This fell to £394 million in 1990–1, through the American slump, but forced a switch to Japanese and Asian campaigning which took electronics investment up to £981 million in 1995–6, three-quarters of inward investment, and an astonishing £5 billion-plus in 1997.

Of high value-added electronics there was not much sign; or rather, a succession of promising enterprises which sprouted, then were taken over, moved out or closed down. Critical mass didn't generate much local sourcing – about 20 per cent – and the threat impended over all these pastel-coloured blocks around the motorways from Ayr to Dundee that a recession in demand, innovation by competitors, or simply the need to re-tool a production line, might lead to closure.

Food processing, another potential leading sector, ran into similar problems. Scotland, with 25 per cent of the British fishing fleet, was hit by both EU fishing policy and the results of consistent overfishing of the North Sea. Salmon farming – a branch with a turnover by 1992 of over £30 million, ran into trouble with epidemics and lochs polluted by phosphates from feedstuffs. Even more acute was the crisis in the beef and butchery industries following the emergencies over BSE (mad cow disease) and e-coli bacteria in 1996. The Roslin Institute's Dolly – the cloned sheep – who swept into the headlines in 1997 wasn't altogether welcome, and indeed genetic complications soon developed.

Scottish financial services had £100 billion under management in 1992 and £170 billion in 1997, and had a particularly dominant role in life assurance. The sector employed 286,000. A promotional body, Scottish Financial Enterprise (SFE), was set up in 1986. But it couldn't be said that a community of investors existed: whizzkids in fund management had more links to London than to other Scottish concerns, and Scottish mutual institutions, such as Scottish Amicable, were vulnerable, particularly to a City of London apprehensive about the concentration of European financial services after monetary union.

III Transport

Transportation and, above all, communications, were the keys to a new, geographically footloose, world industrialisation: yesterday's 'little tigers' became today's inward investors, and Scotland could offer them a labour force more docile than what was to be expected in Seoul or Pusan. In the 1960s, Scots – Sir William Lithgow and George Turnbull – had set up the South Korean shipbuilding and car industries; now these were 'coming home': in 1996 Hyundai promised £2.4 billion for a chip plant in Fife. Scotland was in the paradoxical situation of providing both the cheap labour and the sophisticated finance which made this possible.

The number of cars went up 27 per cent, 1984–94, but motorisation was consolidated rather than increased: up by over 50 per cent in well-set Edinburgh, hardly shifting at all in the housing schemes of the West. The third of society suffering from poverty and unemployment was not helped by immobility, since bus deregulation and privatisation did little for public transport. Bus miles went up 22 per cent and passenger journeys went down 22 per cent, 1985–95 – though deregulation managed to produce traffic jams *caused completely by public transport.* Bus companies – notably the Perth-based Stagecoach Group – used their property assets and local monopolies to become darlings of the City, and cleaned up when privatisation of the railways was driven through by the Scotsman John MacGregor, an otherwise unobtrusive member of John Major's cabinet. Getting hold of lessees seemed unpromising, until the bus companies came forward; while the luxury tour operator Sea Containers and the 'hippy millionaire' Richard Branson scooped the Anglo-Scottish franchises with big promises and even bigger subsidies.

The opening of the Channel Tunnel put Scotland within twenty hours of Brussels by express freight train, which cut costs by 8 per cent. An international depot was established in 1994 at Mossend for this purpose, but through passenger and sleeper trains had not turned up by 1997, and might not turn up at all. Goods traffic fell 40 per cent after the closure of Ravenscraig, but the Wisconsin Central Transport Corporation managed to return freight to the Highland lines and envisaged a 300 per cent increase over a decade. Passenger figures, after gentle decline, recovered. There were no major closures and even the reopening of some thirty miles of track – to Bathgate and Paisley Canal – in the 1980s. Utilisation of lines in the Highlands was low outside the summer season. Did this put them under threat from a lessee, National Express, which had already taken over Scottish Citylink Coaches – at considerable profit to the management which had bought it out? All this was frozen by an early act of the new Labour government, calling in the National Express takeover, while matters were confused by the competing responsibilities of the Secretary of State, the Transport Ministry, and Strathclyde PTA.

IV Getting and Spending

Lothian's wealth per capita in 1996 was £45,324, only £900 less than the sum for London, and 12 per cent greater than the Scottish average. But this was much higher than the average in Strathclyde, with a third living under the poverty line. Although GDP per capita was 99.8 per cent of the UK level, average male earnings, at £335.60, were 95 per cent of the UK figure. This seemed to indicate considerable inequality. Indeed, one of Locate in Scotland's selling points was the cheapness of Scottish labour, even when highly qualified. The expansion of higher education didn't do much for the standard of living of the new graduates. Salaries even in 'growth' areas like computer programming could be as low as £250 a week.

Women were now 52 per cent of the labour force, and their wages were 72 per cent of men's. They had crept up from 45 to 55 per cent of male wages between 1900 and 1971, and though this improved, a gap still remained, largely caused by the falling relative levels of industrial wages. Women made progress in the trade unions, largely thanks to the STUC, their representation on its executive going from only one out of twenty-one to twelve out of thirty-seven, and delegates rising from 7 to 23 per cent between 1971 and 1993. Women were the heroines of a society in which divorce ended one in three of marriages; one in five households were single-parent families. For the married, there seems to have been no diminution of the time spent in child-bearing, cooking and cleaning; the 'new man' was largely a myth. In fact, men were a major problem, in the absence of traditional manual jobs: 30 per cent of the long-term unemployed were aged under 24, and the results of this were seen in crime, violence and drugs.

Urban Scotland advertised its charms, but the malls and car-parks spread out, on the fringes of increasingly choked motorways and by-passes. Industrialised shopping had an ambiguous impact on urban life. In tarted-up town centres, bright young representatives of Scotland's local-state capitalism prided themselves on hooking Armani or Versace. Other streets saw a different shopping culture of shabby low-cost stores for folk coming in from the housing schemes. Affluent Edinburgh could apparently sustain Princes Street and the 'out of town' centre at the Gyle. But by 1996 Glasgow was in trouble again, with a mounting debt and an inadequate catchment area for local finance provoking the threat of major cuts.

A Tory adviser, confronted with a Glasgow housing scheme, wondered whether the black economy he found was capitalism or communism. Such precarious enterprise, even if collapsing at the edges into crime, drink, drugs and despair, held some areas together in ways unthinkable in the 1930s. Yet the ligatures of Adam Ferguson's 'society' still bound: if a potential big-league capitalist emerged, 'a neighbour picked up a phone'. Did the 'makers, movers and menders' of Alasdair Gray's *Lanark* exist in embryo, a market structure on a collectivist base? Or was it enough, as Gray wrote in his 'Postscript' to Agnes Owens' *Gentlemen of the West* (1986), to survive, threaten no-one, and try to be articulate on behalf of folk with low incomes? 'Mac is typical of a huge piece of Britain. Conservatives can draw soothing morals from his existence. I hope they will not.'

Drink mattered less to the Scots, whose overall expenditure was bang on the UK norm. The worry was that the saving was going on drugs. Addiction was scarcely noticeable in 1981; in March 1995 there were 6,359 patients under treatment for drug abuse. How much of a diseconomy was this? One Health Board calculation put the cost to the Glasgow economy alone at £633 million. Was this believable? The problem was finding out, in a culture where market research had displaced sociology.

V Society

Sport and Recreation

In 2002, the World Cup would be staged by Japan and South Korea. The game of Busby, Shankly and Stein would be relayed from places which, two decades earlier, would have been utterly baffled by the FA rules. But so too were the Scots by the new sport-capitalism. Rugby followed golf and football into the big league, encouraged by Rupert Murdoch's television contracts. The Premier League (two-thirds of 3.5 million tickets) and Rangers dominated Scots football to the point of monotony, provoking Fergus McCann, who had taken over Celtic, to suggest combining with the English league. Tourism, at £2.5 billion, became as big as agriculture and mining combined – rising from 1.36 million overseas visitors in 1988 to nearly 2 million in 1995. European visitors were now pulling ahead of those from the USA.

Religion

The fact that almost half of marriages were now civil, compared with only a quarter in 1971, showed that religion continued its downward spiral; the Catholic Church claimed more adherents (800,000) than the Kirk (700,000) but admitted that 120,000 of these had lapsed. Was the Kirk any more relevant to people than the horoscopes which clogged all but the *Scotsman* and the *Herald*? Even the 215,000 members in the BBs, Scouts, Guides and Girls' Brigades fell to 170,000 between 1988 and 1996. The traditional blend of social radicalism and doctrinal conservatism represented by Cardinal Winning of Glasgow suffered a shock akin to those coming the way of the Catholic Church in Ireland when the adventures of the Bishop of Argyll hit the tabloids in 1996. Abortion was tried as a political card; it proved a non-runner in the 1997 election. But Kenyon Wright, Maxwell Craig and others played notable roles in organising the politics of devolution; and coming to terms with religion – in its good or questionable aspects – still marked such thinkers and writers as Kay Carmichael and Alasdair Gray. An eighteenth-century 'common-sense' theism still helped order thought and feeling, though a fundamentalism closer to the American style played a key role in some notable careers: Brian Souter of Stagecoach, Ian Clark of BNOC, Lord Chancellor Mackay. At the other extreme, cases of child abuse, in Orkney and elsewhere, were linked with Satanism. Were luck and superstition, astrology and addiction to the X-Files, made concrete in the country's surpassing addiction to the National Lottery, the new opiates of the people?

Education

Universities burgeoned. In 1993, Ian Lang put the former Scottish central institutions under the control of a Scottish Higher and Further Education Funding Council. Most opted for university status, taking the number from seven to thirteen, and the students accredited to them from 112,000 in 1983 to 180,000 in 1996. About a third of schoolchildren had the equivalent of university entrance qualifications, and post-secondary education attracted 76 per cent of them, compared with 40 per cent in the UK generally. Was this evidence of the *perfervidium ingenium Scotorum*, or of avoiding the dole queue? There was legitimate worry about standards, not least in history, where most schoolchildren believed that James Watt invented the electric light bulb.

Culture

For all its political frustration, the 1980s in Scotland was rich in cultural re-examinations and rediscoveries, provoked by the reaction to 1979 and the challenge of 'Scotland in Europe'. Major achievements in literary and social history – *The History of Scottish Literature, People and Society in Scotland, The Dictionary of Scottish Business Biography* were just the peaks – filled out epochs and individuals who had been at best shadowy when the present book was first drafted. The imaginative achievement of Scots novelists and dramatists – Alasdair Gray, James Kelman, Liz Lochhead, John Byrne – now feeding on the life and problems of urban Scotland, complemented one of Europe's richest and most polyphonic poetics. 1996 was a bad year, with the deaths of Norman MacCaig, Sorley MacLean and George Mackay Brown. But to the innovation of Edwin Morgan was added the architectural statements of Ian Hamilton Finlay, the humanism of Douglas Dunn, and the busy evangelism of the Scottish Poetry

Library. Scottish painting and sculpture – Stephen Conroy, Ken Currie, John Bellany, Eduardo Paolozzi – established a European reputation, following rules unheard of in London.

This may have contributed to a youth culture which was unrespectable rather than rebellious, summed up by the post-chemical literature of such as Irvine Welsh, aimed at 'people who don't read books'. This could yaw between obscenity and violence and a clogged sentimentality or sociological sententiousness like Burns at his raised-pinkie worst. Nevertheless, *Trainspotting* (thanks largely to Danny Boyle's film) became the tenth most important book, the 1996 papers said, since books started. Newspapers were certainly healthy, and for once disproportionately 'Scottish'-owned, with the empires of Gus MacDonald and the mysterious Barclay Brothers.

There was little enough that was distinctive about the new townscapes. London's Terry Farrell and Norman Foster set the Edinburgh and Glasgow scenes, although Charles Rennie Mackintosh staged a ghostly revival, with the completion of some of his unfulfilled designs. Most of the people seemed to have tastes which were pervasively transatlantic. Ryan and Lauren were apparently the most popular children's names in Scotland. Was it all to be jeans, trainers, t-shirts, baseball caps, in-line skating, fast food? Or were the fans of Runrig and the Proclaimers our new democrats in waiting?

VI Politics

Local Government

Sir Robert Calderwood, Chief Executive of Strathclyde, reckoned it took over ten years for the regional system to settle down. Its positive results, notably in industrial, transport and European policy, were only becoming apparent after 1985; yet by 1992 the Conservatives were bent on abolition of the 'two-tier' system. Why? Economy? This didn't square with the costs of 'reform', estimated at around £700 million. Revenge for their eviction from the regions and the hope of recovering some municipal power-bases? This seemed more plausible. The result was, however, disastrous, initially for them, subsequently for local authorities in general. Strathclyde's campaign against water privatisation produced a devastating result for the government, with only 97 per cent voting against in a referendum. Worse was to come. In the first 'single-tier' elections in May 1995, the Conservatives won only 7 per cent of the poll and not a single council.

But first-past-the-post created a series of Labour fiefdoms in which all the problems of one-party rule – nepotism, corruption, freeloading – made themselves felt. Local responsibility for cash-raising was lessened, as suburban communities no longer contributed to central city expenses: something which soon impressed itself on Glasgow, where Labour suspended most of the council leadership in late 1997. Since councillors were fewer, and as many formerly regional functions were now carried out by joint boards or the new water authorities, government was even more remote. With the rise of the full-time councillor, female representation seems also to have declined, to under 13.7 per cent in the late 1980s.

Thatcher's Decade

The electoral system which favoured the Conservatives in England boosted Labour in Scotland. In four-party politics, the Liberals and SNP in 1992 got 35 per cent of the vote and only 17 per cent of MPs; the Conservatives (and this was a good year for them) got 25 per cent of votes and 15 per cent of MPs. The Liberals had done well when, after the split in the Labour Party, the Liberal/SDP Alliance vote rose to 24.5 per cent in 1983, their seats going from three to eight; but in 1992, when their vote almost halved, their seats still stood at nine. The paradox was that this quite un-British political community was, for the first time in nearly a century, to provide a lot of front-bench talent. It was based on very rickety foundations.

The Conservatives' destruction owed much to a combination of dogma and indolence, but they were initially canny. Between 1979 and 1986 George Younger, a 'wet', ex-officer and brewer, tempered Thatcherism, retained the Scottish Development Agency and established a Select Committee on Scottish Affairs – meeting occasionally in the Royal High School – yet his autonomy was checked by a Whitehall ideology and a fast-waning Scottish industrial capitalism. Following Michael Heseltine's resignation over the Westland affair, he became Minister of Defence, the first promotion out of the Secretaryship since Walter Elliot in 1938. It wasn't to be the last.

His successor Malcolm Rifkind, previously reckoned a liberal and devolutionist, proved pliant to London command. He acquiesced in the dismantling of regional economic policy by Lord Young and the demoralisation and dismemberment of the SDA. In 1987 the Scottish Select Committee was suspended because of conflict between Labour MPs and the bored English Tories put in as makeweights. In a post usually occupied by former whips and Scottish business dynasts, Rifkind, a clever, rather lonely man, was attacked by the Tory right after 1987, when Tory MPs fell from twenty-one to ten. Thatcher went over his head to install Michael Forsyth as Scottish Chairman, who imported a highly ideological staff and provoked civil war within the party. This led to Forsyth's removal and (probably) to Rifkind's role in toppling Thatcher on 22 November 1990. Secretary of State for Transport and then, after April 1992, for Defence, Rifkind became Foreign Secretary in 1995.

The SNP left believed that the party's conservatism had cost it nine MPs in 1979, and set out in the '79 group to compete with Labour. Its republican radicalism was premature, and the conflicts contributed to a wretched result in 1983. This gave the Liberals their hour. Under David Steel, who took over as leader in 1976 after the fall of Jeremy Thorpe, the alliance was forged with the ex-right-wing-Labour SDP; but the return of Roy Jenkins for Glasgow Hillhead in 1982 could not conceal its failure to gain adherents. Jenkins' replacement as leader by the opportunistic Dr David Owen brought Steel nothing but trouble in the 1987 campaign.

Table 7.1: European Parliament election results

	1979		1984		1989		1994		1999	
	MEPs	%	MEPs	%	MEPs	%	MEPs	%	MEPs	%
Labour	2	33	5	41	7	41	6	43	3	29
Conservative	5	34	2	26	–	21	–	15	2	20
SNP	1	19	1	18	1	27	2	33	2	27
Lib Dems	–	14	–	16	–	4	–	7	1	10
others	–	–	–	–	–	7	–	2	0	14
turnout		34		33		41		38		25
turnout: England		31		32		36		36		23

In 1979, Labour suffered the further humiliation of a defeat in the first European parliament elections. No left-wing parties had any interest in Europe, and in a low poll the Conservatives took most seats, with the Highlands seat going to Mrs Winifred Ewing of the SNP. Thereafter the Tories dwindled to nothing, while Europe began to preoccupy Scottish regional authorities and pressure groups, frustrated by Whitehall. Then in 1986 the concept of 'Independence in Europe', projected with typical force, brought Jim Sillars back into prominence, and in November 1988 into the Commons as SNP MP for Govan.

Neil Kinnock, remembered in Scotland as an anti-devolutionist, was even less loved than Thatcher. Yet under him Labour underwent a drastic 'modernisation': party and leader ditched unilateralism and Bevanite collectivism to woo the south-eastern voter. (In 1987 Labour had only 16.8 per cent support there, compared with 42 per cent in Scotland.) A new generation, university-educated, and formed in the politics of the student movement, Union debates, and the Labour clubs – John Smith, Gordon Brown, Robin Cook, Martin O'Neill – had come to the fore, not just in Scottish but in Westminster politics: the first time Scots had exercised such authority since the time of ... well ... Ramsay Macdonald.

A Constitution for Scotland?

Macdonald had started his career as a home ruler, and following the 1987 election the theme emerged again. The Campaign for a Scottish Assembly, which had struggled to keep interest alive, got an influential committee to draft *A Claim of Right for Scotland*, published on 6 July 1988. This proposed the summoning of a 210-strong Constitutional Convention composed of MPs, council representatives, trade unionists and the Churches, to deliberate on Scotland's constitutional future. Within a year, Labour and the Liberal Democrats had accepted membership, and the issue was given added urgency by the Govan by-election. But the SNP's poll position soared after Govan and it announced it would only take part if its policy of independence in Europe were included in the referendum options. The other parties wanted a single agreed option, and the Convention's composition obviously favoured the electoral status quo. The SNP withdrew. The Tories announced they weren't interested, and anathematised their dwindling home-rule minority.

The Convention first met in the Kirk's Assembly Hall on 30 March 1989, and its Convener, Canon Kenyon Wright, issued its report *Towards Scotland's Parliament*, in November 1990. The scheme was for a legislature with 'entrenched' powers broadly resembling those of a German *Land*, elected under a form of proportional representation and financed by 'assigned revenues' deducted from the taxes raised in Scotland. The electorate's attention-span for matters constitutional is limited, and, while significant in converting the Labour Party in Scotland to PR, the Convention's ideas were noted by fewer than a quarter. But in late 1991, on the death of the Tory party's one home-ruler MP, Alick Buchanan-Smith, a Liberal Democrat victory and a new, aggressive SNP leader, Alex Salmond, kicked the issue back into life. In late January 1992, Salmond triumphed in an inter-party debate in the Usher Hall and a *Scotsman* poll showed 50 per cent for the SNP's 'independence in Europe' policy. There was much talk of a Conservative initiative on self-government, should they win in the UK and lose in Scotland.

1992: Election Anti-climax

Despite this, on 9 April hardly anything changed. The press was anti-Tory (in contrast to England) but Ian Lang and his team just held their position; a few hundred votes the other way would have been a disaster. One, unregarded, Tory weapon was the poll tax. It had dislodged an unelectable Mrs Thatcher, and prompted the most sustained campaign of civil disobedience ever seen in Scotland, when up to a third refused to pay, but Labour councils suffered falls in revenue, and up to 5 per cent of Labour voters dropped off the electoral register. The SNP gambled on signals of a Labour defeat producing a swing to them, but these came far too late. A one-third increase didn't save Jim Sillars at Govan. Slightly increasing their vote from 24 to 25.7 per cent, taking one seat from Labour and regaining Kincardine, the Conservatives were lulled into a deadly false sense of security.

The Conservative utopia of minimal government and market choice had become illusory. State monopolies were now private monopolies, fitfully and ineffectively controlled; 'people's capitalism' lasted only until the people had sold their shares off at a profit: its logical successor was the National Lottery, not the small and medium-sized enterprise (SME). Government assaults on local authority competence in areas like health and education produced a potential chaos of competing public authorities: school boards, hospital trusts, training and enterprise councils battling it out with local government. This meant that more powers ended up with St Andrew's House, which took over from 'British' institutions in areas like the environment and higher education. Was the result semi-colonial, the Secretary of State a governor, even a *gauleiter*? But there was nothing purposive about the situation; only irritation among the governed and irresolution in the executive.

Where were the mass protests? Occasionally the STUC and left-wing bodies could put several thousands on the streets, but there was nothing resembling the repeated, peaceful demonstrations which felled Communism in East Germany. All parties were suffering substantial membership loss, with the number of fully-paid-up less than 100,000, or 2 per cent of the population. Among the Tories, where nothing was left of the tradition of Walter Elliot and John Buchan, this process seemed to accelerate almost alarmingly. On 14 September 1992, when Major visited Scotland to 'take stock', sterling dropped against the Deutschmark by 15 per cent. His next visit was on 11–12 December for the European summit. Edinburgh launched a miniature festival, and cultural and ethnic delights almost drowned out the further disintegration of the British monarchy. Scots would disgrace themselves, in the eyes of Ian Lang, by demonstrating in favour of autonomy. On a cold December afternoon, 25,000 did so.

John Smith, a universally popular figure, had succeeded Kinnock. When in May 1994 he died suddenly in London the grief was immense; his grave on Iona became a place of pilgrimage. But the by-election which followed nailed the Monklands Labour Party as ingrown and self-serving; there was a frisson of Catholic racketeering (although politics and the Church in Ireland were going through a similar purgative experience). Helen Liddell, former Scottish organiser of the party, only just beat her SNP challenger. The new leader, Tony Blair, was Scots in origin but remote from the lowland Labour culture of most of his front-benchers.

Sir Nicholas Fairbairn died in early 1995, leaving the Commons a drabber place, his family a complex legacy to fight over, and his seat to the SNP. John Major, from being Britain's most popular prime minister ever, in 1991, saw his stock plunge into the cellar, and in mid-1995 John Redwood challenged him for the Tory leadership. Surprisingly, Michael Forsyth, a junior Home Office minister, backed Major and was rewarded with the Scottish Secretaryship when Lang went to the Board of Trade. This was a madeover Forsyth, intent on discussions with the STUC, appointing old foes – notably Jim Sillars and Dick Douglas – to quangos, even wearing a kilt (the first Scottish Secretary anyone could remember who did so). He fought against the 'genocide' of Gaelic culture, and at the end of 1996 secured the return of the Stone of Scone from Westminster Abbey.

1997: 'At hame wi' freedom'?

The election of 1997 was long on professionalism and short on ideology. It became tenser as Blair and his Shadow Secretary of State, George Robertson, vacillated about the power of and the timetable for the Scottish parliament. A general position which aligned Blair with the Conservative record, projected by a well-organised campaign, caused doubts. These were suppressed by the farce of the Tory party, divided over Europe and racked by personal scandals which felled one MP and the party chairman, before the campaign was really under way. On 2 May 1997, the Conservatives in Scotland ceased to exist as a parliamentary party. The SNP, which had gained two seats though only a slight increase in its vote, was now second to Labour. Blair replaced the rather rebarbative Robertson with his chief whip Donald Dewar, clever, witty and above all tactful. He held to his promise of a referendum, which was slated for 11 September. The campaign, centred on the 'second question' of tax-varying powers, initially gave some headway to the 'Think Twice' unionist group, aided by a few finance leaders and Tam Dalyell. Scandals in Govan and Paisley, the latter exposed by the suicide of the Paisley South MP, Gordon McMaster, haunted Labour. Then the death in a Paris accident of the Princess of Wales intervened. The contrast between a decorous truce in the north and uninhibited orgies of grief and anti-monarchical emotion in London suddenly seemed to crystallise civic differences, growing for so long. The 'Scotland FORward' alliance? headed enthusiastically by Dewar, Salmond and the Liberals' Jim Wallace, had to prove itself in a 100-hour campaign, and did. 'Think Twice', already hampered by the non-participation of Rifkind and Forsyth, out after financial pastures new, was finished by the 'fraternal assistance' of Lady Thatcher. The poll was slightly lower than in 1979 but the Yesses reached 74 per cent (turnouts were low in the industrial cities, but promisingly high and positive in the 'new' Scotland of the suburban central belt). The Scots result undoubtedly helped carry Welsh devolution (support for which was, however, up 150 per cent on 1979) by the narrowest of margins on 18 September. Would consensus continue? The Scotland bill proceeded through Parliament – relatively few MPs bothered about it – and became law in June 1998. Elections were slated for 6 May 1999, coinciding with the Council contests and slightly ahead of the European Parliament elections on 10 June. The latter used an all-Scotland list, but the old European seats were used to elect the Scottish Parliament's fifty-six additional or 'list' members. This 'modified d'Hondt' system resembled that of Germany, but gave an advantage of about 4 per cent to the party which commanded most constituency MSPs.

Table 7.2: The referenda of 1979 and 1997 (given on the basis of the regions in 1979)

Region (turnout) (%)	Yes votes 1979 (%)	Yes votes 1997 (%)	Difference 1979–1997 (%)	Region (turnout) (%)	Yes votes 1979 (%)	Yes votes 1997 (%)	Difference 1979–1997 (%)
Borders (64)	40	63	57	Orkney (53)	57	28	103
Central (65)	54	76	40	Shetland (53)	27	62	129
Dumfries (64)	41	61	49	Strathclyde (60)	54	78	44
Fife (61)	57	76	33	Tayside (59)	50	68	36
Grampian (55)	48	68	41	Western Isles (55)	55	79	43
Highland (60)	51	73	43	**Scotland (60)**	**52**	**74 (64*)**	**42**
Lothian (61)	51	75	47	Wales (50)	20	50.3	150

* Scottish percentage voting for tax-varying powers; only Dumfries and Orkney rejected these, very narrowly.

In domestic policy Blair and Brown were mildly redistributory but didn't advertise it, and made gestures favourable to land reform. It looked an uphill fight for Donald Dewar, as the SNP was 10 per cent ahead of Labour in the polls in July 1998, with a majority of voters also favouring 'Independence in Europe'. Labour was also plunged in internal problems. One minister resigned over expenditure cuts, an MP committed suicide. Scandal lapped at local parties in Glasgow, Motherwell and Paisley. Candidate selection was secretive and bungled. Dewar was rattled and Blair buttressed him with the appointment of Helen Liddell – 'the hammer of the Nats' – as Minister of State. Then strategy changed. Liddell vanished into an oubliette in the Scottish Office, and the Chancellor Gordon Brown, popular and unquestionably Scots, fronted the campaign.

By early 1999 economic difficulties, paradoxically, made things run Labour's way. Falls in the price of oil, microchips, farm and fish products made the economics of independence look risky; even the SNP admitted to a likely initial deficit of around £1.7 billion, and Brown's spin-doctors operated with focus groups and an overwhelmingly sympathetic press to denounce independence as 'divorce'. By early April this seemed to have worked, and a principled but risky stand by Alex Salmond against the bombing of Serbia cost him further support. The SNP poll fell to 25 per cent and an outright Labour victory seemed possible.

But at the end of a complex and difficult count (at one point the Lothian tellers went on strike!) an unexpected gap appeared between Labour's first and second votes, and the makings of a revolt against the 'one-party-states' of the West. (Labour got 39 per cent, the SNP 29 per cent, the Lib Dems 14 per cent and the Conservatives 16 per cent, and others 3 per cent of the first votes.) The fiery home ruler Denis Canavan trounced the official Labour man in Falkirk; the Scottish Socialists returned Tommy Sheridan on the Glasgow list and the Greens got Robin Harper in for Edinburgh.

Labour could later reflect that these results were better than the neck-and-neck finish between them and the SNP in the European elections. They went into coalition with the Lib Dems – ironically the great beneficiaries of first-past-the-post – the price being the abolition of tuition fees at the universities, a compromise came later with the Cubie report. Thirty-seven per cent of the MSPs were women, making the parliament the second most feminist after Sweden, and women provided three members of Dewar's Labour–Lib Dem cabinet, which influenced the strong social themes of the first legislative programme.

Table 7.3: Seats by European election groupings
(A = Constituency MSPs; B = % of second vote; C = list MSPs)

	Labour			SNP			Conservative			Lib Dems			Others		
	A	B	C	A	B	C	A	B	C	A	B	C	A	B	C
Highlands & Islands	1	(25)	3	2	(28)	2	0	(15)	2	5	(21)	0	0	(11)	0
North-East	4	(25)	0	2	(32)	4	0	(18)	3	3	(17)	0	0	(8)	0
Mid-Scotland & Fife	6	(33)	0	2	(27)	3	0	(19)	3	1	(13)	1	0	(8)	0
West of Scotland	9	(39)	0	0	(26)	4	0	(16)	2	0	(11)	1	0	(8)	0
Glasgow	10	(44)	0	0	(26)	5	0	(8)	1	0	(7)	1	0	(15)	1
Central Scotland	9	(39)	0	0	(28)	5	0	(9)	1	0	(6)	1	1	(18)	0
Lothians	8	(30)	0	0	(26)	3	0	(16)	2	1	(14)	1	0	(14)	1
South of Scotland	6	(31)	0	1	(25)	3	0	(22)	4	2	(12)	0	0	(10)	0

One incident showed that Scots' freedom had indeed a 'hame' – the Bank of Scotland fixed up a clever deal with the American Rev. Pat Robertson, whose 'Christian Coalition Inc.' combined fundamentalism with no-holds-barred capitalism. On 1 June Robertson denounced Scotland as a 'dark land' because it tolerated homosexuality. Under pressure from Parliament, the Bank broke the contract off. Much less, however, was said during or after the election about other contracts – 'concordats' – which would govern Anglo-Scottish relations, and about the future of such contested areas as the media and social security. Blair appointed John Reid Secretary of State, a high-flyer for an obsolete position. Was Whitehall's grip on Scottish affairs still there? Journalists, ever inconstant, listened to a few MSPs in debates and thought this might be no bad thing.

But on 1 July, an informal, pleasantly chaotic ceremony, with the Queen as honoured guest rather than monarch, rambled from the old Parliament House to the temporary seat of government in the Church of Scotland's Assembly Hall. Powers were handed over, in the shape of a mace inscribed 'Compassion, Justice, Truth, Liberty'. Tom Fleming read one of Iain Crichton Smith's poems:

> our three-voiced country
> sing in a new world,
> joining the other rivers
> without dogma,
> but with friendliness to all around her

and that 'dear friendly ghost', erudite, troubled, benign, seemed somewhere near, about to join Dewar and walk with the others, on 'a journey which started long ago, and which has no end'.

Further Reading

(Places of publication: L = London, E = Edinburgh, G = Glasgow, A = Aberdeen, O = Oxford, C = Cambridge, except where otherwise stated.)

A *Government Papers* (available under the thirty-year rule) are divided between the Public Record Office (Cabinet and British Ministries) and West Register House, Edinburgh (Scottish Office); they are valuable on economic and social issues after the 1930s.

B *Private Collections*: The National Library, Edinburgh, is particularly strong on nationalism (the Scottish Secretariat and J. A. A. Porteous papers) with smaller collections of Elliot, Johnston, and Woodburn papers: Liberal Party papers are in Edinburgh University Library; those of the Labour Party: Scottish Council in Labour Party Headquarters, London.

C *Statistical Sources*: *Census Returns* are important but flawed. Occupational categories change between 1911 and 1921, the 1931 census took place at the pit of the slump, and there was not another until 1951. The *Censuses of Production* of 1907, 1924, 1935, and 1948 and subsequently were used, along with the *Glasgow Herald Trade Reviews*, by R. H. Campbell for his *Rise and Fall of Scottish Industry* (E, 1980). *The Annual Reports* (*AR*) of the Board (later the Department) of Agriculture and Fisheries, and the Scottish Education Department, the Scottish Economic Committee's *Scotland's Industrial Future* (G, 1939) and the *Clydesdale Bank Reports* (1934–9) sum up interwar trends. *Industry and Employment in Scotland*, an annual paper after 1947, was supplemented by the twice-yearly *Digest of Scottish Statistics* (1954–71), dividing into the annual *Scottish Abstract of Statistics* and the twice-yearly *Scottish Economic Bulletin* (since 1971). The SNP publishes regular statistical bulletins, and the Scottish Council's *Input-Output Table* (E, 1977) was the first of several (see *SEB*). There is Scottish material in B. R. Mitchell and P. Deane, *British Historical Statistics* (2 vols, C, 1962 and 1971), A. H. Halsey, *Trends in British Society since 1900* (*TBS*) (1972) and David Butler et al., *British Political Facts* (L, 1994), *The General Election of 1950*, etc., and in F. W. S. Craig's various compilations of election results. The Unionists published a useful *Yearbook for Scotland* until 1970: thereafter see the *Yearbook of Scottish Government* (*YSG*) (E, 1974–93) and *Scottish Affairs* (1993–). *The Third Statistical Account* (*TSA*), conceived in 1943, was finally completed in 1995, though latterly without general county introductions. J. Cunnison and J. B. S. Gilfillan's *Glasgow* (G, 1958) is one of the best volumes. Magnus Linklater and Robin Denniston, eds, *Anatomy of Scotland Today* (L, 1992). D. Daiches, ed., *A Companion to Scottish Culture* (L, 1982). D. Thomson, ed., *The Companion to Gaelic Scotland* (O, 1983) can also be consulted.

D *Bibliographies*: P. D. Hancock's *A Bibliography of Works Relating to Scotland, 1916–1950* (E, 1959–60) can be supplemented by W. H. Marwick's bibliographies in the *Economic History Review* (*EcHR*) in 1952, 1963, and 1972 and C. Allen's in the *YSG* and *SA*. The Scottish Labour History Society's *Labour Records in Scotland* (1977) is likewise supplemented by the annual bibliographical and research surveys in *Scottish Economic and Social History* (1979–) and the *Scottish History Review*.

E *General Introductions and Serial Publications:* M. Lynch, *A History of Scotland* (L, 1991), W. Ferguson, *Scotland, 1689 to the Present* (E, 1968) G. S. Pryde, *Scotland after 1603* (E, 1962), T. C. Smout, *A Century of the Scottish People* (L, 1986) and T. Devine and R. Findlay, ed., *Scotland in the Twentieth Century* (E, 1996) are basic. For the later period see J. G. Kellas, *The Scottish Political System* (*SPS*) (C, 1973, 1989), *Modern Scotland* (*MS*) (L, 1968, 1980), and C. T. Harvie, *Scotland and Nationalism* (L, 1997, 1993) and D. McCrone, *Understanding Scotland* (L, 1992). I. Finlayson, *The Scots* (O, 1988) and M. Pittock, *The Rediscovery of Scotland* (L, 1991) are more literary accounts.

Useful symposia are: J. N. Wolfe, ed., *Government and Nationalism in Scotland* (*GNS*) (E, 1968), T. C. Smout, ed., *Scotland and the Sea* (E, 1992), and G. Brown, ed., *The Red Paper on Scotland* (*RP*) (E, 1975), K. Cargill, ed., *Scotland 2000* (G, 1987), D. McCrone, ed., *The Making of Scotland* (E, 1989) H. Fraser and R. J. Morris, eds, *People and Society in Scotland, 1830–1914* (E, 1990) and A. Dickson and J. H. Treble, eds, *1914 to the Present* (E, 1991); *The Sunday Mail History of Scotland* (G, 1988–9), R. Mitchison, ed., *Why Scottish History Matters* (E, 1991, 1997), I. Donnachie, ed., *The Manufacture of Scottish History* (E, 1992), I. Wood, ed., *Scotland and Ulster* (E, 1994) and J. Calder, ed., *The Enterprising Scot* (E, 1986).

The 1980s also saw treatments of multinationality in the British Isles, such as B. Crick, ed., *National Identities* (1991), C. Crouch and D. Marquand, eds, *The New Centralism* (O, 1988), H. Kearney, *The British Isles: a History of Four Nations* (C, 1989). Such discussions inform K. O. Morgan, *The People's Peace, 1945–1990* (O, 1990) and T. Nairn, *The Enchanted Glass* (L, 1988).

A growing number of European studies include R. Sturm, *Nationalismus in Schottland und Wales* (Bochum, 1981), J. Leruez, *L'Ecosse, une Nation sans Etat* (Paris, 1983), K. White, ed., *Ecosse* (Paris, 1988), C. und L. Ulsamer, *Schottland, das Nordseeöl und die britische Wirtschaft* (Schondorf, 1991) and C. Civardi, *Ecosse* (Paris, 1991), R. Drost-Hüttl, *Die schottische Nationalbewegung, 1886–1945* (Bochum, 1995) and S. Hagemann, *Die schottische Renaissance* (Frankfurt, 1992) and L. Moreno, *Escocia nacion y razon* (Madrid, 1995).

In terms of biography there was *Scottish Biographies* (E, 1938) and then a gap until *Who's Who in Scotland* (E, 1994–). *A Dictionary of Scottish Biography* is being organized from Stirling University; and see W. Knox, *Scottish Labour Leaders, 1920–1950* (E, 1983). *The Dictionary of National Biography* is being re-compiled as the *New DNB*, with due attention to Scotland, by H. G. C. Matthew at Oxford. See, additionally, *Obituaries from the The Times* and *The Times Guide to the House of Commons*, *Keesing's Contemporary Archives* and *Hansard*. Of newspapers and periodicals, the *Glasgow Herald* was indexed until 1968, and the *Scotsman* has been since 1975. Both now have Internet archives. *Scotland* was valuable on economic affairs in the 1950s and 1960s; and *Scottish Business Insider* or the recent period.

F *Economy:* Matters have much improved since 1981, with many important monographs and articles, notably in *Scottish Economic and Social History* (*SESH*) and the commentaries of the Fraser of Allander Institute (*FAI*): P. Payne, 'The End of Steelmaking in Scotland', in *SESH* (1995) supplements his *Colvilles* (O, 1980). J. Hume and M. Moss, *Beardmores* (L, 1980), R. H. Campbell on the N. B. *Loco in Business History* (*BH*) (1978) and on 'The Scottish Office and the Special Areas' in the *Historical Journal* (*HJ*) (1978) are valuable. A. Slaven, *The Economic Development of the West of Scotland 1760–1860* (L, 1975), amplifies *TSA Glasgow* and see also Slaven on John Brown's, 1919–38, in *BH* (1977), and N. K. Buxton on Scottish shipbuilding, also in *BH* (1968), and on economic growth in Scotland (*EcHR* 1980).

The World War I historian still depends on W. R. Scott and J. Cunnison, *The Industries of the Clyde Valley during the War* (O, 1924) and the printed but unpublished *History of the Ministry of*

Munitions (1922); E. M. H. Lloyd, *Experiments in State Control* (O, 1923), has much on the textile industries and A. L. Bowley, *Prices and Wages in the UK*, 1914–20 (O, 1921) on incomes. A. Marwick, *The Deluge* (L, 1966) and A. S. Milward, *The Economic Effects of the Two World Wars in Britain* (L, 1970) set out the UK context. For the Clyde episodes see J. Hinton *The First Shop Stewards Movement* (L, 1973); W. J. Reader, *Weir: Architect of Air Power* (G, 1968), and *The Weir Group* (L, 1971), H. McShane, *No Mean Fighter* (L, 1976), W. Gallacher, *Revolt on the Clyde* (L, 1936), *Last Memoirs* (L, 1966), and N. MacLean Milton, *John Maclean* (L, 1973) have to be taken with caution.

H. W. Richardson, *Economic Recovery in Britain 1932–39* (L, 1967), and B. W. E. Alford, *Depression and Recovery* (L, 1972), sum up the debate on the inter-war economy. There was a spate of publications in the 1930s, including the *Scott Report on West Central Scotland* (E, 1930) and the SEC's *The Highland Economy* and *Light Industries* (E, 1938); see also the *Special Area Commissioners' Reports* (1935–9). More 'partisan' are C. Maclehose, *The Scotland of our Sons* (G, 1936), R. Findlay, *Scotland at the Crossroads* (E, 1937) and J. A. Bowie, *The Future of Scotland* (E, 1939). On agriculture, see J. A. Symon, *Scottish Farming* (L, 1959), D. Jones, ed., *Rural Scotland during the War* (O, 1926), and A. Smith, *Joseph Duncan* (E, 1974). On the Highlands, see D. Turnock, *Patterns of Highland Development* (L, 1970), D. Thomson and I. Grimble, *The Future of the Highlands* (L, 1968), N. Nicholson, *Lord of the Isles* (1965). On banking, see S. G. Checkland, *Scottish Banking* (G, 1975), and R. Saville, *Bank of Scotland: A History, 1695–1995* (E, 1996); on transport, there is a wealth of enthusiasts' accounts, of which J. Thomas's *Regional History of the Railways of Great Britain: Scotland* (Newton Abbot, 1971) acts as introduction, but this has yet to lead to a history of twentieth-century developments. See also the various regional plans and the British Association's *Scientific Survey of S. E. Scotland* (E, 1951).

For the 1945–79 period, J. Gollan presented an intelligent left-wing survey in *Scottish Prospect* (G, 1948), and J. A. A. Porteous, *Scotland and the South* (Stirling, 1947) draws on much SEC material. A. Cairncross, ed., *The Scottish Economy* (SE) (C, 1953) is uneven (it misses out fishing and is weak on manufacturing) but still essential, as is G. McCrone, *Scotland's Economic Progress* (SEP) (L, 1965), and T. L. Johnston et al., *Structure and Growth of the Scottish Economy* (L, 1973) and T. Dickson, ed., *Capital and Class in Scotland* (E, 1983). On trade unions, R. A. Cage, ed., *The Working Class in Glasgow, 1750–1914* (G, 1987) forms a prelude to A. Tuckett, *The STUC: The First Eighty Years, 1987–1977* (E, 1986) and K. Aitken, *The Bairns o' Adam* (E, 1996). J. Foster and C. Woolfson, *The Politics of the UCS Work-in* (L, 1986) and I. MacDougall, ed., *Militant Miners* (E, 1982) are examples of remarkable serial contributions to labour history.

For consumption patterns, see G. T. Murray, *Scotland, the New Future* (G, 1973). On Scotland as a 'problem region', see G. McCrone, *Regional Policy in Britain* (L, 1969), C. H. Lee, *Regional Economic Growth in the United Kingdom since the 1880s* (L, 1971), B. E. Coates and E. M. Rawstron, *Regional Variations in Britain* (L, 1971), and Manners et al., *Regional Development in Britain* (New York, 1972). Two key Scottish Council: Development and Industry (SCDI) reports are J. N. Toothill et al., *The Scottish Economy* (E, 1961) and *Oceanspan* (E, 1970/73); in between comes Labour's ill-fated *Plan for Scotland, 1965–1970* (L, 1966), with its various regional accompaniments; a good commentary is R. Saville, ed., *The Economic Development of Modern Scotland 1950–80* (E, 1985). For individual industries: coal, see W. Ashworth, *The History of the British Coal Industry*, Vol. 5., *1946–82* (O, 1986); textiles, see J. Butt and K. Ponting, eds, *Scottish Textile History* (A, 1987) and W. S. Howe, *The Dundee Textile Industries 1960–77* (A, 1983); oil, see D. G. Mackay and G. A. McKay, *The Political Economy of North Sea Oil* (O, 1975), *SCDI, Oil and Scotland's Future* (E, 1973) in the perspective of C. Harvie, *Fool's Gold* (L, 1994). For the HIDB, see James Grassie, *Highland Experiment* (A, 1984).

For the 1979–97 period, see C. Lythe and M. Majumdar, *The Renaissance of the Scottish Economy* (L, 1982), N. Hood and S. Young, *Multinationalism in Retreat* (E, 1982) and Neil K. Buxton, *Scotland in a Rapidly-Changing World* (E, 1986). C. H. Lee, *Scotland and the United*

Kingdom (M, 1995); Foster, Woolfson and Beck, *Paying for the Piper* (L, 1996); P. Payne, *The Hydro* (A, 1988); Scottish Trades Union Congress, *Scotland: a Land for People* (G, 1987).

G   *Society*: Halsey, *TBS*, the *TSA*, and the regional plans of the 1940s and 1960s contain uneven amounts of data. Compare J. Littlejohn, Westrigg: *The Sociology of a Cheviot Parish* (L, 1964) (Eskdalemuir c. 1940–55), with R. Frankenberg, *Communities in Britain* (L, 1966); an urban equivalent is G. Hutton, ed., *Social Environment in Suburban Edinburgh* (York, 1975). See also the surveys of Glasgow school-leavers by T. Ferguson and J. Cunnison, *The Young Wage-Earner* (L, 1951), *In their Early Twenties* (L, 1956).

Specific subject areas: *Housing*: W. M. Ballantine, *Rebuilding a Nation* (E, 1944), D. Niven, *Scottish Housing* (1979), T. Begg, *50 Special Years* (G, 1987), *The History of the Scottish Special Housing Association* (E, 1978), *The Cullingworth Report* (E, 1967), A. Sutcliffe, ed., *Multi-Storey Living* (1974). *Food*: Boyd Orr, *Food, Health and Income* (1936) is basic; see also D. J. Robertson, 'Consumption' in *SE* and McCrone, SEP. *Health*: R. Levitt in *The Reorganised National Health Service* (1976) has a historical introduction, followed up by D. Hamilton, *The Healers: A History of Medicine in Scotland* (E, 1982) and G. McLachlan, ed., *Improving the Common Wealth: Scottish Health Services, 1900–84* (E, 1987); see also T. T. Paterson in *SE* and the *SA* volumes. R. M. Titmuss, *Problems of Social Policy* (L, 1950) has information on wartime developments. *Unemployment and poverty*: *The Scottish Poor Law Magazine* lasted until 1929; after 1935, the *AR* of the Unemployment Assistance Board; see also W. Hannington, *The Problem of the Distressed Areas* (L, 1937). I. Levitt, *Poverty and Welfare in Scotland, 1890–1948* (E, 1988) and G. Brown and R. Cook, eds, *Scotland, the Real Divide* (E, 1983), and J. Cameron, *Prisons and Punishment in Scotland* (E, 1983).

Education: The *AR* of the *Scottish Education Department*; J. Scotland, *The History of Scottish Education* (L, 1970) and R. M. Knox, *250 Years of Scottish Education* (E, 1953) and *Studies in the History of Scottish Education* (1970), W. Humes and H. Paterson, eds, *Scottish Culture and Scottish Education* (E, 1983), A. MacPherson, *The Leadership Class in Scottish Education* (E, 1986) and A. MacPherson and C. Raab, *Governing Education* (E, 1988). A. S. Neill and R. F. Mackenzie's books provide a dissenting commentary.

Religion: AR of the *Church of Scotland* and various special reports, particularly *God's Will for Church and Nation* (Edinburgh, 1943) are basic, as is the *Scottish Catholic Yearbook*, J. Highet, *The Scottish Churches* (L, 1960), C. Brown, *The Social History of Religion in Scotland* (L, 1987), W. Storrar, *Scottish Identity: a Christian Vision* (E, 1990) and D. Forrester, *Churches and the Political Process in Scotland Today* (E, 1989). Clerical memoirs proliferate; the most useful is A. Muir, *John White* (L, 1960). For religious populism, see S. Bruce, *Militant Protestantism and Modern Scotland* (E, 1986), T. Gallagher and G. Walker, eds, *Sermons and Battle Hymns* (E, 1991) and W. Marshall, *The Billy Boys* (E, 1996).

'No Gods and Precious Few *Women*' was a fair comment; proper recompense will have to wait until after the Millennium, but until then there are *Uncharted Lives: Scottish Women's Experience, 1850–1982* (G, 1984); E. King, *The Thenew Factor* (E, 1993); L. Leneman, *A Guid Cause: The Women's Suffrage Movement in Scotland* (A, 1991); Woman's Claim of Right Group, *A Woman's Claim of Right in Scotland* (E, 1991).

Urban life: G. Gordon, ed., *Perspectives of the Scottish City* (A, 1986), with B. Dicks, *Scottish Urban History* (A, 1983). B. Aspinwall, *Portable Utopia: Glasgow and the United States* (A, 1982). R. Duncan, *Steelopolis: The Making of Motherwell, 1750–1939* (Motherwell, 1991) is only one of a number of good recent histories of industrial towns. For Glasgow, see I. Spring, *Phantom Village* (E, 1989), M. Keating, *The City that Refused to Die* (A, 1988), G. Jarvie and G. Walker, eds, *Ninety-Minute Patriots?* (E, 1993), B. Murray, *The Old Firm, Sectarianism, Sport and Society* (E, 1985).

Oral and other histories worth consulting are B. Kay, *Scots: The Mither Tongue* (E, 1986) and *Odyssey* (G, 1986–8), I. MacDougall, *Voices from the Hunger Marches* (E, 1990), D. Forman, *Son of Adam* (L, 1990), D. Thomson, *Nairn in Darkness and Light* (L, 1987).

H   *Politics and Government*: When S. B. Chrimes, ed., *The General Election in Glasgow, 1950* (G, 1951) came out it was unique until I. Budge and D. W. Urwin, *Scottish Political Behaviour* (L, 1966). But in the last decade there have been I. Hutchinson, *A Political History of Scotland, 1832–1924* (E, 1986), M. Fry, *Patronage and Principle* (A, 1987), J. Mitchell, *Conservatives and the Union* (E, 1990), G. Warner, *History of the Scottish Tory Party* (L, 1988), I. Donnachie et al., *Forward. 100 Years of Labour Politics in Scotland* (E, 1988); in its turn this is being replaced by W. Kenefick and A. McIvor, eds, *Roots of Red Clydeside 1910–1914?* (E, 1996), I. McLean, *The Legend of Red Clydeside* (E, 1982), J. Holford, *Reshaping Labour: Edinburgh in the Great War and After* (Beckenham, 1987). There is no history of Scottish Liberalism, but see R. Douglas, *The History of the Liberal Party, 1895–1970* (L, 1971). R. K. Middlemass, *The Clydesiders* (L, 1965) and B. Pimlott, *The Left in the Thirties* (C, 1977) can be read along with two studies of *The General Strike* (both L, 1976), ed. respectively by M. Morris and J. Skelley.

For nationalism, W. L. Miller, *The End of British Politics: Scots and English Political Behaviour in the Seventies* (O, 1981) gives a framework confirmed by events; in addition see J. Brand, *The National Movement in Scotland* (L, 1978), K. Webb, *The Rise of Nationalism in Scotland* (L, 1977), and H. Hanham *Scottish Nationalism* (L, 1968), M. Keating and D. Bleiman, *Labour and Scottish Nationalism* (L, 1979), R. Finlay, *Independent and Free* (E, 1994), H. Drucker and G. Brown, *Devolution and Nationalism* (E, 1982), L. Paterson, *The Autonomy of Modern Scotland* (E, 1994), T. Nairn, *Auld Enemies* (G, 1992), J. Mitchell, *Strategies for Self-government* (E, 1996).

M. Spaven, *Fortress Scotland* (1983), D. Graham and P. Clarke, *The New Enlightenment* (L, 1985); and there are any number of autobiographies (a) and memoirs (b) with Scots material. I simply list the more important names: H. H. Asquith (ab), J. M. Bannerman (b), Balfour of Burleigh (b), Winston Churchill (b), James Clunie (a), Hugh Dalton (a), Walter Elliot (b), William Gallacher (a), William Graham (b), Jo Grimond (a), Lord Home (ab), Tom Johnston (ab), Jennie Lee (a), John MacCormick (a), Ramsay Macdonald (b), J. MacGovern (a), John Maclean (b), Harold Macmillan (ab), Harry McShane (a), James Maxton (b), Abe Moffat (a), Robert Munro (a), Lord Boyd Orr (a), Lord Pentland (b), Jimmie Reid (a), John Reith (ab), Lord Rosebery (b), Donald Stewart (a), James Stuart (a), William Wolfe (a).

D. Glen, ed., *Whither Scotland* (L, 1971) and N. MacCormick, ed., *The Scottish Debate* (O, 1970) prefaced the exciting but frustrating 1970s. See *YSB* and *SA*, and also H. Drucker, *Breakaway. The Scottish Labour Party* (E, 1978), T. Dalyell, *Devolution: The End of Britain* (L, 1977), and A. Macartney and D. Denver, eds, *Yes or No: The Devolution Referendum* (A, 1981). Post-débâcle came O. D. Edwards, ed., *A Claim of Right for Scotland* (E, 1988), T. Gallagher, ed., *Nationalism in the Nineties* (E, 1991) and R. Levy, *Scottish Nationalism at the Crossroads* (E, 1990), summed up elegantly by A. Marr, *The Battle for Scotland* (L, 1992), and A. Clements, K. Farquharson and K. Wark, *Restless Nation* (E, 1996).

Administration: see Kellas, *SPS*, and Hanham in *GNS*; G. M. Keating and A. Midwinter, *The Government of Scotland* (E, 1983). G. Pottinger, *The Secretaries of State for Scotland 1926–76* (E, 1978) adds a little inside information; and see J. S. Gibson, *The Thistle and the Crown* (E, 1985), M. Cuthbert ed., *Government Spending in Scotland* (E, 1982), F. Bealey and J. Sewel, *The Politics of Independence* (A, 1981), R. Young, *The Search for Democracy* (Paisley, 1977) about the regional epoch.

I   *Culture*. Too many monographs, so general surveys must suffice. Interpretatively, T. Nairn, *The Breakup of Britain* (L, 1977) offers an important revisionist-Marxist model, criticized by C. Beveridge and R. Turnbull, *The Eclipse of Scottish Culture* (E, 1989) and *Scotland after Enlightenment* (E, 1996), who lean to the idealism of G. Davie, *The Crisis of the Democratic Intellect* (E, 1986). R. Crawford, *Devolving English Literature* (O, 1992) and W. Donaldson, *Popular Literature in Victorian Scotland* (A, 1986) provide a preface to C. Craig, ed., *The History of Scottish Literature, Vol. 4. Twentieth Century* (A, 1987) as essential reading. T. Royle, *Companion to Scottish*

Literature (L, 1983) and R. Watson, *History of Scottish Literature* (L, 1985) provide further background. H. MacDiarmid, *Contemporary Scottish Studies* (1927, E, 1976) is important, and see A. Bold, *Hugh MacDiarmid* (L, 1988), I. Murray and R. Tait, *Ten Modern Scottish Novels* (A, 1985). D. Gifford, *Gibbon and Gunn* (E, 1984) and M. Burgess, ed., *The Other Voice: Scottish Women's Writing Since 1808* (E, 1987) are stimulating general studies. For regional literatures, see D. Hewitt and M. Spiller, *Literature of the North* (A, 1963) and C. Withers, *Gaelic in Scotland, 1689–1981* (E, 1984) and *Gaelic Scotland: The Transformation of a Culture Region* (L, 1988).

In the arts, the Penguin *Buildings of Scotland*, region by region, has been coming out since 1979, and D. Macmillan, *Scottish Art, 1460–1990* (E, 1990) is unsurpassed. For the performing arts, see D. Hutchinson, *The Modern Scottish Theatre* (G, 1977), I. Lockerbie, ed., *Image and Identity: Theatre and Cinema in Scotland and Quebec* (Stirling, 1988), G. Bruce, *Festival in the North* (L, 1977), J. Purser, *Music in Scotland* (E, 1990) and for folk song see H. Henderson, *Alias MacAlias* (E, 1992). Cinema is covered by H. F. Hardy, *John Grierson* (L, 1978), C. MacArthur, *Scotch Reels* (L, 1982) and D. Bruce, *Scotland the Movie* (E, 1996). On organisations, there are G. Bruce, *To Foster and Enrich: The Saltire Society, 1935–85* (E, 1988), *The Charter for the Arts in Scotland* (E, 1993), W. H. McDowell, *BBC Broadcasting in Scotland 1923–1983* (E, 1992); and for critiques see C. Kirkwood, *Vulgar Eloquence* (E, 1989), and C. Harvie, *Cultural Weapons* (E, 1992).

Appendix: Chronological Table 1906–2000

Abbreviations: *E*: election; S: Secretary for Scotland (after 1926 Secretary of State): PM: Prime Minister; RC: Royal Commission.

1906   *E Jan.* Liberal landslide: Campbell-Bannerman PM, John Sinclair S.

1908   Asquith PM: Education (Scotland) Act.

1909   'People's Budget'; crisis with Lords; miners affiliate to Labour Party.

1910   *E Jan., Dec.* Liberals continue in power, Parliament Act.

1911   Scottish Exhibition, Glasgow; Agriculture (Scotland) Act.

1912   RC on Scottish Housing set up. T. P. MacKinnon Wood S. Suffragette and Labour unrest; Scottish Unionist party formed from Conservatives and Liberal Unionists.

1914   Crisis over Irish home rule, outbreak of war (4 Aug).

1915   Coalition government (May); battles of Neuve Chapelle, Loos; Labour unrest on Clyde (autumn).

1916   End of 'Red Clyde' by April; H. Tennant S, July; battle of Somme, July–November; Lloyd George PM (6 December), R. Munro (Coalit. Lib.) S.

1917   Report of RC on housing; Bolshevik revolution in Russia (November).

1918   *E Dec.* Women over 30 get vote; Education (Scotland) Act; Battle of Amiens (August); Armistice (11 Nov); sweeping 'Coalition' (mainly Conservative) majority.

1919   40 Hours Strike (end of Jan.)

1920   Major Labour gains in Glasgow municipal elections; Communist Party of Great Britain formed.

1921   Railways Act; 'Sankey' RC on Coal recommends nationalization; 'Triple Alliance' of miners, railway, and transport workers fails (Nov.).

1922   *E Nov.* Coalition ends; sweeping Labour gains; Unionist govt: Bonar Law PM.

1923   *E Dec.* 'Chamberlain' housing act; Baldwin PM, loses support through protectionist programme; 1st Labour government: Macdonald PM, William Adamson S; BBC begins broadcasting.

1924   *E Oct.* Wheatley housing act; Labour falls; Baldwin PM: Sir J. Gilmour S.

1926   General Strike (2–9 May); miners out until November; Secretary becomes Secretary of State.

1927   Union powers restricted; National Party of Scotland founded.

1928   Women over 21 get vote: Scottish Office reorganized; boards abolished.

1929   *E May.* Fusion of Church of Scotland and UF Church; Local Government (Scotland) Act: parish councils and educational authorities abolished. Labour govt; Macdonald PM, Adamson S. Wall Street Crash (October).

1930   Scottish National Development Council formed.

1931   *E Oct.* Macdonald forms National Government, mainly Cons. (August): Sir Archibald Sinclair (Lib.) S. Comes off gold standard (Sept). Crushes Labour.

1932   Liberals leave government over protection; Sir Geoffrey Collins S. ILP disaffiliates from Labour Party; 'Loyalists' form Scottish Socialist Party (SSP).

1933   Hitler in power (May); Labour takes Glasgow.

1934   Scottish National Party formed; Special Areas Act.

1935   *E Nov.* Rearmament started; National govt win. Baldwin PM.

1936   Walter Elliot (Un.) S; Scottish Economic Committee formed; Abdication Crisis; Spanish Civil War; St Andrew's House opened.

1937   Hillington industrial estate started; Chamberlain PM; Barlow Commission into distribution of industry set up.

1938   Empire Exhibition, Glasgow. Films of Scotland started; John Colville (Un.) S,

1939   3 Sept. war breaks out; evacuation.

1940   Barlow RC reports; Churchill PM (May): Ernest Brown (N. Lib.) S; SSP disbanded.

1941   Tom Johnston (Lab.) S (Feb.); Clydebank blitz (March); Council of State formed (October).

1942   Council of Industry formed (May); Cooper committee into Highland power. Beveridge Report (November).

1943   North of Scotland Hydro Electric Board set up.

1945   *E July.* SNP win Motherwell (Apr); caretaker Unionist government; Lord Rosebery (N. Lib.) S; Labour's big majority; Attlee PM; Joe Westwood S.

1946   Bank of England, civil aviation nationalized; national insurance set up; severe winter brings emergency.

1947   Coal, cables nationalized; Arthur Woodburn S; peacetime conscription introduced; first new-town schemes.

1948   National health service set up; transport nationalized; pound devalued.

1950   *E Feb.* Labour's majority reduced to 5; Hector McNeil S; Korean War breaks out.

1951   *E Oct.* Conservatives win; Churchill PM; J. Stuart S. Festival of Britain.

1953   Coronation of Elizabeth II; Korean War ends. RC on Scottish Affairs reports.

1955   *E May.* Eden PM, wins; STV begins broadcasting.

1956   Suez; Russian invasion of Hungary (Oct.–Nov.); split in CPGB.

1957   Macmillan PM. John Maclay S.

1958   Slump in Scottish industry.

1959   *E Oct.* Macmillan wins, but Scottish voting against govt.

1960   Toothill inquiry begun.

1961   Toothill Report; Beeching Report. Government support for industry increased; steel strip mill and motor industry move to Scotland. Michael Noble S.

1962   Scottish Development Department set up.

1963   Sir Alec Douglas-Home PM; Buchanan Report.

1964   *E Oct.* Labour wins. Wilson PM: W. Ross S.

1965   Highland Development Board set up.

1966   *E March.* Labour majority increased. 'A Plan for Scotland'.

1967   Steel nationalized; Scottish Transport Group set up. SNP wins Hamilton; oil exploration begins. Social Work (Scotland) Act.

1968   SNP successes in local elections. Crowther, later Kilbrandon RC into Constitution set up. Conservatives back devolution; Wheatley report on local government.

1970   *E June.* Conservatives win. Heath PM, Gordon Campbell S; SNP support slumps.

1971   Upper Clyde Shipbuilders crisis.

1972   Scottish Economic Planning Department set up. Local Government (Scotland) Act sets up regions and districts.

1973   Miners' strike: three-day week; Yom Kippur war causes threefold rise in oil price. Kilbrandon Report. Britain joins EEC.

1974   *Es Feb, Oct.* Labour wins narrowly, Wilson PM, Ross S. Big SNP gains. Labour

	promises devolution. Labour wins first regional election.
1975	Scottish Development Agency set up. Referendum confirms EEC membership.
1976	First devolution bill; Callaghan PM; Bruce Millan S.
1977	Bill fails; Lib.–Lab. pact enables new bill in autumn. SNP success in district elections.
1978	Scotland and Wales Act (subject to referendum).
1979	*E May.* Act fails to gain 40 per cent of electorate in referendum. Conservatives win general and Euro *Es.* Thatcher PM: George Younger S. Slump in SNP support.
1980	Labour success in district elections; beginning of steel industry contraction.
1981	Closure of Chrysler car factory, Linwood, and Invergordon aluminium works. Social Democrats leave Labour Party.
1982	*March–June* Falklands War; *May* some Conservative success at regional elections.
1983	*E June.* Alliance makes gains from Conservatives.
1984	*March* Miners' strike begins; *June* Conservatives lose 3 European Parliament seats; Labour gains in district elections include (for the first time) Edinburgh.
1985	*March* Miners' strike ends in defeat for NUM; peak year of oil production; shipyard crisis on Clyde.
1986	Gartcosh steelworks closed. Government reshuffle, Younger becomes M. of Defence. Malcolm Rifkind S.; *May* Heavy Conservative losses in regional elections. Replacement for rates announced. July Commonwealth Games in Edinburgh, largely boycotted.
1987	*E June.* Conservative seats fall from 21 to 10.
1988	Poll tax enacted. *July* Piper Alpha oil platform blows up in North Sea, 167 killed; *November* Jim Sillars elected for SNP at Glasgow Govan; *December* Pan-Am Jumbo jet blown up over Lockerbie, 270 dead.
1989	*March* Constitutional Convention meets in Edinburgh; peaceful revolutions throughout Eastern Europe.
1990	*June* Conservatives lose last European seats; *November* Constitutional Convention reports; Mrs Thatcher overthrown; John Major PM; Malcolm Rifkind becomes M of Transport; Ian Lang S.
1991	*Jan–April* Gulf War, much involvement of Scottish troops; electricity boards sold off; *September* Ravenscraig steelworks: complete closure announced for autumn 1992; *November* Liberal Democrats win Kincardine by-election.
1992	*April E* Conservatives slightly improve their position to 11 seats; sharp fall in Labour support at district elections; *July* Ravenscraig closed; *December* European summit in Edinburgh.
1993	*April* railway privatisation carried. *May* opening of Channel Tunnel.
1994	*May* local elections, Conservative wipeout. Death of John Smith. Tony Blair leader of the Labour Party. *June* European elections; crisis over Brent Spar platform; poll on water privatisation with 97 per cent against.
1995	*July* Government reshuffle, Lang to Board of Trade, Michael Forsyth S.
1996	*March* Dunblane killings; *November* return of Stone of Scone; record oil production.
1997	*E May.* Scotrail franchised to National Express. Labour win. No Conservatives returned. Blair PM, Donald Dewar S; *September* Referenda on Scots parliament 74–26 per cent, on Welsh Assembly, 50.3–49.7 per cent.
1998	Legislation for parliament.
1999	Elections for parliament.
2000	Scottish Parliament in Session.

Index

Holiday Inn Express

J. BECK MOBILE

07 93591 9217

HOME

01340 821 035'

Annie home –
Thurs. 22/7.

23rd/24th/26th July

LE CHIEN
DES
BASKERVILLE

Conan DOYLE

Le chien
des
Baskerville

Traduit de l'anglais par A. de Jassard (1905)

PRÉFACE
LE CHIEN DES BASKERVILLE

Arthur Conan Doyle est né le 22 mai 1859 à Édimbourg, dans une vieille famille catholique. L'un de ses ancêtres a été compagnon de Richard Cœur de Lion (c'est du moins ce qu'il prétendra), son grand-père est un caricaturiste célèbre, son père, l'honorable conservateur des monuments historiques de la ville. Arthur choisit de suivre les cours de la faculté de médecine d'Édimbourg, l'une des plus réputées du monde. Pour payer ses études, il assiste des médecins et surtout, parce que ce lecteur de Stevenson est passionné d'aventures, il s'embarque sur un baleinier comme médecin de bord.

Ainsi, en 1880, découvre-t-il le Grand Nord, et la rude vie de marin. À son retour, il publie ses souvenirs de la campagne de pêche dans un journal londonien ; le directeur de la revue, impressionné par son écriture, lui suggère d'abandonner la médecine pour la littérature et le reportage. Mais Doyle repousse la tentation, et passe ses diplômes. Docteur et chirurgien en titre, il s'embarque à nouveau, à destination de l'Afrique. Mais étant tombé gravement malade, il ne va pas au-delà de Lagos.

Puis, il ouvre un cabinet près de Porsmouth. Ses débuts sont difficiles. Ayant perdu la foi, il a refusé l'aide financière proposée par ses oncles catholiques (il sera toute sa vie un anticlérical farouche). Heureusement, il finit par se faire une clientèle ; c'est ainsi qu'il épouse, en 1885, la sœur aînée de l'un de ses jeunes patients, mort entre ses bras… Le couple aura trois enfants. En

1886, Doyle, qui n'a jamais renoncé à l'écriture et apprécie les histoires criminelles, invente les personnages de Sherlock Holmes et du Dr Watson dans son *Étude en rouge*. Mais le succès n'étant pas au rendez-vous, il se tourne vers le roman historique, avec *La Compagnie blanche*, qui lui apporte un peu de notoriété.

Mariant encore écriture et médecine, il ouvre un nouveau cabinet à Londres. Les patients sont plus rares que les lecteurs ; aussi décide-t-il de se consacrer uniquement aux seconds et de ranger définitivement sa trousse. Pour écrire, il s'enferme pendant plusieurs jours dans son bureau, et en interdit l'accès à ses proches (Simenon fera de même lorsqu'il écrira les aventures du commissaire Maigret) ou s'exile à la campagne pendant des semaines… Il alterne les romans policiers et les romans historiques ; Sherlock Holmes commence à devenir célèbre, si célèbre que, las (et jaloux ?) de son succès, son auteur le fait mourir dans *Le Dernier problème*, en 1892. Les lecteurs s'indignent au point que, deux ans plus tard, Conan Doyle sera contraint de le ressusciter dans *La Maison vide*.

Son épouse ayant contracté la tuberculose, Doyle l'emmène faire des séjours en Suisse. En 1894, l'Amérique lui fait un triomphe, grâce à Sherlock Holmes, qui devient le héros d'une pièce dans laquelle le détective, pourtant célibataire endurci, se marie… Conan Doyle, qui n'a pas participé au scénario, a donné son accord ; la pièce sera joué trente ans sans interruption.

En 1899, à 40 ans, Conan Doyle s'engage comme médecin militaire pour participer à la guerre contre les Boers, en Afrique du Sud : est-ce par pur patriotisme, ou pour fuir la tentation ? Il est en effet amoureux de Jean Leckie, une charmante jeune femme, mais refuse d'être infidèle à son épouse, toujours malade. En Afrique du Sud, il dirige un hôpital et rédige un article sur la guerre ; sa défense de la position britannique (dont l'impérialisme est fortement critiqué sur le continent européen) est si brillante que le roi Édouard VII le nomme chevalier.

Arthur Conan Doyle, désormais *sir*, se présente, sans succès, aux élections à Édimbourg. Battu en 1900 et en 1906, il renonce à mendier le suffrage de ses contemporains, sans pour autant renoncer à ses idées : dans une Angleterre encore fortement victorienne, il défend le divorce, dans une Europe colonialiste, il dénonce l'exploitation de l'Afrique et de ses habitants. Sa première épouse étant morte en 1906, il peut convoler avec Jean Leckie, dix ans après leur première rencontre. C'est un auteur à succès : le président américain Théodore Roosevelt, venu assister aux funérailles d'Édouard VII, demande à le rencontrer.

Devant la montée des périls qui mèneront à la Première Guerre mondiale, il prône une alliance avec la France contre l'Allemagne. Ses propositions — créer un corps de sous-mariniers, installer des canots pneumatiques sur les navires de guerre… — sont considérées par les militaires comme les aimables inventions d'un romancier trop imaginatif ! En 1914, toujours patriote, sir Arthur veut s'engager dans l'armée, mais cet honneur lui est refusé : il a 55 ans. Il se console en allant effectuer des reportages sur le front italien. Son fils Kingsley mourra sur le front dans les derniers jours du conflit. Il lui rendra hommage, ainsi qu'à tous les combattants britanniques, dans son *Histoire de la Grande Guerre*, qui fera un triomphe en librairie.

Ce va-t-en-guerre au grand cœur lutte aussi contre l'injustice au sein de son propre pays : pour avoir fait campagne afin d'obtenir la grâce d'un terroriste irlandais (son ami Kipling refusera de s'y associer), il ne sera jamais pair du royaume ; mais il est comme Sherlock Holmes : la gloire, il s'en moque. En 1928 cependant, deux ans avant sa mort, il aura la satisfaction de faire casser le procès qui avait condamné un innocent (mais le vrai coupable ne sera jamais retrouvé, et les journalistes ne manqueront pas de déplorer l'absence de Sherlock Holmes).

Esprit curieux, il s'intéresse à tout, et, comme Victor Hugo, s'adonne au spiritisme. Il en préside même un congrès international à Paris, en 1925. C'est en rentrant d'un voyage en Scandinavie, en 1929, qu'il est victime d'une première attaque d'apoplexie. Pendant sa convalescence, il apprend à peindre. Mais il n'explosera jamais : une nouvelle et définitive attaque l'emporte le 6 juillet 1930, assis dans son fauteuil, car ce *gentleman* avait refusé de s'aliter..

I

M. SHERLOCK HOLMES

Ce matin-là, M. Sherlock Holmes qui, sauf les cas assez fréquents où il passait les nuits, se levait tard, était assis devant la table de la salle à manger. Je me tenais près de la cheminée, examinant la canne que notre visiteur de la veille avait oubliée. C'était un joli bâton, solide, terminé par une boule — ce qu'on est convenu d'appeler, « une permission de minuit ».

Immédiatement au-dessous de la pomme, un cercle d'or, large de deux centimètres, portait l'inscription et la date suivantes : « A M. James Mortimer, ses amis du C. C. H. — 1884. »

Cette canne, digne, grave, rassurante, ressemblait à celles dont se servent les médecins « vieux jeu ».

« Eh bien, Watson, me dit Holmes, quelles conclusions en tirez-vous ? »

Holmes me tournait le dos et rien ne pouvait lui indiquer mon genre d'occupation.

« Comment savez-vous ce que je fais ? Je crois vraiment que vous avez des yeux derrière la tête.

— Non ; mais j'ai, en face de moi, une cafetière en argent, polie comme un miroir. Allons, Watson, communiquez-moi les réflexions que vous suggère l'examen de cette canne. Nous avons eu la malchance de manquer hier son propriétaire et, puisque nous ignorons le but de sa visite, ce morceau de bois acquiert une certaine importance.

— Je pense, répondis-je, suivant de mon mieux la méthode de mon compagnon, que le docteur Mortimer doit être quelque vieux médecin, très occupé et très estimé, puisque ceux qui le connaissent lui ont donné ce témoignage de sympathie.

— Bien, approuva Holmes… très bien !

— Je pense également qu'il y a de grandes probabilités pour que le docteur Mortimer soit un médecin de campagne qui visite la plupart du temps ses malades à pied.

— Pourquoi ?

— Parce que cette canne, fort jolie quand elle était neuve, m'apparaît tellement usée que je ne la vois pas entre les mains d'un médecin de ville. L'usure du bout en fer témoigne de longs services.

— Parfaitement exact ! approuva Holmes.

— Et puis, il y a encore ces mots : « Ses amis du C.C.H. » Je devine qu'il s'agit d'une société de chasse… Le docteur aura soigné quelques-uns de ses membres qui, en reconnaissance, lui auront offert ce petit cadeau.

— En vérité, Watson, vous vous surpassez, fit Holmes, en reculant sa chaise pour allumer une cigarette. Je dois avouer que, dans tous les rapports que vous avez bien voulu rédiger sur mes humbles travaux, vous ne vous êtes pas assez rendu justice. Vous n'êtes peut-être pas lumineux par vous-même ; mais je vous tiens pour un excellent conducteur de lumière. Il existe des gens qui, sans avoir du génie, possèdent le talent de le stimuler chez autrui. Je confesse, mon cher ami, que je suis votre obligé. »

Auparavant, Holmes ne m'avait jamais parlé ainsi. Ces paroles me firent le plus grand plaisir, car, jusqu'alors, son indifférence aussi bien pour mon admiration que pour mes efforts tentés en vue de vulgariser ses méthodes, m'avait vexé. De plus, j'étais fier de m'être assimilé son système au point de mériter son approbation quand il m'arrivait de l'appliquer.

Holmes me prit la canne des mains et l'examina à son tour pendant quelques minutes. Puis, soudainement intéressé, il posa sa cigarette, se rapprocha de la fenêtre et la regarda de nouveau avec une loupe.

« Intéressant, quoique élémentaire, fit-il, en retournant s'asseoir sur le canapé, dans son coin de prédilection. J'aperçois sur cette canne une ou deux indications qui nous conduisent à des inductions.

— Quelque chose m'aurait-il échappé ? dis-je d'un air important. Je ne crois pas avoir négligé de détail essentiel.

— Je crains, mon cher Watson, que la plupart de vos conclusions ne soient erronées. Quand je prétendais que vous me stimuliez, cela signifiait qu'en relevant vos erreurs j'étais accidentellement amené à découvrir la vérité… Oh ! dans l'espèce, vous ne vous trompez pas complètement. L'homme est certainement un médecin de campagne… et il marche beaucoup.

— J'avais donc raison.

— Oui, pour cela.

— Mais c'est tout ?

— Non, non, mon cher Watson… pas tout — tant s'en faut. J'estime, par exemple, qu'un cadeau fait à un docteur s'explique mieux venant d'un hôpital que d'une société de chasse. Aussi, lorsque les initiales « C.C. » sont placées avant celle désignant cet hôpital, les mots « Charing Cross » s'imposent tout naturellement.

— Peut-être.

— Des probabilités sont en faveur de mon explication. Et, si nous acceptons cette hypothèse, nous avons une nouvelle base qui nous permet de reconstituer la personnalité de notre visiteur inconnu.

— Alors, en supposant que C.C.H. signifie « Charing Cross Hospital », quelles autres conséquences en déduirons-nous ?

— Vous ne les trouvez-pas ?… Vous connaissez ma méthode… Appliquez-la !

— La seule conclusion évidente est que notre homme pratiquait la médecine à la ville avant de l'exercer à la campagne.

— Nous devons aller plus loin dans nos suppositions. Suivez cette piste. À quelle occasion est-il le plus probable qu'on ait offert ce cadeau ? Quand les amis du docteur Mortimer se seraient-ils cotisés pour lui donner un souvenir ? Certainement au moment où il quittait l'hôpital pour s'établir… Nous savons qu'il y a eu un cadeau... Nous croyons qu'il y a eu passage d'un service d'hôpital à l'exercice de la médecine dans une commune rurale. Dans ce cas, est-il téméraire d'avancer que ce cadeau a eu lieu à l'occasion de ce changement de situation ?

— Cela semble très plausible.

— Maintenant vous remarquerez que le docteur Mortimer ne devait pas appartenir au service régulier de l'hôpital. On n'accorde ces emplois qu'aux premiers médecins de Londres — et ceux-là ne vont jamais exercer à la campagne. Qu'était-il alors ? Un médecin auxiliaire... Il est parti, il y a cinq ans... lisez la date sur la canne. Ainsi votre médecin, grave, entre deux âges, s'évanouit en fumée, mon cher Watson, et, à sa place, nous voyons apparaître un garçon de trente ans, aimable, modeste, distrait et possesseur d'un chien que je dépeindrai vaguement plus grand qu'un terrier et plus petit qu'un mastiff. »

Je souris d'un air incrédule, tandis que Holmes se renversait sur le canapé, en lançant au plafond quelques bouffées de fumée.

« Je ne puis contrôler cette dernière assertion, dis-je ; mais rien n'est plus facile que de nous procurer certains renseignements sur l'âge et les antécédents professionnels de notre inconnu. »

Je pris sur un rayon de la bibliothèque l'annuaire médical et je courus à la lettre M. J'y trouvai plusieurs Mortimer. Un seul pouvait être notre visiteur.

Je lus à haute voix :

— « Mortimer, James, M.R.C.S.[1], 1882 ; Grimpen, Dartmoor, Devon. Interne de 1882 à 1884 à l'hôpital de Charing Cross. Lauréat du prix Jackson pour une étude de pathologie comparée, intitulée : "L'hérédité est-elle une maladie ?" Membre correspondant de la Société pathologique suédoise. Auteur de "Quelques caprices de l'atavisme" *(The Lancet, 1882)*, "Progressons-nous ?" *(Journal de Pathologie, 1883)*. Médecin autorisé pour les paroisses de Grimpen, Thornsley et High Barrow. »

— Hé ! Watson, il n'est nullement question de société de chasse, fit Holmes avec un sourire narquois ; mais bien d'un

---

1. *Member of royal college Surgeons.* (Membre du collège royal des chirurgiens.)

médecin de campagne, ainsi que vous l'aviez finement pronostiqué, d'ailleurs. Mes déductions se confirment. Quant aux qualificatifs dont je me suis servi, j'ai dit, si je me souviens bien : aimable, modeste et distrait. Or, on ne fait de cadeaux qu'aux gens aimables ; un modeste seul abandonne Londres pour se retirer à la campagne et il n'y a qu'un distrait pour laisser sa canne au lieu de sa carte de visite, après une attente d'une heure dans notre salon.

— Et le chien ? repris-je.

— Le chien porte ordinairement la canne de son maître. Comme elle est lourde, il la tient par le milieu, fortement. Regardez la marque de ses crocs ! Elle vous indiquera que la mâchoire est trop large pour que le chien appartienne à la race des terriers et trop étroite pour qu'on le range dans celle des mastiffs. C'est peut-être… oui, parbleu ! *c'est* un épagneul ! »

Tout en parlant, Holmes s'était levé et arpentait la pièce. Il s'arrêta devant la fenêtre. Sa voix avait un tel accent de conviction que la surprise me fit lever la tête.

« Comment, mon cher ami, dis-je, pouvez-vous affirmer cela ?

— Pour la raison bien simple que j'aperçois le chien à notre porte et que voilà le coup de sonnette de son maître… Restez, Watson ; le docteur Mortimer est un de vos confrères, votre présence me sera peut-être utile… Que vient demander le docteur Mortimer, homme de science, à Sherlock Holmes, le spécialiste en matière criminelle ?… Entrez ! »

M'attendant à voir le type du médecin de campagne que j'avais dépeint, l'apparition de notre visiteur me causa une vive surprise. Le docteur Mortimer était grand, mince, avec un long nez crochu qui débordait entre deux yeux gris, perçants, rapprochés l'un de l'autre et étincelants derrière des lunettes d'or. Il portait le costume traditionnel — mais quelque peu négligé — adopté par ceux de sa profession ; sa redingote était de couleur sombre et son pantalon frangé. Quoique jeune, son dos se voûtait déjà : il marchait la tête penchée en avant et son visage respirait un air de grande bonhomie.

En entrant, il aperçut sa canne dans les mains de Holmes et il se précipita avec une expression joyeuse :

« Quel bonheur ! fit-il. Je ne me souvenais plus où je l'avais laissée… Je ne voudrais pas perdre cette canne pour tout l'or du monde.

— Un cadeau, n'est-ce pas ? interrogea Holmes.

— Oui monsieur.

— De l'hôpital de Charing Cross ?

— De quelques amis que j'y comptais… à l'occasion de mon mariage.

— Ah ! fichtre ! c'est ennuyeux, répliqua Holmes ? en secouant la tête. »

Le docteur Mortimer, légèrement étonné, cligna les yeux.

« Qu'y a-t-il d'ennuyeux ?

— Vous avez dérangé nos petites déductions… Vous dites : votre mariage ?

— Oui. Pour me marier, j'ai quitté l'hôpital… Je désirais me créer un intérieur.

— Allons, fit Holmes, après tout, nous ne nous sommes pas trompés de beaucoup… Et maintenant, docteur Mortimer…

— Non, monsieur ! M. Mortimer, tout bonnement !… Un humble M.R.C.S.

— Et, évidemment, un homme d'un esprit pratique.

— Oh ! un simple *minus habens*, un ramasseur de coquilles sur le rivage du grand océan inconnu de la science. C'est à M. Sherlock Holmes que je parle ?…

— Oui ; et voici mon ami, le docteur Watson.

— Très heureux de faire votre connaissance, monsieur. J'ai souvent entendu prononcer votre nom avec celui de votre ami. Vous m'intéressez vivement ? monsieur Holmes. J'ai rarement vu un crâne aussi dolichocéphalique que le vôtre, ni des bosses supra-orbitales aussi développées. Voulez-vous me permettre de promener mon doigt sur votre suture pariétale ? Un moulage de votre crâne, monsieur, en attendant la pièce originale, ferait l'ornement d'un musée d'anthropologie. Loin de moi toute pensée macabre ! Mais je convoite votre crâne. »

Holmes montra une chaise à cet étrange visiteur.

« Vous êtes un enthousiaste de votre profession, comme je le suis de la mienne, dit-il. Je devine à votre index que vous fumez la cigarette... ne vous gênez pas pour en allumer une. »

Notre homme sortit de sa poche du papier et du tabac, et roula une cigarette avec une surprenante dextérité. Il avait de longs doigts, aussi agiles et aussi mobiles que les antennes d'un insecte.

Holmes demeurait silencieux ; mais ses regards, obstinément fixés sur notre singulier compagnon, me prouvaient à quel point celui-ci l'intéressait.

Enfin Holmes parla.

« Je présume, monsieur, dit-il, que ce n'est pas seulement pour examiner mon crâne que vous m'avez fait l'honneur de venir me voir hier et de revenir aujourd'hui ?

— Non, monsieur, non... bien que je me réjouisse de cet examen. Je suis venu, monsieur Holmes, parce que je reconnais que je ne suis pas un homme pratique et ensuite parce que les circonstances m'ont placé en face d'un problème aussi grave que mystérieux. Je vous considère comme le second parmi les plus habiles experts de l'Europe...

— Vraiment ! Puis-je vous demander le nom de celui que vous mettez en première ligne ? fit Holmes avec un peu d'amertume.

— L'œuvre de M. Bertillon doit fort impressionner l'esprit de tout homme amoureux de précision scientifique.

— Alors, pourquoi ne le consultez-vous pas ?

— J'ai parlé de précision scientifique. Mais, en ce qui concerne la science pratique, il n'y a que vous... J'espère, monsieur, que je n'ai pas involontairement...

— Un peu, interrompit Holmes. Il me semble, docteur, que, laissant ceci de côté, vous feriez bien de m'expliquer exactement le problème pour la solution duquel vous réclamez mon assistance. »

II

LA MALÉDICTION DES BASKERVILLE

« J'ai dans ma poche un manuscrit, commença le docteur.

— Je l'ai aperçu quand vous êtes entré, dit Holmes.

— Il est très vieux.

— Du XVIII⁰ siècle — à moins qu'il ne soit faux.

— Comment le savez-vous ?

— Pendant que vous parliez, j'en ai entrevu cinq ou six centimètres. Il serait un piètre expert celui qui, après cela, ne pourrait préciser la date d'un document à une dizaine d'année près. Avez-vous lu ma petite monographie sur ce sujet ?… Je place le vôtre en 1730.

— Il est exactement de 1742, répondit Mortimer, en sortant le manuscrit de sa poche. Ces papiers m'ont été confiés par sir Charles Baskerville, dont la mort tragique a causé dernièrement un si grand émoi dans le Devonshire. J'étais à la fois son médecin et son ami. D'un esprit supérieur, pénétrant, pratique, il se montrait aussi peu imaginatif que je le suis beaucoup moi-même. Cependant il ajoutait très sérieusement foi au récit contenu dans ce document, et cette foi le préparait admirablement au genre de mort qui l'a frappé. »

Holmes prit le manuscrit et le déplia sur son genou.

« Vous remarquerez, Watson, me dit-il, que les *s* sont indifféremment longs et courts. C'est une des quelques indications qui m'ont permis de préciser la date. »

Par-dessus son épaule, je regardai le papier jauni et l'écriture presque effacée. En tête, on avait écrit : « *Baskerville Hall* », et, au-dessous, en gros chiffres mal formés : « *1742* ».

« Je vois qu'il s'agit de sortilège, fit Holmes.

— Oui ; c'est la narration d'une légende qui court sur la famille de Baskerville.

— Je croyais que vous désiriez me consulter sur un fait plus moderne et plus précis ?

— Très moderne… et sur un point précis, urgent, qu'il faut élucider dans les vingt-quatre heures. Mais ce manuscrit est court et intimement lié à l'affaire. Avec votre permission, je vais vous le lire. »

Holmes s'enfonça dans son fauteuil, joignit les mains et ferma les yeux, dans une attitude résignée.

Le docteur Mortimer exposa le document à la lumière et lut d'une voix claire et sonore le curieux récit suivant :

« On a parlé souvent du chien des Baskerville. Comme je descends en ligne directe de Hugo Baskerville et que je tiens cette histoire de mon père, qui la tenait lui-même du sien, je l'ai écrite avec une conviction sincère en sa véracité. Je voudrais que mes descendants crussent que la même justice qui punit le péché sait aussi le pardonner miséricordieusement, et qu'il n'existe pas de si terrible malédiction qui ne puissent racheter le repentir et les prières. Je voudrais que, pour leur salut, mes petits-enfants apprissent, non pas à redouter les suites du passé, mais à devenir plus circonspects dans l'avenir et à réprouver les détestables passions qui ont valu à notre famille de si douloureuses épreuves.

« Au temps de notre grande révolution, le manoir de Baskerville appartenait à Hugo, de ce nom, homme impie et dissolu. Ses voisins lui auraient pardonné ces défauts, car la contrée n'a jamais produit de saints ; mais sa cruauté et ses débauches étaient devenues proverbiales dans la province.

« Il arriva que Hugo s'éprit d'amour (si, dans ce cas, l'emploi de ce mot ne constitue pas une profanation) pour la fille d'un cultivateur voisin. La demoiselle, réservée et de bonne réputation, l'évitait, effrayée par son mauvais renom.

« Une veille de Saint-Michel, Hugo, de concert avec cinq ou six de ses compagnons de plaisir, se rendit à la ferme et enleva la jeune fille, en l'absence de son père et de ses frères. Ils la conduisirent au château et l'enfermèrent dans un donjon ; puis ils descendirent pour achever la nuit en faisant ripaille, selon leur coutume.

« De sa prison, la pauvre enfant frissonnait, au bruit des chants et des blasphèmes qui montaient jusqu'à elle. Dans sa détresse, elle tenta ce qui aurait fait reculer les plus audacieux : à l'aide du lierre qui garnissait le mur, elle se laissa glisser le long de la gouttière et s'enfuit par la lande vers la maison de son père, distante d'environ trois lieues.

« Quelque temps après, Hugo quitta ses amis pour monter un peu de nourriture à sa prisonnière. Il trouva la cage vide et l'oiseau envolé. Alors, on l'aurait dit possédé du démon. Dégringolant l'escalier, il entra comme un fou dans la salle à manger, sauta sur la table et jura devant toute la compagnie que, si cette nuit même il pouvait s'emparer de nouveau de la fugitive, il se donnerait au diable corps et âme. Tous les convives le regardaient, ahuris. À ce moment l'un d'eux, plus méchant — ou plus ivre — que les autres, proposa de lancer les chiens sur les traces de la jeune fille.

« Hugo sortit du château, ordonna aux valets d'écurie de seller sa jument, aux piqueurs de lâcher la meute et, après avoir jeté aux chiens un mouchoir de la prisonnière, il les mit sur le pied. L'homme, en jurant, les bêtes, en hurlant, dévalèrent vers la plaine, sous la clarté morne de la lune.

« Tout ceci s'était accompli si rapidement que, tout d'abord, les convives ne comprirent pas. Mais bientôt la lumière se fit dans leur esprit. Ce fut alors un vacarme infernal ; les uns demandaient leurs pistolets, les autres leur cheval, ceux-ci de nouvelles bouteilles de vin. Enfin, le calme rétabli, la poursuite commença. Les chevaux couraient ventre à terre sur la route que la jeune fille avait dû prendre pour rentrer directement chez elle.

« Les amis de Hugo galopaient depuis deux kilomètres, quand ils rencontrèrent un berger qui faisait paître son troupeau sur la lande. En passant, ils lui crièrent s'il avait vu la bête de chasse. On raconte que la peur empêcha l'homme de répondre immédiatement. Cependant il finit par dire qu'il avait aperçu l'infortunée jeune fille poursuivie par les chiens.

« — J'ai vu plus que cela, ajouta-t-il ; j'ai vu galoper en silence, sur les talons du sire de Baskerville, un grand chien noir, que je prie le ciel de ne jamais découpler sur moi. »

« Les ivrognes envoyèrent le berger à tous les diables et continuèrent leur course.

« Mais le sang se figea bientôt dans leurs veines. Le galop d'un cheval résonna sur la lande et la jument de Hugo, toute blanche d'écume, passa près d'eux, les rênes flottantes, la selle vide.

« Dominés par la peur, les cavaliers se serrèrent les uns contre les autres ; mais ils ne cessèrent pas la poursuite, quoique chacun, s'il eût été seul, eût volontiers tourné bride.

« Ils arrivèrent sur les chiens. La meute était réputée pour sa vaillance et ses bonnes qualités de race ; cependant les chiens hurlaient lugubrement autour d'un buisson poussé sur le bord d'un profond ravin. Quelques-uns faisaient mine de s'éloigner, tandis que d'autres, le poil hérissé, les yeux en fureur, regardaient en bas, dans la vallée.

« La compagnie, complètement dégrisée, s'arrêta. Personne n'osant avancer, les trois plus audacieux descendirent le ravin.

« La lune éclairait faiblement l'étroite vallée formée par le fond de la gorge. Au milieu, la pauvre jeune fille gisait inanimée, à l'endroit où elle était tombée, morte de fatigue ou de peur. Ce ne fut ni son cadavre, ni celui de Hugo, étendu sans mouvement à quelques pas de là, qui effraya le plus les trois sacripants. Ce fut une horrible bête, noire, de grande taille, ressemblant à un chien, mais à un chien ayant des proportions jusqu'alors inconnues.

« La bête tenait ses crocs enfoncés dans la gorge de Hugo. Au moment où les trois hommes s'approchaient, elle arracha un lambeau de chair du cou de Baskerville et tourna vers eux ses prunelles de feu et sa gueule rouge de sang… Le trio, secoué par la peur, s'enfuit en criant.

« On prétend que l'un des trois hommes mourut dans la nuit ; les deux autres restèrent frappés de folie jusqu'à la mort.

« C'est ainsi, mes enfants, que l'on raconte la première apparition du chien qui, depuis cette époque, a, dit-on, si cruellement éprouvé notre famille. J'ai écrit cette histoire, parce que les amplifications et les suppositions inspirent toujours plus de terreur que les choses parfaitement définies.

« Plusieurs membres de la famille, on ne peut le nier, ont péri de mort violente, subite et mystérieuse. Aussi devons-nous confier à l'infinie bonté de la Providence qui punit rarement l'innocent au delà de la troisième ou de la quatrième génération, ainsi qu'il est dit dans l'Écriture sainte.

« Je vous recommande à cette Providence, mes chers enfants, et je vous conseille d'éviter, par mesure de prudence, de traverser la lande aux heures obscures où l'esprit du mal chemine. »

(De Hugo Baskerville à ses fils Roger et John, sous la recommandation expresse de n'en rien dire à leur sœur Élisabeth.)

Lorsque le docteur Mortimer eut achevé sa lecture, il remonta ses lunettes sur son front et regarda Sherlock Holmes. Ce dernier bâilla, jeta le bout de sa cigarette dans le feu et demanda laconiquement :

« Eh bien ?

— Vous ne trouvez pas ce récit intéressant ?

— Si ; pour un amateur de contes de fées. »

Mortimer sortit de sa poche un journal soigneusement plié.

« Maintenant, monsieur Holmes, fit-il, je vais vous lire quelque chose de plus récent. C'est un numéro de la *Devon County Chronicle*, publié le 14 mai de cette année et contenant les détails de la mort de sir Charles Baskerville, survenue quelques jours avant cette date. »

Mon ami prit une attitude moins indifférente. Le docteur rajusta ses lunettes et commença :

« La mort récente de sir Charles Baskerville, désigné comme le candidat probable du parti libéral aux prochaines élections du Mid-Devon, a attristé tout le comté. Quoique sir Charles n'ait résidé à Baskerville Hall que peu de temps, l'amabilité de ses manières et sa grande générosité lui avaient gagné l'affection et le respect de tous ceux qui le connaissaient.

« En ces temps de "nouveaux riches"[1], il est réconfortant de voir des rejetons d'anciennes familles ayant traversé de mauvais

---

1. En français dans le texte.

jours reconstituer leur fortune et restaurer l'antique grandeur de leur maison.

« On sait que sir Charles avait gagné beaucoup d'argent dans l'Afrique du Sud. Plus sage que ceux qui poursuivent leurs spéculations jusqu'à ce que la chance tourne contre eux, il avait réalisé ses bénéfices et était revenu en Angleterre. Il habitait Baskerville depuis deux ans et nourrissait le grandiose projet de reconstruire le château et d'améliorer le domaine, projet que la mort vient d'interrompre. N'ayant pas d'enfants, il voulait que tout le pays profitât de sa fortune, et ils sont nombreux ceux qui déplorent sa fin prématurée. Nous avons souvent relaté dans ces colonnes ses dons généreux à toutes les œuvres charitables du comté.

« L'enquête n'a pu préciser les circonstances qui ont entouré la mort de sir Charles Baskerville ; mais, au moins, elle a dissipé certaines rumeurs engendrées sur la superstition publique.

« Sir Charles était veuf ; il passait pour quelque peu excentrique. Malgré sa fortune considérable, il vivait très simplement. Son personnel domestique consistait en un couple, nommé Barrymore : le mari servant de valet de chambre et la femme, de bonne à tout faire.

« Leur témoignage, confirmé par celui de plusieurs amis, tend à montrer que, depuis quelque temps, la santé de sir Charles était fort ébranlée. Il souffrait de troubles cardiaques se manifestant par des altérations du teint, de la suffocation et des accès de dépression nerveuse. Le docteur Mortimer, ami et médecin du défunt, a témoigné dans le même sens.

« Les faits sont d'une grande simplicité. Tous les soirs, avant de se coucher, sir Charles avait l'habitude de se promener dans la fameuse allée des Ifs, de Baskerville Hall. La déposition des époux Barrymore l'a pleinement établi.

« Le 4 mai, sir Charles fit part de son intention bien arrêtée de partir le lendemain pour Londres. Il donna l'ordre à Barrymore de préparer ses bagages. Le soir, il sortit pour sa promenade nocturne, pendant laquelle il fumait toujours un cigare.

« On ne le vit pas revenir.

« À minuit, Barrymore, trouvant encore ouverte la porte du château, s'alarma et, allumant une lanterne, il se mit à la recherche de son maître.

« Il avait plu dans la journée ; les pas de sir Charles s'étaient imprimés dans l'allée. Au milieu de cette allée, une porte conduit sur la lande. Des empreintes plus profondes indiquaient que sir Charles avait stationné à cet endroit. Ensuite il avait dû reprendre sa marche, car on ne retrouva son cadavre que beaucoup plus loin.

« Il est un point de la déclaration de Barrymore qui reste encore inexplicable : il paraîtrait que la forme des empreintes s'était modifiée à partir du moment où sir Charles Baskerville avait repris sa promenade. Il semble n'avoir plus marché que sur la pointe des pieds.

« Un certain Murphy — un bohémien — se trouvait à cette heure tout près de là, sur la lande ; mais, d'après son propre aveu, il était complètement ivre. Il déclare cependant avoir entendu des cris, sans pouvoir indiquer d'où ils venaient. On n'a découvert sur le corps de sir Charles aucune trace de violence, quoique le rapport du médecin mentionne une convulsion anormale de la face — convulstion telle que le docteur Mortimer s'est refusé tout d'abord à reconnaître dans le cadavre le corps de son ami. On a remarqué fréquemment ce symptôme dans les cas de dyspnée et de mort occasionnée par l'usure du cœur. L'autopsie a corroboré ce diagnostic, et le jury du coroner a rendu un verdict conforme aux conclusions du rapport médical.

« Nous applaudissons à ce résultat. Il est, en effet, de la plus haute importance que l'héritier de sir Charles s'établisse au château et continue l'œuvre de son prédécesseur si tristement interrompue. Si la décision prosaïque du coroner n'avait pas définitivement détruit les histoires romanesques murmurées dans le public à propos de cette mort, on n'aurait pu louer Baskerville Hall.

« L'héritier du défunt — s'il vit encore — est M. Henry Baskerville, fils du plus jeune frère de sir Charles. Les dernières lettres du jeune homme étaient datées d'Amérique ; on a télégraphié dans toutes les directions pour le prévenir de l'héritage qui lui échoit. »

Le docteur Mortimer replia son journal et le replaça dans sa poche.

« Tels sont les faits de notoriété publique, monsieur Holmes, dit-il.

— Je vous remercie, dit Sherlock, d'avoir appelé mon attention sur ce cas, certainement intéressant par quelques points… Ainsi donc cet article résume tout ce que le public connaît ?

— Oui.

— Apprenez-moi maintenant ce qu'il ne connaît pas. »

Holmes se renversa de nouveau dans son fauteuil et son visage reprit son expression grave et impassible.

« En obtempérant à votre désir, fit le docteur Mortimer, qui commençait déjà à donner les signes d'une violente émotion, je vais vous raconter ce que je n'ai confié à personne. Je me suis tu devant le coroner, parce qu'un homme de science y regarde à deux fois avant d'endosser une superstition populaire… Moi aussi, je crois qu'il serait impossible de louer Baskerville Hall, si quelque chose venait en augmenter l'horrible réputation. Pour ces deux raisons, j'en ai dit moins que je n'en savais — il ne pouvait en résulter pratiquement rien de bon. Mais, avec vous, je n'ai plus les mêmes motifs de garder le silence. »

Et Mortimer nous fit le récit suivant :

« La lande est presque inhabitée, et ceux qui vivent dans le voisinage les uns des autres sont étroitement liés ensemble. Voilà la raison de mon intimité avec sir Charles Baskerville. À l'exception de M. Frankland, de Lafter Hall, et de M. Stapleton, le naturaliste, il n'y a pas, à plusieurs milles à la ronde, de gens bien élevés.

« Sir Charles se plaisait dans la retraite, mais sa maladie opéra entre nous un rapprochement qu'un commun amour de la science cimenta rapidement. Il avait apporté du sud de l'Afrique un grand nombre d'observations scientifiques et nous avons passé ensemble plus d'une bonne soirée à discuter l'anatomie comparée du Bushman et du Hottentot.

« Pendant les derniers mois de sa vie, je constatai la surexcitation progressive de son système nerveux. La légende que je viens de vous lire l'obsédait à tel point que rien au monde n'aurait pu l'amener à franchir la nuit la grille du château. Quelque incroyable que cela vous paraisse, il était sincèrement convaincu qu'une terrible fatalité pesait sur sa famille, et, malheureusement, les archives de sa maison étaient peu encourageantes.

« La pensée d'une présence occulte, incessante, le hantait. Bien souvent il me demanda si, au cours de mes sorties nocturnes, je n'avais jamais aperçu d'être fantastique ni entendu d'aboiements de chien. Il renouvela maintes fois cette dernière question — et toujours d'une voix vibrante d'émotion.

« Je me souviens parfaitement d'un incident qui a précédé sa mort de quelques semaines. Un soir, j'arrivai au château en voiture. Par hasard, sir Charles se trouvait sur sa porte. J'étais descendu de mon tilbury et je lui faisais face. Tout à coup ses regards passèrent par-dessus mon épaule et j'y lus aussitôt une expression de terreur. Je me retournai juste à temps pour distinguer confusément, au détour de la route, quelque chose que je pris pour un énorme veau noir.

« Cette apparition émut tellement sir Charles qu'il courut à l'endroit où il avait vu l'animal et qu'il le chercha partout des yeux. Mais la bête avait disparu. Cet incident produisit une déplorable impression sur son esprit.

« Je passai toute la soirée avec lui, et ce fut pour expliquer l'émotion ressentie qu'il confia à ma garde l'écrit que je vous ai lu. Ce petit épisode n'a d'importance que par la tragédie qui a suivi ; sur le moment, je n'y en attachai aucune et je jugeai puérile l'exaltation de mon ami.

« Enfin, sur mes instances, sir Charles se décida à partir pour Londres. Le cœur était atteint, et la constante angoisse qui le poignait — quelque chimérique qu'en fût la cause — avait une répercussion sur ma santé. Je pensais que les distractions de la ville le remettraient promptement. M. Stapleton, consulté, opina dans le même sens.

« Au dernier instant, la terrible catastrophe se produisit.

« La nuit du décès de sir Charles Baskerville, Barrymore, le valet de chambre qui avait fait la lugubre découverte, m'envoya chercher par un homme d'écurie. Je n'étais pas encore couché et, une heure plus tard, j'arrivais au château.

« Je contrôlai tous les faits mentionnés dans l'enquête : je suivis la trace des pas dans l'allée des Ifs et je vis à la grille l'endroit où le défunt s'était arrêté. À partir de cet endroit, je remarquai la nouvelle forme des empreintes. Sur le sable fin, il n'y avait d'autres pas que ceux de Barrymore ; puis j'examinai attentivement le cadavre, auquel on n'avait pas encore touché.

« Sir Charles était étendu, la face contre terre, les bras en croix, les doigts crispés dans le sol et les traits tellement convulsés sous l'empire d'une violente émotion que j'aurais à peine osé certifier son identité.

« Le corps ne portait aucune blessure... Mais la déposition de Barrymore était incomplète. Il a dit qu'auprès du cadavre il n'existait nulle trace de pas... Il n'en avait pas vu... Elles ne m'ont pas échappé, à moi... nettes et fraîches... à quelque distance du lieu de la scène !...

— Des empreintes de pas ?

— Oui, des empreintes de pas.

— D'homme ou de femme ? »

Mortimer nous considéra une seconde d'une façon étrange. Sa voix n'était plus qu'un faible murmure, quand il répondit :

« Monsieur Holmes, j'ai reconnu l'empreinte d'une patte de chien gigantesque ! »

III

LE PROBLÈME

Je confesse que ces mots me causèrent un frisson. Il y avait dans la voix du docteur Mortimer un tremblement qui prouvait que son propre récit l'avait profondément ému.

Penché en avant, Holmes l'écoutait avec, dans les yeux, cette lueur qui décèle toujours chez lui un vif intérêt.

« Vous avez vu cela ? interrogea-t-il.

— Aussi nettement que je vous vois.

— Et vous n'en avez rien dit ?

— Pourquoi en aurais-je parlé ?

— Comment expliquez-vous que vous soyez le seul à avoir remarqué ces empreintes ?

— Elles commençaient seulement à une vingtaine de mètres du cadavre… personne n'y avait fait attention. Si je n'avais pas connu la légende, il est probable que j'aurais agi comme tout le monde.

— Y a-t-il beaucoup de chiens de berger sur la lande ?

— Beaucoup… Mais celui-là n'était pas un chien de berger.

— Vous dites que vous le jugez de grande taille ?

— Énorme.

— Et qu'il n'avait pas approché le cadavre ?

— Non.

— Quelle nuit faisait-il ?

— Humide et froide.

— Pleuvait-il ?

— Non.

— Décrivez-moi l'allée des Ifs.

— Elle est formée par une double rangée de vieux ifs, hauts de douze pieds et absolument impénétrables. On se promène sur la partie comprise entre les arbustes, large de huit pieds.

— Entre les ifs et cette partie, sablée sans doute, n'y a-t-il rien ?

— Si. Il existe, de chaque côté, une bande de gazon d'environ six pieds.

— La bordure d'ifs, m'avez-vous dit, est coupée par une porte ?

— Oui… qui donne accès sur la lande.

— Il n'y a pas d'autre ouverture ?

— Aucune.

— De telle sorte qu'on n'arrive à l'allée des Ifs que par la maison ou par cette porte ?

— On peut également s'y rendre par une serre construite à l'extrémité de l'allée.

— Sir Charles a-t-il poussé sa promenade jusque-là ?

— Non, cinquante mètres le séparaient encore de cette serre.

— Maintenant, voudriez-vous me dire, docteur Mortimer ? — et ce détail a son importance — si les empreintes que vous avez relevées se trouvaient sur le sable de l'allée ou sur le gazon ?

— Je n'ai pu distinguer aucune empreinte sur le gazon.

— Existaient-elles seulement sur le même côté que la porte ?

— Oui, sur le bord de l'allée sablée, du même côté que la porte.

— Vous m'intéressez excessivement... Autre chose, cette porte était-elle fermée ?

— Fermée et cadenassée.

— Quelle est sa hauteur ?

— Quatre pieds.

— Alors, quelqu'un aurait pu la franchir ?

— Facilement.

— Près de la porte, y avait-il des marques particulières ?

— Non.

— Ah !... A-t-on fait des recherches de ce côté ?

— Personne autre que moi.

— Et vous n'avez rien découvert ?

— Sir Charles avait dû piétiner sur place. Évidemment, il était resté en cet endroit cinq ou dix minutes.

— Comment le savez-vous ?

— Parce que, deux fois, les cendres de son cigare se sont détachées.

— Très bien déduit, approuva Holmes. Watson, reprit-il, voici un collègue selon notre cœur... Mais ces marques ?

— Le piétinement les avait rendues confuses. En dehors de l'empreinte des pas de sir Charles, il m'a été impossible d'en distinguer d'autres. »

De sa main, Sherlock Homes frappa son genou dans un geste d'impatience.

« Encore si j'avais été là ! s'écria-t-il. Le cas m'apparaît d'un intérêt palpitant. Cette page de gravier sur laquelle j'aurais pu lire tant de choses, la pluie et le sabot des paysans curieux l'auront faite indéchiffrable. Ah ! docteur Mortimer, pourquoi ne m'avez-vous pas appelé ? Vous êtes bien coupable !

— Je ne pouvais vous appeler, monsieur Holmes, sans révéler tous ces faits, et je vous ai déjà donné les raisons pour lesquelles je désirais garder le silence. D'ailleurs… d'ailleurs…

— Pourquoi cette hésitation ?

— Dans certain domaine, le détective le plus expérimenté et le plus subtil demeure impuissant.

— Insinuez-vous que ces faits appartiennent au domaine surnaturel ?

— Je ne le dis pas positivement.

— Mais vous le pensez évidemment.

— Depuis le drame, monsieur Holmes, on m'a raconté divers incidents qu'il est malaisé de classer parmi les événements naturels.

— Par exemple ?

— J'ai appris qu'avant la terrible nuit plusieurs personnes ont vu sur la lande un animal dont le signalement se rapportait à celui du démon des Baskerville… L'animal ne rentre dans aucune espèce cataloguée. On convient qu'il avait un aspect épouvantable, fantastique, spectral. J'ai questionné ces gens — un paysan obtus, un maréchal ferrant et un fermier. Aucun n'a varié sur le portrait de la sinistre apparition. Elle incarnait bien exactement le chien vomi par l'enfer, d'après la légende. La terreur règne dans le district en souveraine maîtresse, et il pourrait se vanter d'être téméraire celui qui s'aventurerait la nuit sur la lande.

— Et vous, un homme de science, vous admettez une manifestation surnaturelle ?

— Je ne sais que croire. »

Holmes haussa les épaules.

« Jusqu'ici, dit-il, j'ai borné mes investigations aux choses de ce monde. Dans la limite de mes faibles moyens, j'ai combattu le mal… mais ce serait une tâche bien ambitieuse que de s'attaquer au démon lui-même. Cependant, il vous faut bien admettre la matérialité des empreintes !

— Le chien originel était assez matériel pour déchiqueter le cou d'un homme, et néanmoins il était bien d'essence infernale !

— Je vois que vous avez passé aux partisans du surnaturel… Maintenant, répondez encore à ceci : Puisque vous pensez ainsi, pourquoi êtes-vous venu me consulter ? Vous me demandez en même temps de ne pas rechercher les causes de la mort de sir Charles Baskerville et vous me priez de m'occuper de ces recherches.

— Je ne vous en ai pas prié.

— Alors en quoi puis-je vous aider ?

— En m'indiquant l'attitude que je dois garder vis-à-vis de sir Henry Baskerville, qui arrive à Waterloo station — ici le docteur Mortimer tira sa montre — dans une heure un quart.

— Est-ce lui qui hérite ?

— Oui. À la mort de sir Charles, nous avons fait une enquête sur ce jeune homme et nous avons appris qu'il se livrait à l'agriculture, au Canada. Les renseignements fournis sur son compte sont excellents à tous égards… je ne parle pas à cette heure comme le médecin, mais comme l'exécuteur testamentaire de sir Charles Baskerville.

— Il n'y a pas d'autres prétendants à la fortune du défunt, je présume ?

— Pas d'autres, le seul parent dont nous ayons pu retrouver la trace se nomme — ou mieux se nommait Roger Baskerville, il était le troisième frère de sir Charles. Le second frère, mort jeune, n'a eu qu'un fils, Henry ; on considérait le troisième frère, Roger, comme la brebis galeuse de la famille. Il perpétuait l'ancien type des Baskerville et continuait, m'a-t-on affirmé, les errements du vieil Hugo. Le séjour de l'Angleterre lui paraissant malsain, il s'expatria dans l'Amérique centrale, où il mourut de la fièvre jaune ; en 1876, Henry est donc le dernier des Baskerville… Dans une heure cinq minutes, je le rencontrerai à Waterloo station… Il m'a télégraphié de Southampton qu'il arriverait ce matin… Que dois-je faire, monsieur Holmes ?

— Pourquoi n'irait-il pas dans la demeure de ses ancêtres ?

— Cela semble tout naturel, n'est-ce pas ? Et cependant il faut se souvenir que les Baskerville qui ont habité le château ont tous péri de mort violente. J'ai la conviction que, si sir Charles avait pu me parler avant son décès, il m'aurait instamment recommandé de ne pas y conduire le dernier représentant de sa race et l'héritier de sa grande fortune. D'autre part, il est incontestable que la prospérité de ce misérable pays dépend absolument de la présence de sir Henry. Tout le bien commencé par sir Charles sera perdu, si le château reste désert. Je suis venu vous demander un avis, monsieur Holmes, parce que je crains de me laisser entraîner par mon intérêt, trop évident en l'espèce. »

Holmes resta songeur pendant un moment.

Puis il dit :

« En d'autres termes, voici quelle est votre opinion : Vous estimez qu'une influence diabolique rend le séjour de Dartmoor insalubre aux Baskerville. Ai-je bien exprimé votre pensée ?

— Ne suis-je pas fondé à le prétendre ?

— J'en conviens. Mais, si votre théorie sur le surnaturel est exacte, notre jeune homme peut aussi bien en subir les effets à Londres que dans le Devonshire. J'ai peine à admettre un diable dont les pouvoirs s'arrêteraient aux limites d'une paroisse — tout comme ceux d'un conseil de fabrique.

— Vous traiteriez probablement la question plus sérieusement, monsieur Holmes, si vous viviez en contact permanent avec ces choses-là. Ainsi, d'après vous, ce jeune homme ne courrait pas plus de dangers dans le Devonshire qu'à Londres ?... Il arrivera dans cinquante minutes. Que me conseillez-vous de faire ?

— Je vous conseille de prendre un cab, d'appeler votre caniche qui gratte à ma porte d'entrée et d'aller au-devant de sir Henry Baskerville, à Waterloo station.

— Et ensuite ?

— Ensuite vous ne lui direz rien jusqu'à ce que j'aie réfléchi.

— Combien de temps comptez-vous réfléchir ?

— Vingt-quatre heures. Docteur Mortimer, je vous serais très reconnaissant de revenir me voir ici, demain matin, à dix heures. Pour mes dispositions futures, j'aurais besoin que vous ameniez avec vous sir Henry.

— Comptez-y, monsieur Holmes. »

Le docteur Mortimer griffonna le rendez-vous sur sa man-
chette et sortit.

Holmes l'arrêta sur le haut de l'escalier.

« Encore une question, docteur Mortimer. Vous m'avez dit
qu'avant la mort de sir Charles Baskerville plusieurs personnes
avaient aperçu sur la lande l'étrange apparition ?

— Oui ; trois personnes.

— L'a-t-on revue après ?

— Je n'en ai plus entendu parler.

— Merci. Au revoir. »

Holmes retourna s'asseoir avec cet air de satisfaction interne
qui signifiait qu'il entrevoyait une tâche agréable.

« Sortez-vous, Watson ? me demanda-t-il.

— Oui ; à moins que je ne vous sois de quelque utilité.

— Non, mon cher ami, je ne réclame votre concours qu'au
moment d'agir. Savez-vous que cette affaire est superbe, unique
en son genre à certains points de vue… Lorsque vous passerez
devant la boutique de Bradley, priez-le donc de m'envoyer une
livre de son tabac le plus fort… Vous seriez bien aimable de me
laisser seul jusqu'à ce soir… Nous nous communiquerons alors
nos impressions sur le très intéressant problème que nous a soumis ce matin le docteur Mortimer. »

Holmes aimait à s'isoler ainsi pendant les heures de contention
mentale au cours desquelles il pesait le pour et le contre des choses. Il édifiait alors des théories contradictoires, les discutait et
fixait son esprit sur les points essentiels.

Je passai mon après-midi au cercle et ne repris que le soir le
chemin de Baker street.

Il était près de neuf heures, lorsque je me retrouvai assis dans
le salon de Sherlock Holmes.

En ouvrant la porte, ma première impression fut qu'il y avait
le feu à la maison. La fumée obscurcissait tellement la pièce
qu'on voyait à peine la flamme de la lampe placée sur la table.

Je fis quelques pas dans le salon et mes craintes s'apaisèrent
aussitôt : ce n'était que la fumée produite par un tabac grossier.

Elle me saisit à la gorge et me fit tousser.

Enfin, à travers cet épais nuage, je finis par découvrir Holmes, enveloppé dans sa robe de chambre, enfoui dans un large fauteuil et tenant entre ses dents le tuyau d'une pipe en terre très culottée.

Plusieurs rouleaux de papier jonchaient le tapis autour de lui.

« Pris froid, Watson ? dit-il.

— Non… c'est cette atmosphère empoisonnée.

— Elle doit être, en effet, un peu épaisse.

— Épaisse ! Elle est irrespirable !

— Eh bien, ouvrez la fenêtre. Je parie que vous n'avez pas bougé de votre cercle !

— Mon cher Holmes… certainement. Mais comment… »

Sherlock Holmes se moqua de mon ahurissement.

« Vous êtes d'une naïveté délicieuse, fit-il. Cela me réjouit d'exercer à vos dépens les modestes dons que je possède. Voyons, un monsieur auquel on ne connaît pas d'amis intimes sort par un temps pluvieux, boueux… Il revient le soir, immaculé, le chapeau et les bottines aussi luisants que le matin… Qu'en concluriez-vous ? Qu'il a été cloué quelque part toute la journée… N'est-ce pas évident ?

— En effet, c'est plutôt évident.

— Il y a de par le monde une foule de choses évidentes que personne n'observe. Et moi, où croyez-vous que je sois allé ?

— Vous êtes également resté cloué ici.

— Erreur !… J'ai visité le Devonshire.

— Par la pensée ?

— Oui. Mon corps n'a pas quitté ce fauteuil et a consommé en l'absence de ma pensée — j'ai le regret de le constater — la valeur de deux grands bols de café et une incroyable quantité de tabac. Après votre départ, j'ai envoyé chercher à Stamford la carte officielle de la lande de Dartmoor et mon esprit l'a parcourue en tous sens. À cette heure, je me flatte de pouvoir y retrouver mon chemin sans guide.

— Cette carte est donc établie à une grande échelle ?

— Très grande. »

Holmes en déplia une partie qu'il tint ouverte sur ses genoux.

« Voici le district qui nous intéresse, fit-il. Là, au centre, vous apercevez Baskerville Hall.

— Avec cette ceinture de bois ?

— Oui. Bien que l'allée des Ifs ne soit désignée par aucun nom, je jurerais qu'elle s'étend le long de cette ligne, avec la lande à droite. Ici, cet amas de maisons représente le hameau de Grimpen où notre ami, le docteur Mortimer, a installé son quartier général. Constatez que, dans un rayon de six kilomètres, il n'y a que de rares habitations. Voici encore Lafter Hall, dont il est question dans le vieux grimoire. La construction indiquée plus loin doit abriter le naturaliste… Stapleton, si je me souviens bien de son nom. Enfin, j'aperçois deux fermes : High Tor et Foulmire. À quatorze milles de là, se dresse la prison de Princetown. Autour et entre ces quelques maisons se déroule la lande, morne, désolée. C'est là que se passa le drame ; c'est là que nous essayerons de le reconstituer.

— L'endroit est sauvage ?

— Plutôt. Si le diable désirait se mêler des affaires des hommes…

— Ainsi donc, vous aussi, vous penchez vers une intervention surnaturelle ?

— Le diable ne peut-il pas se servir d'agents en chair et en os ?… Dès le début, deux questions se dressent devant nous. La première : Y a-t-il eu crime ? La seconde : Quel est ce crime et comment l'a-t-on commis ? Si les conjectures du docteur Mortimer sont fondées et si nous nous trouvons en présence de forces échappant aux lois ordinaires de la nature, certes le mieux est de ne pas pousser plus loin nos investigations. Mais nous devons épuiser toutes les autres hypothèses, avant de nous arrêter à celle-ci… Nous ferions bien de fermer cette fenêtre, qu'en pensez-vous ? Je reconnais que je suis bizarre, mais il me semble qu'une concentration d'atmosphère favorise toujours une concentration de pensée. Je ne vais pas jusqu'à m'enfermer dans une boîte pour réfléchir… Ce serait cependant la conséquence logique de mes convictions… De votre côté, avez-vous creusé l'affaire ?

— Oui, beaucoup, pendant le courant de la journée.

— Quelle est votre opinion ?

— Je me déclare fort embarrassé.

— Cette affaire ne ressemble pas, en effet, à toutes les autres… Elle en diffère par plusieurs points… Ce changement dans les empreintes de pas, par exemple… Comment l'expliquez-vous ?

— Mortimer dit que sir Charles Baskerville a parcouru une partie de l'allée sur la pointe des pieds.

— Il n'a fait que répéter la déclaration de quelque imbécile au cours de l'enquête. Pourquoi se promènerait-on dans une allée sur la pointe des pieds ?

— Alors ?

— Il courait, Watson !… Sir Charles courait désespérément !… Il courait pour se sauver, jusqu'au moment où la rupture d'un anévrisme l'a jeté la face contre terre.

— Pourquoi fuyait-il ?

— Là gît le problème. Des indices me portent à croire qu'il était déjà terrassé par la peur, avant même de commencer à courir.

— Sur quelles preuves appuyez-vous ce raisonnement ?

— J'admets que la cause de sa peur se trouvait sur la lande. S'il en était ainsi — et cela paraît probable — seul un homme affolé aurait couru en tournant le dos à sa maison, au lieu de se diriger vers elle. Si l'on tient pour véridique le récit du bohémien, sir Charles courait, en appelant au secours, dans la direction où il était le plus improbable qu'il lui en arrivât… Et puis, qu'attendait-il, cette nuit-là ? Pourquoi attendait-il dans l'allée des Ifs plutôt qu'au château ?

— Vous croyez qu'il attendait quelqu'un ?

— Le docteur Mortimer nous a montré un sir Charles Baskerville vieux et infirme. Nous pouvons accepter les promenades vespérales… mais, ce soir-là, le sol était humide et la nuit froide. Est-il admissible qu'il se soit arrêté pendant cinq ou dix minutes, ainsi que le docteur Mortimer, avec une sagacité que je ne lui soupçonnais pas, l'a déduit très logiquement de la chute des cendres de son cigare ?

— Puisqu'il sortait tous les soirs.

— Il ne me paraît pas très vraisemblable qu'il s'attardât tous les soirs à la porte donnant sur la lande. Toutes les dépositions, au contraire, indiquent qu'il évitait cette lande. Or, cette nuit-là, il s'était posté à cet endroit… Il partait le lendemain pour Londres… La chose prend corps, Watson ; elle devient cohérente !… Voulez-vous me passer mon violon ?… Ne pensons plus à cette affaire pour le moment, et attendons la visite du docteur Mortimer et de sir Henry Baskerville. »

IV

SIR HENRY BASKERVILLE

Ce matin-là, nous déjeunâmes de bonne heure.

Sherlock Holmes, en robe de chambre, attendait l'arrivée de nos visiteurs. Ils furent exacts au rendez-vous : dix heures sonnaient à peine, quand on introduisit le docteur Mortimer, suivi du jeune baronnet.

Il pouvait avoir trente ans. Petit, alerte, les yeux noirs, il était très solidement bâti. Il avait des sourcils très fournis qui donnaient à son visage une expression énergique.

Il portait un vêtement complet de couleur rougeâtre. Son teint hâlé attestait de nombreuses années passées au grand air, et cependant le calme de son regard et la tranquille assurance de son maintien dénotaient un homme bien élevé.

« Voici sir Henry Baskerville », dit Mortimer.

— Lui-même, ajouta le jeune homme. Et ce qu'il y a de plus étrange, monsieur Holmes, c'est que, si mon ami ici présent ne m'avait pas proposé de me présenter à vous, je serais venu de mon propre mouvement. Vous aimez les énigmes… Eh bien, j'en ai reçu une, ce matin, qui exige, pour la deviner, plus de temps que je ne puis lui consacrer. »

Holmes s'inclina.

« Veuillez vous asseoir, sir Henry, fit-il. Dois-je comprendre que depuis votre court séjour à Londres, vous avez été l'objet de quelque aventure ?

— Oh ! rien de bien important, monsieur Holmes. Une plaisanterie, si je ne me trompe… cette lettre — mérite-t-elle ce nom ? — qui m'a été remise ce matin. »

Et sir Henry posa une enveloppe sur la table.

Nous nous approchâmes tous pour la regarder.

Le papier était de couleur grisâtre et de qualité commune.

Une main malhabile avait écrit l'adresse suivante : « Sir Henri Baskerville, Northumberland hotel ».

La lettre portait le timbre du bureau de Charing Cross et avait été mise à la poste la veille au soir.

« Qui savait que vous descendiez à Northumberland hotel ? » demanda Holmes en regardant attentivement notre visiteur.

— Personne. Je m'y suis seulement décidé après ma rencontre avec le docteur Mortimer.

— Sans doute M. Mortimer y logeait déjà ?

— Non ; j'étais descendu chez un ami, répondit le docteur. Il était impossible de prévoir que nous irions dans cet hôtel.

— Hum ! fit Sherlock. Quelqu'un me paraît très au courant de vos mouvements ».

Holmes tira de l'enveloppe la moitié d'une feuille de papier écolier pliée en quatre.

Il l'ouvrit et la développa sur la table.

Au milieu, des caractères imprimés, réunis ensemble et collés, formaient une seule phrase.

Elle était ainsi conçue :

« Si vous attachez de la valeur à votre raison ou à votre vie, prenez garde à la lande. »

Seul, le mot « lande », était écrit à la main.

« Peut-être m'apprendrez-vous, monsieur Holmes, dit sir Henry Baskerville, ce que signifie tout cela et quel est l'homme qui s'intéresse tant à moi ?

— Qu'en pensez-vous, docteur Mortimer ? Vous conviendrez, en tout cas, qu'il n'y a là rien de surnaturel.

— J'en conviens, monsieur. Mais cet avis ne peut-il être envoyé par une personne convaincue que nous sommes en présence de faits surnaturels ?

— Quels faits ? demanda vivement sir Henry. Il me semble, messieurs, que vous connaissez mieux mes affaires que je ne les connais moi-même.

— Avant de sortir de cette pièce, répliqua Sherlock Holmes, vous en saurez autant que nous, je vous le promets. Pour le moment — et avec votre permission — nous allons nous renfermer dans l'examen de ce fort intéressant document. Il a été probablement confectionné hier soir et mis à la poste aussitôt. Avez-vous le *Times* d'hier, Watson ?

— Il est là, sur le coin de votre table.

— Ayez l'obligeance de me le passer… la page intérieure, s'il vous plaît… celle qui contient les *leading* articles. »

Holmes parcourut rapidement les colonnes du journal de la Cité.

« Le principal article traite la question de la liberté de commerce, fit-il. Permettez-moi de vous en lire un passage :

« C'est un leurre de croire que les tarifs "protecteurs encouragent votre commerce" et votre industrie nationale. Si vous "attachez de la valeur à vos importations, prenez garde à une trop longue application de cette législation, qui aura vite abaissé les conditions générales de la vie dans cette île… La raison vous en "démontrera tout le danger."

« Quel est votre avis sur ceci, Watson ? » s'écria joyeusement Holmes, en se frottant les mains, avec une satisfaction manifeste.

Le docteur Mortimer considéra Holmes avec un air d'intérêt professionnel, tandis que sir Henry tourna vers moi des regards étonnés.

« Je n'entends pas grand'chose aux questions de tarifs et d'économie politique, dit ce dernier. D'ailleurs il me semble que cette lettre nous a un peu détournés de notre sujet.

— Au contraire, sir Henry, je crois que nous y sommes en plein. Watson est plus initié que vous à ma méthode, et cependant je crains qu'il n'ait pas saisi l'importance de cette citation.

— Non, répliquai-je, je ne vois pas quel rapport…

— Il en existe un — et très intime. *« Vous »*, *« votre »*, *« votre »*, *« vie »*, *« raison »*, *« attachez de la valeur »*, *« prenez garde à »*... Comprenez-vous maintenant où l'on a pris ces mots ?

— Mais oui ! s'écria sir Henry. C'est très adroit.

— Et s'il me restait un doute, continua Holmes, le seul fait que les mots « *prenez garde* », et « *attachez de la valeur* » sont détachés d'un seul coup de ciseaux le dissiperait ».

— Réellement, monsieur Holmes, ceci dépasse tout ce que j'aurais pu imaginer, dit Mortimer, en examinant mon ami avec stupéfaction. Je comprendrais qu'on eût deviné que ces mots avaient été découpés dans un journal… Mais indiquer lequel et ajouter qu'ils proviennent d'un *leading* article, c'est vraiment étonnant ! Comment l'avez-vous découvert ?

— Je présume, docteur, que vous savez distinguer le crâne des nègres de celui des Esquimaux ?

— Très certainement.

— Pourquoi ?

— C'est mon métier. Les différences sautent aux yeux… L'os frontal, l'angle facial, la courbe des maxillaires, le…

— Eh bien, le reste est mon métier, à moi ! Les différences me sautent également aux yeux. Je trouve tout autant de dissemblance entre les caractères du *Times* et ceux d'une méchante feuille de chou qu'entre vos nègres et vos Esquimaux. Pouvoir reconnaître les uns des autres les caractères d'imprimerie, voilà la science la plus élémentaire d'un expert en crime. J'avoue néanmoins qu'au temps de ma jeunesse je confondis le *Leeds Mercury* avec les *Western Morning News*. Un premier-Londres du *Times* est absolument reconnaissable, et ces mots ne pouvaient avoir été pris que là. La lettre étant d'hier, il devenait donc presque certain que je les trouverais dans le numéro paru à cette date.

— Ainsi, demanda sir Henry Baskerville, quelqu'un les a découpés avec des ciseaux ?...

— Avec des ciseaux à ongles, précisa Holmes. Remarquez que la lame en était très courte, puisque celui qui les maniait s'y est pris à deux fois pour les mots « prenez garde à » et « attachez de la valeur ».

— En effet. Ainsi quelqu'un a découpé les mots avec de petits ciseaux à ongles et les a fixés ensuite à l'aide de colle…

— Non, de gomme, rectifia Holmes.

—… À l'aide de gomme, sur le papier, continua sir Henry. Expliquez-moi aussi pourquoi le mot « lande » est écrit à la main ?

— Parce que l'article ne le contient pas. Les autres mots sont usuels ; on peut les rencontrer dans tous les journaux plus facilement que « lande » beaucoup moins commun.

— J'accepte votre explication, monsieur Holmes. Avez-vous lu autre chose dans ce message ?

— J'y ai puisé une ou deux indications, bien qu'on ait pris toutes sortes de précautions pour donner le change. Observez que l'adresse — d'une écriture mal formée — est mise à la main. Or, le *Times* est le journal des intelligences cultivées. Nous pouvons en conclure que la lettre a été composée par un homme instruit, qui désirait passer pour quelqu'un qui ne le serait pas. Ensuite les efforts pour déguiser l'écriture suggèrent l'idée que vous connaissez cette écriture ou que vous pourrez la connaître un jour. Vous observerez en outre que les mots ne sont pas collés suivant une ligne droite ; il y en a de placés plus haut que d'autres. « Vie », par exemple, est tout à fait hors de la ligne. Faut-il attribuer ce manque de soin à la négligence du découpeur ou bien à son agitation ou à sa précipitation ? Je penche pour cette dernière interprétation. Ce message était important et vraisemblablement celui qui le composait y apportait toute son attention. Si nous admettons la précipitation, il faut chercher qu'elle en était la cause, car la même lettre jetée à la boîte le matin de bonne heure au lieu du soir, aurait touché quand même sir Henry avant sa sortie de l'hôtel. Le correspondant de sir Henry craignait-il d'être interrompu ?… Et par qui ?

— Nous entrons à présent dans le domaine des hypothèses, fit le docteur Mortimer.

— Disons plutôt, répliqua Holmes, dans le domaine des probabilités… et choisissons la plus vraisemblable. Cela s'appelle appliquer l'imagination à la science. N'avons-nous pas toujours à notre disposition quelque fait matériel pour asseoir nos spécu-

lations ? Vous allez m'accuser encore de me livrer à des hypothèses, mais j'ai la certitude que cette lettre a été écrite dans un
hôtel.

— Qu'est-ce qui vous fait dire cela ? s'écria Mortimer.

— Si vous examiner attentivement cette lettre, vous verrez
que la plume et l'encre laissaient à désirer. La plume a craché
deux fois dans un même mot et elle a couru trois fois à sec dans
l'adresse — courte cependant… La plume était donc mauvaise et
l'encrier contenait peu d'encre. Or, la plume et l'encrier d'un
particulier sont rarement dans cet état, et il est plus rare encore
qu'ils le soient simultanément… Tandis que vous connaissez les
plumes et les encriers d'hôtels ? Aussi je n'hésite pas à dire que
nous devons fouiller les corbeilles à papier des hôtels qui avoisi-
nent Charing Cross, jusqu'à ce que nous ayons retrouvé le
numéro mutilé du *Times*. Grâce à lui, nous mettrons la main sur
l'expéditeur de ce singulier message… Tiens ! tiens !

Holmes avait élevé à la hauteur de ses yeux le papier sur
lequel on avait collé les mots et il l'examinait avec soin.

« Eh bien ? demandai-je.

— Rien, dit-il, en reposant le feuillet sur la table. Ce papier est
tout blanc, sans même de filigrane… Je crois que nous avons tiré
de cette curieuse lettre tous les indices qu'elle pouvait fournir.
Maintenant, sir Henry, vous est-il arrivé quelque chose depuis
votre descente du train ?

— Non, monsieur Holmes… Je ne me souviens pas.

— N'avez-vous pas remarqué que quelqu'un vous ait observé
ou suivi ?

— Il me semble marcher à travers les ténèbres d'un sombre
feuilleton, répondit notre visiteur. Pourquoi diable m'aurait-on
surveillé ou suivi ?

— Ça m'en a tout l'air cependant. N'avez-vous pas autre
chose à nous communiquer, avant que nous entrions dans l'étude
de cette sorte de surveillance qui vous entoure ?

— Cela dépend de ce que vous jugez digne de vous être
communiqué.

— Tout ce qui sort de la marche ordinaire de la vie en vaut la
peine. »

Sir Henry sourit.

« Je ne connais presque rien de la vie anglaise, dit-il, puisque j'ai passé la majeure partie de mon existence aux États-Unis ou au Canada. Je ne pense pas toutefois que la perte d'une bottine soit ici un événement qui sorte de la « marche ordinaire de la vie ».

— Vous avez perdu une de vos bottines ?

— Seulement égaré, intervint Mortimer… Vous la retrouverez en rentrant à l'hôtel. Quelle nécessité d'ennuyer M. Holmes avec de semblables futilités ?

— Il m'a interrogé, je réponds, repartit sir Henry.

— Parfaitement, dit Holmes. Dites-moi tout, quelque négligeables que ces incidents puissent vous paraître. Ainsi, vous avez perdu une bottine ?

— Tout au moins égaré. J'ai placé la paire à la porte de ma chambre, la nuit dernière, et, ce matin, il ne m'en restait plus qu'une. Questionné, le garçon n'a pu me donner aucune explication. Le pire, c'est que je les avais achetées la veille, dans le Strand, et que je ne les avais jamais portées.

— Si vous ne les avez jamais portées pourquoi les faire nettoyer ?

— Le cuir, fauve, n'avait pas encore été poli… Je désirais qu'il le fût.

— Ainsi hier, dès votre arrivée à Londres, vous êtes sorti immédiatement et vous avez acheté des bottines ?

— J'ai acheté différentes choses… Le docteur Mortimer m'a accompagné. Dame ! Si je dois jouer au grand seigneur, il faut bien que j'en aie les habits… Dans le Far-West, je ne soignais pas beaucoup ma tenue… Parmi mes emplettes, figurait cette paire de bottines jaunes… Je les ai payées six dollars… et on m'en a volé une avant même que j'aie pu m'en servir.

— Je ne vois pas l'utilité de ce vol, dit Holmes. Je partage l'avis du docteur Mortimer… vous les retrouverez bientôt.

— Il me semble, messieurs, dit le baronnet, que nous avons assez causé de moi. Le moment est venu de me dire, à votre tour, tout ce que vous savez.

— Ce désir est très légitime, répondit Sherlock Holmes. Docteur Mortimer, recommencez donc pour sir Henry votre récit d'hier matin ».

Ainsi encouragé, notre ami tira ses papiers de sa poche et narra toute l'histoire que le lecteur connaît déjà.

Sir Henry Baskerville l'écouta avec la plus profonde attention. De temps en temps un cri de surprise lui échappait.

Lorsque le docteur Mortimer cessa de parler, il s'écria :

— « J'ai donc recueilli un héritage maudit !… Certes, dès ma plus tendre enfance, j'ai entendu parler de ce chien. C'est l'histoire favorite de la famille, mais je ne pensai jamais à la prendre au sérieux. Quant à la mort de mon oncle… Il me semble que ma tête bout… je ne puis lier deux idées… Je me demande si ce que vous venez de m'apprendre exige une enquête judiciaire ou un exorcisme.

— Précisément.

— Puis, il y a cette lettre adressée à mon hôtel… Elle tombe à propos.

— Elle montre que quelqu'un connaît mieux que nous ce qui se passe sur la lande, dit Mortimer.

— Et aussi que ce quelqu'un vous veut du bien, puisqu'il vous prévient du danger, ajouta Holmes.

— Ma présence là-bas contrarie peut-être certains projets…

— C'est encore possible… Merci, docteur Mortimer, de m'avoir soumis un problème qui renferme un aussi grand nombre d'intéressantes alternatives. Maintenant, sir Henry Baskerville, il ne nous reste plus qu'un seul point à décider : oui ou non, devez-vous aller au château ?

— Pourquoi n'irais-je pas ?

— Il paraît y avoir du danger.

— Un danger provenant du démon familial ou d'êtres humains ?

— C'est ce qu'il faut éclaircir.

— Quelle que soit votre décision, mon parti est pris. Il n'existe en enfer aucun diable, monsieur Holmes, ni sur terre aucun homme capables de m'empêcher d'aller dans la demeure de mes ancêtres. Voilà mon dernier mot. »

Les sourcils de sir Henry se froncèrent et son visage, pendant qu'il parlait, tourna au rouge pourpre.

Il était évident que le dernier rejeton des Baskerville avait hérité le caractère emporté de ses aïeux.

Il reprit :

« J'ai besoin de méditer plus longuement sur tout ce que vous m'avez appris. Il est malaisé de se décider aussi rapidement. Accordez-moi une heure de recueillement… Onze heures et demie sonnent, je retourne directement à mon hôtel… Acceptez, ainsi que M. Watson, une invitation à déjeuner pour deux heures. Je vous répondrai alors plus clairement.

— Cela vous convient-il, Watson ? me demanda Holmes.

— Parfaitement.

— Dans ce cas, attendez-nous… Faut-il faire avancer une voiture ?

— Je vous accompagnerai dans votre promenade, fit Mortimer.

— À deux heures… c'est entendu ? répéta sir Henry.

— Oui, à bientôt », répondîmes-nous, Holmes et moi.

Nous entendîmes le pas de nos visiteurs résonner dans l'escalier et la porte de la rue se refermer sur eux.

Aussitôt Holmes abandonna son attitude rêveuse et se réveilla homme d'action.

« Vite ! votre chapeau, Watson ! » dit-il.

Il courut en robe de chambre vers son cabinet de toilette, d'où il ressortit quelques secondes après en redingote.

Nous descendîmes l'escalier quatre à quatre, et nous nous précipitâmes dans la rue.

À deux cent mètres devant nous, nous aperçûmes le docteur Mortimer et sir Henri Baskerville se dirigeant vers Oxford street.

Je demandai à mon ami :

« Voulez-vous que je coure et que je les arrête ?

— Gardez-vous-en bien, Watson. Votre compagnie me suffit, si la mienne ne vous déplaît pas… Ces messieurs avaient raison… il fait très bon marcher ce matin. »

Holmes hâta le pas, jusqu'à ce que nous eussions diminué de moitié la distance qui nous séparait de nos nouveaux amis.

Alors, laissant entre eux et nous un intervalle d'environ cent mètres, nous parcourûmes Oxford street, puis Regent street.

Bientôt Holmes poussa un cri de joie. Je suivis la direction de son regard et je vis un *hansom-cab*, rangé le long du trottoir, reprendre sa marche en avant. Un voyageur l'occupait…

« Voilà notre homme ! s'écria Holmes. Venez vite ! Nous pourrons au moins le dévisager, faute de mieux ! »

Comme dans un éclair, je vis une barbe noire broussailleuse et des yeux perçants qui nous regardaient à travers la glace du cab. Aussitôt la trappe par laquelle on communique de l'intérieur avec le cocher s'ouvrit et un ordre fut donné. Le véhicule partit à fond de train vers Trafalgar square.

Holmes chercha immédiatement autour de lui une voiture vide et n'en trouva pas. Dans une course folle, il se jeta au milieu des embarras de la rue. Mais le cab avait trop d'avance sur mon ami, qui le perdit de vue peu après.

« Sapristi ! dit Holmes, avec amertume, en se dégageant tout haletant des files de voitures, quelle malchance et aussi quelle imprévoyance de ma part ! Si vous êtes juste, Watson, vous enregistrerez cet échec à mon passif. »

J'interrogeai Sherlock :

« Quel homme était-ce ?

— Je n'en ai pas la moindre idée ;

— Un espion ?

— D'après ce que nous avons entendu, il est certain qu'une ombre a marché dans les pas de Baskerville depuis son arrivée à Londres. Comment aurait-on su rapidement qu'il avait choisi Northumberland hotel ? Si on l'a espionné le premier jour, j'en conclus qu'on l'espionnera le second. Vous vous souvenez bien que, tout à l'heure, pendant la lecture des papiers du docteur Mortimer, je me suis approché deux fois de la fenêtre ?

— Oui, je me le rappelle.

— Je regardais si personne ne flânait dans la rue. Je n'avais rien remarqué de suspect. Ah ! nous avons affaire avec un homme habile Watson ! La chose se complique. Bien qu'il me soit encore impossible de démêler si nous nous trouvons en présence d'une intervention amicale ou hostile, je reconnais qu'il en existe une. Quand nos amis nous ont quittés, je les ai suivis pour découvrir leur invisible surveillant. Cet homme est si rusé qu'au lieu d'aller à pied, il a préféré prendre un cab. Il pouvait ainsi rester en arrière de ceux qu'il observait ou les devancer pour échapper à leur attention. Ce procédé offrait aussi l'avantage de conserver leur contact, si l'envie leur venait de monter en cab ; mais il avait un désavantage évident.

— Celui de livrer son auteur à la discrétion du cocher ?

— Évidemment.

— Quel malheur que nous n'ayons pas son numéro !

— Mon cher Watson, j'ai été maladroit, j'en conviens… Toutefois, vous n'imaginez pas sérieusement que j'aie oublié de l'inscrire là ! »

Et Holmes se frappa le front.

Il reprit :

« J'ai lu sur le cab le numéro 2704. Mais cela nous importe peu pour le moment.

— Qu'auriez-vous pu faire de plus ?

— Si j'avais remarqué le cab, j'aurais tourné sur mes talons et pris une autre direction. J'aurais eu alors toute facilité pour en héler un autre, et, à une distance respectueuse, j'aurais trotté dans les pas du premier jusqu'à Northumberland hotel. Là, j'aurais attendu. Puis, lorsque notre inconnu aurait accompagné sir Henry Baskerville chez lui, nous l'aurions filé à notre tour. Tandis que, par une précipitation intempestive, dont notre adversaire a su profiter avec une décision rare, nous nous sommes trahis et nous avons perdu sa trace. »

Tout en causant et en flânant devant les magasins de Regent street, nous avions cessé de voir le docteur Mortimer et son compagnon.

« Il est inutile que nous les suivions plus loin, dit Holmes. L'ombre s'est évanouie et ne reparaîtra plus. D'autres cartes nous restent encore dans les mains, jouons-les avec résolution. Reconnaîtriez-vous l'homme assis dans le cab ?

— Je ne reconnaîtrais que sa barbe.

— Moi aussi… Mais je jurerais bien qu'elle est fausse. Un homme, engagé dans une « filature » aussi délicate, ne peut porter une telle barbe que pour dissimuler ses traits… Entrons ici, Watson. »

Holmes pénétra dans un de ces bureaux de quartier où des commissionnaires se tiennent à toute heure du jour et de la nuit à la disposition du public.

Le directeur le reçut avec force salutations.

« Ah ! Wilson, fit mon ami, je vois avec plaisir que vous n'avez pas oublié le léger service que je vous ai rendu.

— Certes non, monsieur. Vous avez sauvé ma réputation et peut-être même ma vie.

— Vous exagérez, mon garçon. Je me souviens que vous aviez, parmi vos boys, un gamin nommé Cartwright, qui fit preuve d'une certaine adresse, au cours de l'enquête.

— Oui, monsieur ; il est toujours ici.

— Faites-le monter… Pouvez-vous me procurer la monnaie de ce billet de cinq livres ? »

Un jeune garçon de quatorze ans, à la mine intelligente et futée, répondit au coup de sonnette du directeur.

Il vint se placer devant Holmes, qu'il regarda respectueusement.

« Donne-moi l'Annuaire des hôtels, lui dit mon ami. Voici, Cartwright, le nom des vingt-trois hôtels qui sont dans le voisinage immédiat de Charing Cross… Tu les vois bien ?

— Oui, monsieur.

— Tu les visiteras tous, les uns après les autres.

— Oui, monsieur.

— Tu commenceras par donner au concierge de chacun d'eux un shilling… Voici vingt-trois shillings.

— Oui, monsieur.

— Tu leur demanderas de te remettre les corbeilles à papier d'hier. Tu leur diras qu'on a laissé à une mauvaise adresse un télégramme important que tu tiens à retrouver… Comprends-tu ?

— Oui, monsieur.

— Ce qu'il te faudra réellement chercher, ce n'est pas un télégramme, mais une page intérieure du *Times* dans laquelle on aura pratiqué des coupures à l'aide de ciseaux. Voilà ce numéro du *Times* et la page en question… Tu la reconnaîtras facilement, n'est-ce pas ?

— Oui, monsieur.

— Dans chaque hôtel, le concierge te renverra au garçon du hall, auquel tu donneras aussi un shilling… Je te remets encore vingt-trois autres shillings. Probablement, dans vingt hôtels sur vingt-trois, on te répondra que le contenu des corbeilles de la veille a été jeté ou brûlé. Dans les trois derniers hôtels, on te conduira à des tas de papiers parmi lesquels tu devras rechercher cette page du *Times*. Tu as très peu de chances de la retrouver… Voici dix shillings de plus pour faire face à l'imprévu. Envoie-moi à Baker street, avant ce soir, le résultat de tes investigations. Maintenant, Watson, procurons-nous par télégramme l'identité du cocher qui conduit le cab 2704. Puis, en attendant l'heure de nous présenter à Northumberland hotel, nous entrerons dans une des expositions de peinture de Bond street. »

V

FILS CASSÉS

Sherlock Holmes possédait à un suprême degré la faculté de détacher son esprit des pensées les plus absorbantes.

Pendant deux heures, il parut avoir oublié l'étrange affaire à laquelle nous étions mêlés, et il se plongea dans l'examen des peintures de l'école belge. Il ne voulut même parler que d'art — dont il n'avait d'ailleurs que des notions très imparfaites — pendant le trajet qui séparait Bond street de Northumberland hotel.

« Sir Henry Baskerville vous attend dans sa chambre, nous dit le commis de l'hôtel. Il a bien recommandé qu'on le prévienne dès que vous serez arrivé.

— Y aurait-il de l'indiscrétion à parcourir votre registre ? demanda Holmes.

— Pas du tout. »

À la suite du nom de Baskerville, le livre ne contenait que celui de deux voyageurs : Théophile Johnson et sa famille, de Newcastle, et Mme Oldmore et sa fille, de High Lodge, Alton.

— C'est certainement le Johnson que je connais, dit Holmes au portier… Un avocat, n'est-ce pas ?… Avec toute la barbe grise… atteint d'une légère claudication ?

— Non, monsieur. Ce Johnson est un gros marchand de charbon, très ingambe, à peu près de votre âge.

— Vous devez faire erreur sur sa profession.

— Non, monsieur. Depuis plusieurs années, il descend dans cet hôtel et nous le connaissons tous.

— Alors, c'est différent. Et Mme Oldmore ? Je crois me rappeler ce nom. Excusez ma curiosité ; mais souvent, en venant voir un ami, on en rencontre un autre.

— Elle est impotente. Son mari a exercé pendant quelques années les fonctions de maire à Gloucester. Nous la comptons parmi nos meilleurs clients.

— Merci de votre explication. Je regrette de ne pouvoir me recommander auprès de vous de son amitié. »

Tout en montant l'escalier, Sherlock Holmes reprit à voix basse :

« Nous avons fixé un point important : nous savons que ceux qui s'occupent si activement de notre ami ne sont point logés dans le même hôtel que lui. Cela prouve que quelque intérêt qu'ils aient à l'espionner, ainsi que nous l'avons constaté, ils ne désirent pas être vus par lui. Ceci est très suggestif.

— En quoi ?

— En ceci… Mon Dieu ! mais que diable arrive-t-il ? »

Comme nous tournions dans le corridor de l'hôtel, nous nous heurtâmes à sir Henry Baskerville lui-même.

Le visage rouge de colère, il tenait à la main une vieille bottine toute poudreuse.

Il paraissait si furieux qu'il avait peine à parler. Quant il put donner un libre cours à son emportement, il s'exprima, en accentuant davantage le jargon du Far-West dont il s'était servi le matin.

« On se paye donc ma tête dans cet hôtel, criait-il. S'ils n'y prennent garde, je leur montrerai qu'on ne se moque pas du monde de la sorte ! Sacrebleu ! si le garçon ne retrouve pas la bottine qui me manque, il m'entendra ! Certes, monsieur Holmes, je comprends la plaisanterie ; mais celle-ci dépasse les bornes !...

— Vous cherchez encore votre bottine ?

— Oui, monsieur... et je prétends qu'il faudra bien qu'on la retrouve.

— Vous disiez qu'il s'agissait d'une bottine en cuir fauve ?

— Oui... Mais, maintenant, c'est une noire qu'on a égarée.

— Non ?

— Je dis ce que je dis. Je n'en ai que trois paires : des jaunes, neuves ; des noires, vieilles, et celles que je porte aux pieds. La nuit dernière, on m'a pris une bottine jaune et, ce matin, on m'en a pris une noire. Eh bien ! l'avez-vous ? Parlerez-vous, idiot, au lieu de rester là à me regarder ? »

Un domestique, Allemand d'origine, venait d'apparaître :

« Non, monsieur, répondit-il ; je ne l'ai pas... Je l'ai demandée dans tout l'hôtel.

— On retrouvera cette bottine avant ce soir ou je préviendrai le gérant que je quitte immédiatement sa boîte.

— On la retrouvera, monsieur... je vous le promets, si vous daignez prendre patience.

— Faites bien attention que c'est la dernière chose que je consens à perdre dans cette caverne de voleurs. Je vous demande pardon, monsieur Holmes, de vous ennuyer de ces futilités.

— Pas du tout... la chose en vaut la peine.

— Est-ce vraiment votre avis ?

— Certainement. Mais comment expliquez-vous ceci ? questionna Holmes.

— Je ne cherche même pas à l'expliquer. C'est bien la chose la plus curieuse, la plus folle qui me soit jamais arrivée.

— La plus curieuse... peut-être, répliqua Holmes, pensif.

— Qu'en concluez-vous, vous même ? demanda à son tour sir Henry.

— Rien encore. Votre cas est très compliqué. Si je rapproche de la mort de votre oncle les événements qui vous sont personnels, je ne crois pas que, sur les cinq cents affaires dont j'ai dû m'occuper, il y en ait une plus ardue. Mais nous tenons plusieurs fils, et il faut espérer que les uns et les autres nous conduiront à la solution. Peu importe que nous perdions du temps à débrouiller nos nombreux écheveaux… Tôt ou tard nous mettrons la main sur le bon. »

Pendant le déjeuner, il fut peu question de ce qui nous avait réunis.

Lorsque nous retournâmes au salon, Holmes demanda à Baskerville quelles étaient ses intentions.

« Retourner au château ?

— Quand ?

— À la fin de la semaine.

— À tout prendre, dit Holmes, je considère que c'est le parti le plus sage. J'ai la conviction qu'on vous espionne à Londres. Or, au milieu de cette population de plusieurs millions d'habitants, il n'est pas facile de savoir en face de qui nous nous trouvons, pas plus que de découvrir le dessein que l'on poursuit. Puis, si l'on vous veut du mal, nous serons impuissants à l'empêcher… Avez-vous remarqué, docteur Mortimer, qu'on vous suivait ce matin, depuis le moment où vous êtes sortis de l'hôtel jusqu'à celui où vous y êtes revenus ? »

Mortimer fit un soubresaut.

« Suivis ! Par qui ?

— Ça, je ne puis malheureusement pas vous l'apprendre. Existe-t-il, parmi vos voisins ou vos connaissances de Dartmoor, un homme portant une longue barbe noire ?

— Non. Attendez !… Sir Barrymore, le valet de chambre de sir Charles, porte toute sa barbe… elle est noire.

— Ah !… Où habite ce Barrymore ?

— On lui a confié la garde du château.

— Il faut que nous sachions s'il est là ou si, par hasard, il n'aurait pas déserté son poste pour venir à Londres.

— Comment faire ?

— Donnez-moi une feuille de télégramme. »

Sherlock Holmes griffonna quelques mots.

Il lut :

« Tout est-il préparé pour recevoir sir Henry ? » Cela suffira. J'envoie cette dépêche à M. Barrymore, château de Baskerville. Quel est le bureau de poste le plus proche ? Grimpen… Très bien. Nous allons expédier au directeur de ce bureau un télégramme ainsi conçu : « Remettez en mains propres la dépêche destinée à M. Barrymore. Si absent, retournez-la à sir Henry Baskerville, Northumberland hotel. » Nous apprendrons ainsi, avant ce soir, si, oui ou non, Barrymore est à son poste dans le Devonshire.

— Parfait, dit sir Henry. À propos, docteur Mortimer, parlez-nous un peu de ce Barrymore.

— Il est le fils d'un vieil intendant des Baskerville. Ils habitent le château depuis quatre générations. D'après ce que l'on m'a dit, sa femme et lui sont des gens très honorables.

— Il n'en est pas moins vrai, dit Baskerville, que tant qu'aucun membre de la famille ne résidera au château, ces gens-là y trouveront un bon gîte et n'auront rien à faire.

— C'est exact.

— Les Barrymore figuraient-ils sur le testament de sir Charles ? demanda Holmes.

— Pour cinq cents livres sterling chacun.

— Ah ! Connaissaient-ils cette libéralité ?

— Oui. Sir Charles aimait à parler de ses dispositions testamentaires.

— C'est très intéressant.

— J'aime à croire, fit Mortimer, que vos soupçons ne s'étendent pas à tous ceux qui ont reçu un legs de sir Charles… il m'a laissé mille livres.

— Vraiment !… Et à qui encore ?

— Il a légué à des particuliers des sommes insignifiantes et d'autres, très considérables, à des œuvres de bienfaisance.

— À combien s'élevait le montant de sa fortune ?

— À sept cent quarante mille livres. »

Holmes ouvrit de grands yeux étonnés.

« Je ne me figurais pas que sir Charles possédât une somme aussi gigantesque.

— Sir Charles passait pour être riche, mais jusqu'au jour de l'inventaire, nous ne soupçonnions pas l'étendue de sa fortune, dont le montant total approchait bien d'un million de livres.

— Peste ! Voilà un magot pour lequel un homme peut risquer son va-tout… Encore une question, docteur Mortimer. En supposant qu'il arrive malheur à notre jeune ami — pardonnez-moi, sir Henry, cette désagréable hypothèse — à qui reviendra cette fortune ?

— Roger Baskerville, le plus jeune frère de sir Charles, étant mort garçon, cette fortune irait à des cousins éloignés, les Desmond. James Desmond est un vieux clergyman du Westmoreland.

— Merci. Ces détails sont du plus grand intérêt. Connaissez-vous M. James Desmond ?

— Oui, je l'ai aperçu une fois chez sir Charles. Il a un aspect vénérable et mène, dit-on, une vie exemplaire. Je me souviens qu'il a résisté aux sollicitations de sir Charles, qui insistait pour lui faire accepter une donation assez importante.

— Ainsi, cet homme, simple de goûts, deviendrait l'héritier des millions de sir Charles ?

— Certainement… D'après l'ordre des successions, il hériterait du domaine. Il recueillerait également toutes les valeurs, à moins qu'il n'en soit décidé autrement par le précédent propriétaire qui peut, par testament, en disposer à son gré.

— Avez-vous fait votre testament, sir Henry ? demanda Sherlock Holmes.

— Non. Je n'en ai pas eu encore le temps, puisque je ne sais que d'hier comment sont les choses. Mais, en tout cas, les valeurs mobilières suivront le domaine et le titre… Telle était la volonté de mon pauvre oncle. Comment le propriétaire de Baskerville, s'il était pauvre, entretiendrait-il le château ? Maison, terres, argent doivent se confondre sur la même tête.

— Parfaitement… J'approuve votre départ immédiat pour le Devonshire. Je ne mets qu'une restriction à ce projet : vous ne pouvez partir seul.

— Le docteur Mortimer m'accompagne.

— Mais le docteur Mortimer a ses occupations et sa maison est située à plusieurs milles du château. Avec la meilleure volonté du monde, il lui serait impossible de vous porter secours. Non, sir Henry, il faut que vous emmeniez avec vous une personne de confiance qui restera sans cesse à vos côtés.

— Pouvez-vous venir, monsieur Holmes ?

— Au moment critique, je tâcherai de me trouver là : Mais vous comprendrez qu'avec les consultations qu'on me demande de tous côtés et les appels qu'on m'adresse de tous les quartiers de Londres, je ne puisse m'absenter pour un temps indéterminé. Ainsi, à cette heure, un des noms les plus honorés de l'Angleterre se trouve en butte aux attaques d'un maître chanteur, et je suis seul capable d'arrêter ce scandale. Dans ces conditions, comment aller à Dartmoor ?

— Alors, qui me recommanderiez-vous ? »

Holmes posa sa main sur mon bras.

« Si mon ami consentait à accepter cette mission, dit-il, personne ne serait plus digne que lui de la remplir. Il possède toute ma confiance. »

Cette proposition me prit au dépourvu et, sans me donner le temps de répondre, sir Henry saisit ma main, qu'il serra chaleureusement.

« Je vous remercie de votre obligeance, docteur Watson, dit-il. Vous me connaissez maintenant et vous en savez autant que moi sur cette affaire. Si vous acceptez de m'accompagner au château de Baskerville et de me tenir compagnie là-bas, je ne l'oublierai jamais. »

Les expéditions aventureuses ont toujours exercé sur moi une irrésistible fascination ; de plus, les paroles élogieuses prononcées par Holmes à mon adresse, ainsi que la précipitation du baronnet à m'agréer pour compagnon, me décidèrent rapidement.

« Je viendrai avec plaisir, répondis-je. Je trouverai difficilement un meilleur emploi de mon temps.

— Vous me tiendrez exactement au courant de tout, dit Holmes. Lorsque la crise arrivera — et elle arrivera certainement —

je vous dicterai votre conduite. J'espère que vous serez en mesure de partir samedi, n'est-ce pas, sir Henry ?

— Cette date convient-elle au docteur Watson ? demanda ce dernier.

— Absolument.

— Alors, à samedi ! À moins d'avis contraire, nous nous retrouverons à la gare de Paddington, au train de dix heures trente. »

Nous nous levions pour prendre congé, quand Baskerville poussa un cri de triomphe.

Il se baissa dans un des coins de la chambre et tira une bottine jaune de dessous une armoire.

« La bottine qui me manquait ! s'écria-t-il.

— Puissent toutes vos difficultés s'aplanir aussi aisément ! dit Sherlock Holmes.

— C'est très curieux, intervint le docteur Mortimer ; avant le déjeuner, j'ai soigneusement cherché par toute la pièce.

— Moi, aussi, fit Baskerville. Je l'ai bouleversée de fond en comble. Il n'y avait pas la moindre bottine.

— Dans ce cas, le garçon l'aura rapportée pendant que nous déjeunions. »

On appela le domestique, qui déclara ne rien savoir et ne put fournir aucun renseignement.

Un nouvel incident venait donc de s'ajouter à cette série de petits mystères qui s'étaient succédé si rapidement.

En négligeant la mort tragique de sir Charles, nous nous trouvions en présence de faits inexplicables survenus dans l'espace de deux jours : la réception de la lettre découpée dans le *Times*, l'espion à barbe noire blotti dans le cab, la perte de la bottine jaune, puis de la vieille bottine noire, et enfin la trouvaille de la bottine jaune.

Durant notre retour à Baker street, Homes demeura silencieux. Je voyais à ses sourcils froncés, à sa mine préoccupée, que son esprit, — comme le mien, d'ailleurs — s'efforçait à relier entre eux ces épisodes étranges et en apparence incohérents.

Tout l'après-midi et jusqu'à bien avant dans la soirée, Holmes s'abîma dans ses pensées et s'enveloppa de nuages de fumée.

À l'heure du dîner, on lui apporta deux télégrammes.

Le premier contenait ceci :

« Le directeur de la poste de Grimpen m'annonce que Barry-more est au château.

« BASKERVILLE. »

Le second était ainsi conçu :

« Selon votre ordre, j'ai visité vingt-trois hôtels ; je n'ai découvert dans aucun le numéro découpé du *Times*.

« CARTWRIGHT. »

Le visage d'Holmes exprima une vive contrariété.

« Voici déjà deux fils qui se brisent dans nos mains, fit-il. Rien ne me passionne plus qu'une affaire dans laquelle tout se retourne contre moi. Il nous faut chercher une autre piste.

— Nous avons encore celle du cocher qui conduisait l'espion.

— Oui. J'ai télégraphié au bureau de la police pour qu'on m'envoyât son nom et son adresse… Tenez, je ne serais pas surpris que ce fût la réponse à ma demande. »

Un coup de sonnette retentissait en effet à la porte d'entrée.

Bientôt après, on introduisit dans le salon un homme qui était le cocher lui-même.

Il s'avança, en roulant son chapeau entre ses doigts.

« J'ai reçu du bureau central, dit-il, un message m'avertissant que, dans cette maison, un bourgeois avait pris des renseignements sur le 2704. Je conduis depuis sept ans sans avoir mérité un seul reproche… J'arrive tout droit de la remise pour que vous m'expliquiez bien en face ce que vous avez contre moi.

— Je n'ai rien contre vous, mon brave homme, dit Holmes. Au contraire, si vous répondez clairement à mes questions, je tiens un demi-souverain à votre disposition.

— Alors, y a pas d'erreur, dit le cocher, j'aurai fait une bonne journée. Que voulez-vous savoir ?

— D'abord votre nom et votre adresse, pour le cas où j'aurais encore besoin de vous.

— John Clayton, 3, Turpey street. Je remise à Shipley, près de Waterloo station. »

Sherlock Holmes nota ces renseignements.

« Maintenant, Clayton, reprit-il, parlez-moi du voyageur qui est venu ce matin surveiller cette maison et qui, ensuite, a suivi deux messieurs dans Regent street. »

Le cocher parut étonné et quelque peu embarrassé.

« Je ne vois pas la nécessité de vous parler d'une chose que vous connaissez déjà aussi bien que moi, dit-il. La vérité, c'est que ce voyageur m'avoua être un détective et me recommanda de ne souffler mot de lui à personne.

— Mon ami, reprit Holmes gravement, l'affaire est très sérieuse et vous vous mettriez dans un très vilain cas si vous cherchiez à me cacher quoi que ce soit. Ainsi ce monsieur vous a dit qu'il était détective ?

— Oui.

— Quand vous l'a-t-il dit ?

— En me quittant.

— Vous a-t-il dit autre chose ?

— Il s'est nommé. »

Holmes me jeta un regard triomphant.

« Vraiment !… Il s'est nommé !… Quelle imprudence !… Et quel nom vous a-t-il donné ?

— Son nom ? répéta le cocher… Sherlock Holmes. »

Jamais réponse ne démonta mon ami comme celle qui venait de lui être faite.

Pendant un instant, il sembla ahuri.

« Touché, Watson !… bien touché !… Le coup a été bien envoyé, et je sens devant moi une arme aussi rapide et aussi souple que celle que je manie… Ainsi donc votre voyageur s'appelait Sherlock Holmes ?

— Oui, monsieur, il m'a donné ce nom-là.

— Parfait. Où l'avez-vous « chargé » et qu'est-il arrivé ensuite ?

— Il m'a hélé à neuf heures et demie, dans Trafalgar square. Il m'a dit qu'il était détective et m'a offert deux guinées pour la journée. Je devais aller où bon lui semblerait, sans jamais lui

poser de questions. Je me suis bien gardé de refuser cette offre.
Je l'ai conduit près de Northumberland hotel, où nous avons
attendu la sortie de deux messieurs qui sont montés dans un cab
à la station voisine. Nous avons suivi cette voiture jusqu'à ce
qu'elle se soit arrêtée près d'ici.

— À ma porte ? dit Holmes.

— Je n'en suis pas certain ; mais le bourgeois, lui, savait où
les autres allaient. Il est descendu à peu près au milieu de la rue
et j'ai « poireauté » une heure et demie. Alors les deux messieurs
sont repassés à pied, et nous les avons suivis de nouveau dans
Baker street et dans…

— Je sais, interrompit Holmes.

— Nous avions remonté les trois quarts de Regent street… À
ce moment, à travers la trappe, mon voyageur m'a crié de filer
vers Waterloo station aussi vite que possible. J'ai fouetté la
jument et, dix minutes plus tard, nous étions rendus à destination. Il m'a payé deux guinées, comme un « bon zigue », et il est
rentré dans la gare. En me quittant, il s'est retourné et m'a dit :
« Vous serez peut-être content d'apprendre que vous avez conduit
M. Sherlock Holmes ». Voilà comment j'ai appris son nom.

— Je comprends… Et vous ne l'avez plus revu ?

— Non… Il avait disparu dans la gare.

— Faites-moi le portrait de M. Sherlock Holmes. »

Le cocher se gratta la tête :

« Il n'est pas facile à peindre. Il paraît quarante ans… Il est de
taille moyenne… cinq ou six centimètres de moins que vous. Il
était habillé comme un gommeux et portait une barbe noire coupée en carré… Il m'a semblé très pâle… Je ne puis vous en dire
plus long.

— La couleur de ses yeux ? »

Le cocher parut chercher dans ses souvenirs et répondit :

« Je ne me la rappelle pas.

— D'autres détails vous ont-ils frappé ?

— Non.

— Bien, fit Holmes. Voici votre demi-souverain. Vous en
aurez un autre, si vous m'apportez de nouveaux renseignements.
Bonne nuit.

— Bonne nuit, monsieur, et merci. »

John Clayton partit très satisfait.

Holmes se retourna vers moi avec un haussement d'épaules et un sourire découragé.

« Voilà un troisième fil qui casse et nous ne sommes pas plus avancés qu'au début, dit-il. Le rusé coquin !… Il connaissait le numéro de ma maison et la visite projetée par sir Henry Baskerville !… Dans Regent street, il a flairé qui j'étais… il s'est douté que j'avais pris le numéro de sa voiture et que je rechercherais le cocher !… Ah ! Watson, cette fois nous aurons à lutter contre un adversaire digne de nous. Il m'a fait mat à Londres ; je vous souhaite meilleure chance dans le Devonshire… Mais je ne suis plus aussi tranquille.

— Sur quoi ?

— Sur votre sort, là-bas. C'est une vilaine affaire, Watson… vilaine et dangereuse… Plus je l'examine et moins elle me plaît. Ouis, oui, mon cher ami, riez à votre aise !… Je vous jure que je serai très heureux de vous revoir sain et sauf dans notre logis de Baker street. »

VI

LE CHÂTEAU DE BASKERVILLE

Au jour indiqué, sir Henry Baskerville et le docteur Mortimer se trouvèrent prêts, et nous partîmes pour le Devonshire, ainsi que cela avait été convenu.

Sherlock Holmes m'accompagna à la gare, afin de me donner en voiture ses dernières instructions.

« Je ne vous troublerai pas, me dit-il, par l'exposé de mes théories ou par la confidence de mes soupçons. Je désire simplement que vous me teniez au courant des faits jusque dans leurs plus petits détails. Reposez-vous sur moi du soin d'en tirer les déductions qu'ils comporteront.

— Quelle espèce de faits dois-je vous communiquer ? demandai-je.

— Tous ceux qui vous paraîtront toucher à l'affaire — même de loin… Renseignez-vous sur les relations du jeune Baskerville avec ses voisins et sur tout ce que vous pourrez recueillir de nouveau concernant la mort de sir Charles. Je me suis livré, ces jours derniers, à quelques enquêtes dont le résultat, je le crains fort, aura été négatif. Une seule chose me semble certaine : M. James Desmond, l'héritier présomptif, est un parfait galant homme ; cette persécution n'émane pas de lui. Nous devons donc éliminer ce clergyman de nos calculs. Il ne reste plus que les personnes qui entoureront sir Henry Baskerville sur la lande.

— Ne pensez-vous pas qu'il serait bon de se débarrasser immédiatement du couple Barrymore ?

— Non, nous commettrions une faute. Innocents, ce serait une cruelle injustice ; coupables, ce serait renoncer à la possibilité de les confondre. Non, non, conservons-les sur notre liste de suspects. Si je me souviens bien, il y a au château un cocher et, sur la lande, deux fermiers. Nous y trouvons également notre ami le docteur Mortimer — que je tiens pour absolument honnête — et sa femme — sur laquelle nous manquons de renseignements. Il y a aussi le naturaliste Stapleton et sa sœur, qu'on dit très attrayante ; puis c'est M. Frankland, de Lafter Hall, qui représente un facteur inconnu, ainsi que deux ou trois autres voisins. Vous devrez porter vos investigations sur ces gens-là.

— J'agirai de mon mieux.

— Je suppose que vous emportez des armes ?

— Oui, j'ai cru bien faire de m'en munir.

— Certainement. Jour et nuit ayez votre revolver à portée de la main, et ne vous relâchez jamais de vos mesures de prudence. »

Nos amis avaient déjà retenu un wagon de 1re classe et nous attendaient sur le quai.

« Non, nous n'avons rien de neuf à vous apprendre, fit le docteur Mortimer, en répondant à une question de mon ami. Je ne puis vous affirmer qu'une chose : personne ne nous a suivis depuis deux jours. Nous ne sommes jamais sortis sans avoir regardé de tous côtés, et un espion n'aurait pas échappé à notre vigilance.

— Vous ne vous êtes pas quittés, je présume ?

— Seulement hier, après midi. Quand je suis à Londres, je consacre toujours quelques heures aux distractions… je les ai passées au musée de l'Académie de chirurgie.

— Et moi, je suis allé voir le beau monde, à Hyde Park, dit Baskerville. Il ne s'est rien produit d'extraordinaire.

— C'était tout de même imprudent, répliqua gravement Holmes, en secouant la tête. Je vous prie, sir Henry, de ne plus vous absenter seul, si vous ne voulez pas vous exposer à de grands malheurs. Avez-vous retrouvé votre bottine ?

— Non ; elle est bien perdue.

— C'est vraiment très curieux. Allons, adieu ! « ajouta-t-il, comme le train commençait à glisser le long du quai.

Puis il reprit :

« Souvenez-vous, sir Henry, de l'une des phrases de la légende que le docteur Mortimer nous a lue : "Évitez la lande à l'heure où l'esprit du mal chemine".

Je passai la tête par la portière pour regarder encore le quai, que nous avions déjà laissé bien loin derrière nous, et j'aperçus la grande silhouette de Sherlock Holmes, immobile et tournée vers nous.

Le voyage me parut court et agréable.

J'employai le temps à faire plus ample connaissance avec mes compagnons et à jouer avec le caniche de Mortimer.

Peu d'heures après notre départ, le sol changea de couleur ; de brun, il devint rougeâtre. Le granit avait remplacé la pierre calcaire.

Des vaches rousses ruminaient dans de gras pâturages, dénotant un pays plus fertile, mais plus humide.

Le jeune Baskerville, le visage collé aux vitres du wagon, contemplait avec intérêt le paysage et s'enthousiasmait à la vue des horizons familiers du Devonshire.

« Depuis que j'ai quitté l'Angleterre, dit-il, j'ai parcouru la moitié du monde, mais je n'ai jamais rien trouvé de comparable à ceci.

— Il est rare de rencontrer un habitant du Devonshire, fis-je observer, qui ne soit pas épris de son comté.

— Cela dépend tout autant de l'individu que du comté, repartit Mortimer. Un examen superficiel de notre ami révèle chez lui la tête du Celte où sont fortement développées les bosses de l'enthousiasme et de l'attachement. Le crâne du pauvre sir Charles présentait les particularités d'un type très rare, moitié gaélique et moitié hibernien… Vous étiez fort jeune, n'est-ce pas, sir Henry, lorsque vous vîntes au château de Baskerville pour la dernière fois ?

— À la mort de mon frère, j'avais une dizaine d'années et je ne suis jamais venu au château. Nous habitions un petit cottage sur la côte méridionale de l'Angleterre. Je suis parti de là pour rejoindre un ami en Amérique. La contrée que nous traversons est aussi nouvelle pour moi que pour le docteur Watson ; cela vous explique l'extrême curiosité que la lande excite en moi.

— Vous allez pouvoir la satisfaire, dit Mortimer, en désignant la fenêtre du wagon… Vous devez l'apercevoir d'ici. »

Dans le lointain, au-dessus de la verdure des champs et dominant une pente boisée, se dressait une colline grise, mélancolique, terminée par une cime dentelée dont les arêtes, à cette distance, perdaient de leur netteté et de leur vigueur. Cela ressemblait à quelque paysage fantastique entrevu à travers un rêve.

Baskerville tint longtemps les yeux fixés sur ce coin du ciel, et je lus sur son visage mobile l'impression que faisait sur son esprit la vue de cette contrée où ceux de sa race avaient vécu si longtemps et avaient laissé de si profondes traces de leur passage.

Il était assis en face de moi, dans le coin d'un prosaïque wagon, vêtu de son complet gris, parlant avec cet accent américain fortement prononcé, et, pendant que je détaillais sa figure énergique, je pressentais plus que jamais qu'il était vraiment le descendant de cette longue lignée d'hommes ardents et courageux.

Il y avait de l'orgueil, de la vaillance et de la force sous ces épais sourcils, ainsi que dans ces narines mobiles et dans ces yeux couleur de noisette.

Si, sur cette lande d'aspect sauvage, nous devions entreprendre une enquête difficile et périlleuse, nous aurions dans sir Henry un compagnon avec lequel on pouvait tenter l'aventure, certains qu'il saurait en partager bravement tous les dangers.

Le train stoppa à une petite station.

Nous descendîmes. Dehors, au-delà d'une petite barrière peinte en blanc, attendait une voiture attelée de deux cobs.

Notre arrivée constituait sûrement un grand événement, car le chef de gare et les hommes d'équipe se précipitèrent au-devant de nous pour prendre nos bagages.

C'était une simple halte au milieu de la campagne. Je fus donc très surpris de remarquer que, de chaque côté de la porte, deux soldats se tenaient appuyés sur leur fusil. Quand nous passâmes auprès d'eux, ils nous dévisagèrent avec insistance.

Le cocher, petit, trapu, salua sir Henry Baskerville, et, quelques minutes plus tard, nous roulions sur la route blanche et poudreuse.

Nous traversions un pays vallonné, couvert de pâturages.

Le toit de quelques maisons s'élevait au-dessus des frondaisons épaisses des arbres ; mais au-delà de cette campagne paisible, illuminée par les rayons du soleil couchant, la longue silhouette de la lande se détachait en noir sur l'azur du ciel.

La voiture s'engagea dans un chemin de traverse.

Nous gravîmes ainsi des sentiers abrupts, bordés de hauts talus tapissés de mousse et de scolopendres, où, pendant des siècles, le passage des roues avait creusé de profondes ornières. Des fougères rouillées par la rosée, des ronces aux baies sanglantes étincelaient aux derniers feux du soleil.

Nous franchîmes un petit pont de granit et nous côtoyâmes un ruisseau qui fuyait rapidement sur un lit de cailloux grisâtres. La route et le ruisseau suivaient une vallée plantée de chênes rabougris et de sapins étiques.

Baskerville saluait chaque tournant du chemin par une exclamation de surprise. Tout lui semblait beau, tandis que j'éprouvais une indéfinissable tristesse à l'aspect de cette campagne qui portait les stigmates irrécusables de l'hiver déjà prochain.

Tout à coup Mortimer s'écria :

« Regardez donc ça ! »

Une petite colline, une sorte d'éperon formé par la lande et s'avançant dans la vallée, se dressait devant nous. Sur la cime, semblable à une statue équestre, nous aperçûmes un soldat à cheval, le fusil appuyé sur son bras gauche, prêt à faire feu. Il gardait la route par laquelle nous arrivions.

« Que signifie ceci, Perkins ? » demanda Mortimer au cocher.

Celui-ci se retourna à demi sur son siège.

« Un condamné s'est échappé, il y a trois jours, de la prison de Princetown. On a placé des sentinelles sur tous les chemins et dans toutes les gares. On ne l'a pas encore retrouvé, et les fermiers des environs sont bien ennuyés.

— Je comprends… ils toucheraient cinq livres de récompense en échange d'un petit renseignement.

— Oui, monsieur. Mais cinq livres de récompense représentent bien peu de chose en comparaison du danger qu'ils courent d'avoir le cou coupé. Ah ! ce n'est pas un condamné ordinaire ! Il est capable de tout.

— Qui est ce ?

— Selden, l'assassin de Notting Hill. »

Je me souvenais parfaitement de ce crime. Il était un de ceux qui avaient le plus intéressé Sherlock Holmes, en raison des circonstances particulièrement féroces qui entourèrent le crime et de l'odieuse brutalité avec laquelle l'assassin accomplit son forfait. Cependant on avait commué la sentence de mort prononcée contre le coupable, sur des doutes conçus à propos de sa responsabilité mentale.

Notre voiture avait gravi une pente et, devant nous, se déroulait l'immense étendue de la lande. Un vent glacial qui la balayait nous fit frissonner.

Ainsi donc quelque part sur cette plaine désolée, se terrait comme une bête sauvage, cette infernale créature dont le cœur devait maudire l'humanité qui l'avait rejetée de son sein.

Il ne manquait plus que cela pour compléter la lugubre impression produite par cette vaste solitude, cette bise glacée et ce ciel qui s'assombrissait davantage à chaque instant.

Sir Henry Baskerville lui-même devint taciturne et serra plus étroitement autour de lui les pans de son manteau.

Maintenant, les plaines fertiles s'étendaient derrière et au-dessous de nous.

Nous voulûmes les contempler une dernière fois. Les rayons obliques du soleil abaissés sur l'horizon teintaient d'or les eaux du ruisseau et faisaient briller la terre rouge fraîchement remuée par le soc de la charrue.

Devant nous, la route, avec ses pentes rudes parsemées d'énormes rochers roussâtres, prenait un aspect de plus en plus sauvage.

De loin en loin, nous passions près d'un cottage, construit et couvert en pierres, dont aucune plante grimpante n'atténuait la rigidité des lignes.

Soudain, nous vîmes une dépression de terrain, ayant la forme d'un entonnoir, où croissaient des chênes entrouverts, ainsi que des sapins échevelés et tordus par des siècles de rafale.

Deux hautes tours effilées pointaient au-dessus des arbres.

Le cocher les désigna avec son fouet.

« Le château de Baskerville », dit-il.

Les joues empourprées, les yeux enflammés, sir Henry s'était levé et regardait.

Quelques minutes après, nous atteignîmes la grille du château, enchâssée dans des piliers rongés par le temps, mouchetés de lichens et surmontés de têtes de sangliers, armes de Barkerville.

Le pavillon du portier n'était plus qu'une ruine de granit noir au-dessus de laquelle s'enchevêtrait un réseau de chevrons dépouillés du toit qu'ils supportaient jadis. En face, s'élevait un nouveau bâtiment dont la mort de sir Charles avait arrêté l'achèvement.

La porte s'ouvrait sur une avenue où les roues de la voiture s'enfoncèrent dans un lit de feuilles mortes. Les branches des arbres séculaires qui la bordaient se rejoignaient au-dessus de nos têtes pour former comme un sombre tunnel.

Baskerville frissonna, en apercevant cette lugubre allée à l'extrémité de laquelle on découvrait le château.

« Est-ce ici ? demanda-t-il à voix basse.

— Non ; l'allée des Ifs se trouve de l'autre côté.

— Je ne m'étonne pas que, dans un endroit pareil, l'esprit de mon oncle se soit détraqué. Il n'en faut pas davantage pour déprimer un homme. Avant six mois j'aurai installé là, ainsi que devant le château, une double rangée de lampes électriques. »

L'avenue aboutissait à une large pelouse au-delà de laquelle on distinguait le château.

À la clarté pâlissante de ce soir d'automne, je vis que le centre était formé par une construction massive, avec un portail formant saillie.

La façade disparaissait sous les lierres. Les fenêtres et quelques écussons aux armes des Baskerville coupaient çà et là l'uniformité de cette sombre verdure.

De cette partie centrale, montaient les deux tours, antiques, crénelées, percées de nombreuses meurtrières. À droite et à gauche de ces tours, on avait ajouté une aile d'un style plus moderne.

« Soyez le bienvenu au château de Baskerville, sir Henry », dit une voix.

Un homme de haute taille s'était avancé pour ouvrir la portière de la voiture.

Une silhouette de femme se profilait dans l'encadrement de la porte. Elle sortit à son tour et aida l'homme à descendre les bagages.

« Je vous demande la permission de rentrer directement chez moi, sir Henry, fit Mortimer. Ma femme m'attend.

— Vous ne voulez pas dîner avec nous ?

— Non ; il faut que je m'en aille. Je dois avoir des malades qui me réclament. J'aurais été heureux de vous montrer le château, mais Barrymore sera un meilleur guide que moi. Au revoir, et, si je puis vous rendre service, n'hésitez pas à me faire appeler à tout heure du jour ou de la nuit. »

Le roulement de la voiture qui emmenait le docteur s'éteignit bientôt dans le lointain.

Sir Henry et moi nous entrâmes dans le château et la porte se referma lourdement sur nous.

Nous nous trouvâmes dans une grande pièce dont le plafond, très élevé, était soutenu par de fortes solives de chêne noircies par le temps.

Dans une cheminée monumentale, un feu de bois pétillait sur de hauts chenets. Nous en approchâmes nos mains engourdies par le froid du voyage.

Nous examinâmes curieusement les hautes et longues fenêtres aux vitraux multicolores, les lambris de chêne, les têtes de cerfs et les armes accrochées aux murs — le tout triste et sombre sous la lumière atténuée d'une lampe accrochée au milieu du plafond.

« C'est bien ainsi que je me représentais le château, me dit sir Henry. Cela ne ressemble-t-il pas à quelque vieux tableau d'intérieur ? La demeure n'a pas changé depuis cinq cents ans qu'y vivent mes ancêtres ! »

Tandis qu'il jetait les yeux autour de lui, son visage bronzé s'éclaira d'un enthousiasme juvénile. Mais, à un moment, la lumière le frappa directement, alors que de longues traînées d'ombre couraient contre les murs, formant au-dessus de sa tête et derrière lui comme un dais funéraire.

Barrymore était revenu de porter les bagages dans nos chambres. Il se tenait devant nous dans l'attitude respectueuse d'un domestique de grande maison. Il avait très bonne apparence, avec sa haute taille, sa barbe noire coupée en carré et sa figure qui ne manquait pas d'une certaine distinction.

« Désirez-vous qu'on vous serve immédiatement, monsieur ? demanda-t-il.

— Est-ce prêt ?

— Dans quelques minutes. Vous trouverez de l'eau chaude dans vos chambres… Ma femme et moi, sir Henry, nous serons heureux de rester auprès de vous jusqu'à ce que vous ayez pris vos nouvelles dispositions. Maintenant l'entretien de cette maison va exiger un personnel plus nombreux.

— Pourquoi « maintenant » ?

— Je veux dire que sir Charles menait une existence très retirée et que nous suffisions à son service. Vous, — c'est tout naturel — vous recevrez davantage et, nécessairement, vous devrez augmenter votre domesticité.

— Dois-je en conclure que vous avez l'intention de me quitter ?

— Oui, mais seulement lorsque vous nous y autoriserez.

— Votre famille n'est-elle pas au service des Baskerville depuis plusieurs générations ? Je regretterais de commencer ma vie ici en me séparant de serviteurs tels que vous. »

Je crus découvrir quelques traces d'émotion sur le pâle visage du valet de chambre.

« Ma femme et moi nous partageons ce sentiment, reprit Barrymore. Mais à dire vrai, nous étions très attachés à sir Charles ; sa mort nous a donné un coup et nous a rendu pénible la vue de tous ces objets qui lui appartenaient. Je crains que nous ne puissions plus supporter le séjour du château.

— Qu'avez-vous l'intention de faire ?

— Nous sommes décidés à entreprendre quelque petit commerce ; la générosité de sir Charles nous en a procuré les moyens… Ces messieurs veulent-ils que je les conduise à leur chambre ? »

Une galerie courait autour du hall. On y accédait par un escalier à double révolution. De ce point central, deux corridors, sur lesquels s'ouvraient les chambres, traversaient toute la longueur du château.

Ma chambre était située dans la même aile que celle de sir Henry et presque porte à porte.

Ces pièces étaient meublées d'une façon plus moderne que le reste de la maison ; le papier, clair, et les innombrables bougies, allumées un peu partout, effacèrent en partie la sombre impression ressentie dès notre arrivée.

Mais la salle à manger, qui communiquait avec le hall, était pleine d'ombre et de tristesse. On dressait encore la table sur une espèce d'estrade autour de laquelle devaient autrefois se tenir les domestiques.

À l'une des extrémités de la pièce, une loggia, réservée pour des musiciens, dominait la salle.

À la lueur des torches et avec la haute liesse des banquets du bon vieux temps, cet aspect pouvait être adouci. Mais de nos jours, en présence de deux messieurs vêtus de noir, assis dans le cercle de lumière projeté par une lampe voilée d'un abat-jour, la voix détonnait et l'esprit devenait inquiet.

Toute une lignée d'ancêtres habillés de tous les costumes des siècles passés, depuis le chevalier du règne d'Élisabeth jusqu'au petit maître de la Régence, nous fixait du haut de ses cadres et nous gênait par sa muette présence.

Nous parlâmes peu et je me sentis soulagé, une fois le repas terminé, quand nous allâmes fumer une cigarette dans la salle de billard.

« Vrai ! ça n'est pas un endroit folâtre, dit sir Henry. Je crois qu'on peut s'y faire, mais je me sens encore dépaysé. Je ne m'étonne pas qu'à vivre seul dans cette maison, mon oncle soit devenu un peu toqué… Vous plaît-il que nous nous retirions de bonne heure dans nos chambres ?… Demain matin, les choses nous sembleront peut-être plus riantes. »

Avant de me coucher, j'ouvris mes rideaux pour jeter un coup d'œil sur la campagne. Ma fenêtre donnait sur la pelouse, devant la porte du hall. Au-delà, deux bouquets d'arbres s'agitaient en gémissant sous le souffle du vent.

Une partie du disque de la lune apparaissait dans une déchirure des nuages. À cette pâle clarté, je vis, derrière les arbres, la dentelure des roches, ainsi que l'interminable et mélancolique déclivité de la lande.

Je refermai mon rideau avec la sensation que cette dernière impression ne le cédait en rien à celles déjà éprouvées.

Et cependant elle devait être suivie d'une autre non moins pénible !

La fatigue me tenait éveillé. Je me retournais dans mon lit, à la recherche d'un sommeil qui me fuyait sans cesse.

Dans le lointain, une horloge à carillon sonnait tous les quarts ; elle rompait seule le silence de mort qui pesait sur la maison.

Tout à coup un bruit parvint à mon oreille, distinct, sonore, reconnaissable.

C'était un gémissement de femme — le gémissement étouffé de quelqu'un en proie à un inconsolable chagrin.

Je me dressai sur mon séant et j'écoutai avidement.

Le bruit était proche et venait certainement de l'intérieur du château.

Les nerfs tendus, je demeurai ainsi plus d'une demi-heure ; mais je ne perçus plus que le carillon de l'horloge et le frôlement des branches de lierre contre les volets de ma fenêtre.

VII

M. STAPLETON, DE MERRIPIT HOUSE

Le lendemain, la splendeur du matin dissipa un peu l'impression de tristesse laissée dans nos esprits par notre première inspection du château de Baskerville.

Pendant que je déjeunais avec sir Henry, le soleil éclaira les fenêtres à meneaux, arrachant des teintes d'aquarelle à tous les vitraux armoriés qui les garnissaient ; sous ses rayons dorés, les sombres lambris prenaient l'éclat du bronze. On aurait difficilement reconnu la même pièce qui, la veille, nous avait mis tant de mélancolie à l'âme.

« Je crois, dit le baronnet, que nous ne devons nous en prendre qu'à nous-mêmes de ce que nous avons éprouvé hier. La maison n'y était pour rien... Le voyage nous avait fatigués ; notre promenade en voiture nous avait gelés... ; tout cela avait influé sur notre imagination. Ce matin, nous voilà reposés, bien portants et tout nous paraît plus gai.

— Je ne suis pas de votre avis, répondis-je, en ce qui concerne le jeu de notre imagination. Ainsi n'avez-vous pas entendu quelqu'un — une femme, je crois — pleurer toute la nuit ?

— Oui, dans un demi-sommeil, il me semble bien avoir entendu ce bruit. J'ai écouté un instant ; mais, le silence s'étant rétabli, j'en ai conclu que je rêvais.

— Moi, je l'ai perçu très distinctement et je jurerais que c'étaient des gémissements de femme... Il faut que nous éclaircissions ce fait. »

Sir Henry sonna Barrymore et lui demanda quelques explications.

Aux questions de son maître, je crus voir le visage, déjà pâle, du valet de chambre, pâlir encore davantage.

« Il n'y a que deux femmes dans la maison, sir Henri, dit-il : la fille de cuisine, qui couche dans l'autre aile du château, et ma femme. Or, je puis vous affirmer qu'elle est absolument étrangère au bruit dont vous parlez. »

Le domestique mentait certainement, car, après le déjeuner, je rencontrai Mme Barrymore dans le corridor. Elle se trouvait en pleine lumière. C'était une grande femme, impassible, aux traits accentués, ayant, sur les lèvres, un pli amer. Elle avait les yeux rouges et, à travers ses paupières gonflées, son regard se posa sur moi.

Elle avait dû pleurer toute la nuit, et, s'il en était ainsi, son mari ne pouvait l'ignorer. Alors pourquoi avait-il accepté le risque de cette découverte en déclarant le contraire ? Pourquoi ce ton affirmatif ? Et pourquoi — surtout — sa femme pleurait-elle si convulsivement ?

Déjà une atmosphère de mystère et d'obscurité se formait autour de cet homme au teint pâle, porteur d'une superbe barbe noire.

N'était-ce pas lui qui, le premier, avait découvert le cadavre de sir Charles Baskerville ? N'était-il pas le seul témoin qui pût nous renseigner sur les circonstances de la mort du vieux gentilhomme ? Qu'y avait-il d'impossible à ce qu'il fût le voyageur entrevu dans le cab, à Londres ? Sa barbe ressemblait étonnamment à celle de l'inconnu.

Le cocher nous avait bien dépeint son client comme un homme plutôt petit… Mais ne pouvait-il pas s'être trompé ?

Comment tirer cette affaire au clair ?

Évidemment le plus pressé était d'interroger le directeur du bureau de poste de Grimpen et de savoir si le télégramme adressé à Barrymore lui avait été remis en mains propres. Quelle que fût la réponse, j'aurais au moins un détail à communiquer à Sherlock Holmes.

Sir Henry avait de nombreux documents à compulser ; je mis à profit ce temps pour exécuter mon projet.

Une promenade très agréable sur la lande me conduisit à un petit hameau au milieu duquel s'élevaient deux constructions de meilleure apparence que les autres. L'une était l'auberge ; l'autre, la maison du docteur Mortimer.

Le directeur de la poste, qui se livrait également au commerce de l'épicerie, se souvenait fort bien du télégramme.

« Certainement, monsieur, me dit-il, on a remis la dépêche à Barrymore, ainsi que l'indiquait l'adresse.

— Qui l'a remise ?

— Mon fils, ici présent. »

Le fonctionnaire épicier interpella un gamin qui baguenaudait dans un coin.

« James, demanda-t-il, la semaine dernière, tu as bien remis une dépêche à M. Barrymore ?

— Oui, papa.

— A M. Barrymore lui-même ? insistai-je.

— À ce moment-là, il était au grenier et je n'ai pu la donner à lui-même ; mais je l'ai remise à Mme Barrymore, qui m'a promis de la lui porter aussitôt.

— As-tu vu M. Barrymore ?

— Non, monsieur ; je vous ai dit qu'il était au grenier.

— Puisque tu ne l'as pas vu, comment sais-tu qu'il se trouvait au grenier ?

— Sa femme devait savoir où il était, intervint le directeur de la poste. N'aurait-il pas reçu le télégramme ? S'il y a erreur, que M. Barrymore se plaigne ! »

Il me semblait inutile de poursuivre plus loin mon enquête. Ainsi, malgré la ruse inventée par Sherlock Holmes, nous n'avions pas acquis la preuve du séjour de Barrymore au château pendant la semaine précédente.

Supposons le contraire… Supposons que l'homme qui, le dernier, avait vu sir Charles vivant, ait été le premier à espionner son héritier dès son arrivée en Angleterre.

Alors, quoi ?

Était-il l'instrument de quelqu'un ou nourrissait-il de sinistres projets pour son propre compte ?

Quel intérêt avait-il à persécuter la famille Baskerville ?

Je pensai à l'étrange avertissement découpé dans les colonnes du *Times*. Était-ce l'œuvre de Barrymore ou bien celle d'un tiers qui s'évertuait à contrecarrer ses desseins ?

Sir Henry avait émis la version la plus plausible : si on éloignait les Baskerville du château, Barrymore et sa femme y trouveraient un gîte confortable et pour un temps indéfini.

Certes, une semblable explication ne suffisait pas pour justifier le plan qui paraissait enserrer le baronnet comme dans les mailles d'un invisible filet.

Holmes lui-même avait convenu que jamais, au cours de ses sensationnelles enquêtes, on ne lui avait soumis de cas plus complexe.

Tout en retournant au château par cette route solitaire, je faisais des vœux pour que mon ami, enfin débarrassé de ses préoccupations, revînt vite me relever de la lourde responsabilité qui pesait sur moi.

Soudain je fus tiré de mes réflexions par un bruit de pas. Quelqu'un courait derrière moi, en m'appelant par mon nom.

Croyant voir le docteur Mortimer, je me retournai ; mais, à ma grande surprise, un inconnu me poursuivait.

J'aperçus un homme de taille moyenne, mince, élancé, blond, la figure rasée, âgé de trente-cinq ans environ, vêtu d'un complet gris et coiffé d'un chapeau de paille. Il portait sur le dos la boîte en fer-blanc des naturalistes et tenait à la main un grand filet vert à papillons.

« Je vous prie d'excuser mon indiscrétion, docteur Watson, dit-il, en s'arrêtant tout haletant devant moi. Sur la lande, pas n'est besoin des présentations ordinaires. Mortimer, notre ami commun, a dû vous parler de moi… Je suis Stapleton, de Merripit house.

— Votre filet et votre boîte me l'auraient appris, répliquai-je, car je sais que M. Stapleton est un savant naturaliste. Mais comment me connaissez-vous ?

— Je suis allé faire une visite à Mortimer et, tandis que vous passiez sur la route, il vous a montré à moi par la fenêtre de son cabinet. Comme nous suivions le même chemin, j'ai pensé que je vous rattraperais et que je me présenterais moi-même. J'aime à croire que le voyage n'a pas trop fatigué sir Henry ?

— Non, merci ; il est en excellente santé.

— Tout le monde ici redoutait qu'après la mort de sir Charles le nouveau baronnet ne vînt pas habiter le château. C'est beaucoup demander à un homme jeune et riche de s'enterrer dans un pareil endroit, et je n'ai pas à vous dire combien cette question intéressait la contrée ; sir Henry, je suppose, ne partage par les craintes superstitieuses du populaire ?

— Je ne le pense pas.

— Vous connaissez certainement la légende de ce maudit chien que l'on accuse d'être le fléau de la famille ?

— On me l'a contée.

— Les paysans de ces parages sont extraordinairement crédules. Beaucoup jureraient avoir rencontré sur la lande ce fantastique animal. »

Stapleton parlait, le sourire sur les lèvres, mais il me sembla lire dans ses yeux qu'il prenait la chose plus au sérieux.

Il reprit :

« Cette histoire hantait l'imagination de sir Charles, et je suis sûr qu'elle n'a pas été étrangère à sa fin tragique.

— Comment cela ?

— Ses nerfs étaient tellement exacerbés que l'apparition d'un chien quelconque devait produire un effet désastreux sur son cœur, mortellement atteint. J'imagine qu'il a réellement vu quelque chose de ce genre dans sa dernière promenade, le long de l'allée des Ifs. J'appréhendais sans cesse un malheur, car j'aimais beaucoup sir Charles et je lui savais le cœur très malade.

— Comment l'aviez-vous appris ?

— Par mon ami, le docteur Mortimer.

— Alors vous croyez qu'un chien a poursuivi sir Charles et que la peur a occasionné sa mort ?

— Pouvez-vous me fournir une meilleure explication ?

— Il ne m'appartient pas de conclure.

— Quelle est l'opinion de M. Sherlock Holmes ? »

Pendant quelques secondes, cette question me coupa la parole. Mais un regard sur la figure placide et sur les yeux assurés de mon compagnon me montra qu'elle ne cachait aucune arrière-pensée.

« Nous essayerions vainement de prétendre que nous ne vous connaissons pas, docteur Watson, continua Stapleton. Les hauts faits de votre ami le détective sont parvenus jusqu'à nous et vous ne pouviez les célébrer sans vous rendre vous-même populaire. Lorsque Mortimer vous a nommé, j'ai aussitôt établi votre identité. Vous êtes ici parce M. Sherlock Holmes s'intéresse à l'affaire, et je suis bien excusable de chercher à connaître son opinion.

— Je regrette de n'être pas en mesure de répondre à cette question.

— Puis-je au moins vous demander s'il nous honorera d'une visite ?

— D'autres enquêtes le retiennent à la ville en ce moment.

— Quel malheur ! Il jetterait un peu de lumière sur tout ce qui reste si obscur pour nous. Quant à vos recherches personnelles, si vous jugez que je vous sois de quelque utilité, j'espère que vous n'hésiterez pas à user de moi. Si vous m'indiquiez seulement la nature de vos soupçons ou de quel côté vous allez pousser vos investigations, il me serait possible de vous donner dès maintenant un avis ou une aide.

— Je vous affirme que je suis simplement en visite chez mon ami sir Henry et que je n'ai besoin d'aide d'aucune sorte.

— Parfait ! dit Stapleton. Vous avez raison de vous montrer prudent et circonspect. Je regrette de vous avoir adressé cette question indiscrète, et je vous promets de m'abstenir dorénavant de la plus légère allusion à ce sujet. »

Nous étions arrivés à un endroit où un étroit sentier tapissé de mousse se branchait sur la route pour traverser ensuite la lande.

Sur la droite, un monticule escarpé, caillouteux, avait dû être exploité autrefois comme carrière de granit. Le versant qui nous faisait face était taillé à pic ; dans les anfractuosités de la roche, poussaient des fougères et des ronces.

Dans le lointain, un panache de fumée montait perpendiculairement dans le ciel.

« Quelques minutes de marche dans ce sentier perdu nous conduiront à Merripit house, dit Stapleton. Voulez-vous me consacrer une heure ?… Je vous présenterai à ma sœur. »

Mon premier mouvement fut de refuser. Mon devoir me commandait de retourner auprès de sir Henry.

Mais je me souvins de l'amas de papiers qui recouvrait sa table et je me dis que je ne lui étais d'aucun secours pour les examiner.

D'ailleurs Holmes ne m'avait-il pas recommandé d'étudier tous les habitants de la lande ?

J'acceptais donc l'invitation de Stapleton et nous nous engageâmes dans le petit chemin.

« Quel endroit merveilleux que la lande ! dit mon compagnon, en jetant un regard circulaire sur les ondulations de la montagne qui ressemblaient à de gigantesques vagues de granit. On ne se lasse jamais du spectacle qu'elle offre à l'œil de l'observateur. Vous ne pouvez imaginer quels secrets étonnants cache cette solitude !… Elle est si vaste, si dénudée, si mystérieuse !

— Vous la connaissez donc bien ?

Je ne suis ici que depuis deux ans. Les gens du pays me considèrent comme un nouveau venu… Nous nous y installâmes peu de temps après l'arrivée de sir Charles… Mes goûts me portèrent à explorer la contrée jusque dans ses plus petits recoins… Je ne pense pas qu'il existe quelqu'un qui la connaisse mieux que moi.

— Est-ce donc si difficile ?

— Très difficile. Voyez-vous, par exemple, cette grande plaine, là-bas, vers le nord, avec ces proéminences bizarres ? Qu'y trouvez-vous de remarquable ?

— On y piquerait un fameux galop.

— Naturellement, vous deviez me répondre cela… Que de vies humaines cette erreur n'a-t-elle pas déjà coûté ? Apercevez-vous ces places vertes disséminées à sa surface ?

— Le sol paraît y être plus fertile. »

Stapleton se mit à rire.

« C'est la grande fondrière de Grimpen, fit-il. Là-bas, un faux pas conduit à une mort certaine — homme ou bête. Pas plus tard qu'hier, j'ai vu s'y engager un des chevaux qui errent sur la lande. Il n'en est plus ressorti… Pendant un moment, sa tête s'est agitée au-dessus de la vase, puis le bourbier l'a aspiré ! On ne la traverse pas sans danger dans la saison sèche ; mais après la saison d'automne, l'endroit est terriblement dangereux. Et cependant je puis m'y promener en tous sens et en sortir sans encombre. Tenez ! voilà encore un de ces malheureux chevaux ! »

Une forme brune allait et venait au milieu des ajoncs. Tout à coup, une encolure se dressa, en même temps qu'un hennissement lugubre réveilla tous les échos de la lande.

Je me sentis frissonner de terreur ; mais les nerfs de mon compagnon me parurent beaucoup moins impressionnables que les miens.

« C'est fini ! me dit-il. La fondrière s'en est emparée… Cela fait deux en deux jours !… Et ils seront suivis de bien d'autres. Pendant la sécheresse, ils ont l'habitude d'aller brouter de ce côté, et, lorsqu'ils s'aperçoivent que le sol est devenu moins consistant, la fondrière les a déjà saisis.

— Et vous dites que vous pouvez vous y aventurer ?

— Oui. Il existe un ou deux sentiers dans lesquels un homme courageux peut se risquer… Je les ai découverts.

— Quel désir vous poussait donc à pénétrer dans un lieu si terrible ?

— Regardez ces monticules — au-delà ! Ils représentent de vrais îlots de verdure découpés dans l'immensité de la fondrière. C'est là qu'on rencontre les plantes rares et les papillons peu communs… Si le cœur vous dit d'aller les y chercher ?…

— Quelque jour j'essayerai. »

Stapleton me regarda avec étonnement :

« Au nom du ciel, s'écria-t-il, abandonnez ce funeste projet ! Je vous affirme que vous n'avez pas la plus petite chance de vous tirer de là vivant. Je n'y parviens qu'en me servant de points de repère très compliqués.

— Hein ? fis-je… Qu'y a-t-il encore ? »

Un long gémissement, indiciblement triste, courut sur la lande. Bien qu'il eût ébranlé l'air, il était impossible de préciser d'où il venait.

Commencé sur une modulation sourde, semblable à un murmure, il se changea en un profond rugissement, pour finir en un nouveau murmure, mélancolique, poignant.

« Hé ! curieux endroit, la lande ! répéta Stapleton.

— Qu'était-ce donc ?

— Les paysans prétendent que c'est le chien de Baskerville qui hurle pour attirer sa proie. Je l'ai déjà entendu une ou deux fois, mais jamais aussi distinctement. »

Avec un tressaillement de crainte au fond du cœur, je regardai cette vaste étendue de plaine, mouchetée de larges taches vertes formées par les ajoncs.

Sauf deux corbeaux qui croassaient lugubrement sur la cime d'un pic, une immobilité de mort régnait partout.

« Vous êtes un homme instruit, dis-je, vous ne pouvez croire à de pareilles balivernes ! À quelle cause attribuez-vous ce bruit étrange ?

— Les fondrières rendent parfois des sons bizarres, inexplicables… La boue se tasse… L'eau sourd ou quelque chose…

— Non, non, répondis-je ; c'était une voix humaine.

— Peut-être bien, répondit Stapleton. Avez-vous jamais entendu s'envoler un butor ?

— Non, jamais.

— C'est un oiseau très rare — a peu près complètement disparu de l'Angleterre — mais, dans la lande, rien n'est impossible. Oui, je ne serais pas étonné d'apprendre que c'est le cri du dernier butor qui vient de frapper nos oreilles.

— Quel bruit étrange !…

— Ce pays est plein de surprises. Regardez le flanc de la colline… Que croyez-vous apercevoir ? »

Je vis une vingtaine de tas de pierre grises amoncelées circulairement.

« Je ne sais pas… Des abris de bergers ?

— Non. Nos dignes ancêtres habitaient là. L'homme préhisto-rique vivait sur la lande et comme, depuis cette époque, personne ne l'a imité, nous y retrouvons encore presque intacts les vesti-ges de son passage. Ceci vous représente des wigwams recou-verts de leur toiture. Si la curiosité vous prenait de les visiter, vous y verriez un foyer, une couchette…

— On dirait une petite ville. À quelle époque était-elle peu-plée ?

— L'homme néolithique… la date nous manque.

— Que faisait-il ?

— Il menait paître son troupeau sur les pentes et, lorsque les armes de bronze remplacèrent les haches de pierre, il fouillait les entrailles de la terre à la recherche du zinc. Voyez cette grande tranchée sur la colline opposée… Voilà la preuve de ce que j'avance. Ah ! vous rencontrerez de bien curieux sujets d'étude sur la lande ! Excusez-moi un instant, docteur Watson… c'est sûrement un cyclopelte !… »

Un petit insecte avait traversé le chemin et Stapleton s'était aussitôt élancé à sa poursuite.

À mon grand désappointement, la bestiole vola droit vers la fondrière, et ma nouvelle connaissance, bondissant de touffe en touffe, courait après elle, son grand filet vert se balançant dans l'air. Ses vêtements gris, sa démarche irrégulière, sautillante, saccadée, le faisaient ressembler lui-même à une gigantesque phalène.

Je m'étais arrêté pour suivre sa chasse, et j'éprouvais un mélange d'admiration pour son extraordinaire agilité et de crainte pour le danger auquel il s'exposait dans cette perfide fon-drière. Un bruit de pas me fit retourner ; une femme s'avançait vers moi dans le chemin.

Elle venait du côté où le panache de fumée dénonçait l'empla-cement de Merripit house ; mais la courbure de la lande l'avait cachée à mes yeux jusqu'au moment où elle se trouva près de moi.

Je reconnus en elle miss Stapleton dont on m'avait parlé. Cela me fut aisé, car, indépendamment du petit nombre de femmes

qui vivent sur la lande, on me l'avait dépeinte comme une personne d'une réelle beauté.

La femme qui s'approchait de moi répondait au portrait qu'on
m'avait tracé de la sœur du naturaliste.

Impossible de concevoir un plus grand contraste entre un frère
et une sœur.

Stapleton était quelconque, avec ses cheveux blonds et ses
yeux gris, tandis que la jeune fille avait ce teint chaud des brunes
— si rare en Angleterre. Son visage un peu altier, mais finement
modelé, aurait paru impassible dans sa régularité, sans l'expression sensuelle de la bouche et la vivacité de deux yeux noirs lar-
gement fendus. Sa taille parfaite, moulée dans une robe de coupe
élégante, la faisait ressembler, sur ce chemin désert, à une
étrange apparition.

Au moment où je me retournais, elle regardait son frère. Alors
elle hâta le pas.

J'avais ôté mon chapeau et j'allais prononcer quelques mots
d'explication, lorsque ses paroles imprimèrent une autre direction à mes pensées.

« Allez-vous-en ! s'écria-t-elle. Retournez vite à Londres. »

Si grande fut ma surprise, que j'en demeurai stupide.

En me regardant, ses yeux brillaient et son pied frappait le sol
avec impatience.

« Pourquoi m'en aller ? demandai-je.

— Je ne puis vous le dire. »

Elle parlait d'une voix basse, précipitée, avec un léger grasseyement dans sa prononciation.

Elle reprit :

« Pour l'amour de Dieu, faites ce que je vous recommande.
Retournez vite et ne remettez jamais plus les pieds sur la lande !

— Mais j'arrive à peine.

— Pourquoi ne tenir aucun compte d'un avertissement dicté
pour votre seul intérêt ?… Retournez à Londres !… Partez ce
soir même… Fuyez ces lieux à tout prix ! Prenez garde ! Voici
mon frère… pas un mot de ce que je vous ai dit… Soyez donc
assez aimable pour me cueillir cette orchidée, là-bas… La lande
est très riche en orchidées… vous en jugerez par vous-même,

bien que vous soyez venu à une saison trop avancée pour jouir de toutes les beautés de la nature. »

Stapleton avait renoncé à sa poursuite et retournait vers nous, essoufflé, et le teint coloré par la course.

« Eh bien, Béryl ? » dit-il.

Il me sembla que le ton de cette interpellation manquait de cordialité.

« Vous avez bien chaud, Jack.

— Oui ; je poursuivais un cyclopelte. Ils sont très rares, surtout à la fin de l'automne. Quel malheur de n'avoir pu l'attraper ! »

Il parlait avec un air dégagé, mais ses petits yeux gris allaient sans cesse de la jeune fille à moi.

« Je vois que les présentations sont faites, continua-t-il.

— Oui. Je disais à sir Henry qu'il était un peu tard pour admirer les beautés de la lande.

— À qui penses-tu donc parler ?

— À sir Henri Baskerville.

— Non, non, me récriai-je vivement… pas à sir Henry, mais à un simple bourgeois, son ami… Je me nomme le docteur Watson. »

Une expression de contrariété passa sur le visage de miss Stapleton.

« Nous avons joué aux propos interrompus, dit-elle.

— Vous n'avez pas eu le temps d'échanger beaucoup de paroles ? demanda son frère, avec son même regard interrogateur.

— J'ai causé avec le docteur Watson, comme si, au lieu d'un simple visiteur, il eût été un habitant permanent de la lande.

— Que peut lui importer que la saison soit trop avancée pour les orchidées !… Nous ferez-vous le plaisir de nous accompagner jusqu'à Merripit house ? » ajouta le naturaliste, en se tournant vers moi.

Quelques instants après, nous arrivions à une modeste maison ayant autrefois servi d'habitation à un herbager de la lande, mais que l'on avait réparée depuis et modernisée.

Un verger l'entourait. Les arbres, comme tous ceux de la lande, étaient rabougris et pelés. L'aspect de ce lieu remplissait l'âme d'une vague tristesse.

Nous fûmes reçus par un vieux bonhomme qui paraissait monter la garde autour de la maison.

À l'intérieur, les pièces étaient spacieuses et meublées avec une élégance qui trahissait le bon goût de la maîtresse de la maison.

Tandis que, par la fenêtre entrouverte, je jetais un coup d'œil sur le paysage sauvage qui se déroulait devant moi, je me demandais quelle raison avait amené dans ce pays perdu cet homme d'un esprit cultivé et cette superbe créature.

« Singulier endroit pour y planter sa tente, n'est-ce pas ? fit Stapleton, répondant ainsi à ma pensée. Et cependant nous nous sommes arrangés pour y être heureux, pas, Béryl ?

— Très heureux, répliqua la jeune fille, dont le ton me parut toutefois manquer de conviction.

— Je dirigeais jadis une école, continua Stapleton, dans le nord de l'Angleterre... Pour un homme de mon tempérament, la besogne était trop machinale et trop dépourvue d'intérêt. Mais j'aimais à vivre ainsi au milieu de la jeunesse, à façonner ces jeunes intelligences à ma guise et à leur inculquer mes idées et mes préférences. La malchance s'en mêla : une épidémie se déclara dans le village et trois enfants moururent. Mon établissement ne se releva jamais de ce coup et la majeure partie de mes ressources se trouva engloutie. Si je ne regrettais la charmante compagnie de mes écoliers, je me réjouirais de cet incident. Avec mon amour immodéré pour la botanique et la zoologie, je rencontrerais difficilement un champ plus ouvert à nos recherches, car ma sœur est aussi éprise que moi des choses de la nature. Ceci, docteur Watson, répond à une question que j'ai lue sur votre visage, pendant que vous regardiez sur la lande.

— Je me disais, en effet, que ce séjour devait être bien triste, sinon pour vous, du moins pour votre sœur.

— Non, non, dit vivement miss Stapleton ; je ne connais pas la tristesse.

— Nous avons nos études, nos livres et de bons voisins, paraphrasa mon hôte. Le docteur Mortimer est un véritable savant... Puis nous possédions dans ce pauvre sir Charles un délicieux compagnon. Nous l'appréciions beaucoup, et nous ressentons plus que je ne puis le dire le vide causé par sa mort… Serais-je indiscret en me présentant cet après-midi au château pour rendre visite à sir Henry ?

— Je suis sûr que vous lui ferez le plus grand plaisir.

— Alors prévenez-le de ma venue. Nous nous emploierons de tout notre pouvoir pour qu'il s'habitue ici… Désirez-vous, docteur Watson, visiter ma collection de lépidoptères ? Je ne crois pas qu'il en existe de plus complète dans tout le sud de l'Angleterre. Pendant que vous l'admirerez on nous préparera un lunch. »

J'avais hâte de reprendre auprès de sir Henry mes fonctions de garde du corps. D'ailleurs, la solitude de la lande, la mort du malheureux cheval aspiré par la fondrière, le bruit étrange que le public associait à l'horrible légende des Baskerville, tout cela m'étreignait le cœur. J'ajouterai encore l'impression produite par l'avis de miss Stapleton, avis si précis et si net que je ne pouvais l'attribuer qu'à quelque grave raison.

Je résistai donc à toutes les instances de mon hôte et je repris, par le même étroit sentier, le chemin du château.

Mais il devait exister un raccourci connu des habitants du pays, car, avant que j'eusse rejoint la grande route, je fus très étonné de voir miss Stapleton, assise sur un quartier de roche, au croisement de deux voies.

Elle avait marché très vite, et la précipitation de la course avait empourpré ses joues.

« J'ai couru de toutes mes forces afin de vous devancer, me dit-elle. Je n'ai même pas pris le temps de mettre un chapeau… Je ne m'arrête pas… Mon frère s'apercevrait de mon absence. Je voulais vous dire combien je déplorais la stupide erreur que j'ai commise en vous confondant avec sir Henry. Oubliez mes paroles, elles ne vous concernent en rien.

— Comment les oublierais-je, miss Stapleton, répliquai-je. Je suis l'ami de sir Henry, et le souci de sa sécurité m'incombe tout particulièrement. Apprenez-moi pourquoi vous souhaitiez si ardemment qu'il retournât à Londres.

— Caprice de femme, docteur Watson ! Lorsque vous me connaîtrez davantage, vous comprendrez que je ne puisse pas toujours fournir l'explication de mes paroles ou de mes actes.

— Non, non… Je me rappelle le frémissement de votre voix, l'expression de votre regard… Je vous en prie, je vous en supplie, soyez franche, miss Stapleton ! Depuis que j'ai posé le pied sur ce pays, je me sens environné de mystères. La vie sur la lande ressemble à la fondrière de Grimpen : elle est parsemée d'îlots de verdure auprès desquels l'abîme vous guette, et aucun guide ne s'offre à vous éloigner du danger. Que vouliez-vous dire ? Apprenez-le-moi et je vous promets de communiquer votre avertissement à sir Henry. »

Pendant une minute, un combat se livra dans l'âme de la jeune fille. Toutefois, ses traits avaient repris leur expression résolue, lorsqu'elle me répondit :

« Vous prêtez à mes paroles plus d'importance qu'elles n'en comportent. La mort de sir Charles nous a très vivement impressionnés, mon frère et moi. Nous étions très liés… Sa promenade favorite consistait à se rendre chez nous par la lande. Cette espèce de sort qui pesait sur sa famille hantait son cerveau, et, lorsque se produisit le tragique événement, je crus ses craintes fondées jusqu'à un certain point. Quand on annonça qu'un nouveau membre de la famille Baskerville allait habiter le château, mes appréhensions se réveillèrent et j'ai pensé bien faire en le prévenant du danger qu'il courait. Voilà le mobile auquel j'ai obéi.

— Mais quel est ce danger ?

— Vous connaissez bien l'histoire du chien ?

— Je n'ajoute aucune foi à de pareilles absurdités.

— J'en ajoute, moi. Si vous possédez quelque influence sur sir Henry, emmenez-le loin de ce pays qui a déjà été si fatal à sa famille. Le monde est grand… Pourquoi s'obstinerait-il à vivre au milieu du péril ?

— Précisément parce qu'il y a du péril. Sir Henry est ainsi fait. Je crains qu'à moins d'un avis plus motivé que celui que vous m'avez donné il ne me soit impossible de le déterminer à partir.

— Je ne puis vous dire autre chose… je ne sais rien de précis.

— Me permettez-vous de vous adresser une dernière question, miss Stapleton ? Quand vous m'avez parlé tout à l'heure, puisqu'il vous était impossible de m'en apprendre davantage, pourquoi redoutiez-vous tant que votre frère ne vous entendît. Il n'y avait rien dans vos paroles que ni lui — ni personne d'ailleurs — ne pût écouter.

— Mon frère désire que le château soit habité ; il estime que le bonheur des pauvres gens de la lande l'exige. Tout avis poussant sir Henry à s'éloigner l'aurait mécontenté... J'ai accompli maintenant mon devoir et je n'ajouterai plus un mot. Je retourne vite à la maison pour que mon frère ne se doute pas que nous avons causé ensemble. Adieu. »

Miss Stapleton reprit le chemin par lequel elle était venue, tandis que, le cœur oppressé de vagues alarmes, je continuais ma route vers le château.

VIII

PREMIER RAPPORT DU DOCTEUR WATSON

J'ai sous les yeux, éparses sur ma table, les lettres que j'écrivais à Sherlock Holmes au fur et à mesure que se déroulèrent les événements. Une page manque ; mais, sauf cette lacune, elles sont l'expression exacte de la vérité. De plus, elles montrent mes impressions et mes craintes d'alors plus fidèlement que ne pourrait le faire ma mémoire, quelque ineffaçable souvenir qu'elle ait gardé de ces heures tragiques.

Je vais donc reproduire ces lettres afin de relater les faits selon leur enchaînement.

Château de Baskerville, 13 octobre.

« Mon cher Holmes,

« Mes dépêches et mes lettres précédentes vous ont à peu près tenu au courant de tout ce qui s'est passé jusqu'à ce jour dans ce coin du monde, certainement oublié de Dieu.

« Plus on vit ici, plus l'influence de la lande pénètre l'âme du sentiment de son immensité, mais aussi de son charme effrayant.

« Dès qu'on a foulé ce sol, on perd la notion de l'Angleterre moderne. On heurte à chaque pas les vestiges laissés par les hommes des temps préhistoriques. Où qu'on dirige sa promenade, on rencontre les demeures de cette race éteinte, ses tombeaux et les énormes monolithes qui marquent, à ce que l'on suppose, l'emplacement de ses temples.

« Si celui qui examine ces huttes de pierres grisâtres adossées au flanc raviné des collines apercevait un homme, la barbe et les cheveux incultes, le corps recouverts d'une peau de bête, sortant de l'une d'elles et assujettissant sur la corde de son arc une flèche terminée par un silex aigu, celui-là se croirait transporté à un autre âge et jurerait que la présence en ces lieux de cet être, depuis longtemps disparu, est plus naturelle que la sienne propre.

« On se demande avec stupeur comment des êtres humains ont pu vivre en aussi grand nombre sur cette terre toujours réputée stérile. Je ne connais rien des choses de l'antiquité, mais je présume qu'il a existé des races pacifiques et opprimées qui ont dû se contenter des territoires dédaignés par les autres peuples plus conquérants.

« Tout ceci est étranger à la mission que vous m'avez confiée et n'intéressera que médiocrement votre esprit si merveilleusement pratique. Je me rappelle encore votre superbe indifférence à propos du mouvement terrestre. Que vous importe celui des deux, de la terre ou du soleil, qui tourne autour de l'autre !

« Je reviens aux faits concernant sir Henry Baskerville.

« Depuis ces derniers jours, je ne vous ai adressé aucun rapport, parce que, jusqu'à cette date, je n'avais rien de marquant à vous signaler.

« Mais il vient de se produire un fait important que je dois vous raconter. Néanmoins, avant de le faire, je veux vous présenter certains facteurs du problème que nous avons à résoudre.

« L'un d'entre eux est ce prisonnier évadé, errant sur la lande, et dont je vous ai succinctement entretenu. Il y a toutes sortes de bonnes raisons de croire qu'il a quitté le pays — pour la plus grande tranquillité des habitants du district.

« Une semaine s'est écoulée depuis son évasion et on ne l'a pas plus vu qu'on n'a entendu parler de lui. Il serait inconcevable qu'il eût pu tenir la lande pendant tout ce temps.

« Certes, quelques-unes de ces huttes de pierre lui auraient aisément servi de cachette ; mais de quoi se serait-il nourri dans ce pays où, à moins de tuer les moutons qui paissent l'herbe rase des collines, il n'y a rien à manger.

« Nous pensons donc qu'il s'est enfui, et les hôtes des fermes écartées goûtent de nouveau un paisible sommeil.

« Ici, nous sommes quatre hommes capables de nous défendre ; il n'en est pas de même chez les Stapleton et j'avoue qu'en pensant à leur isolement, je me sens inquiet pour eux.

« Le frère, la sœur, un vieux serviteur et une domestique vivent éloignés de tout secours. Ils se trouveraient sans défense, si un gaillard décidé à tout, comme ce criminel de Notting Hill, parvenait à s'introduire dans leur maison.

« Sir Henry et moi, nous préoccupant de cette situation, nous avions décidé que Perkins, le cocher, irait coucher chez Stapleton ; mais ce dernier s'y est opposé.

« Notre ami le baronnet témoigne un intérêt considérable à notre jolie voisine. Cela n'a rien d'étonnant, dans cette contrée déserte où les heures pèsent lourdement sur un homme aussi actif que sir Henry… Puis miss Béryl Stapleton est bien attirante ! Il y a en elle quelque chose d'exotique, de tropical, qui forme un singulier contraste avec son frère, si froid, si impassible.

« Cependant Stapleton évoque l'idée de ces feux qui couvent sous les cendres. Il exerce une très réelle influence sur sa sœur, car j'ai remarqué qu'en parlant elle cherchait constamment son regard pour y lire une approbation. L'éclat métallique des prunelles de cet homme et ses lèvres minces, d'un dessin si ferme, dénotent une nature autoritaire. Vous le trouveriez digne de toute votre attention.

« L'après-midi du jour où j'avais rencontré Stapleton, il vint à Baskerville, et, le lendemain matin, il nous conduisit à l'endroit où l'on suppose que se passèrent, d'après la légende, les faits relatifs à ce misérable Hugo Baskerville.

« Nous marchâmes pendant quelques milles sur la lande jusqu'à un site tellement sinistre d'aspect, qu'il n'en fallait pas davantage pour accréditer cette légende.

« Une étroite vallée, enserrée entre deux pics rocheux, conduisait à un espace gazonné sur lequel avaient poussé des fleurettes des champs.

« Au milieu, se dressaient deux grandes pierres usées et comme affilées à leurs extrémités, au point de ressembler aux monstrueuses canines d'un animal fabuleux.

« Rien dans ce décor ne détonnait avec la scène du drame de jadis.

« Très intéressé, sir Henry demanda plusieurs fois à Stapleton s'il croyait véritablement aux interventions surnaturelles dans les affaires des hommes. Il parlait sur un ton badin, mais il était évident qu'il outrait son langage.

« Stapleton se montra circonspect dans ses réponses ; mais il était non moins évident que, par égard pour l'état d'esprit du baronnet, il dissimulait une partie de sa pensée. Il nous cita le cas de plusieurs familles ayant souffert d'influences malignes, et il nous laissa sous l'impression qu'il partageait la croyance populaire en la matière.

« En revenant, nous nous arrêtâmes à Merripit house pour y déjeuner.

« Ce fut là que sir Henry fit la connaissance de miss Stapleton.

« Dès cette première rencontre, la jeune fille me parut avoir profondément impressionné l'esprit de notre ami, et je me tromperais fort si ce sentiment ne fut pas réciproque.

« Pendant que nous rentrions au château, le baronnet me parla sans cesse de notre voisine et, depuis lors, il ne s'est pas écoulé de jour que nous n'ayons vu quelqu'un, du frère ou de la sœur.

« Ils ont dîné hier ici et l'on a causé vaguement d'une visite que nous leur ferions la semaine prochaine.

« Vous comprenez qu'une semblable union ravirait Stapleton. Cependant, lorsque sir Henry devenait trop empressé auprès de la sœur, j'ai surpris maintes fois dans les yeux du frère un regard non équivoque de désapprobation. Il doit être partagé entre l'affection qu'il a pour elle et la crainte de l'existence solitaire qu'il mènerait après son départ. Toutefois, ce serait le comble de l'égoïsme que de s'opposer à un aussi brillant mariage.

« J'ai la conviction que Stapleton ne souhaite pas que cette intimité se change en amour, et j'ai souvent remarqué qu'il se donnait beaucoup de mal pour empêcher leurs tête-à-tête.

« Soit dit en passant, la recommandation que vous m'avez faite de ne jamais laisser sir Henry sortir seul deviendrait bien difficile à suivre, si une intrigue d'amour venait s'ajouter à nos autres embarras. Mes bons rapports avec sir Henry se ressentiraient certainement de l'exécution trop rigoureuse de vos ordres.

« L'autre jour — mardi, pour préciser — le docteur Mortimer a déjeuner avec nous. Il avait pratiqué des fouilles dans un tumulus, à Long Down, et y avait trouvé un crâne de l'époque préhistorique qui l'avait rempli de joie. Je ne connais pas de maniaque qui lui soit comparable !

« Les Stapleton arrivèrent peu après le docteur, et Mortimer, sur la demande de sir Henry, nous conduisit tous à l'allée des Ifs pour nous expliquer comment l'événement avait dû se produire, la fatale nuit.

« Quel lugubre promenade que cette allée des Ifs !

« Imaginez un chemin bordé de chaque côté par la muraille épaisse et sombre d'une haie taillée aux ciseaux avec, à droite et à gauche, une étroite bande de gazon.

« L'extrémité de l'allée opposée au château aboutit à une serre à moitié démolie.

« Au milieu de cette allée, une porte s'ouvre sur la lande. C'est à cet endroit que, par deux fois, sir Charles a secoué les cendres de son cigare. Cette porte, de bois peint en blanc, ne ferme qu'au loquet. Au-delà s'étend l'immensité de la lande.

« Je me souviens de votre théorie sur l'affaire et j'essayai de reconstituer la scène.

« Tandis que le vieux gentilhomme s'était arrêté, il avait vu arriver du dehors quelque chose qui le terrifia tellement qu'il en perdit l'esprit et qu'il courut, qu'il courut, jusqu'à ce qu'il tomba foudroyé par la peur et l'épuisement.

« Voilà le long couloir de verdure par lequel il a fui.

« Que fuyait-il ?

« Un chien de berger ? ou bien un chien noir, silencieux, monstrueux, fantastique ?

« S'agissait-il, au contraire, d'un guet-apens qui ne relevait en rien de l'ordre surnaturel ?

« Le pâle et vigilant Barrymore en savait-il plus long qu'il ne voulait en dire ?

« Tout cela était vague, sombre — plus sombre surtout à cause du crime que je soupçonnais.

« Depuis ma dernière lettre, j'ai fait la connaissance d'un autre voisin, M. Frankland, de Lafter Hall, qui habite à quatre milles de nous, vers le sud.

« C'est un homme âgé, rouge de teint, blanc de cheveux et colérique. La législation anglaise le passionne et il a dissipé en procès une grande fortune. Il plaide pour le seul plaisir de plaider. On le trouve toujours disposé à soutenir l'une ou l'autre face d'une question ; aussi ne doit-on pas s'étonner que cet amusement lui ait coûté fort cher.

« Un jour, il supprime un droit de passage et défie la commune de l'obliger à le rétablir. Le lendemain, il démolit de ses propres mains la clôture d'un voisin et déclare la servitude prescrite depuis un temps immémorial, défiant cette fois le propriétaire de le poursuivre pour violation de propriété.

« Il est ferré sur les droits seigneuriaux et communaux et il applique ses connaissances juridiques, tantôt en faveur des paysans de Fenworthy et tantôt contre eux, de telles sorte que, périodiquement et selon sa plus récente interprétation de la loi, on le porte en triomphe dans le village ou on l'y brûle en effigie.

« On prétend qu'il soutient en ce moment sept procès, ce qui absorbera probablement le restant de sa fortune et lui enlèvera toute envie de plaider dans l'avenir.

« Cette bizarrerie de caractère mise à part, je le crois un bon et brave homme, et je ne vous en parle que pour satisfaire votre désir de connaître tous ceux qui nous entourent.

« Pour l'instant, il a une autre marotte. En sa qualité d'astronome amateur, il possède un excellent télescope qu'il a installé sur son toit et à l'aide duquel il passe son temps à interroger la lande, afin de découvrir le prisonnier échappé de Princetown.

« S'il employait seulement son activité à ce but louable, tout serait pour le mieux ; mais la rumeur publique fait circuler le bruit qu'il a l'intention de poursuivre le docteur Mortimer pour avoir ouvert un tombeau sans l'autorisation des parents du défunt — il s'agit du crâne de l'âge néolithique retiré du tumulus de Long Down. En un mot, il rompt la monotonie de notre existence et apporte une note gaie dans ce milieu, qui en a réellement besoin.

« Maintenant que je vous ai entretenu du prisonnier évadé, des Stapleton, du docteur Mortimer, de Frankland, laissez-moi finir par un fait très important : il concerne les Barrymore.

« Vous vous souvenez du télégramme envoyé de Londres pour nous assurer que Barrymore se trouvait bien ici.

« Je vous ai déjà informé que le témoignage du directeur de la poste de Grimpen n'était concluant ni dans un sens ni dans l'autre.

« Je dis à sir Henry ce qu'il en était. Immédiatement il appela Barrymore et lui demanda s'il avait reçu lui-même le télégramme.

« Barrymore répondit affirmativement.

« — Le petit télégraphiste vous l'a-t-il remis en mains propres ? » interrogea sir Henry.

« Barrymore parut étonné et réfléchit quelques instants :

« — Non, fit-il ; j'étais au grenier à ce moment-là ; ma femme me l'y a monté.

« — Est-ce vous qui avez envoyé la réponse ?

« — Non, j'ai dit à ma femme ce qu'il fallait répondre et elle est redescendue pour écrire. »

« Dans la soirée, le valet de chambre revint de lui-même sur ce sujet :

« — Je cherche vraiment, sir Henry, à comprendre l'objet de vos questions, dit-il. J'espère qu'elles ne tendent pas à établir que j'ai fait quoi que ce soit pour perdre votre confiance. »

« Sir Henry affirma qu'il n'en était rien. Il acheva de le tranquilliser en lui donnant presque toute son ancienne garde-robe.

« Mme Barrymore m'intéresse au plus haut degré. C'est une femme un peu corpulente, bornée, excessivement respectable et de mœurs puritaines. Vous imagineriez difficilement une nature plus glaciale.

« Je vous ai raconté comment je l'entendis sangloter, la nuit de mon arrivée au château. Depuis, j'ai surpris maintes fois des traces de larmes sur son visage. Quelque profond chagrin lui ronge le cœur.

« Est-ce le souvenir d'une faute qui la hante ?

« Ou bien Barrymore jouerait-il les tyrans domestiques ?

« J'ai toujours pressenti qu'il y avait quelque chose d'anormal et de louche dans les manières de cet homme. L'aventure de la nuit dernière a fortifié mes soupçons.

« Et cependant elle semble de bien petite importance par elle-même !

« Vous savez si, en temps ordinaire, mon sommeil est léger… Il est plus léger encore, depuis que vous m'avez placé de garde auprès de sir Henry.

« Or, la nuit dernière, vers deux heures du matin, je fus réveillé par un bruit de pas glissant furtivement dans le corridor.

« Je me levai et j'ouvris ma porte pour risquer un œil.

« Une ombre noire allongée — celle d'un homme tenant une bougie à la main — traînait sur le tapis.

« L'homme était en bras de chemise et pieds nus.

« Je ne voyais que les contours de son ombre ; mais, à ses dimensions, je reconnus qu'elle ne pouvait appartenir qu'à Barrymore.

« Il marchait lentement, avec précaution. Il y avait dans son allure quelque chose d'indéfinissable — de criminel et de craintif à la fois.

« Je vous ai écrit que le balcon qui court autour du hall coupe en deux le corridor et que ce dernier se prolonge à droite et à gauche jusqu'à chaque extrémité du château.

« J'attendis que Barrymore eût disparu, puis je le suivis.

« Lorsque j'arrivai au tournant du balcon, il avait atteint le fond du corridor et, à une clarté qui passait par l'entrebâillement d'une porte, je vis qu'il était entré dans une chambre.

« Toutes ces chambres sont nues et inoccupées ; son expédition n'en devenait que plus incompréhensible pour moi.

« En étouffant le bruit de mes pas, je me glissai le long du passage et j'avançai ma tête par l'ouverture de la porte.

« Barrymore était blotti dans le coin de la fenêtre, sa bougie tout près de la vitre. Son profil, à demi tourné vers moi, me permit de constater l'expression d'attente impatiente peinte sur son visage, tandis qu'il scrutait les ténèbres de la lande.

« Pendant quelques minutes, son regard eut une fixité étonnante. Puis il poussa un profond soupir, et, avec un geste de mauvaise humeur, il éteignit sa bougie.

« Toujours aussi furtivement, je regagnai ma chambre et, bientôt après, j'entendis Barrymore retourner également chez lui.

« Une heure s'écoula. Alors je perçus vaguement dans un demi-sommeil, le grincement d'une clef dans une serrure ; mais je ne pus distinguer d'où venait ce bruit.

« Comment deviner ce que cela signifie ? Il se passe certainement dans cette maison des choses mystérieuses que nous finirons bien par découvrir, un jour ou l'autre.

« Je ne vous importunerai pas de mes théories, puisque vous ne réclamez de moi que des faits. Mais, ce matin, j'ai eu une longue conversation avec sir Henry, et nous avons dressé un plan de campagne basé sur ma découverte de la nuit précédente.

« Je ne vous en entretiendrai pas aujourd'hui ; il fera l'objet de mon prochain rapport, dont la lecture ne manquera pas de vous intéresser. »

IX

DEUXIÈME RAPPORT DU DOCTEUR WATSON
LA LUMIÈRE SUR LA LANDE

Baskerville, 15 octobre.

« Mon cher Holmes,

Si, pendant quelques jours, je vous ai laissé sans nouvelles, vous conviendrez que je répare aujourd'hui le temps perdu.

« Les événements se précipitent autour de nous.

« Dans mon dernier rapport, je terminais en vous narrant la promenade nocturne de Barrymore. Aujourd'hui, voici une abondante moisson de renseignements qui vous surprendront grandement — ou bien je me tromperais fort.

« Les choses ont pris une tournure que je ne pouvais prévoir. Pendant les quarante-huit heures qui viennent de s'écouler, il est survenu quelques éclaircissements qui, si j'ose m'exprimer ainsi, ont, d'un autre côté, rendu la situation plus compliquée.

« Je vais tout vous conter ; vous jugerez vous-même.

« Le lendemain de mon aventure, j'allai examiner avant le déjeuner la chambre dans laquelle Barrymore avait pénétré la nuit précédente.

« Je remarquai que la fenêtre par laquelle notre homme regardait si attentivement la lande avait une particularité, celle de donner le plus près sur la campagne. Par une échappée ménagée entre deux rangées d'arbres, une personne placée dans la situation occupée par le valet de chambre, pouvait découvrir un assez vaste horizon, alors que, des autres croisées, elle n'en aurait aperçu qu'un coin très restreint.

« Il résultait de cette constatation que Barrymore avait choisi cette fenêtre dans le dessein de voir quelque chose ou quelqu'un sur la lande. Mais, comme la nuit était obscure, on ne pouvait supposer qu'il eût l'intention de voir quelqu'un.

« Je pensai tout d'abord à une intrigue d'amour. Cela expliquait et ses pas furtifs et les pleurs de sa femme.

« Barrymore est un fort beau garçon, bien fait pour séduire une fille de la campagne.

« Cette supposition paraissait donc très vraisemblable. De plus, la porte, ouverte après mon retour dans ma chambre, indiquait qu'il était sorti pour courir à quelque rendez-vous clandestin.

« Le lendemain matin, je raisonnais donc ainsi et je vous communique l'orientation de mes soupçons, bien que la suite ait prouvé combien peu ils étaient fondés.

« La conduite de Barrymore pouvait s'expliquer le plus naturellement du monde ; cependant je ne crus pas devoir taire ma découverte à sir Henry.

« J'eus un entretien avec le baronnet et je lui fis part de tout ce que j'avais vu.

« — Je savais que Barrymore se promenait toutes les nuits, me dit-il, et je voulais le questionner à ce sujet. Deux ou trois fois, à la même heure que vous, je l'ai entendu aller et venir dans le corridor.

« — Peut-être va-t-il toutes les nuits à cette fenêtre, insinuai-je.

« — Peut-être. Guettons-le ; nous aurons vite appris la raison de ces promenades. Je me demande ce que ferait votre ami Holmes, s'il se trouvait ici.

« — Il s'arrêterait certainement au parti que vous proposez, répondis-je ; il suivrait Barrymore.

« — Alors, nous le suivrons aussi.

« — Ne nous entendra-t-il pas ?

« — Non ; il est un peu sourd… En tout cas, il faut que nous tentions l'aventure. Cette nuit, nous veillerons dans ma chambre et nous attendrons qu'il ait passé. »

« Sir Henry se frottait les mains de plaisir. Évidemment, il se réjouissait de cette perspective qui apportait un changement dans la monotonie de son existence.

« Le baronnet s'est mis en rapports avec l'architecte qui avait dressé pour sir Charles les plans de la réfection du château. Il a traité avec un entrepreneur de Londres, et les réparations vont bientôt commencer.

« Il a commandé des décorateurs et des tapissiers de Plymouth et, sans nul doute, notre jeune ami ne veut rien négliger pour tenir l'ancien rang de sa famille.

« Lorsque la maison sera réparée et remeublée, il n'y manquera plus que la présence d'une femme.

« Entre nous, il existe des indices caractéristiques de la prompte exécution de ce projet — pour peu que la dame y consente. En effet, j'ai rarement rencontré un homme plus emballé sur une femme que ne l'est sir Henry sur notre belle voisine, miss Stapleton. Cependant je crains bien que leur voyage sur le fleuve du Tendre ne soit très mouvementé.

« Aujourd'hui, par exemple, la surface de l'onde chère aux amoureux a été ridée par un coup de vent inattendu, qui a causé un vif mécompte à notre ami.

« Lorsque notre conversation sur Barrymore eut pris fin, sir Henry mit son chapeau et se disposa à sortir.

« Naturellement, j'en fis autant.

« — Où allez-vous, Watson ? me demanda-t-il en me regardant avec curiosité.

« — Cela dépend… Devez-vous traversez la lande ?

« — Oui.

« — Alors vous connaissez mes instructions. Je regrette de vous importuner de ma personne, mais vous n'ignorez pas qu'Holmes m'a recommandé avec instance de ne pas vous perdre de vue, surtout quand vous iriez sur la lande. »

« Sir Henry posa en riant sa main sur mon épaule.

« — Mon cher ami, fit-il, malgré toute sa perspicacité, Holmes n'a pas prévu certaines choses qui se sont passées depuis mon arrivée ici. Vous me comprenez ?… Je jurerais bien que vous êtes le dernier homme qui consentirait à jouer auprès de moi le rôle de trouble-fête. Il faut que je sorte seul. »

« Ces paroles me plaçaient dans une situation embarrassante. Je ne savais trop que dire ni que faire et, avant que mon irrésolution cessât, sir Henry avait enlevé sa canne du portemanteau et s'était éloigné.

« À la réflexion, ma conscience me reprocha amèrement de n'avoir pas exigé, sous un prétexte quelconque, que le baronnet me gardât auprès de lui.

« Je me représentais la posture que j'aurais vis-à-vis de vous, si je retournais à Baker street vous avouer que ma désobéissance à vos ordres avait causé un malheur.

« Je vous assure qu'à cette pensée, le sang me brûla les joues.

« Je me dis que je pouvais encore rattraper mon promeneur et je partis immédiatement dans la direction de Merripit house.

« Je courus de toute la vitesse de mes jambes jusqu'au point où la route bifurque sur la lande. Sir Henry demeurait invisible.

« Alors, craignant d'avoir suivi une mauvaise direction, j'escaladai une colline — celle que l'on avait exploitée comme carrière de granit — du haut de laquelle ma vue embrassait presque tout le pays.

« Immédiatement, j'aperçus le baronnet à cinq cents mètres devant moi. Il s'était engagé dans le petit sentier. Une femme, qui ne pouvait être que miss Stapleton, marchait à côté de lui.

« Certainement un accord existait déjà entre eux et je surprenais un rendez-vous convenu.

« Ils allaient, lentement, absorbés par leur conversation.

« Je vis miss Stapleton faire de rapides mouvements avec sa main, comme pour souligner ce qu'elle disait, tandis que sir Henry l'écoutait attentivement et secouait parfois négativement la tête.

« Je me dissimulai derrière un rocher, curieux de voir comment tout cela finirait.

« Me jeter au travers de leur entretien, c'eût été commettre une impertinence dont je me sentais incapable. Mais, d'autre part, ma consigne m'ordonnait de marcher dans les pas de sir Henry.

« Espionner un ami est un acte odieux. Cependant je me résolus à l'observer du haut de ma cachette et de lui confesser plus tard ma faute. J'étais certains qu'il conviendrait avec moi de la difficulté de ma situation et qu'il approuverait le parti que j'avais pris, bien que, si un danger soudain l'eût menacé, je me fusse trouvé trop éloigné pour le secourir promptement.

« Sir Henry et sa compagne, perdus dans leur absorbante conversation, s'étaient arrêtés au milieu du sentier.

« Tout à coup j'eus la sensation de n'être pas le seul témoin de leur entrevue.

« Quelque chose de vert, flottant dans l'air, attira mon attention. Un nouveau regard me montra ce quelque chose fixé à l'extrémité d'un bâton porté par un homme qui enjambait les quartiers de roches.

« Je reconnus Stapleton et son filet.

« La distance qui le séparait du couple était moins grande que celle qui m'en séparait moi-même, et il paraissait se diriger du côté des deux jeunes gens.

« À ce moment, sir Henry attira miss Stapleton vers lui. Il avait passé son bras autour de la taille de Béryl, qui se recula, en détournant son visage. Il se pencha vers elle ; mais elle étendit la main pour se protéger.

« Une seconde après, je les vis s'éloigner précipitamment l'un de l'autre et faire demi-tour.

« Stapleton avait provoqué cette brusque séparation. Il accourait au-devant d'eux, son ridicule filet se balançant sur son épaule. Il gesticulait comme un possédé et sa surexcitation était telle qu'il dansait presque en face des amoureux.

« Je ne pouvais imaginer ce qui se passait. Toutefois, je crus deviner que Stapleton gourmandait sir Henry ; que ce dernier présentait des explications et que sa colère croissait à mesure que l'autre refusait de les accepter.

« La dame gardait un silence hautain.

« Finalement Stapleton tourna sur ses talons et fit de la main un signe péremptoire à sa sœur. Celle-ci, après un regard plein d'hésitation adressé à sir Henry, se décida à marcher aux côtés de son frère.

« Les gestes de colère du naturaliste indiquaient que la jeune fille n'échappait pas à son mécontentement.

« Après les avoir considérés l'un et l'autre pendant l'espace d'une minute, le baronnet, la tête basse et l'air abattu, reprit lentement le chemin par lequel il était venu.

« Je ne pouvais deviner ce que tout cela signifiait, mais je me sentais honteux d'avoir assisté à cette scène, à l'insu de mon ami.

« Je dégringolai vivement la colline pour aller à la rencontre de sir Henry. Son visage était pourpre de colère et ses sourcils froncés, comme ceux d'un homme poussé à bout.

« — Allô ! Watson, d'où sortez-vous ? me dit-il. J'aime à croire que vous ne m'avez pas suivi ? »

« Je lui expliquai tout : comment j'avais jugé impossible de le laisser s'engager seul sur la lande et comment j'avais assisté à ce qui venait d'arriver.

« Pendant un moment, ses yeux flambèrent ; mais ma franchise le désarma et il eut un triste sourire.

« — On aurait pensé, reprit-il, que cette solitude offrirait un abri sûr !… Ah ! ouiche, tout le pays semble s'y être réuni pour me voir faire ma cour — et quelle misérable cour ! Où aviez-vous loué un fauteuil ?

« — Sur la colline.

« — Au dernier rang ! Son frère, à elle, était assis aux premières loges !… L'avez-vous aperçu s'approcher de vous ?

« — Oui.

« — Aviez-vous jamais remarqué qu'il fût toqué ?

« — Non.

« — Moi non plus. Jusqu'à ce jour, je le jugeais sain d'esprit… Mais, à cette heure, je vous affirme que l'un de nous deux mérite une camisole de force. À propos de quoi en a-t-il après moi ?… Voilà déjà plusieurs semaines, Watson, que nous vivons côté à côte… Parlez-moi franchement… Y a-t-il un empêchement à ce que je sois un bon mari pour une femme que j'aimerais ?

« — Je n'en vois pas.

« — Stapleton ne peut arguer de ma situation mondaine… C'est donc ma personne qu'il méprise !… Qu'a-t-il contre moi ? Je n'ai jamais fait de tort à personne, que je sache ? Et cependant il ne m'autorise pas à toucher le bout des doigts de sa sœur.

« — Non ?

« — Si, et bien plus encore. Écoutez, Watson… Je ne connais miss Stapleton que depuis quelques semaines, mais, le jour où je l'ai rencontrée pour la première fois, j'ai senti que Dieu l'avait faite pour moi — et elle pareillement. Elle était heureuse de se trouver près de moi, je le jurerais ! Il passe dans les yeux des femmes des lueurs qui sont plus éloquentes que des paroles… Son frère ne nous permettait pas de rester seuls ensemble et, aujourd'hui seulement, j'ai saisi l'occasion de causer avec elle sans témoins.

« Notre rencontre l'a comblée de joie… mais ce n'était pas d'amour qu'elle désirait m'entretenir, et, si elle avait pu m'en empêcher, elle n'aurait pas souffert que je lui en eusse parlé.

« Elle a commencé à insister sur le danger que je cours ici et sur l'inquiétude dans laquelle elle vivrait, si je ne quittais pas Baskerville.

« Je lui ai répondu que, depuis que je la connaissais, je n'étais plus pressé de partir et que, si réellement elle souhaitait mon départ, le meilleur moyen d'en venir à ses fins était de s'arranger pour m'accompagner.

« Je lui proposai de l'épouser, mais, avant qu'elle eût pu me répondre, son espèce de frère arrivait sur nous avec des façons d'énergumène. Ses joues blêmissaient de rage et, dans ses yeux, de sinistres éclairs de folie s'allumaient.

« Que faisais-je avec madame ?… Comment avais-je l'audace de lui rendre des hommages qui lui étaient odieux ?… Mon titre de baronnet autorisait-il donc une conduite aussi cavalière ?

« Si Stapleton n'avait pas été le frère de Béryl, j'aurais mieux su que lui répondre. En tout cas, je lui ai dit quels sentiments m'inspirait sa sœur et que j'espérais qu'elle me ferait l'honneur de devenir ma femme.

« Au lieu de le calmer, ce discours l'irrita encore davantage. À mon tour, je m'emportai et je ripostai un peu plus aigrement que je ne l'aurais dû, Béryl étant présente à notre altercation.

« Leur départ précipité a terminé cette scène pénible et vous voyez en moi l'homme le plus bouleversé de tout le comté. »

« Je risquai une ou deux explications ; mais j'étais en réalité tout aussi troublé que sir Henry.

« Le titre de notre ami, sa fortune, son âge, ses manières, son physique, tout militait en sa faveur. On ne pouvait rien lui reprocher — rien que le fatal destin qui s'acharnait sur sa famille.

« Pourquoi repousser brusquement ses avances, sans même prendre l'avis de la personne qui en était l'objet ? Et pourquoi miss Stapleton avait-elle obéi à son frère, sans protester autrement que par son effarement ?

« Dans l'après-midi, une visite du naturaliste fit cesser nos conjectures. Il venait s'excuser de sa conduite grossière.

« Après un long entretien avec sir Henry, dans le cabinet de ce dernier, tout malentendu fut dissipé, et l'on convint que, pour fêter cette réconciliation, nous irions dîner le vendredi suivant à Merripit house.

« — Cette démarche de Stapleton ne modifie pas mon appréciation sur lui, me dit sir Henry… Je le considère toujours comme un peu toqué… Je ne puis oublier l'expression de son regard, quand il courut sur moi ce matin. Cependant je dois reconnaître qu'il s'est excusé de fort bonne grâce.

« — Vous a-t-il donné une explication de sa conduite ?

« — Oui. Il prétend qu'il a reporté sur sa sœur toutes ses affections. Cela est très naturel et je me réjouis de ces sentiments à son égard… Il m'a dit qu'ils avaient toujours vécu ensemble, menant une existence de cénobites, et que la pensée de la perdre lui était intolérable. Il a ensuite ajouté qu'il ne s'était pas tout d'abord aperçu de mon attachement pour miss Stapleton, mais que, lorsqu'il avait vu de ses propres yeux l'impression produite sur moi par sa sœur et qu'il avait compris qu'un jour viendrait peut-être où il serait forcé de se séparer d'elle, il avait ressenti un tel choc que, pendant une minute, il ne fut plus conscient de ses paroles ou de ses actes.

« Il se confondit en excuses et reconnut de quelle folie et de quel égoïsme il se rendait coupable, en voulant retenir éternellement autour de lui une aussi belle personne que sa sœur. Il conclut en convenant que, si elle devait le quitter, il valait mieux que ce fût pour épouser un voisin tel que moi.

« — Vraiment ?

« — Il s'appesantit sur la rudesse du coup et sur le temps qu'il lui faudrait pour s'y accoutumer. Il s'engagea à ne plus s'opposer à mes projets, si je lui promettais de n'en plus parler de trois mois et si, pendant ce temps, je me contentais de l'amitié de miss Béryl, sans lui demander son amour. Je promis tout ce qu'il désirait et cela clôtura le débat. »

« Voilà donc un de nos petits mystères éclairci.

« Nous savons maintenant pourquoi Stapleton regardait avec défaveur l'amoureux de sa sœur — même lorsque cet amoureux est un parti aussi enviable que sir Henry.

« Passons maintenant à un autre fil que j'ai débrouillé dans cet écheveau pourtant si emmêlé. Je veux parler des gémissements nocturnes, du visage éploré de Mme Barrymore et des pérégrinations clandestines de son mari.

« Félicitez-moi, mon cher Holmes… Dites-moi que je n'ai pas déçu l'espoir que vous aviez placé dans mes qualités de détective, et que vous ne regrettez pas le témoignage de confiance dont vous m'avez honoré en m'envoyant ici. Il ne m'a fallu qu'une nuit pour tirer tout cela au clair !

« En disant une nuit, j'exagère. Deux nuits m'ont été nécessaires, car, la première, nous avons fait chou blanc.

« Nous étions restés dans la chambre de sir Henry à fumer des cigarettes jusqu'à trois heures du matin. Sauf le carillon de l'horloge du hall, aucun bruit ne frappa nos oreilles.

« Ce fut une veillée peu réjouissante, qui se termina par notre assoupissement dans les bras de nos fauteuils respectifs.

« Nous ne nous décourageâmes pas pour cela, et nous convînmes de recommencer.

« La nuit suivante, nous baissâmes la lampe et, la cigarette aux lèvres, nous nous tînmes cois.

« Ah ! combien les heures s'écoulèrent lentement ! Cependant nous avions pour nous soutenir l'ardeur du chasseur qui surveille le piège dans lequel il espère voir tomber la bête de chasse.

« Une heure sonna… puis deux heures.

« Pour la seconde fois, nous allions nous séparer bredouilles, lorsque d'un même mouvement nous nous levâmes de nos sièges.

« Un pas glissait furtivement le long du corridor.

« Quand il se fut évanoui dans le lointain, le baronnet, très doucement, ouvrit la porte et nous sortîmes de la chambre.

« Notre homme avait déjà dépassé le balcon du hall.

« Le corridor était plongé dans les ténèbres. Nous le parcourûmes jusqu'à l'autre aile du château.

« Nous arrivâmes assez tôt pour apercevoir la silhouette d'un homme barbu, de haute taille, qui marchait sur la pointe des pieds, en courbant les épaules.

« Il poussa la même porte que l'avant-veille. La lueur de la bougie en dessina lumineusement l'encadrement et piqua d'un rayon de clarté jaune l'obscurité du corridor.

« Avec des précautions infinies, nous nous dirigeâmes de ce côté, tâtant du pied chaque lame du parquet avant de lui confier le poids de notre corps.

« Nous avions au préalable enlevé nos bottines ; mais le plancher vermoulu fléchissait et criait sous nos pas.

« Parfois il nous semblait impossible que Barrymore ne nous entendît pas.

« Fort heureusement, il est sourd, et la préoccupation de ne pas faire de bruit l'absorbait entièrement.

« Nous atteignîmes enfin la porte derrière laquelle il avait disparu et nous jetâmes un coup d'œil dans la chambre.

« Barrymore, une bougie à la main, était presque collé contre la fenêtre et regardait attentivement à travers les carreaux — dans la même position que les nuits précédentes.

« Nous n'étions convenus de rien. Mais le caractère résolu du baronnet le porte naturellement à aller droit au but.

« Il pénétra dans la chambre.

« Au bruit, Barrymore se retira vivement de la fenêtre et nous apparut, tremblant, livide, haletant. Ses yeux noirs, rendus plus brillants par la pâleur exsangue de la face avaient, en nous regardant, sir Henry et moi, une expression d'étonnement et d'effroi.

« — Que faites-vous là, Barrymore ? demanda le baronnet.

« — Rien, monsieur. »

« Sa frayeur était si grande qu'il pouvait à peine parler, et le tremblement de sa main agitait à tel point la bougie que les ombres dansaient sur la muraille.

« — C'est la fenêtre, reprit-il… Je fais une ronde, toutes les nuits, pour m'assurer qu'elles sont bien fermées.

« — Au second étage ?

« — Oui, monsieur… toutes les fenêtres.

« — Écoutez-moi, Barrymore ! dit sir Henry sévèrement. Nous sommes décidés à vous arracher la vérité… Cela vous évitera des ennuis dans l'avenir. Allons, pas de mensonges ! Que faisiez-vous à cette fenêtre ? »

« Le pauvre diable nous adressa un regard désespéré et croisa ses mains dans un geste de muette supplication.

« — Je ne faisais rien de mal, monsieur… Je tenais une bougie contre cette fenêtre.

« — Dans quel but ?

« — Ne me le demandez pas, sir Henry !… ne me le demandez pas !… Je vous jure que ce secret ne m'appartient pas et que je ne puis vous le dire. S'il n'intéressait que moi seul, je vous le confierais sans hésiter. »

« Une pensée soudaine me traversa l'esprit et je pris la bougie des mains tremblantes du valet de chambre.

« — Ce doit être un signal, dis-je au baronnet. Voyons si l'on y répondra. »

« J'imitai la manœuvre de Barrymore et, regardant au dehors, j'essayai de percer les ténèbres de la nuit.

« De gros nuages voilaient la lune.

« Je distinguai vaguement la ligne sombre formée par la cimes des arbres, et, au-delà, une vaste étendue plus éclairée : la lande.

« Tout à coup un cri de joie m'échappa.

« Un point lumineux avait surgi dans le lointain.

« — Le voilà ! m'écriai-je.

« — Non, monsieur… Non, ce n'est rien ! répliqua le valet de chambre… Je vous assure…

« — Promenez votre bougie devant la fenêtre, Watson, me dit le baronnet. Tenez, l'autre lumière remue également. Maintenant, coquin, nierez-vous que c'était un signal ? Parlez ! Quel est là-bas votre complice et contre qui conspirez-vous ? »

« Le visage de Barrymore exprima aussitôt une défiance manifeste :

« — C'est mon affaire et non la vôtre !… Vous ne saurez rien !…

« — Alors quittez mon service… immédiatement !

« — Très bien, monsieur.

« — Je vous chasse ! Vous devriez être honteux de votre conduite… Votre famille a vécu pendant plusieurs siècles sous le même toit que la mienne et je vous trouve mêlé à quelque complot tramé contre moi !…

« — Non, monsieur… non, pas contre vous », fit une voix de femme.

« Nous nous retournâmes, et, sur le seuil de la chambre, nous aperçûmes Mme Barrymore, plus pâle et plus terrifiée que son mari.

« Enveloppée dans un châle, en jupons, cet accoutrement l'aurait rendue grotesque, n'avait été l'intensité des sentiments imprimés sur son visage.

« — Il nous faut partir, Élisa, lui dit Barrymore. C'en est fait… Prépare nos paquets.

« — Oh ! Jean, Jean, répondit-elle, je suis la cause de ton renvoi… Il n'y a que moi seule de coupable !… Il n'a fait que ce que je lui ai demandé…

« — Parlez, alors ! commanda sir Henry. Que voulez-vous dire ?

« — Mon malheureux frère meurt de faim sur la lande. Nous ne pouvons le laisser périr si près de nous… Au moyen de cette bougie, nous lui annonçons que nous lui avons préparé des vivres, et la lueur que vous avez aperçue là-bas nous indique l'endroit où nous devons les lui apporter.

« — Votre frère est ?…

« — Le prisonnier évadé de Princetown… Selden l'assassin.

« — Voilà la vérité, monsieur, fit Barrymore. Je vous ai dit que ce secret ne m'appartenait pas et qu'il m'était impossible de vous l'apprendre. Vous le connaissez maintenant, et vous voyez que, s'il y a un complot, il n'est pas dirigé contre vous. »

« Ainsi se trouvent expliqués les expéditions nocturnes de Barrymore et les échanges de signaux entre le château et la lande.

« Sir Henry et moi, nous regardions avec stupéfaction Mme Barrymore. Cette personne d'aspect si respectable était donc du même sang que l'un des plus célèbres criminels de l'Angleterre ?

« — Oui, monsieur, reprit-elle, je m'appelle Selden, et *il* est mon frère. Nous l'avons trop gâté dans son enfance… Il a fini par croire que le monde n'avait été créé que pour son plaisir et qu'il était libre d'y faire ce que bon lui semblait… Devenu grand, il fréquenta de mauvais compagnons, et le chagrin causé par son inconduite hâta la mort de notre pauvre mère.

« De crime en crime, il descendit toujours plus bas, et il ne dut qu'à la miséricorde divine d'échapper à l'échafaud. Mais pour moi, mon bon monsieur, il est toujours resté le petit enfant aux cheveux bouclés que j'avais soigné, avec lequel j'avais joué autrefois, en sœur aînée aimante et dévouée.

« Il connaît ces sentiments, et c'est ce qui l'a déterminé à s'évader de prison. Il est venu me retrouver, certain d'avance que je ne refuserais pas de l'aider.

« Une nuit, il arriva ici, exténué de fatigue et de faim, traqué par la police ; que devions-nous faire ?

« Nous le recueillîmes, nous le nourrîmes et nous prîmes soin de lui.

« Lorsqu'on annonça votre venue ici, mon frère pensa qu'il serait plus en sûreté sur la lande que partout ailleurs. Il attend dans sa cachette que l'oubli se fasse autour de son nom.

« Toutes les deux nuits, nous plaçons une bougie devant la fenêtre pour nous assurer de sa présence ; s'il nous répond par le même signal, mon mari va lui porter des vivres.

« Nous espérons toujours qu'il pourra fuir ; mais tant qu'il sera là, nous ne l'abandonnerons pas.

« Voilà, monsieur, aussi vrai que je suis une honnête femme, la vérité tout entière. Vous conviendrez que, si quelqu'un mérite un blâme ce n'est pas mon mari, mais moi seule, pour l'amour de qui il a tout fait. »

« Mme Barrymore parlait avec un air de sincérité qui entraînait la conviction.

« — Est-ce vrai, Barrymore ? demanda le baronnet.

« — Oui, sir Henry… absolument.

« — Je ne puis vous blâmer d'avoir assisté votre femme. Oubliez ce que j'ai dit. Rentrez chez vous ; nous causerons de tout cela demain matin. »

« Lorsque les deux époux furent sortis, nous regardâmes encore par la fenêtre.

« Sir Henry l'avait ouverte toute grande. Le vent glacial de la nuit nous cinglait le visage.

« Au loin, le point lumineux brillait toujours.

« — Je me demande comment Selden ose allumer cette bougie, dit sir Henry.

« — Peut-être la dispose-t-il de façon à ne la rendre visible que du château.

« — Très vraisemblablement. À combien évaluez-vous la distance qui nous sépare d'elle ?

« — Heu ! Elle doit être près du *Cleft-Tor*.

« — À un mille ou deux ?

« — À peine.

« — C'est juste… Puisque Barrymore doit y porter des provisions, elle ne peut se trouver à une trop grande distance… Et dire que ce misérable attend à côté de sa bougie ! Vraiment, Watson, j'ai envie de sortir et d'arrêter cet homme ! »

« Un désir semblable avait traversé mon esprit. Je ne l'aurais certainement pas eu, si les Barrymore s'étaient spontanément confiés à nous. Mais nous avions dû leur arracher leur secret.

« Et puis cet homme ne constituait-il pas un danger permanent pour la société ? N'était-il pas un scélérat endurci, indigne de pitié ? En somme, nous ne faisions que notre devoir en essayant de le replonger dans le cachot où il serait inoffensif.

« Si nous n'exécutions pas ce projet, qui sait si d'autres ne payeraient pas de leur vie le prix de notre indifférence !…

« Qui sait, par exemple, si, quelque nuit, il ne s'attaquerait pas à nos voisins, les Stapleton ! Je soupçonne sir Henry d'avoir obéi à cette pensée, en se montrant si décidé à tenter cette aventure.

« — Je vous accompagne, lui dis-je.

« — Alors prenez votre revolver et chaussez vos bottines. Plus tôt nous partirons, mieux cela vaudra… le drôle n'aurait qu'à souffler sa bougie et qu'à filer… »

« Cinq minutes plus tard, nous étions dehors, en route pour notre expédition.

« Nous marchions à travers les taillis, au milieu du triste sifflement du vent d'automne et du bruissement des feuilles mortes.

« L'air de la nuit était chargé d'humidité et la terre dégageait l'âcre senteur des plantes en décomposition.

« De temps en temps, la lune pointait entre deux nuages ; mais bientôt les nuées se rejoignaient et recouvraient toute la surface du ciel. Au moment où nous mettions le pied sur la lande, une pluie menue commença à tomber.

« Devant nous, la lueur jaune brillait toujours.

« — Êtes-vous armé ? dis-je tout bas à sir Henry.

« — J'ai un fusil de chasse à répétition.

« — Il faudra surprendre Selden et nous emparer de lui, avant qu'il soit en état de nous résister, repris-je ; il paraît que c'est un garçon déterminé.

« — Dites-donc, Watson, que penserait M. Sherlock Holmes de nous voir ainsi sur la lande, "à l'heure où l'esprit du mal chemine" ?

« Comme en réponse à ces paroles, il s'éleva dans la vaste solitude de la lande ce cri étrange que j'avais déjà entendu sur les bords de la grande fondrière de Grimpen.

« Porté par le vent dans le silence de la nuit, arriva jusqu'à nous ce long murmure, bientôt suivi d'un hurlement sonore et terminé par une sorte de lugubre gémissement. Il retentit à plusieurs reprises, strident, sauvage, menaçant, ébranlant l'atmosphère entière.

« Le baronnet me saisit le bras et, malgré l'obscurité, je le vis blêmir.

« — Mon Dieu ! Watson, qu'y a-t-il ?

« — Je l'ignore. C'est un bruit de la lande… Je l'ai déjà entendu une fois. »

« Le cri ne se renouvela pas et un silence de mort s'abattit sur nous. Nous prêtâmes attentivement l'oreille, mais en vain.

« — Watson, me dit le baronnet, c'était le hurlement d'un chien. »

« Mon sang se glaça dans mes veines. Pendant que sir Henry parlait, un tremblement secouait sa voix et montrait toute la soudaine terreur qui s'était emparée de lui.

« — Comment appellent-ils ce bruit ? ajouta-t-il.

« — Qui : ils ?

« — Les gens du pays.

« — Ce sont des paysans ignorants… Que vous importe le nom par lequel ils le désignent.

« — Dites-le-moi toujours, Watson ? »

« J'hésitai. Cependant, je ne pus éluder la question.

« — Ils prétendent que c'est le hurlement du chien des Baskerville. »

« Sir Henry soupira et resta un moment silencieux.

« — Un chien, soit ! fit-il enfin. En tout cas, il me semble que le son venait de là-bas, à plusieurs milles de distance.

« — Il est difficile d'en indiquer la direction.

« — Il s'élevait et diminuait selon le vent. N'est-ce pas du côté de la grande fondrière de Grimpen ?

« — Oui.

« — Ne croyez-vous pas aussi que c'était un hurlement de chien ? Je ne suis plus un enfant… N'appréhendez pas de me dire la vérité.

« — Lorsque je l'entendis pour la première fois, Stapleton m'accompagnait. Il m'affirma que ce pouvait être l'appel d'un oiseau de passage.

« — Non, non… c'était bien un chien… Mon Dieu ! y aurait-il quelque chose de vrai dans toutes ces histoires ? Suis-je réellement menacé d'un danger de provenance mystérieuse ? Vous ne croyez pas n'est-ce pas, Watson ?

« — Non… certainement non.

« — Autre chose est de plaisanter de cela, à Londres, ou d'entendre un cri pareil, ici, sur la lande… Et mon oncle ? N'a-t-on pas remarqué près de son cadavre l'empreinte d'une patte de chien ? Tout cela se tient. Je ne me crois pas poltron, Watson ; mais ce bruit a figé mon sang. Tâtez mes mains !

« — Il n'y paraîtra plus demain, dis-je à sir Henry en manière d'encouragement.

« — J'ai peur de ne pouvoir chasser ce cri de ma pensée… Que conseillez-vous de faire maintenant ?

« — Retournons au château.

« — Jamais de la vie ! Nous sommes venus pour arrêter Selden, nous l'arrêterons. Le prisonnier nous aura à ses trousses, et nous, un chien-fantôme aux nôtres !… En avant ! Nous verrons bien si le diable a lâché sur la lande tous les démons de l'enfer. »

« Toujours guidés par la petite lueur qui scintillait devant nous, nous reprîmes notre marche, en trébuchant à chaque pas dans les broussailles.

« Par une nuit noire comme une gueule de four, on se trompe facilement dans l'évaluation de la distance à laquelle on croit apercevoir une lumière. Elle nous paraissait parfois très éloignée, tandis qu'à certains moments nous l'aurions crue seulement à quelques mètres de nous.

« Nous la découvrîmes enfin. En la collant avec sa propre cire, on avait fiché une bougie dans une crevasse de rochers. Cette précaution avait le double avantage de la préserver du vent et de ne la rendre visible que du château.

« Un bloc de granit dissimulait notre présence.

« Accroupis derrière cet abri, nous avançâmes la tête pour examiner ce phare minuscule.

« Cette simple bougie, brûlant au milieu de la lande sans autre signe de vie autour d'elle, était un bizarre spectacle.

« — Que faire ? murmura sir Henry à mon oreille.

« — Attendre, répondis-je sur le même ton. Notre homme doit se tenir à proximité de sa lumière. Tâchons de l'apercevoir. »

« À peine avais-je achevé ces mots que mon désir fut réalisé.

« Sur les rochers, qui surplombaient la crevasse où brûlait la bougie, se profilait la silhouette d'un homme dont la figure bestiale décelait toutes les plus basses passions.

« Souillé de boue, avec sa barbe inculte et ses longs cheveux emmêlés, on aurait pu le prendre pour un de ces êtres primitifs, ensevelis depuis des siècles dans les sarcophages de la montagne.

« La clarté de la bougie montait jusqu'à lui et se jouait dans ses yeux, petits, astucieux, qui scrutaient fiévreusement à droite et à gauche l'épaisseur des ténèbres, comme ceux d'une bête sauvage qui a éventé la présence des chasseurs.

« Quelque chose avait évidemment éveillé ses soupçons. Peut-être avions-nous omis un signal convenu entre Barrymore et lui. Ou bien le drôle avait-il des raisons de croire qu'un danger le menaçait… Toujours est-il que je lisais ses craintes sur son horrible visage.

« À chaque instant il pouvait sortir du cercle lumineux qui l'entourait et disparaître dans la nuit.

« Je bondis en avant suivi de sir Henry.

« Au même moment, le prisonnier proféra un épouvantable blasphème et fit rouler sur nous un quartier de roche, qui se brisa sur le bloc de granit derrière lequel nous nous abritions.

« Pendant l'espace d'un éclair, je le vis très distinctement, tandis qu'il se levait pour fuir ; il était de petite taille, trapu et très solidement charpenté.

« Par un heureux hasard, la lune vint à déchirer son voile de nuages. Nous escaladâmes le monticule. Parvenus au sommet, nous distinguâmes Selden qui en descendait précipitamment la pente escarpée, en faisant voler les cailloux de tous côtés, tel un chamois.

« J'aurais pu l'abattre d'un coup de revolver ; mais je n'avais emporté cette arme que pour me défendre en cas d'attaque, et non pas pour tirer sur un fuyard sans défense.

« Nous étions, sir Henry et moi, d'excellents coureurs parfaitement entraînés. Seulement nous nous rendîmes bien vite compte que nous ne rattraperions pas notre homme.

« Longtemps, à la clarté de la lune, nous le suivîmes jusqu'à ce qu'il ne fût plus qu'un point imperceptible, glissant rapidement à travers les rochers qui hérissaient une colline éloignée.

« Nous courûmes jusqu'à perte d'haleine ; mais l'espace entre lui et nous s'élargissait de plus en plus. Finalement nous nous arrêtâmes, exténués, pour nous asseoir et le regarder disparaître au loin.

« Ce fut à ce moment que survint la chose du monde la plus extraordinaire et la plus inattendue.

« Nous venions de nous relever, et nous nous disposions à reprendre le chemin du château, abandonnant cette inutile poursuite.

« Vers notre droite, la lune s'abaissait sur l'horizon. Déjà la cime d'un pic avait mordu la partie inférieure de son disque argenté.

« Alors, là, sur ce pic, se dessina, noir comme une statue d'ébène sur ce fond éclatant de lumière, le profil d'un homme.

« Ne croyez pas, mon cher Holmes, que j'ai été le jouet d'une illusion. Je vous assure que, de ma vie, je n'ai rien vu de plus distinct.

« Autant qu'il m'a été possible d'en juger, cet homme m'a paru grand et mince. Il se tenait debout, les jambes un peu écartées, les bras croisés, la tête basse, dans l'attitude de quelqu'un méditant sur l'immensité qui se déroule devant lui.

« On aurait pu le prendre pour le génie de ce terrible lieu.

« Ce n'était pas Selden, car cet homme se trouvait très loin de l'endroit où le prisonnier avait disparu à nos yeux. D'ailleurs, il paraissait beaucoup plus grand que le frère de Mme Barrymore.

« J'étouffai un cri de surprise, et j'allais le montrer au baronnet, lorsqu'il s'éclipsa pendant le temps que je me mis à saisir le bras de mon ami.

« La crête de la colline avait entamé plus profondément le disque de la lune ; mais, sur le pic, il ne restait plus de trace de cette muette apparition.

« Je voulus me diriger de ce côté et fouiller cette partie de la lande ; j'y renonçai, elle était trop distante de nous.

« Les nerfs du baronnet vibraient encore sous le cri qui lui rappelait la sombre histoire de sa famille. Je ne le sentais pas d'humeur à tenter de nouvelles aventures.

« Sir Henry n'avait pas vu l'homme du pic ; il ne pouvait partager le frisson que son étrange présence et sa majestueuse attitude avaient fait passer dans tout mon être.

« — Quelque sentinelle ! dit-il… depuis l'évasion de Selden, la lande en est couverte. »

« Malgré la vraisemblance de cette explication, je ne suis pas convaincu.

« J'irai aux preuves.

« Aujourd'hui nous écrivons au directeur de la prison de Princetown pour lui indiquer les parages où se cache le contumace.

« Mais quel malheur que nous n'ayons pu nous emparer de lui et le ramener triomphalement à son cachot !

« Telles sont, mon cher Holmes, les aventures de la dernière nuit.

« Vous ne vous plaindrez pas de l'étendue de mon rapport. Certes, il contient force détails qui ne touchent que de très loin à l'affaire. Toutefois, il me semble qu'il vaut mieux que vous soyez tenu au courant de tout ; vous trierez vous-même les renseignements utiles qui vous aideront à asseoir votre opinion.

« Avouez que nous avons fait quelques pas en avant.

« En ce qui concerne les Barrymore, nous avons découvert le mobile de leurs actions et, de ce côté le terrain est déblayé.

« Seule la lande avec ses mystères et ses étranges habitants, demeure toujours plus insondable que jamais.

« Peut-être, dans ma prochaine lettre, pourrai-je vous fournir quelques éclaircissements sur ce qui s'y passe.

« Le mieux serait que vous vinssiez au plus tôt. En tout cas, vous recevrez d'autres nouvelles sous peu de jours. »

X
EXTRAITS DU JOURNAL DE WATSON

Jusqu'ici j'ai cité certains passages des rapports que j'adressais presque journellement à Sherlock Holmes. Aujourd'hui, j'en suis arrivé à un point de mon récit où je me vois forcé d'abandonner ce procédé et d'avoir recours à mes souvenirs personnels, aidé en cela par le journal que j'ai tenu à cette époque. Quelques extraits me remettront en mémoire les détails de ces scènes fixées dans mon esprit d'une manière indélébile.

Je reprends donc au matin qui suivit notre vaine poursuite de Selden et nos autres aventures sur la lande.

« *16 octobre*. — Journée triste, brumeuse ; il bruine presque sans relâche.

« D'épais nuages enveloppent le château ; parfois ils se déchirent et laissent entrevoir les ondulations de la lande striée de minces filets d'argent, ruisselets occasionnellement créés par la pluie dévalant sur le flanc raviné des collines.

« Tout est mélancolie — au dehors comme au dedans.

« Le baronnet subit maintenant le contre-coup des émotions trop vives de la nuit précédente.

« Moi-même, je me sens oppressé. Il me semble qu'un péril nous menace — péril sans cesse présent et d'autant plus terrible que je ne puis le préciser.

« N'ai-je pas raison de craindre ? Cette longue série d'incidents ne dénote-t-elle pas une influence maligne s'exerçant autour de nous ? C'est d'abord la fin tragique du dernier commensal du château de Baskerville qui meurt de la même mort que son ancêtre Hugo. Puis viennent les affirmations des paysans relatives à la présence sur la lande d'un animal extraordinaire. N'ai-je pas entendu deux fois de mes propres oreilles, un bruit qui ressemblait à l'aboiement lointain d'un chien ?

« Mais il est incroyable, inadmissible, que ce bruit soit dû à une cause surnaturelle. Comment un chien-fantôme marquerait-il sur le sol l'empreinte de ses pas et remplirait-il l'air de ses hurlements ?

« Stapleton peut avoir de ces superstitions ; Mortimer également.

« Mais moi ?

« Je me flatte de posséder une qualité inappréciable : le sens commun — et rien ne me fera croire à de pareilles absurdités. Ma crédulité me rabaisserait au niveau de ces paysans ignares qui ne se contentent pas d'affirmer l'existence d'un animal fantastique, mais qui le dépeignent comme lançant du feu par la gueule et par les yeux.

« Holmes n'ajouterait aucune foi à ces inventions — et je suis son agent.

« Mais, d'autre part, les faits sont les faits, et, à deux reprises différentes, j'ai entendu ces cris sur la lande.

« Supposons pour un instant qu'un animal prodigieux, d'une espèce inconnue, erre la nuit dans la campagne. Sa présence ne suffirait-elle pas à tout expliquer ?

« Alors, où ce chien se cacherait-il ? Où prendrait-il sa nourriture ? D'où viendrait-il et pourquoi ne l'aurait-on jamais aperçu à la clarté du jour ?

« On doit avouer qu'une explication naturelle de ces faits offre presque autant de difficulté que l'admission d'une intervention surnaturelle.

« En dehors du chien, il reste toujours le fait matériel de l'homme aperçu dans le cab et de la lettre qui mettait sir Henry en garde contre les dangers de la lande.

« Ceci, au moins, appartient bien au domaine de la réalité ; mais ce peut être l'œuvre d'un ami aussi bien que celle d'un ennemi.

« À cette heure, où se trouvait cet ami ou cet ennemi ? N'a-t-il pas quitté Londres ou nous a-t-il accompagnés jusqu'ici ? Serait-ce… Oui, serait-ce l'inconnu que j'ai entrevu sur le pic ?

« Je reconnais que je ne l'ai vu que l'espace d'une minute, et cependant je suis prêt à jurer certaines choses le concernant. D'abord, il ne ressemble à aucune des personnes que j'ai rencontrées dans le pays, et je connais maintenant tous nos voisins. Cet homme était plus grand que Stapleton et plus mince que Frankland.

« Il se rapprocherait davantage de l'aspect de Barrymore. Mais le valet de chambre était resté au château, derrière nous, et je suis sûr qu'il ne pouvait nous avoir suivis.

« Alors un inconnu nous espionne ici, de même qu'un inconnu nous espionnait à Londres. Si je mets jamais la main sur cet homme, nous toucherons au terme de nos embarras.

« Tous mes efforts vont tendre vers ce seul but.

« Mon premier mouvement fut de confier mes projets à sir Henry. Mon second — beaucoup plus sage — me poussa à jouer la partie tout seul et à parler le moins possible de ce que je comptais entreprendre.

« Le baronnet est préoccupé. Ce bruit perçu sur la lande a ébranlé ses nerfs. Je ne viendrai pas augmenter ses angoisses ; mais je vais prendre toutes mes mesures pour réussir.

« Ce matin, il s'est passé au château une petite scène qui mérite d'être racontée.

« Barrymore demanda à sir Henry la faveur d'un entretien. Ils allèrent s'enfermer quelque temps dans la bibliothèque.

« Je demeurai dans la salle de billard d'où j'entendis plusieurs fois un bruit de voix montées à un diapason assez aigu. Je me doutais bien de ce qui faisait l'objet de leur discussion.

« Enfin, le baronnet ouvrit la porte et m'appela :

« — Barrymore, me dit-il, estime qu'il a un grief contre nous. Il pense qu'il était peu délicat de notre part de nous mettre à la recherche de son beau-frère, alors qu'il nous avait parlé en confidence de sa présence sur la lande. »

« Le valet de chambre se tenait devant nous, très pâle, mais aussi très calme.

« — Peut-être, répondit-il, ai-je eu le tort de m'emporter… S'il en est ainsi, veuillez me pardonner, sir Henry. Tout de même j'ai été fort surpris d'apprendre ce matin que vous aviez donné la chasse à Selden. Le pauvre garçon a déjà bien assez de monde à ses trousses, sans que j'en grossisse le nombre par mon fait.

« — Si vous aviez parlé spontanément, reprit le baronnet, la chose serait toute différente. Mais vous n'êtes entré — ou mieux votre femme n'est entrée dans la voie des aveux, que contrainte par nous et lorsqu'il vous était difficile à tous deux de faire autrement.

« — Je ne m'attendais pas, sir Henry, à ce que vous vous prévaudriez de notre confiance… non, je ne m'y attendais pas !

« — Cet homme constitue un danger public. Il existe, disséminées sur la lande, des maisons isolées… et c'est un misérable que rien n'arrêterait. Il n'y a qu'à le regarder pour s'en convaincre. Prenez, par exemple, l'intérieur de M. Stapleton… Le naturaliste est l'unique défenseur de son foyer. Non, la sécurité ne régnera dans les environs que lorsque Selden sera bel et bien sous les verrous.

« — Selden ne s'introduira dans aucune maison, monsieur, je vous en donne solennellement ma parole d'honneur. D'ailleurs, il débarrassera bientôt le pays de sa présence. Je vous assure, sir Henry, qu'avant peu de jours toutes les démarches seront terminées pour qu'il s'embarque à destination de l'Amérique du Sud. Au nom du ciel, je vous supplie de ne pas le dénoncer à la justice… On a renoncé à le rechercher ; qu'il vive, tranquille, les quelques jours qui le séparent encore de son départ ! Appeler de nouveau sur lui l'attention de la police, c'est nous causer de graves ennuis, à ma femme et à moi… Je vous en prie, monsieur, ne dites rien.

« — Quel est votre avis, Watson ? » me demanda sir Henry.

« Je haussai les épaules :

« — S'il allait se faire pendre ailleurs, répondis-je, ce serait une charge de moins pour les contribuables.

« — Oui ; mais en attendant, comment l'empêcher de commettre des méfaits ? répliqua mon jeune ami.

« — Ne craignez pas cela de lui, insista Barrymore. Nous lui avons procuré tout ce dont il pouvait avoir besoin. Et puis, commettre un crime équivaudrait à révéler l'endroit où il se cache.

« — C'est vrai, convint sir Henry... Soit ! Barrymore, nous ne dirons rien.

« — Dieu vous bénisse, monsieur, et je vous remercie du fond du cœur. Si l'on avait repris son frère, ma pauvre femme en serait morte. »

« Le baronnet parut regretter aussitôt sa promesse, car, en s'adressant à moi, il reprit :

« — En somme, nous protégeons et nous encourageons un criminel... Enfin, après les paroles de Barrymore, je ne me sens plus le courage de livrer cet homme... Allons, ne parlons plus de cela... Vous pouvez vous retirer. »

« Avec toutes sortes de protestations de gratitude, le domestique se disposait à sortir.

« Tout à coup il hésita et revint sur ses pas.

« — Vous vous êtes montré si bon pour moi, dit-il en s'adressant à sir Henry, que je tiens à vous en témoigner ma reconnaissance. Je sais une chose que j'aurais déjà racontée, si je ne l'avais apprise postérieurement à la clôture de l'enquête. Je n'en ai encore soufflé mot à personne... C'est à propos de la mort de ce pauvre sir Charles. »

« À ces mots, nous nous dressâmes, le baronnet et moi.

« — Savez-vous comment il est mort ?

« — Non, monsieur ; il ne s'agit pas de cela.

« — De quoi, alors ?

« — De la raison pour laquelle sir Charles se trouvait à la porte de la lande. Il attendait une femme.

« — Il attendait une femme ! Lui ?

« — Oui, monsieur.

« — Le nom de cette femme ?

« — J'ignore son nom, mais je puis vous donner ses initiales.

« — Quelles sont-elles ?

« — L. L.

« — Comment les connaissez-vous ?

« — Voici. Le matin de sa mort, votre oncle avait reçu une lettre. Il en recevait journellement un grand nombre… Il avait le cœur généreux et tous ceux qui se trouvaient dans le besoin ne manquaient pas de s'adresser à lui. Par extraordinaire, ce matin-là, le courrier n'apporta qu'une lettre… Je la remarquai davantage… Elle venait de Coombe Tracey… Une femme en avait écrit la suscription.

« — Après ?

« — Je n'y pensai plus, et, sans ma femme, je ne m'en serais certainement plus souvenu. Seulement, il y a quelques jours, en nettoyant le cabinet de sir Charles — on n'y avait pas touché depuis le jour de sa mort — Élisa trouva au fond de la cheminée les cendres d'une lettre qu'on avait brûlée. Auparavant, on l'avait déchirée en menus morceaux. Cependant, sur une petite bande de papier — une fin de page — on pouvait encore lire l'écriture qui se détachait en gris sur le vélin calciné. Il nous sembla que c'était un *post-scriptum*. Nous lûmes : "Je vous en prie, je vous en supplie, vous êtes un homme d'honneur, brûlez cette lettre et venez ce soir, à dix heures, à la porte de la lande". On avait signé des deux initiales L. L.

« — Avez-vous conservé cette bande de papier ?

« — Non, monsieur ; dès que nous la touchâmes, elle tomba en poussière.

« — Sir Charles avait-il reçu d'autres lettres de cette même écriture ?

« — Je ne prenais pas garde à ses lettres. Je n'aurais prêté aucune attention à celle-là, si d'autres l'avaient accompagnée.

« — Vous ne soupçonnez pas qui peut être L. L. ?

« — Non, monsieur… pas plus que vous-même. Je crois que si nous parvenions à percer l'anonymat de cette dame, nous en saurions plus long sur la mort de sir Charles.

« — Je ne m'explique pas, Barrymore, pourquoi vous avez caché un détail de cette importance.

« — Que voulez-vous, monsieur ?... Le malheur nous avait frappés, nous aussi... Selden, mon beau-frère !... Et puis nous aimions beaucoup sir Charles... il nous avait fait tant de bien !... Raconter ce détail n'aurait pas ressuscité notre pauvre maître ; nous nous sommes tus par égard pour lui... Dame ! il faut toujours se montrer prudent, lorsque la réputation d'une femme est en jeu. Le meilleur d'entre nous...

« — En quoi la mémoire de mon oncle aurait-elle souffert ?

« — En tout cas, je ne pensais pas que cette révélation dût la servir. Mais maintenant j'aurais mal reconnu votre bonté, si je ne vous avais pas dit tout ce que je savais sur ce sujet.

« — Très bien, Barrymore ; vous pouvez vous retirer. »

« Lorsque le valet de chambre fut sorti, sir Henry se retourna vers moi.

« — Eh bien, Watson, votre opinion sur ce fait nouveau ?

« — Je crois qu'il plonge l'affaire dans des ténèbres plus épaisses qu'auparavant.

« — C'est également mon avis. Ah ! si nous découvrions qui est cette L. L., tout se trouverait singulièrement éclairci. Nous avons fait néanmoins un grand pas. Nous savons qu'il existe une femme qui, si nous la retrouvons, devra nous expliquer ce nouvel incident. Quel est votre avis ?

« — Communiquer d'abord ceci à Sherlock Holmes ; nous tenons peut-être la clef du mystère qu'il cherche encore à cette heure.

Je montai dans ma chambre et je rédigeai immédiatement pour Sherlock Holmes la relation de cette intéressante conversation. Mon ami devait être fort occupé à Londres, car les notes que je recevais de Baker street étaient rares, courtes, sans commentaires sur les renseignements transmis par moi, et ne contenaient que de brèves recommandations au sujet de ma mission.

Probablement, le cas de chantage soumis à Holmes absorbait tous ses instants. Cependant je pensai que ce nouveau facteur introduit dans l'affaire de Baskerville appellerait sûrement son attention et raviverait son intérêt. Je souhaitais du fond du cœur qu'il fût près de moi.

« *17 octobre.* — La pluie n'a cessé de tomber toute la journée, fouettant les vitres et les feuilles du lierre qui tapisse le château.

« Malgré moi, je songeais au prisonnier évadé qui errait sans abri sur la lande morne et glaciale. Le pauvre diable ! Quels que soient ses crimes, il faut lui tenir compte de ce qu'il a souffert.

« Ce souvenir en évoque d'autres ; celui de l'homme entrevu à travers la glace du cab et la silhouette qui se profila sur le ciel, au sommet du pic. Était-il également dehors, sous ce déluge, cet ami des ténèbres, ce veilleur inconnu ?

« Vers le soir, je passai mon manteau en caoutchouc et je sortis sur la lande.

« La pluie me battait le visage ; le vent sifflait à mes oreilles. J'étais en proie aux plus sombres pensées. Que Dieu vienne en aide à ceux qui s'engagent à cette heure sur la fondrière de Grimpen, car la terre ferme n'est déjà plus qu'un immense marécage !

« Je gravis le pic Noir, celui sur lequel j'avais aperçu le veilleur solitaire, et du haut de sa cime rocheuse, je contemplai à mon tour la plaine dénudée qui s'étendait à mes pieds.

« Les rafales de pluie s'écrasaient sur la surface rouge de la terre et les nuages, lourds, aux teintes d'ardoise, formaient comme de grises couronnes aux sommets des collines fantastiques.

« À gauche, dans un bas-fond à moitié caché par les embruns, les deux tourelles du château de Baskerville se dressaient au-dessus des arbres du parc. Elles représentaient, avec les huttes préhistoriques qui se pressaient sur le flanc des coteaux, les seuls indices de vie humaine que je pusse apercevoir.

« Je ne découvris aucune trace de l'homme entrevu, deux nuits auparavant, à l'endroit même où je me trouvais.

« En revenant à Baskerville par un petit sentier, je rencontrai Mortimer en dogcart.

« Le docteur s'était montré plein d'attentions pour nous. Il ne se passait pas de jour qu'il ne vînt au château s'informer de ce que nous devenions.

« Mortimer insista pour me faire monter dans sa voiture ; il voulait me reconduire un bout de chemin.

« Il me fit part de la préoccupation que lui causait la perte de son caniche. Le chien s'était échappé sur la lande et, depuis lors, son maître ne l'avait plus revu.

« Je prodiguai à ce bon docteur toutes sortes de consolations, mais je revis dans mon esprit le cheval disparaissant dans la fondrière de Grimpen, et je me dis que notre ami ne retrouverait plus son fidèle compagnon.

« — À propos, Mortimer, lui dis-je, tandis que la voiture nous cahotait, je présume que vous connaissez toutes les personnes qui habitent ici, dans un rayon de plusieurs milles.

« — Vous avez raison.

« — Dans ce cas, pourriez-vous m'apprendre quelle est la femme dont le nom et le prénom commencent tous les deux par la lettre L ? »

« Le docteur réfléchit pendant un instant.

« — Non, fit-il. Il existe bien quelques laboureurs et quelques bohémiens dont j'ignore le nom ; mais, parmi les femmes de bourgeois ou de fermiers, je n'en vois pas qui aient ces initiales. Attendez un peu ! reprit-il après une pause… Il y a Laura Lyons… ses initiales sont bien L. L ;… seulement elle demeure à Coombe Tracey.

« — Qui est-elle ? demandai-je.

« — C'est la fille de Frankland.

« — Quoi ! de ce vieux toqué de Frankland ?

« — Parfaitement, elle a épousé un artiste, nommé Lyons, qui venait prendre des croquis sur la lande. Il s'est conduit envers elle comme un goujat… il l'a abandonnée. S'il faut en croire la rumeur publique, il n'avait pas tous les torts. Quant à Frankland, il ne veut plus entendre parler de sa fille, sous prétexte qu'elle s'est mariée malgré lui — et peut-être aussi pour deux ou trois autres raisons. En tout cas, abandonné de son mari et de son père, la jeune femme n'a pas beaucoup d'agrément.

« — De quoi vit-elle ?

« — Je crois que Frankland lui envoie quelques subsides… bien maigres probablement, car ses affaires sont peu prospères. Quels que soient les torts de Laura, on ne pouvait la laisser dans cette affreuse misère. Son histoire a transpiré, et plusieurs de nos amis ont fait leur possible pour l'aider à gagner honnêtement sa vie. Stapleton, sir Charles et moi-même, nous y avons contribué dans la mesure de nos moyens. Nous voulions la placer à la tête d'une entreprise de dactylographie. »

« Mortimer essaya de connaître le pourquoi de ces questions. Je m'arrangeai de façon à satisfaire sa curiosité, sans toutefois lui en dire trop long, car je ne jugeais pas utile de lui confier mes projets.

« Je me promis d'aller le lendemain matin à Coombe Tracey. J'espérais que, si je parvenais à joindre cette Laura Lyons, de si équivoque réputation, j'aurais fait un grand pas vers l'éclaircissement de tous ces mystères enchevêtrés les uns dans les autres.

« Au cours de ma conversation avec Mortimer, je dus user de l'astuce du serpent. À un moment, le docteur me pressa de questions embarrassantes ; je m'en tirai en lui demandant d'un air fort innocent à quelle catégorie appartenait le crâne de Frankland. À partir de cet instant, nous ne parlâmes plus que de phrénologie. — Je ne pouvais avoir passé inutilement de si longues années auprès de Sherlock Holmes !

« À noter encore pour ce jour-là une conversation avec Barrymore, qui m'a fourni un atout que je compte bien jouer au moment opportun.

« Nous avions retenu Mortimer à dîner. Le soir, le baronnet et lui se livrèrent à d'interminables parties d'écarté.

« Barrymore m'avait servi le café dans la bibliothèque, et je profitai de ce que nous étions seuls pour lui poser quelques questions.

« — Votre cher beau-frère est-il parti, lui dis-je, ou bien vagabonde-t-il toujours sur la lande ?

« — Je l'ignore, monsieur. J'aime à croire que nous en sommes enfin débarrassés, car il ne nous a jamais procuré que des ennuis. Je lui ai porté des provisions pour la dernière fois, il y a trois jours ; depuis, il ne nous a pas donné signe de vie.

« — Ce jour-là, l'avez-vous vu ?

« — Non, monsieur. Mais, le lendemain, les provisions avaient disparu.

« — Donc, il était encore là.

« — Oui... à moins que ce ne soit l'*autre* qui les ait prises. »

« La tasse que je portais à mes lèvres s'arrêta à mi-chemin de son parcours et je regardai Barrymore avec étonnement.

« — Vous saviez qu'un autre homme se cachait sur la lande !

« — Oui, monsieur.

« — L'avez-vous aperçu ?

« — Non, monsieur.

« — Alors comment l'avez-vous appris ?

« — Selden m'en a parlé... cet homme se cache également ; mais, d'après ce que je suppose, ce n'est pas un convict... Tout cela me semble louche, docteur Watson... je vous le dis en vérité, cela me semble très louche. »

« Barrymore avait prononcé ces paroles avec un grand accent de sincérité.

« — Écoutez-moi, répliquai-je. Je n'ai d'autre souci que l'intérêt de votre maître et ma présence à Baskerville n'a d'autre but que de lui prêter mon concours. Dites-moi bien franchement ce qui vous paraît louche. »

« Barrymore hésita un instant ; regrettait-il déjà sa confidence et éprouvait-il de la difficulté à expliquer ses propres sentiments ?

« Enfin, il agita ses mains vers la fenêtre fouettée par la pluie, et, désignant la lande dans un geste de colère, il s'écria :

« — Ce sont tous les potins qui courent !... Il y a quelque anguille sous roche... On prépare quelque scélératesse ; ça, j'en jurerais ! Je ne me sentirai heureux que lorsque sir Henry sera reparti pour Londres.

« — Quelle est la cause de vos alarmes ?

« — Souvenez-vous de la mort de sir Charles !... Le juge d'instruction nous a dit qu'elle était singulière... Rappelez-vous les bruits de la lande pendant la nuit ! Une fois le soleil couché, aucun homme, même à prix d'argent, n'oserait s'y aventurer... Et puis cet étranger qui se cache là-bas, guettant, attendant ! Qu'attend-il ? Que signifie tout cela ? Certainement rien de bon pour celui qui porte le nom de Baskerville. Je ne serai vraiment soulagé d'un grand poids que le jour où les nouveaux serviteurs de sir Henry prendront leur service au château.

« — Parlons de cet inconnu, fis-je, en ramenant la conversation sur le seul sujet qui m'intéressât. Pouvez-vous m'apprendre quelque chose sur son compte ? Que vous a raconté Selden ? Sait-il pourquoi cet homme se cache ? Quelles sont ses intentions ?...

« — Mon beau-frère l'a aperçu une ou deux fois ; mais, comme il est peu communicatif, il ne s'est pas montré prodigue de renseignements. Tout d'abord Selden a cru que cet inconnu appartenait à la police ; mais, comme il cherchait également la solitude, mon beau-frère a vite reconnu son erreur. D'après ce que Selden a pu en juger, ce nouvel habitant de la lande aurait les allures d'un gentleman. Que fait-il là ?... Mon parent l'ignore.

« — Où vit-il ?

« — Sur le versant de la colline, au milieu de ces huttes de pierres habitées autrefois par nos ancêtres.

« — Comment se procure-t-il de la nourriture ?

« — Un jeune garçon prend soin de lui et lui apporte tout ce dont il a besoin. Selden croit que le gamin va s'approvisionner à Coombe Tracey.

« — Fort bien, Barrymore, répondis-je. Nous reprendrons plus tard cette conversation. »

« Le valet de chambre sorti, je m'approchai de la fenêtre. Dehors, il faisait noir. À travers les vitres recouvertes de buée, je contemplai les nuages que le vent chassait dans le ciel et la cime des arbres qui se courbait sous la bourrasque.

« La nuit, déjà dure pour les gens calfeutrés dans une maison confortable, devait être terrible pour ceux qui n'avaient d'autre abri sur la lande qu'une hutte de pierre !

« Fallait-il qu'elle fût profonde, la haine qui poussait un homme à errer à une pareille heure et dans un tel endroit ! Seul un mobile bien puissant pouvait justifier une semblable séquestration du monde !

« Ainsi donc, dans une hutte de la lande, se trouvait la solution du problème que je brûlais du désir de résoudre.

« Je jurai que vingt-quatre heures ne s'écouleraient pas sans que j'eusse tenté tout ce qu'il est humainement possible de faire pour aller jusqu'au tréfonds même de ce mystère. »

XI

L'HOMME DU PIC NOIR

L'extrait de mon journal particulier qui forme le chapitre précédent m'a conduit jusqu'au 18 octobre, date à laquelle commença à se précipiter la conclusion de ces étranges événements.

Tous les incidents des jours suivants sont gravés dans ma mémoire d'une façon indélébile, et je puis les conter par le menu sans recourir aux notes prises à cette époque.

Je recommence donc mon récit au lendemain du jour où j'avais établi deux faits d'une importante gravité : le premier, que Mme Laura Lyons, de Coombe Tracey, avait écrit à sir Charles Baskerville et pris rendez-vous avec lui pour le lieu et l'heure mêmes où il avait trouvé la mort ; le second, que l'inconnu de la lande se terrait dans les huttes de pierre, sur le versant de la colline.

Ces deux points acquis, je compris néanmoins que mon intelligence ou mon courage ne suffiraient pas pour mener à bien mon entreprise, si je ne parvenais à jeter un supplément de lumière sur ceux encore obscurs.

La veille, le docteur Mortimer et sir Henry avaient joué aux cartes jusqu'à une heure avancée de la nuit, et je n'avais pas eu l'occasion d'entretenir le baronnet de ce que j'avais appris sur Mme Laura Lyons.

Pendant le déjeuner, je lui fis part de ma découverte, et je lui demandai s'il lui plairait de m'accompagner à Coombe Tracey.

Tout d'abord, il se montra enchanté de cette petite excursion ; puis, après mûre réflexion, il nous parut préférable à tous deux que je la fisse seul. Plus la visite serait cérémonieuse, plus il nous serait difficile d'obtenir des renseignements.

Je quittai sir Henry — non sans quelques remords — et je courus vers cette nouvelle piste.

En arrivant à Coombe Tracey, j'ordonnai à Perkins de dételer les chevaux, et je m'enquis de la dame que je venais interroger.

Je la trouvai sans peine : elle habitait au centre de la petite localité.

La bonne m'introduisit dans le salon, sans m'annoncer.

Une femme, assise devant une machine à écrire, se leva et s'avança vers moi avec un sourire de bienvenue.

Quand elle se trouva en face d'un étranger, ce sourire s'évanouit ; elle se rassit et s'informa de l'objet de ma visite. À première vue, Mme Laura Lyons produisait l'impression d'une très jolie femme. Ses yeux et ses cheveux avaient cette chaude coloration de la noisette ; ses joues, quoique marquées de quelques taches de rousseur, possédaient l'éclat exquis des brunes avec, aux pommettes, ce léger vermillon qui brille au cœur de la rose thé.

La première impression, je le répète, engendrait l'admiration. La critique ne naissait qu'à un second examen. Le visage avait quelque chose de défectueux — une expression vulgaire, peut-être une dureté de l'œil ou un relâchement de la lèvre en altéraient la parfaite beauté. Mais la remarque de ces défectuosités ne venait qu'après une étude plus approfondie des traits.

Sur le moment, je n'éprouvai que la sensation d'être en présence d'une très jolie femme, qui me demandait le motif de ma visite.

Jusqu'alors, je ne m'étais nullement douté de la délicatesse de ma démarche.

« J'ai le plaisir, dis-je, de connaître monsieur votre père. »

Ce préambule était maladroit, la dame me le fit aussitôt comprendre.

« Il n'existe rien de commun entre mon père et moi, répliqua-t-elle, et ses amis ne sont pas les miens. Si je n'avais eu que mon père, à cette heure je serais morte de faim. Fort heureusement, sir Charles Baskerville et quelques autres âmes généreuses…

— Je suis précisément venu vous voir à propos de sir Charles Baskerville, interrompis-je. »

À ces mots, les taches de rousseur devinrent plus apparentes sur les joues de Mme Lyons.

« Que puis-je vous dire sur lui ? demanda-t-elle, tandis que ses doigts jouaient nerveusement sur les touches de sa machine à écrire.

— Vous le connaissiez, n'est-ce pas ?

— Je vous ai déjà dit que je lui étais redevable de grands services. Si je puis me suffire à moi-même, je le dois surtout à l'intérêt que lui avait inspiré ma triste situation.

— Lui écriviez-vous ? »

La dame releva vivement la tête ; un éclair de colère passa dans ses beaux yeux veloutés.

« Dans quel but toutes ces questions ? interrogea-t-elle sèchement.

— Dans quel but ? répétai-je… Pour éviter un scandale public… Il vaut mieux que je vous adresse ces questions, ici, dans l'intimité, sans que l'affaire qui m'amène franchisse cette enceinte. »

Mme Lyons garda le silence et ses joues devinrent excessivement pâles.

Puis en me jetant un regard de défi :

« Soit ! dit-elle, je vous répondrai. Que désirez-vous savoir ?

— Correspondiez-vous avec sir Charles ?

— Oui ; je lui ai écrit une ou deux fois pour le remercier de sa délicate générosité.

— Vous rappelez-vous les dates de vos lettres ?

— Non.

— Vous êtes-vous rencontrés ?

— Oui ; une ou deux fois… quand il est venu à Coombe Tracey. C'était un homme très simple, qui faisait le bien sans ostentation.

— Puisque vous l'avez peu vu et que vous ne lui avez écrit que fort rarement, comment pouvait-il connaître assez vos besoins pour vous aider ainsi qu'il l'a fait, d'après vos propres aveux ? »

Mme Lyons rétorqua cette objection avec une extrême promptitude :

« Plusieurs personnes connaissant mon dénuement s'étaient associées pour me secourir. L'une d'elles était M. Stapleton, voisin et ami intime de sir Charles Baskerville. Excessivement bon, il consentit à parler de moi à sir Charles. »

Je savais déjà que, dans plusieurs circonstances, le vieux gentilhomme s'était servi de l'intermédiaire de Stapleton pour distribuer ses aumônes. Le récit de la dame paraissait donc très vraisemblable.

Je continuai :

« Avez-vous écrit à sir Charles pour lui donner un rendez-vous ? »

La colère empourpra de nouveau les joues de Mme Lyons :

« Vraiment, monsieur, répondit-elle, vous me posez là une question bien extraordinaire.

— Je le regrette, madame, mais je dois la renouveler.

— Je vous répondrai : certainement non !

— Pas même le jour de la mort de sir Charles ? »

La rougeur du visage de Mme Laura Lyons fit place à une pâleur cadavérique.

Ses lèvres desséchées s'entrouvrirent à peine pour laisser tomber un « non », que je vis, plutôt que je ne l'entendis.

— Votre mémoire vous trahit sûrement, dis-je. Je puis vous citer un passage de votre lettre. Le voici : « Je vous en prie, "je vous en supplie, vous êtes un homme" d'honneur, brûlez cette lettre et soyez ce "soir, à dix heures, à la porte de la "lande".

Je crus que Mme Lyons allait s'évanouir ; mais, par un suprême effort de volonté, elle se ressaisit.

« Je croyais un galant homme incapable d'une telle action ! bégaya-t-elle.

— Vous êtes injuste pour sir Charles… Il a brûlé votre lettre. Mais quelquefois une lettre, même carbonisée, reste encore lisible… Reconnaissez-vous l'avoir écrite ?

— Oui, je l'ai écrite ! » s'écria-t-elle.

Et répandant son âme dans un torrent de mots, elle ajouta :

« Oui, je l'ai écrite ! Pourquoi le nierais-je ? Je n'ai pas à en rougir !... Je désirais qu'il me secourût et j'espérais l'y amener, s'il consentait à m'écouter. Voilà pourquoi je lui ai demandé une entrevue.

— Pourquoi avoir choisi cette heure tardive ?

— Parce que j'avais appris le matin que sir Charles partait le lendemain pour Londres et que son absence se prolongerait pendant plusieurs mois.

— Mais pourquoi lui donner rendez-vous dans le jardin plutôt que dans le château ?

— Pensez-vous qu'il soit convenable qu'une femme seule aille, à cette heure-là, chez un célibataire ?

— Qu'arriva-t-il au cours de votre entrevue ?

— Je ne suis pas allée à Baskerville.

— Madame Lyons !

— Je vous le jure sur tout ce que j'ai de plus sacré !... Non, je ne suis pas allée à Baskerville... Un événement imprévu m'en a empêchée.

— Quel est-il ?

— Il est d'ordre tout intime. Je ne puis vous le dire.

— Alors vous reconnaissez avoir donné rendez-vous à sir Charles à l'heure et à l'endroit où il a trouvé la mort, mais vous niez être venue à ce rendez-vous ?

— Je vous ai dit la vérité. »

À maintes reprises, j'interrogeai Mme Lyons sur ce fait ; ses réponses ne varièrent pas.

« Madame, lui dis-je en me levant pour clore cette longue et inutile visite, par votre manque de confiance et de franchise, vous assumez une lourde responsabilité et vous vous placez dans une situation très fausse. Si vous me forcez à requérir l'intervention de la justice, vous verrez à quel point vous serez sérieusement compromise ! Si vous n'avez pas trempé dans ce tragique événement, pourquoi avez-vous nié tout d'abord la lettre envoyée par vous à sir Charles à cette date ?

— Je craignais qu'on ne tirât de ce fait une conclusion erronée et que je ne fusse ainsi mêlée à un scandale.

— Pourquoi avez-vous tant insisté pour que sir Charles brûlât votre lettre ?

— Vous devez le savoir, puisque vous l'avez lue.

— Je ne prétends pas avoir lu cette lettre.

— Vous m'en avez cité un passage.

— Le *post-scriptum* seulement. Ainsi que je vous l'ai dit, la lettre avait été brûlée et cette partie demeurait seule lisible. Je vous demande encore une fois pourquoi vous insistiez si fort pour que sir Charles brûlât cette lettre, reçue quelques heures avant sa mort ?

— Ceci est également d'ordre intime.

— Raison de plus pour éviter une enquête publique.

— Eh bien, je vais vous l'apprendre. Si vous connaissez un peu ma malheureuse histoire, vous devez savoir que j'ai fait un mariage ridicule et que je le déplore pour plusieurs raisons.

— Je le sais.

— Par ses persécutions quotidiennes, mon mari — que je déteste — m'avait rendu la vie commune odieuse. Mais il a la loi pour lui et je suis tous les jours exposée à ce qu'il m'oblige à réintégrer le foyer conjugal. À l'époque où j'écrivis cette lettre à sir Charles, j'avais appris que je pourrais reconquérir mon indépendance, moyennant certains frais qu'il fallait consigner. Il s'agissait de tout ce qui m'est le plus cher au monde — tranquillité d'esprit, bonheur, respect de moi-même — de tout ! Je connaissais sir Charles, et je me disais que, s'il entendait mon histoire de ma propre bouche, il ne repousserait pas mes prières.

— Alors pourquoi n'êtes-vous pas allée le retrouver ?

— Dans l'intervalle, j'avais reçu du secours d'un autre côté.

— Pourquoi ne pas écrire une seconde fois à sir Charles pour lui expliquer tout cela ?

— Je l'eusse certainement fait si les journaux du lendemain matin n'avaient pas annoncé sa mort. »

Le récit de Mme Lyons était vraisemblable et cohérent. Pour en contrôler la véracité, il ne me restait plus qu'à vérifier si, vers cette époque, elle avait introduit une action en divorce contre son mari.

D'autre part, il me paraissait inadmissible qu'elle osât affirmer ne pas être allée à Baskerville, si elle s'y était réellement rendue ; elle aurait dû s'y faire porter en voiture et ne rentrer à Coombe Tracey qu'aux premières heures du matin. Or, comment tenir ce voyage secret ?

Selon toute probabilité, Mme Lyons m'avait confessé toute la vérité — ou tout au moins une partie de la vérité.

Je m'en retournai confus et découragé.

— Ainsi donc, une fois encore, je me heurtais à un obstacle qui me barrait la voie au bout de laquelle j'espérais trouver la clef du mystère que j'avais mission de découvrir.

Et cependant, plus je songeais au visage et à l'attitude de Mme Lyons, plus j'avais le pressentiment qu'elle me cachait quelque chose.

Pourquoi était-elle devenue si pâle ?

Pourquoi avais-je dû lutter pour lui arracher certaines explications ?

Pourquoi enfin avait-elle gardé le silence au moment du drame ?

Et ses explications mêmes ne la rendaient pas aussi innocente à mes yeux qu'elle aurait voulu le paraître.

Pour l'instant, je résolus de ne pas pousser plus loin mes investigations du côté de Mme Lyons et de chercher, au contraire, la solution du problème parmi les huttes de pierre de la lande.

Le renseignement fourni par Barrymore était très vague. Je m'en convainquis pendant mon retour au château, à la vue de cette succession de collines qui portaient toutes les traces de l'habitation des anciens hommes.

La seule indication précise consistait à affecter à l'inconnu une de ces antiques demeures de pierre. Or, j'en comptais plus de cent disséminées un peu partout sur la lande.

Cependant, depuis que j'avais vu l'homme juché sur le sommet du pic Noir, j'avais un point de repère pour me guider. Je me promis de concentrer mes recherches autour de ce point.

De là-haut, je pouvais explorer successivement toutes les huttes, jusqu'à ce que j'eusse découvert la bonne. Si j'y rencontrais mon inconnu, je saurais bien, mon revolver aidant, lui arracher son secret. Il faudra qu'il m'apprenne qui il est et pourquoi il nous espionne depuis si longtemps !

Il nous avait échappé au milieu de la foule de Regent street ; dans cette contrée déserte, la même manœuvre serait plus difficile.

Si, au contraire, la hutte était vide, je m'y installerais aussi longtemps qu'il le faudrait pour attendre le retour de son hôte.

Holmes l'avait manqué à Londres… Quel triomphe pour moi si je réussissais là où mon maître avait échoué !

Dans cette enquête, la malchance s'était acharnée contre nous. Mais tout à coup la fortune tourna et commença à me sourire.

Le messager de bonheur se présenta sous les traits de M. Frankland qui, la figure rubiconde encadrée par ses favoris grisonnants, se tenait sur le pas de la porte de son jardin. La grande route que je suivais passait devant cette porte.

« Bonjour, docteur Watson ! s'écria-t-il avec une bonne humeur inaccoutumée. Vos chevaux ont besoin de repos… Entrez donc vous rafraîchir… Vous me féliciterez. »

Depuis que je connaissais la conduite de Frankland envers sa fille, je n'éprouvais plus aucune sympathie pour lui. Mais comme je souhaitais un prétexte pour renvoyer Perkins et la voiture au château, l'occasion me parut excellente.

Je mis pied à terre et je fis dire à sir Henry par le cocher que je rentrerais pour l'heure du dîner.

Puis je pénétrai dans la maison de Frankland.

« C'est un grand jour pour moi, fit cet original, un de ces jours qu'on marque avec un caillou blanc. J'ai remporté aujourd'hui un double succès. Je voulais apprendre aux gens de ce pays que la loi est la loi et qu'il existe un homme qui ne craint pas de l'invoquer. J'avais revendiqué un droit de passage au beau milieu du parc du vieux Middleton, monsieur, sur un espace de cent mètres et devant la porte de la maison. Qu'en pensez-vous ?… Ils verront bien, ces grands seigneurs, qu'ils ne nous écraseront pas toujours sous le sabot ferré de leurs chevaux !… Ensuite, j'avais entouré de clôtures le bois où les habitants de Fenworthy ont coutume d'aller en pique-nique. Les maroufles croient vraiment qu'on a abrogé les lois qui protègent la propriété et qu'ils peuvent déposer partout leurs papiers graisseux et leurs tessons de bouteilles ! Ces deux procès ont été jugés, docteur Watson, et j'ai obtenu gain de cause dans les deux affaires. Je n'avais plus remporté de succès pareil depuis le jour où j'avais fait condamner sir John Morland parce qu'il tirait des lapins sur sa propre garenne.

— Comment diable vous y êtes-vous pris ?

— Feuilletez les recueils de jurisprudence… Vous y lirez : « Frankland *c.* Morland, Cour du Banc de la Reine… » Ça m'a coûté cinq mille francs, mais j'ai eu mon jugement !

— Quel profit en avez-vous tiré ?

— Aucun, monsieur, aucun… Je suis fier de dire que je n'avais aucun intérêt dans l'affaire… Je remplis mon devoir de citoyen… Par exemple, je ne doute pas que les gens de Fenworthy ne me brûlent ce soir en effigie. La dernière fois qu'ils se sont livrés à ce petit divertissement, j'avais averti la police qu'elle eût à intervenir… La police du comté est déplorablement conduite, monsieur ; elle ne m'a pas accordé la protection à laquelle j'avais droit ! Le procès Frankland *c.* la Reine portera la cause devant le public… J'ai prévenu les agents qu'ils se repentiront de leur attitude envers moi — et déjà ma prédiction se réalise.

— Comment ? demandai-je.

— Je pourrais leur apprendre ce qu'ils meurent d'envie de connaître ; mais, pour rien au monde, je n'aiderais des coquins de cette espèce. »

Depuis un moment, je cherchais un prétexte pour échapper aux bavardages de ce vieux fou. En entendant ces paroles, je voulus en savoir davantage.

Je connaissais suffisamment le caractère de Frankland pour être certain que le moindre signe d'intérêt arrêterait immédiatement ses confidences.

— « Quelque délit de braconnage sans doute ? dis-je d'un air indifférent.

— Ah ! ouiche !… La chose est bien plus importante… Que pensez-vous du contumace qui erre sur la lande ? »

Je le regardai, stupéfait.

« Insinueriez-vous que vous savez où il est ?

— J'ignore l'endroit précis où il se cache ; mais je pourrais tout de même procurer à la police le moyen de lui mettre la main au collet. Que faudrait-il pour s'emparer de lui ? Découvrir le lieu où il vient chercher sa nourriture et, de là, le suivre à la trace. »

Certainement Frankland touchait à la vérité.

« Vous avez raison, répondis-je. Mais comment avez-vous deviné qu'il habitait la lande ?

— J'ai vu, de mes yeux vu, le commissionnaire qui lui apporte ses provisions. »

Je tremblai pour Barrymore, car c'était chose dangereuse que de se trouver à la merci de cet incorrigible bavard.

La phrase qui suivit me rassura.

« C'est un jeune garçon qui lui sert de pourvoyeur, ajouta Frankland. À l'aide du télescope que j'ai installé sur mon toit, je l'aperçois tous les jours, parcourant à la même heure le même chemin. Qui irait-il retrouver, sinon le prisonnier évadé ? »

Ce renseignement marquait le retour de la bonne fortune. Et cependant je ne l'accueillis par aucun témoignage d'intérêt.

Un enfant !… Barrymore n'avait-il pas affirmé qu'un enfant ravitaillait l'inconnu ? Alors Frankland se trouvait sur la piste de mon inconnu, et non pas sur celle de Selden ! Que de longues et pénibles recherches n'éviterais-je pas s'il consentait à partager ce secret avec moi !

Il me fallait jouer serré, feindre l'incrédulité et l'indifférence.

« Il est plus probable, repris-je, que c'est le fils de quelque berger de la lande qui porte le dîner de son père. »

La moindre velléité de contradiction mettait le vieil entêté hors de lui. Il me lança un mauvais regard et ses favoris gris se hérissèrent comme les poils d'un chat sauvage.

« Un fils de fermier !… Vraiment ? fit-il en désignant de la main la lande solitaire que nous apercevions à travers la croisée. Voyez-vous le pic Noir, là-bas ? »

Je fis un signe affirmatif.

« Voyez-vous plus loin, reprit-il, cette colline peu élevée couronnée de buissons ? C'est la partie la plus pierreuse de la lande… Un berger voudrait-il y établir son parc ?… Tenez, votre supposition est tout bonnement absurde ! »

Je répondis humblement que j'avais parlé dans l'ignorance de tous ces détails.

Mon humilité désarma Frankland, qui continua ses confidences.

« Je vous assure que j'ai de bonnes raisons de croire que je me trompe pas. Maintes fois, j'ai vu ce jeune garçon, chargé de son paquet, parcourir le même chemin. Chaque jour, et souvent deux fois par jour, j'ai pu… Mais attendez donc, docteur Watson ! Mes yeux me trompent-ils ? N'y a-t-il pas quelque chose qui se meut sur le versant de la colline ? »

Plusieurs milles nous séparaient du point indiqué.

Cependant je distinguai une forme se dessinant en noir sur les teintes vertes et grises du paysage.

« Venez, monsieur, venez ! s'écria Frankland, en se précipitant vers l'escalier. Vous verrez par vous-même et vous jugerez. »

Un énorme télescope, monté sur un trépied, encombrait le faîte de la maison.

Avidement, Frankland y appliqua son œil et poussa un cri de satisfaction.

« Vite, docteur Watson, vite, avant qu'il ait disparu ! »

À mon tour, je collai mon œil à la lentille, et j'aperçus un jeune garçon qui, un paquet sur l'épaule, grimpait la colline. Arrivé au sommet, sa silhouette se profila sur l'azur du ciel. Il regarda autour de lui, de l'air inquiet de ceux qui redoutent d'être poursuivis ; puis il s'éclipsa derrière l'autre versant.

« Eh bien, ai-je raison ? demanda Frankland.

— J'en conviens. Voilà un garçon qui me paraît engagé dans une expédition secrète.

— Un agent de police lui-même ne se tromperait pas sur la nature de l'expédition. Mais je ne leur communiquerai rien et je vous requiers, docteur Watson, d'imiter mon silence. Pas un mot !… Vous comprenez ?

— Je vous le promets.

— La police s'est indignement conduite envers moi… indignement ! Quand le procès Frankland contre la Reine dévoilera l'ensemble des faits, un frisson d'indignation secouera tout le comté. Rien ne pourrait me décider à seconder la police… la police qui aurait été ravie si, au lieu de mon effigie, on avait brûlé ma modeste personne ! Vous vous tairez, n'est-ce pas ?… Acceptez donc de vider un flacon en l'honneur de mes récentes victoires ! »

Je résistai à toutes les sollicitations de Frankland et j'eus toutes les peines du monde à le dissuader de m'accompagner au château.

Je suivis la grande route jusqu'au moment où Frankland devait me perdre de vue ; puis je me dirigeai vers la colline derrière laquelle le jeune garçon avait disparu.

Les choses prenaient une tournure favorable et je jurai d'employer toute mon énergie et toute ma persévérance à profiter des chances que le hasard mettait à ma disposition.

Le soleil était à son déclin lorsque je parvins au sommet de la colline. Les longues pentes qui dévalaient vers la plaine revêtaient, du côté de l'occident, des teintes dorées, tandis que, de l'autre côté, l'ombre croissante les colorait d'un gris sombre.

Le brouillard, au-dessus duquel le Belliver et le pic du Renard faisaient encore saillie, montait lentement sur l'horizon.

Aucun bruit ne troublait le silence de la lande.

Un grand oiseau gris — une mouette ou un courlis — planait dans le ciel bleu. Lui et moi, nous semblions être les deux seules créatures vivantes s'agitant entre l'arc immense du firmament et le désert qui se développait au-dessous.

Ce paysage aride, cette impression de solitude, ce mystère, ainsi que les dangers de l'heure présente, tout cela me glaçait le cœur.

Le gamin entrevu à travers le télescope de Frankland restait invisible.

Mais, en bas, dans la déchirure de la colline, se dressaient de nombreuses huttes de pierre dont l'agglomération affectait la forme d'un immense cercle. Il en était une qui conservait encore

une toiture suffisante pour abriter quelqu'un contre les intempé-
ries des saisons.

À cette vue, mon cœur battit à tout rompre.

Mon inconnu gîtait certainement là ! Je touchais à sa cachette
— son secret était à portée de ma main !

Avec autant de précaution que Stapleton s'approchant, le filet
levé, d'un papillon posé sur une fleur, je fis quelques pas en avant.

Un sentier, à peine frayé à travers les blocs de rochers, conduisait à une ouverture béante qui tenait lieu de porte.

À l'intérieur, tout était silencieux. De deux choses l'une :
l'inconnu s'y trouvait blotti ou bien il rôdait sur la lande.

Mes nerfs vibraient sous la solennité du moment.

Jetant ma cigarette, je saisis la crosse de mon revolver, et,
courant précipitamment vers la porte, je regardai dans la hutte.

Elle était vide.

Une rapide inspection me montra qu'elle était habitée. Je vis
des couvertures, doublées de toile cirée, étendues sur la large
dalle de pierre où les hommes néolithiques avaient coutume de
reposer. Des cendres s'amoncelaient dans un foyer rudimentaire.
On avait placé dans un coin quelques ustensiles de cuisine et une
jarre pleine d'eau.

De vieilles boîtes de conserves mises en tas indiquaient que le
lieu était occupé depuis assez longtemps, et, dès que mes yeux
furent habitués à cette demi-obscurité, je distinguai une miche de
pain et une bouteille de cognac entamées.

Au centre de la hutte, une grande pierre plate remplaçait la
table absente. On y avait posé un paquet enveloppé d'étoffe —
le même sans doute qu'une heure auparavant le gamin portait sur
ses épaules. Il contenait un morceau de pain frais, de la langue
fumée et deux petits pots de confiture.

Lorsque je le replaçai sur la pierre, après l'avoir examiné, je
tressaillis à la vue d'une feuille de papier sur laquelle une main
inexpérimentée avait, d'une grosse écriture, griffonné ces mots :

« Le docteur Watson est allé à Coombe Tracey. »

Pendant une minute, je demeurai immobile, ce papier à la
main, me demandant ce que signifiait ce laconique message.

C'était donc moi — et non pas sir Henry — qu'espionnait l'inconnu ! N'osant pas me suivre lui-même, il avait lancé quelqu'un à mes trousses — le gamin, sans doute — et j'avais son rapport sous les yeux !

Peut-être, depuis mon arrivée sur la lande, n'avais-je pas fait un pas ou dit un mot qui n'eût été observé et rapporté !

Je ressentis alors le poids d'une force invisible, d'un filet tendu autour de nous avec une adresse si surprenante et nous enserrant si légèrement, qu'il ne fallait rien moins qu'une circonstance solennelle pour deviner qu'on était enveloppé dans ses mailles.

D'autres rapports avaient dû précéder celui-ci. Je les cherchai partout. Je n'en trouvai de traces nulle part — par plus d'ailleurs que d'indices révélateurs de la personnalité et des intentions de l'homme qui vivait dans cette retraite. De mon examen de la hutte, je ne pouvais déduire que deux choses : sa sobriété spartiate et son mépris du confort de la vie.

Songeant à la pluie torrentielle des jours précédents et regardant les pierres disjointes qui formaient son toit, je compris combien fort et inébranlable devait être le dessein qui le retenait sous un semblable abri.

Cet homme était-il un ennemi implacable ou un ange gardien ?

Je me promis de ne pas quitter la hutte sans l'avoir appris.

Au dehors, le soleil empourprait l'horizon sous le flot de ses derniers rayons. Ses reflets teintaient de rouge les flaques marécageuses de la grande fondrière. Dans le lointain, pointaient les deux tours du château de Baskerville et, plus loin, un panache de fumée montant dans l'espace marquait l'emplacement du village de Grimpen. Entre les deux, derrière la colline, s'élevait la maison de Stapleton.

Tout était calme, doux, paisible, dans ce glorieux crépuscule. Et cependant, tout en l'admirant, mon âme ne partageait pas la paix de la nature. J'éprouvais comme une vague terreur à la pensée de l'entrevue que chaque minute rendait plus prochaine.

Les nerfs tendus, mais le cœur très résolu, je m'assis dans le coin le plus obscur de la hutte et j'attendis avec une impatience fébrile l'arrivée de son hôte.

Je l'entendis enfin venir.

Je perçus le bruit d'un talon de botte sonnant sur les cailloux du chemin.

Les pas se rapprochaient de plus en plus.

Je me blottis dans mon coin et j'armai mon revolver, déterminé à ne me montrer qu'au moment où l'inconnu aurait pénétré dans la hutte.

Une longue pause m'apprit qu'il s'était arrêté.

Puis les pas se rapprochèrent encore et une ombre se dessina dans l'encadrement de la porte.

« Quelle belle soirée, mon cher Watson ! me dit une voix bien connue. Je crois vraiment que nous serons mieux dehors que dedans ».

XII

MORT SUR LA LANDE

Pendant une ou deux minutes, la surprise me suffoqua ; j'eus toutes les peines du monde à en croire mes oreilles. Cependant je me ressaisis et, en même temps que je reprenais ma respiration, je sentis mon âme soulagée du poids de la terrible responsabilité qui l'oppressait. Cette parole froide, incisive, ironique, ne pouvait appartenir qu'à un seul homme.

« Holmes ! m'écriai-je… Holmes !

— Venez ! me dit-il… Et ne faites pas d'imprudence avec votre revolver. »

Je me courbai pour passer sous le linteau de la porte, et, près de la hutte, j'aperçus mon ami, assis sur une pierre. À la vue de mon visage étonné, ses yeux gris papillotèrent de joie.

Holmes paraissait amaigri, fatigué, mais toujours aussi vif et aussi alerte. Dans son complet de cheviotte, avec son chapeau de drap sur la tête, on l'aurait pris pour un simple touriste visitant la lande. Soigneux de sa personne comme un chat de sa fourrure

— c'est une de ses caractéristiques — il s'était arrangé pour avoir son menton aussi finement rasé et son linge aussi irréprochable que s'il fût sorti de son cabinet de toilette de Baker street.

« Je n'ai jamais été plus heureux de voir quelqu'un, fis-je, en lui secouant les mains.

— Ni plus étonné, hein ?

— Je l'avoue.

— Croyez bien que ma surprise a égalé la vôtre. Comment supposer que vous auriez retrouvé ma retraite momentanée… Jusqu'à vingt mètres d'ici, je ne me serais pas douté que vous occupiez la hutte.

— Vous avez reconnu l'empreinte de mes pas ?

— Non, Watson. Je ne me livrerais pas à une recherche aussi ardue. Seulement, si vous désirez vous cacher de moi, je vous conseille de changer de marchand de tabac. Lorsque je trouve un bout de cigarette portant la marque de Bradley, Oxford street, je devine que mon ami Watson n'est pas loin. Regardez, en voilà une à peu près intacte dans le sentier. Vous l'avez jetée, sans doute, au moment de faire irruption dans la hutte vide ?

— Oui.

— Je l'aurais parié !… Et, connaissant votre admirable ténacité, j'étais certain de vous y trouver embusqué, une arme à portée de votre main, attendant ainsi le retour de celui qui l'habite. Vous pensiez donc qu'elle servait de refuge à un criminel ?

— J'ignorais le nom de son hôte de passage, mais j'étais déterminé à découvrir son identité.

— Très bien, Watson. Mais comment aviez-vous appris la présence d'un étranger sur la lande ? Peut-être m'avez-vous vu, la nuit où vous avez donné la chasse au convict — cette nuit où je fus assez imprudent pour m'exposer à la clarté de la lune ?

— En effet, je vous ai vu, cette nuit-là.

— Alors, vous avez fouillé toutes les huttes, jusqu'à ce que vous soyez arrivé à celle-ci ?

— Non ; j'ai guetté votre jeune commissionnaire et j'ai su où venir tout droit.

« — Je comprends… le vieux bonhomme au télescope !… J'aurais dû m'en méfier lorsque, pour la première fois, je vis ses lentilles étinceler aux feux du soleil. »

Holmes se leva et jeta un coup d'œil dans l'intérieur de la hutte.

« Ah ! reprit-il, Cartwright m'a ravitaillé… Tiens, un papier !… Vous êtes donc allé à Coombe Tracey ?

— Oui.

— Voir Mme Laura Lyons ?

— Parfaitement.

— Bonne idée ! Nos enquêtes suivaient une route parallèle, et, à l'heure où nous combinerons nos renseignements respectifs, nous ne serons pas loin d'avoir fait la lumière.

— Si vous saviez, mon cher Holmes, combien je suis heureux de vous retrouver ici !… Ce mystère, cette responsabilité pesaient trop lourdement sur mes pauvres nerfs. Mais pourquoi diable êtes-vous venu à Dartmoor et qu'y faisiez-vous ? Je vous croyais toujours à Baker street, occupé à débrouiller cette affaire de chantage.

— J'avais intérêt à ne pas vous détromper.

— Ainsi, vous vous moquez de moi et, qui plus est, vous me refusez votre confiance ! fis-je avec quelque amertume. Je méritais mieux que cela, Holmes.

— Mon cher ami, dans ce cas, comme dans beaucoup d'autres, votre concours m'a été très utile, et je vous prie de me pardonner ce semblant de méfiance. En vérité, je ne me suis caché de vous que par souci de votre propre sécurité, et, seul, le sentiment du danger que vous couriez m'a poussé à venir examiner par moi-même la situation. Auprès de sir Henry et de vous, j'aurais partagé votre manière de voir et ma présence aurait mis en garde nos redoutables adversaires. Notre séparation, au contraire, m'a permis d'atteindre un résultat que je n'aurais pas osé espérer, si j'avais vécu au château. Je reste un facteur inconnu, prêt à se lancer dans la bagarre au moment opportun.

— Pourquoi ne pas me prévenir ?

— Cela ne nous aurait été d'aucune utilité et aurait peut-être amené ma découverte. Vous auriez eu à me parler ; avec le cœur compatissant que je vous connais, vous m'auriez apporté des provisions de toutes sortes, que sais-je ?... Enfin nous aurions couru un risque inutile. Cartwright — le gamin de l'*Express Office*, vous vous rappelez ? — m'avait accompagné ; il a pourvu à mes besoins peu compliqués : une miche de pain et un col propre. Que faut-il de plus ? Ensuite, il représentait une paire d'yeux supplémentaires, surmontant deux pieds excessivement agiles. J'ai tiré grand profit des uns et des autres.

— Mes rapports ont donc été perdus ! » m'écriai-je.

Au souvenir de la peine et de l'orgueil éprouvés en les rédigeant, ma voix tremblait.

Holmes tira de sa poche un paquet de papiers.

« Les voilà, vos rapports, dit-il... lus et relus, je vous l'assure. J'avais pris toutes mes précautions pour qu'on me les réexpédiât sans retard de Baker street. Je tiens à vous féliciter du zèle et de l'intelligence que vous avez déployés dans une affaire aussi difficile. »

Je gardais encore rancune à Holmes du tour qu'il m'avait joué, mais la spontanéité et la chaleur de ses louanges dissipèrent bien vite mon ressentiment. Dans mon for intérieur, je convenais qu'il avait raison et qu'il était préférable, pour la réussite de nos projets, que sa présence sur la lande demeurât ignorée.

« Je vous aime mieux ainsi, dit mon ami, en voyant s'éclaircir mon visage rembruni. Et maintenant, racontez-moi votre visite à Mme Laura Lyons... J'ai deviné sans peine que vous alliez là-bas pour causer avec elle... Je suis convaincu qu'elle seule, à Coombe Tracey, peut nous rendre quelques services. Si vous n'aviez pas tenté cette démarche aujourd'hui, moi, je l'aurais faite demain. »

Le soleil s'était couché. Peu à peu l'obscurité envahissait la lande. Le vent ayant fraîchi, nous entrâmes dans la hutte pour y chercher un abri. Là, assis dans la pénombre, je narrai à Holmes ma conversation avec la fille de Frankland ; le récit l'intéressa à tel point que je dus le recommencer.

« Tout ceci est fort important, me dit Sherlock, lorsque j'eus terminé. Vous avez éliminé du problème une inconnue que j'étais incapable de dégager : peut-être savez-vous qu'il existe une grande intimité entre Mme Lyons et Stapleton ?

— Je l'ignorais.

— Si, une très grande intimité. Ils se rencontrent. Ils s'écrivent ; il y a entre eux une entente parfaite. C'est une arme puissante entre nos mains… Si je pouvais seulement l'utiliser pour détacher sa femme de lui…

— Sa femme ? interrompis-je.

— Oui, sa femme. Je vous donne des renseignements en échange des vôtres. La dame qui passe ici pour Mlle Stapleton est en réalité la femme du naturaliste.

— Grands dieux, Holmes ! Êtes-vous sûr de ce que vous dites ? Comment aurait-il permis que le baronnet en devînt amoureux ?

— L'amour de sir Henry ne devait nuire qu'à lui-même. Stapleton — vous en avez été témoin vous-même — ne veillait qu'à une chose : empêcher sir Henry de courtiser sa femme. Je vous répète que la dame n'est pas mademoiselle, mais bien madame Stapleton.

— Pourquoi ce mensonge ?

— Son mari prévoyait qu'elle servirait mieux ses projets, si le baronnet se croyait en face d'une jeune fille à marier. »

Tous mes secrets pressentiments, tous mes vagues soupçons prirent un corps et se concentrèrent sur le naturaliste. Dans cet homme impassible, terne, avec son chapeau de paille et son filet à papillons, je découvrais maintenant quelque chose de terrible — un être infiniment patient, diaboliquement rusé, qui dissimulait une âme de meurtrier sous un visage souriant.

« Alors c'est lui qui nous a espionnés à Londres ? demandai-je à Holmes. Notre ennemi, le voilà donc ?

— Oui. J'explique ainsi l'énigme.

— Et la lettre d'avis ? Elle émanait de sa femme ?

— Parfaitement. »

Des ténèbres qui nous environnaient, je voyais poindre une monstrueuse infamie.

« Ne vous trompez-vous pas, Holmes ? insistai-je. Comment avez-vous découvert qu'ils étaient mariés ?

— La première fois que Stapleton vous rencontra, il eut le tort de vous confier une partie de sa véritable biographie. Depuis, il a dû regretter bien souvent ce moment de franchise… J'appris par vous qu'il avait ouvert autrefois une école dans le nord de l'Angleterre. Rien n'est plus aisé que de retrouver les traces d'un magister. Il existe des agences à l'aide desquelles on peut identifier tout homme ayant exercé cette profession. Quelques recherches me montrèrent qu'on avait supprimé une école dans d'assez vilaines circonstances… Son propriétaire — le nom différait — avait disparu ainsi que sa femme. Les signalements concordaient. Lorsque je sus que l'homme s'adonnait à l'entomologie, je ne conservai plus de doutes sur son identité. »

Le nuage se déchirait insensiblement ; toutefois beaucoup de points restaient encore dans l'ombre.

Je questionnai de nouveau Sherlock Holmes.

« Si cette femme est vraiment Mme Stapleton, dis-je, que vient faire ici Mme Laura Lyons ?

— Vos enquêtes ont élucidé ce point. Votre entrevue avec cette jeune femme a considérablement déblayé la situation… J'ignorais l'existence d'un projet de divorce entre son mari et elle. Si les tribunaux prononçaient la séparation, elle espérait que Stapleton, qu'elle croyait célibataire, l'épouserait.

— Qu'adviendra-t-il, lorsqu'elle connaîtra la vérité ?

— Elle nous sera un précieux allié. Demain nous irons la voir ensemble… Mais ne pensez-vous pas, Watson, que vous avez abandonné votre poste depuis bien longtemps ? Votre place, mon ami, est au château de Baskerville. »

Les dernières lueurs du crépuscule venaient de s'éteindre dans la direction de l'occident, et la nuit était descendue sur la lande. Quelques étoiles clignotaient sur la surface violacée du ciel.

« Une dernière question, Holmes ! fis-je, en me levant. Il ne peut y avoir de secrets entre vous et moi… Que signifie tout ceci ? Où Stapleton veut-il en arriver ? »

Sherlock baissa la voix pour me répondre.

« À un meurtre, Watson… à un meurtre longuement prémédité, froidement exécuté avec d'odieux raffinements. Ne me demandez pas de détails. Mes filets se resserrent autour du meurtrier — autant que les siens autour de sir Henry — et, grâce à votre appui, je le sens déjà à ma merci. Un seul danger nous menace : c'est qu'il frappe avant que nous soyons prêts à frapper nous-mêmes. Encore un jour — deux au plus — et j'aurai réuni toutes mes preuves. Jusque-là veillez sur le baronnet avec la sollicitude d'une tendre mère pour son enfant malade. Votre sortie d'aujourd'hui s'imposait, et cependant je souhaiterais que vous n'eussiez pas quitté sir Henry… Écoutez ! »

Un cri perçant, cri d'horreur et d'angoisse, éclata dans le silence de la lande et nous glaça le sang.

« Oh ! mon Dieu ! balbutia-je. Que se passe-t-il ? Pourquoi ce cri ? »

Holmes s'était dressé vivement. Sa silhouette athlétique se profilait dans l'encadrement de la porte, les épaules voûtées, la tête penchée en avant, ses yeux fouillant l'épaisseur des ténèbres.

« Silence ! dit-il tout bas… Silence ! »

Ce cri n'était parvenu jusqu'à nous qu'en raison de sa violence. Tout d'abord il avait surgi des profondeurs lointaines de la lande. Maintenant il se rapprochait, plus fort et plus pressant que jamais.

« Où est-ce ? reprit Holmes, en sourdine. Où est-ce, Watson ? »

Au tremblement de sa voix, je reconnus que cet homme d'airain était remué jusqu'au fond de l'âme.

J'indiquai un point dans la nuit.

« Là, répondis-je.

— Non, là », rectifia Holmes.

Une fois encore, ce cri, toujours plus proche et plus strident, passa sur la lande.

Il s'y mêlait un nouveau son, un grondement profond, rythmé quoique menaçant, qui s'élevait et s'abaissait, semblable au murmure continu de la mer.

« Le chien ! s'écria Holmes. Venez, Watson, venez vite ! Pourvu que nous n'arrivions pas trop tard ! »

Mon ami partit comme une flèche ; je courais sur ses talons.

D'un endroit quelconque de ce sol tourmenté, en avant de nous, monta un dernier appel désespéré, suivi du bruit sourd que fait un corps en s'abattant comme une masse.

Nul autre bruit ne troubla plus le calme de cette nuit sans vent.

Je vis Holmes porter la main à son front, comme un homme affolé. Il frappait du pied avec impatience.

« Ce Stapleton nous a vaincus, dit-il. Nous arriverons trop tard.

— Non, non ! répondis-je… sûrement non !

— J'ai été assez insensé pour ne pas lui mettre la main au collet !… Et vous, Watson, voyez ce que nous coûte votre sortie du château ! Mais par Dieu ! si sir Henry est mort, nous le vengerons ! »

En aveugles, nous marchions dans l'obscurité, trébuchant contre les quartiers de roches, escaladant les collines, dégringolant les pentes, dans la direction des appels déchirants que nous avions entendus.

Du haut de chaque sommet, Holmes regardait avidement autour de lui ; mais l'ombre était épaisse sur la lande et rien ne bougeait sur cette immense solitude.

Holmes me demanda :

« Apercevez-vous quelque chose, Watson ?

— Non, rien.

— Écoutez ! »

Sur notre gauche, on avait poussé un faible gémissement.

De ce côté, une ligne de rochers formait une sorte de falaise, surplombant un escarpement parsemé de grosses pierres. Au bas, nous distinguâmes vaguement quelque chose de noir et d'informe.

La face contre terre, un homme gisait sur le sol, la tête repliée sous lui, suivant un angle horrible à voir, les épaules remontées et le corps en boule, dans le mouvement de quelqu'un qui va exécuter un saut périlleux. L'attitude était si grotesque que, sur le moment, je ne pus admettre que le gémissement qui avait appelé notre attention fût un râle d'agonie. Pas une plainte, pas un souffle ne sortait de cette masse noire sur laquelle nous étions penchés.

Holmes promena sa main sur ce corps inerte, mais il la retira aussitôt avec une exclamation d'horreur. Je frottai une allumette et je vis que ses doigts étaient ensanglantés… Un filet de sang suintait du crâne de la victime.

L'allumette nous permit de voir autre chose encore : le corps de sir Henry Baskerville. — Nous faillîmes nous évanouir.

Nous ne pouvions pas ne pas reconnaître ce burlesque complet de cheviotte rougeâtre — celui que le baronnet portait le matin où il se présenta pour la première fois à Baker street.

Nous l'aperçûmes l'espace d'une seconde, au moment où l'allumette jeta une dernière clarté avant de s'éteindre — de même que s'éteignait en nos âmes notre suprême lueur d'espoir.

Holmes soupira profondément, et, malgré l'obscurité, je le vis pâlir.

« La brute ! Oh ! la brute ! m'écriai-je, les mains crispées. Je ne me pardonnerai jamais d'avoir causé ce malheur.

— Je suis tout autant à blâmer que vous, Watson… Pour satisfaire mon amour-propre professionnel, pour réunir un faisceau de preuves irréfutables, j'ai laissé tuer mon client !… C'est le plus gros échec de toute ma carrière… Mais comment pouvais-je prévoir que, malgré mes avis réitérés, sir Henry s'aventurerait seul sur la lande !… Oui, comment pouvais-je le prévoir ?

— Dire que nous avons entendu ses appels — et quels appels, mon Dieu ! — et qu'il nous a été impossible de le sauver ! Où est ce chien qui l'a tué ? Il doit errer parmi ces roches… Et Stapleton ? Où se cache-t-il ? Il le payera cher, ce meurtre !

— Oui, mais ce soin me regarde, répondit Holmes avec énergie. L'oncle et le neveu sont morts, le premier, de la frayeur ressentie à la vue d'un animal qu'il croyait surnaturel ; le second, d'une chute faite en voulant échapper à la bête. Il ne nous reste plus qu'à prouver la complicité de l'homme et du chien. Malheureusement, nous ne pouvons affirmer l'existence de ce dernier que pour l'avoir entendu aboyer, car sir Henry est évidemment mort à la suite de sa chute. Mais, quelque rusé que soit Stapleton, je jure bien que je le tiendrai en mon pouvoir avant la nuit prochaine. »

Le cœur serré, abattus par l'épouvantable accident qui termi-
nait si brusquement notre longue et ingrate mission, nous nous
tenions chacun d'un côté de ce cadavre.

La lune se levait. Nous gravîmes le sommet des roches du
haut desquels cet infortuné sir Henry était tombé et, de ce point
culminant, nous promenâmes nos regards sur la lande, irréguliè-
rement illuminée par les pâles rayons de l'astre de la nuit.

Dans le lointain, à plusieurs milles de distance, brillait, dans la
direction de Grimpen, une petite lumière jaune. Elle ne pouvait
venir que de la demeure isolée de Stapleton. Je me tournai vers
elle et, montrant le poing dans un geste de menace :

« Pourquoi n'avons-nous pas arrêté cet homme ? dis-je à
Sherlock Holmes.

— Les preuves suffisantes nous manquent. Le coquin est
habile et rusé au suprême degré. En justice, il ne faut pas se
contenter de savoir, il faut encore prouver. À la première fausse
manœuvre, le drôle nous aurait échappé certainement.

— Alors qu'allons-nous faire ?

— La journée de demain sera bien remplie. Pour cette nuit,
bornons-nous à rendre les derniers devoirs à notre pauvre ami. »

Nous nous rapprochâmes du cadavre de sir Henry. J'eus un
accès de douleur à la vue de ces membres tordus par les dernières
convulsions de l'agonie, et mes yeux se remplirent de larmes.

Holmes avait poussé un cri et s'était penché sur le cadavre. Il
riait, il dansait, en se frottant les mains. Était-ce bien là mon
compagnon, si flegmatique, si maître de lui ?

« Une barbe ! une barbe ! s'écria-t-il. Cet homme a une barbe !

— Une barbe ? répétai-je, de plus en plus étonné.

— Ce n'est pas le baronnet… c'est… oui, c'est mon voisin le
convict ! »

Fiévreusement, nous retournâmes le cadavre en le plaçant sur
le dos. Une barbe, raidie par le sang coagulé, dressa sa pointe
vers le ciel.

Impossible de se méprendre sur ce front proéminent ni sur ces
yeux caves. Je reconnus le visage aperçu quelques jours auparavant au-dessus de la bougie placée dans une anfractuosité de
roche — le visage de Selden l'assassin.

La lumière se fit aussitôt dans mon esprit. Je me souvins que le baronnet avait donné ses vieux effets à Barrymore. Celui-ci les avait remis à son beau-frère pour l'aider à fuir. Bottines, chemise, chapeau, tout avait appartenu à sir Henry.

Certes, cet homme avait trouvé la mort dans des circonstances particulièrement tragiques, mais les juges ne l'avaient-ils pas déjà condamné ?

Le cœur transporté d'allégresse, je racontai à Holmes que le baronnet avait fait cadeau de sa vieille garde-robe à son valet de chambre.

« Ces vêtements ont occasionné la mort de ce pauvre diable, me répondit Sherlock. Pour dresser son chien, Stapleton s'est servi d'un objet soustrait à sir Henry — probablement de la bottine volée à l'hôtel — et la bête a poursuivi Selden. Une chose cependant me paraît inexplicable. Comment, dans les ténèbres, le convict a-t-il su que le chien lui donnait la chasse ?

— Il l'a entendu probablement.

— Parce qu'un chien aboie sur la lande, un homme de la rudesse de Selden ne s'expose pas, en criant comme un forcené, au risque d'une arrestation. Il devait être arrivé au paroxysme de la terreur. D'ailleurs, de la durée de ses appels, je puis conclure qu'il a couru longtemps devant le chien et à une assez grande distance de lui. Comment savait-il que l'animal avait pris sa piste ?

— En supposant que nos conjectures soient vraies, je trouve plus inexplicable encore…

— Je ne suppose rien, interrompit Sherlock Holmes.

— Alors, ripostai-je, pourquoi aurait-on lâché ce chien sur la lande, cette nuit ? Je ne présume pas qu'on le laisse continuellement vagabonder. Stapleton l'aura mis en liberté parce qu'il avait de bonnes raisons de croire que sir Henry sortirait ce soir.

— Il est plus difficile de répondre à mes points d'interrogation qu'aux vôtres. Nous serons bientôt fixés sur ce qui vous préoccupe, tandis que les questions que je me pose demeureront éternellement un mystère pour nous… En attendant, nous voilà bien embarrassés de ce cadavre. Nous ne pouvons l'abandonner en pâture aux vautours et aux renards.

— Je propose de le placer dans une de ces huttes, jusqu'à ce que nous ayons prévenu la police.

— Accepté, dit Holmes. À nous deux, nous l'y porterons facilement… Mais qui vient là, Watson ?… C'est Stapleton lui-même ! Quelle audace ! Pas un mot qui donne l'éveil… pas un mot, sinon toutes mes combinaisons s'effondreront. »

Sur la lande, une forme indécise s'avançait vers nous ; je distinguais le cercle rouge d'un cigare allumé. Sous la lumière incertaine de la lune, je reconnus la démarche saccadée du naturaliste.

À notre vue, il s'arrêta ; puis, presque aussitôt, il continua son chemin.

« Hé quoi, docteur Watson, vous ici ? fit-il. Vous êtes le dernier homme que je comptais rencontrer à cette heure sur la lande. Mais que vois-je ? Un blessé ! Ce n'est pas ?… Dites-moi vite que ce n'est pas sir Henry ! »

Il passa rapidement devant moi et se baissa pour regarder le cadavre. Je l'entendis aspirer l'air profondément ; en même temps son cigare s'échappa de ses doigts.

« Quel est cet homme ? bégaya-t-il.

— Selden, le prisonnier évadé de la prison de Princetown. »

Stapleton tourna vers nous un visage hagard. Par un suprême effort, il refoula au fond de son être son désappointement et sa stupeur. Ses regards se portaient alternativement sur Holmes et sur moi.

« Quelle déplorable aventure ! » reprit-il enfin.

Et s'adressant plus particulièrement à moi, il ajouta :

« De quoi est-il mort ?

— Nous croyons, répondis-je, qu'il se sera cassé la tête en tombant de ces rochers. Nous nous promenions sur la lande mon ami et moi, lorsque nous avons entendu des cris.

— Moi aussi… Je ne suis même accouru que pour cela. J'avais des inquiétudes au sujet de sir Henry. »

Je ne pus m'empêcher de demander :

« Pourquoi plutôt au sujet de sir Henry que de toute autre personne ?

— Je l'avais invité à passer la soirée chez nous. J'étais fort surpris qu'il ne fût pas venu et, naturellement, en entendant crier, j'ai redouté quelque malheur… Auriez-vous par hasard entendu autre chose ? »

Bien que Stapleton eût prononcé négligemment cette dernière phrase il nous couvait des yeux tout en parlant.

« Non… n'est-ce pas, Watson ? répliqua Holmes.

— Non.

— Mais pourquoi cette question ? interrogea mon ami d'un air innocent.

— Vous connaissez les sottes histoires que racontent les paysans sur un chien-fantôme… On prétend qu'il hurle parfois la nuit sur la lande… Je me demandais si, par hasard, cet étrange bruit n'aurait pas retenti ce soir.

— Pas que je sache, répondis-je.

— Quel est votre avis sur l'accident survenu à ce pauvre diable ? continua Stapleton.

— Les transes perpétuelles dans lesquelles il vivait et les privations auxquelles l'exposait son genre de vie ont probablement ébranlé sa raison. Dans un accès de folie, il s'est mis à courir sur le plateau et, en tombant du haut de ces roches, il se sera fracturé le crâne.

— Cela me paraît très vraisemblable, approuva Stapleton, avec un soupir qui témoignait d'un soulagement interne. Et vous, monsieur Holmes, quel est votre avis ? »

Mon ami esquissa un vague salut.

« Je trouve, dit-il, que vous acceptez bien facilement les solutions.

— Depuis la venue du docteur Watson, reprit le naturaliste, nous vous attendions tous les jours… Vous arrivez pour assister à un drame.

— Oui. Demain, en retournant à Londres, j'emporterai avec moi un pénible souvenir.

— Vous repartez demain ?

— J'en ai l'intention.

— Je souhaite que votre visite ait fait un peu de lumière sur ces événements qui troublent la contrée. »

Holmes haussa les épaules :

« On ne cueille pas toujours autant de lauriers que l'on croit, fit-il. Pour dégager la vérité, il faut des faits et non des légendes ou des rumeurs. J'ai complètement échoué dans ma mission. »

Mon ami parlait sur un ton de franchise et d'indifférence parfaitement joué.

Cependant Stapleton ne le perdait pas des yeux. Il se retourna vers moi, en disant :

« Je voudrais bien transporter chez moi le cadavre de ce malheureux, mais je crains d'effrayer ma sœur. Recouvrons-lui le visage… Il restera ainsi sans danger jusqu'à demain matin. »

Nous fîmes ce que conseillait Stapleton. Puis, malgré son insistance pour nous emmener à Merripit house, Holmes et moi nous reprîmes le chemin de Baskerville, laissant le naturaliste rentrer seul chez lui.

En nous retournant nous vîmes sa silhouette s'éloigner lentement à travers l'immensité de la lande.

« Nous touchons au moment critique, me dit Sherlock, tandis que nous marchions silencieusement. Cet homme est joliment fort ! Au lieu de sir Henry, c'est Selden qui tombe victime de ses machinations… Avez-vous remarqué comment il a supporté ce coup, qui en aurait paralysé bien d'autres. Je vous l'ai dit à Londres, Watson, et je vous le répète ici, nous n'avons jamais eu à combattre d'ennemi plus digne de nous.

— Je regrette qu'il vous ait vu.

— Je le regrettais aussi, tout d'abord. Mais il n'y avait pas moyen d'éviter cette rencontre.

— Pensez-vous que votre présence au château modifie ses plans ? demandai-je.

— Elle peut le rendre plus prudent ou, au contraire, le pousser à la témérité. Comme la plupart des criminels habiles, il est capable de trop compter sur son habileté et de croire qu'il nous a dupés.

— Pourquoi ne l'avons-nous pas arrêté ?

— Mon cher Watson, vous êtes un homme d'action, vous ! Votre tempérament vous porte aux actes d'énergie. Mais supposons, par exemple, que nous l'ayons arrêté tout à l'heure, qu'en serait-il résulté de bon pour nous ? Quelles preuves fournirions-nous contre lui ? C'est en cela qu'il est rusé comme un démon. Si nous tenions un complice qui fût en mesure de déposer devant les juges, passe encore ! J'admets même que nous nous emparions de ce chien... Il ne constituerait pas une preuve suffisante pour qu'on nouât une corde autour du cou de son maître.

— Il y a la mort de sir Charles.

— L'examen de son cadavre n'a révélé aucune trace de blessure. Vous et moi, nous savons qu'une frayeur l'a tué et nous connaissons la cause de cette frayeur. Mais comment faire pénétrer cette certitude dans le cœur de douze jurés imbéciles ? Comment prouver l'intervention du chien ? Où est la marque de ses crocs ? D'ailleurs, un chien ne mord jamais un cadavre, et sir Charles était trépassé, lorsque l'animal l'atteignit. Nous devrions établir tout cela, vous dis-je, et nous sommes loin de pouvoir le faire.

— Et le drame de cette nuit ?

— Il ne nous a rien apporté de concluant. Quelle relation directe existe-t-il entre le chien et la mort de Selden ? Avons-nous vu la bête ?

— Non ; mais nous l'avons entendue.

— Je vous l'accorde. Prouvez-moi qu'elle poursuivait le convict... Pour quelle raison, cette poursuite ? Moi, je n'en trouve pas... Non, mon cher Watson, il faut nous résigner à la pensée que nous ne pouvons formuler aucune accusation précise et nous efforcer de recueillir des preuves indiscutables.

— Comment y arriver ?

— Par Mme Laura Lyons. Lorsque nous l'aurons renseignée sur le compte de Stapleton, elle nous sera d'un grand secours. J'ai mes plans, moi aussi ! Attendons-nous à de graves événements pour la journée de demain... Toutefois, avant vingt-quatre heures, j'espère bien avoir définitivement le dessus. »

Holmes borna là ses confidences. Il continua à marcher, perdu dans ses réflexions, jusqu'à la porte du château de Baskerville.

« Entrez-vous ? lui demandai-je.

— Pourquoi pas ? Je n'ai plus de raisons de me cacher... Encore un mot, Watson. Ne parlez pas du chien à sir Henry...

Qu'il pense de la mort de Selden ce que Stapleton voulait que nous crussions nous-mêmes ! Il n'en sera que plus dispos pour l'épreuve qu'il subira demain. Vous m'avez dit qu'il est invité à dîner à Merripit house ?

— Je le suis également.

— Vous vous excuserez… Sir Henry doit seul accepter l'invitation. Nous inventerons un bon prétexte à votre absence. Et maintenant allons prier le baronnet de nous donner à souper. »

XIII

FILETS TENDUS

En raison des derniers événements, sir Henry attendait depuis quelques jours l'arrivée de Sherlock Holmes. Aussi se montra-t-il plus satisfait que surpris de le voir. Toutefois il ouvrit de grands yeux en s'apercevant que mon ami n'avait pas de bagages et ne lui donnait aucune explication sur cette absence de valise.

Nous procurâmes à Sherlock tout ce dont il pouvait avoir besoin et, après un dîner servi bien longtemps après l'heure accoutumée, nous apprîmes au baronnet ce qu'il nous importait qu'il connût de mon aventure.

Auparavant, j'avais eu la corvée de raconter à Barrymore et à sa femme la mort de Selden. Cette nouvelle causa au valet de chambre un soulagement sans égal ; mais Mme Barrymore porta son tablier à ses yeux et pleura amèrement. Pour tout le monde, le convict était un être violent, moitié brute et moitié démon ; pour elle, il demeurait toujours l'enfant volontaire qui s'attachait à ses jupes, à l'époque où elle était jeune fille.

« J'ai erré tristement dans la maison depuis le départ matinal de Watson, dit le baronnet. Je mérite des compliments pour la façon dont j'ai tenu ma promesse. Si je ne vous avais pas juré de ne pas sortir seul, j'aurais pu passer une meilleure soirée… Les Stapleton m'avaient prié d'aller dîner chez eux.

— Je suis certain que vous auriez passé une meilleure soirée, répondit Holmes sèchement. En tout cas, vous n'avez pas l'air de vous douter que nous avons pleuré votre mort. »

Sir Henry releva la tête.

« Comment cela ? demanda-t-il.

— Ce pauvre diable de Selden portait des vêtements qui vous avaient appartenu. Je crains fort que votre domestique, de qui il les tenait, n'ait maille à partir avec la police.

— C'est impossible. Autant qu'il m'en souvienne, ces vêtements n'étaient pas marqués à mon chiffre.

— Tant mieux pour Barrymore… et pour vous aussi, car, tous, dans cette affaire, vous avez agi contre les prescriptions de la loi. Je me demande même si, en ma qualité de détective consciencieux, mon premier devoir ne serait pas d'arrêter toute la maisonnée… Les rapports de Watson vous accablent…

— Faites ! » dit le baronnet en riant.

Puis, redevenant sérieux, il ajouta :

« Quoi de neuf, à propos de votre affaire ? Avez-vous un peu débrouillé l'écheveau ? Je ne crois pas que, depuis votre arrivée ici, nous ayons fait un pas en avant, Watson et moi.

— Avant qu'il soit longtemps, j'espère avoir déblayé le terrain et rendu votre situation sensiblement plus claire. Tout cela est très difficile, très compliqué. Il existe encore quelques points sur lesquels la lumière est nécessaire… Mais elle est en marche, la lumière !

— Watson vous a certainement appris que nous avions acquis une certitude, reprit le baronnet. Nous avons entendu le chien hurler sur la lande, et je jurerais bien que la légende accréditée dans le pays n'est pas une vaine superstition. Autrefois, quand je vivais en Amérique, dans le Far-West, j'ai eu des chiens et je ne puis me méprendre sur leurs hurlements. Si vous parvenez à museler celui-là, je vous proclamerai partout le plus grand détective des temps modernes.

— Je crois que je le musellerai et que je l'enchaînerai facilement, à la condition que vous consentiez à m'aider.

— Je ferai tout ce que vous me commanderez.

— Parfait… Je vous demande en outre de m'obéir aveuglément, sans vous enquérir des raisons qui me guident.

— Je m'y engage.

— Si vous tenez cette promesse, nous avons les plus grandes chances de résoudre bientôt le problème qui vous intéresse. Je n'ai aucun doute… »

Sherlock Holmes s'arrêta soudain pour regarder en l'air, au-dessus de ma tête.

La lumière de la lampe tombait d'aplomb sur son visage, qui avait pris une expression si attentive, si immobile, qu'il ressemblait à une tête de statue personnifiant l'étonnement et la réflexion.

« Qu'y a-t-il ? » criâmes-nous, le baronnet et moi.

Lorsque les yeux de Sherlock se reportèrent sur nous, je vis qu'il réprimait une violente émotion intérieure.

« Excusez l'admiration d'un connaisseur, dit-il à sir Henry, en étendant la main vers la série de portraits qui couvraient le mur. Watson me dénie toute compétence en matière d'art, par pure jalousie, parce que nous ne sommes pas de la même école. Vous avez là une fort belle collection de portraits.

— Je suis heureux de vous les entendre vanter, fit sir Henry, avec surprise. Je ne connais pas grand-chose à tout cela, et je ne puis mieux juger un cheval qu'un tableau. Je ne croyais pas que vous eussiez le temps de vous occuper de ces bagatelles.

— Je sais apprécier le beau, quand je l'ai sous les yeux. Tenez, ceci est un Kneller… Je parierais que cette dame en soie bleue, là-bas, ainsi que ce gros gentilhomme en perruque, doivent être des Reynolds. Des portraits de famille, je suppose ?

— Tous.

— Savez-vous le nom de ces ancêtres ?

— Barrymore m'en a rebattu les oreilles, et je crois que je puis réciter ma leçon.

— Quel est ce gentilhomme avec un télescope ?

— Il s'appelait le vice-amiral de Baskerville et servit aux Indes sous Rodney. Celui qui a cet habit bleu et ce rouleau de papiers à la main fut sir William Baskerville, président des commissions de la Chambre des communes, sous Pitt.

— Et ce cavalier, en face de moi… celui qui porte un habit de velours noir garni de dentelles ?

— Il mérite qu'on vous le présente, car il est la cause de tous nos malheurs. Il se nomme Hugo, Hugo le maudit, celui pour qui l'enfer a vomi le chien des Baskerville. Nous ne sommes pas près de l'oublier. »

Intéressé et surpris, j'examinai le portrait.

« Vraiment ! dit Holmes. Il a l'air d'un homme simple et paisible, mais cependant on devine dans ses yeux une pensée de mal qui sommeille. Je me le figurais plus robuste et d'aspect plus brutal.

— L'authenticité du portrait n'est pas douteuse ; le nom et la date — 1647 — se trouvent au dos de la toile. »

Pendant le dîner, Holmes parla peu. Le portrait du vieux libertin exerçait sur lui une sorte de fascination, et ses yeux ne s'en détachèrent pas.

Ce ne fut que plus tard, à l'heure où sir Henry se retira dans sa chambre, que mon ami me communiqua ses pensées.

Nous redescendîmes dans la salle à manger, et, là, son bougeoir à la main, Holmes attira mon attention sur la vieille peinture que le temps avait recouverte de sa patine.

« Apercevez-vous quelque chose ? » me demanda Sherlock.

J'examinai ce visage long et sévère, encadré par un grand chapeau à plumes, une abondante chevelure bouclée et une collerette de dentelles blanches. La physionomie, point bestiale, avait toutefois un air faux et mauvais, avec sa bouche en coup de sabre, ourlée de lèvres minces, et ses yeux insupportablement fixes.

« Ressemble-t-il à quelqu'un que vous connaissiez ? me demanda Sherlock Holmes.

— Il a quelque chose des maxillaires de sir Henry, répondis-je.

— Un phénomène de suggestion, probablement. Attendez un instant ! »

Holmes monta sur une chaise et, élevant son bougeoir qu'il tenait de la main gauche, il arrondit son bras sur le portrait, de façon à cacher le large chapeau à plumes et les boucles de cheveux.

« Grand Dieu ! » m'écriai-je étonné.

Le visage de Stapleton venait de surgir de la toile.

« Voyez-vous, maintenant ? fit Holmes. Mes yeux sont exercés à détailler les traits des visages et non pas les accessoires. La première qualité de ceux qui se vouent à la recherche des criminels consiste à savoir percer les déguisements.

— C'est merveilleux. On dirait le portrait de Stapleton.

— Oui. Nous nous trouvons en présence d'un cas intéressant d'atavisme — aussi bien au physique qu'au moral. Il suffit d'étudier des portraits de famille pour se convertir à la théorie de la réincarnation. Ce Stapleton est un Baskerville — la chose me paraît hors de doute.

— Un Baskerville — avec des vues sur la succession, repartis-je.

— Exactement. L'examen de ce portrait nous a procuré le plus intéressant des chaînons qui nous manquaient… Nous le tenons, Watson, nous le tenons ! Je jure qu'avant demain soir, il se débattra dans nos filets aussi désespérément que ses propres papillons. Une épingle, un bouchon, une étiquette, et nous l'ajouterons à notre collection de Baker street !… »

En s'éloignant du portrait, Holmes fut pris d'un de ces accès de rire peu fréquents chez lui. Je l'ai rarement entendu rire ; mais sa gaieté a toujours été fatale à quelqu'un.

Le lendemain matin, je me levai de bonne heure. Holmes avait été plus matinal que moi, puisque, de ma fenêtre, je l'aperçus dans la grande allée du parc.

« Nous aurons aujourd'hui une journée bien remplie », fit-il, en se frottant les mains, à la pensée de l'action prochaine. « Les filets sont tendus et la "traîne" va commencer. Avant la fin du jour, nous saurons si nous avons ramené le gros brochet que nous guettons ou s'il a passé à travers les mailles.

— Êtes-vous allé déjà sur la lande ?

— De Grimpen, j'ai envoyé à la prison de Princetown un rapport sur la mort de Selden. Je ne pense pas m'avancer trop, en promettant que personne de vous ne sera inquiété à ce sujet. J'ai écrit aussi à mon fidèle Cartwright. Le pauvre garçon se serait lamenté sur la porte de ma hutte, comme un chien sur le tombeau de son maître, si je n'avais eu la précaution de le rassurer sur mon sort.

— Et maintenant, qu'allons-nous faire en premier lieu ?

— Causez avec sir Henry… Justement, le voici.

— Bonjour, Holmes, dit le baronnet. Vous ressemblez à un général en chef dressant un plan avec son chef d'état-major.

— Votre comparaison est exacte… Watson me demandait les ordres.

— Je vous en demande aussi pour moi.

— Très bien. Vous êtes invité à dîner ce soir chez les Stapleton ?

— Oui ; vous y viendrez également. Ce sont des gens très accueillants… Ils seront très heureux de vous voir.

— Je crains que nous ne soyons obligés, Watson et moi, d'aller à Londres aujourd'hui.

— À Londres ?

— Oui ; j'ai le pressentiment que, dans les présentes conjonctures, notre présence là-bas est indispensable. »

La figure du baronnet s'allongea considérablement.

« J'espérais que vous étiez venus ici pour m'assister. Quand on est seul, le séjour du château et de la lande manque de gaieté.

— Mon cher ami, répliqua Holmes, vous devez vous fier aveuglément à moi et exécuter fidèlement mes ordres. Vous direz aux Stapleton que nous aurions été très heureux de vous accompagner, mais que des affaires urgentes nous ont rappelés à Londres. Vous ajouterez que nous comptons revenir bientôt dans le Devonshire. Voulez-vous ne pas oublier de faire cette commission à vos amis ?

— Si vous y tenez.

— Certainement… C'est très important. »

Je vis au front rembruni de sir Henry que notre désertion — il qualifiait ainsi intérieurement notre départ — l'affectait péniblement.

« Quand désirez-vous partir ? interrogea-t-il, d'un ton sec.

— Aussitôt après déjeuner… Nous irons en voiture à Coombe-Tracey… Afin de vous prouver que son absence sera de courte durée, Watson laissera ici tous ses bagages. »

Et, se retournant vers moi, Holmes continua :

« Watson, envoyez donc un mot aux Stapleton pour leur dire que vous regrettez de ne pouvoir accepter leur invitation.

— J'ai bien envie de vous suivre à Londres, fit le baronnet. Pourquoi resterais-je seul ici ?

— Parce que le devoir vous y retient… Parce que vous m'avez engagé votre parole d'exécuter tous mes ordres, et que je vous commande de demeurer ici.

— Très bien alors… je resterai…

— Encore une recommandation, reprit Sherlock. Je veux que vous alliez en voiture à Merripit house et qu'ensuite vous renvoyiez votre cocher, en disant aux Stapleton que vous rentrerez à pied au château.

— À pied… À travers la lande ?

— Oui.

— Mais c'est précisément la chose que vous m'avez le plus expressément défendue !

— Aujourd'hui vous pouvez faire cette promenade en toute sécurité. Si je n'avais la plus entière confiance dans la solidité de vos nerfs et la fermeté de votre courage, je ne vous y autoriserais pas… Il est essentiel que les choses se passent ainsi.

— Je vous obéirai.

— Si vous tenez à votre existence, ne suivez, sur la lande, d'autre route que celle qui conduit de Merripit house au village de Grimpen… C'est d'ailleurs votre chemin tout naturel pour retourner au château.

— Je ferai ce que vous me commandez.

— À la bonne heure, approuva Holmes. Je partirai le plus tôt possible, après déjeuner, de façon à arriver à Londres dans le courant de l'après-midi.

Ce programme ne manquait pas de me surprendre, bien que, la nuit précédente, Holmes eût dit à Stapleton que son séjour à Baskerville ne se prolongerait pas au-delà du lendemain. Il ne m'était jamais venu à l'idée que Sherlock pût m'emmener avec lui — pas plus que je ne comprenais que nous fussions absents l'un et l'autre, à un moment que mon ami lui-même qualifiait de très critique.

Il n'y avait qu'à obéir en silence. Nous prîmes congé de notre pauvre sir Henry et, une couple d'heures plus tard, nous arrivions à la gare de Coombe Tracey. La voiture repartit pour le château et nous passâmes sur le quai où nous attendait un jeune garçon.

« Avez-vous des ordres à me donner, monsieur ? demanda-t-il à Sherlock Holmes.

— Oui, Cartwright. Vous prendrez le train pour Londres… Aussitôt en ville, vous expédierez en mon nom à sir Henry un télégramme pour le prier de m'envoyer à Baker street, sous pli recommandé, le portefeuille que j'ai laissé tomber dans le salon.

— Oui, monsieur.

— Allez donc voir maintenant au télégraphe si l'on n'a pas un message pour moi. »

Cartwright revint avec une dépêche. Holmes me la tendit.

Elle était ainsi conçue :

« Selon votre désir, j'arrive avec un mandat d'arrêt en blanc. Serai à Grimpen à cinq heures quarante.

« LESTRADE. »

« Ceci, me dit Holmes, répond à un de mes télégrammes de ce matin. Ce Lestrade est le plus habile détective de Scotland Yard, et nous pouvons avoir besoin d'aide… Tâchons, Watson, d'utiliser notre temps. Nous n'en trouverons pas de meilleur emploi qu'en allant rendre visite à votre connaissance, Mme Laura Lyons. »

Le plan de campagne de Sherlock Holmes commençait à devenir évident. Par le baronnet, il voulait convaincre les Stapleton de notre départ, alors que nous devions reprendre clandestinement le chemin de Grimpen, pour nous trouver là au moment où notre présence serait nécessaire. Le télégramme, expédié de Londres par Cartwright, achèverait de dissiper les soupçons des Stapleton, si sir Henry leur en parlait.

Je voyais déjà les filets se resserrer davantage autour du brochet que nous désirions capturer.

Mme Laura Lyons nous reçut dans son bureau. Sherlock Holmes ouvrit le feu avec une franchise et une précision qui la déconcertèrent un peu.

« Je suis en train de rechercher, dit-il, les circonstances qui ont accompagné la mort de feu Charles Baskerville. Mon ami le docteur Watson m'a fait part de ce que vous lui aviez raconté et aussi de ce que vous lui aviez caché à ce sujet.

— Qu'ai-je caché ? demanda Mme Lyons, devenue subitement défiante.

— Vous avouez avoir prié sir Charles de venir à la porte du parc, à dix heures du soir. Nous savons que le vieux gentilhomme a trouvé la mort à cette heure et à cet endroit. Pourquoi avez-vous passé sous silence la relation qui existe entre ces différents événements ?

— Il n'existe entre eux aucune relation.

— Permettez-moi de vous faire remarquer qu'en tout cas, la coïncidence est au moins extraordinaire. J'estime cependant que nous parviendrons à établir cette relation. Je veux agir franchement avec vous, madame Lyons. Un meurtre a été commis, nous en sommes certains, et l'enquête peut impliquer non seulement votre ami M. Stapleton, mais encore sa femme. »

Laura Lyons quitta brusquement son fauteuil.

« Sa femme ! s'écria-t-elle.

— C'est aujourd'hui le secret de Polichinelle. Celle que l'on croyait sa sœur est bien réellement sa femme. »

Mme Lyons se rassit. Ses mains s'étaient à tel point crispées sur les bras du fauteuil que ses ongles — roses quelques minutes auparavant — avaient blanchi sous la violence de l'étreinte.

« Sa femme ! répéta-t-elle. Sa femme ! Il était donc marié ? »

Sherlock Holmes se contenta de hausser les épaules.

« Prouvez-le-moi !... Prouvez-le-moi, reprit-elle... Et si vous m'apportez cette preuve... »

L'éclair qui passa alors dans ses yeux en dit plus long que tous les discours.

« Je suis venu dans cette intention, continua Holmes, en tirant plusieurs papiers de sa poche. Voici d'abord une photographie du couple prise à York, il y a plusieurs années. Lisez la mention écrite au dos : "M. et Mme Vandeleur..." Vous le reconnaîtrez sans peine, — et elle aussi, si vous l'avez vue. Voilà trois signalements de M. et Mme Vandeleur, signés par des témoins dignes de foi, le ménage tenait à cette époque l'école de Saint-Olivier. Lisez ces attestations et voyez si vous pouvez douter de l'identité de ces gens. »

Mme Lyons prit les documents, les parcourut et tourna ensuite vers nous un visage consterné.

« Monsieur Holmes, dit-elle, cet homme m'a proposé de m'épouser, si je divorçais d'avec mon mari. Il m'a menti, le lâche, d'une inconcevable façon. Il ne m'a jamais dit un mot de vérité… Et pourquoi ?… pourquoi ? Je croyais qu'il n'agissait que dans mon seul intérêt. Mais maintenant je me rends compte que je n'étais qu'un instrument entre ses mains… Pourquoi me montrerais-je généreuse envers celui qui m'a si indignement trompée ? Pourquoi tenterais-je de le soustraire aux conséquences de ses actes déloyaux ? Interrogez-moi ! Demandez-moi ce que vous voulez savoir, je vous répondrai sans ambages… Je vous jure qu'au moment d'écrire à sir Charles Baskerville, je n'aurais même pas osé rêver qu'il arriverait malheur à ce vieillard que je considérais comme le meilleur de mes amis.

— Je vous crois absolument, madame, dit Sherlock Holmes. Je comprends que le récit de ces événements vous soit très pénible et peut-être vaudrait-il mieux qu'il vînt de moi… Reprenez-moi si je commets quelque erreur matérielle. L'envoi de cette lettre vous fut suggéré par Stapleton ?

— Il me l'a dictée.

— Je présume qu'il fit miroiter à vos yeux le secours que sir Charles vous enverrait pour faire face aux dépenses nécessitées par votre instance en divorce.

— Très exact.

— Puis, après le départ de votre lettre, il vous dissuada d'aller au rendez-vous ?

— Il me dit qu'il se sentirait froissé si un autre homme me remettait de l'argent pour une semblable destination. Il ajouta que, quoique pauvre, il dépenserait volontiers jusqu'à son dernier sou pour abattre l'obstacle qui nous séparait.

— Ah ! il se montrait d'une logique irréfutable, dit Holmes… Ensuite, vous n'avez plus entendu parler de rien jusqu'au moment où vous avez lu dans les journaux les détails de la mort de sir Charles ?

— Non.

— Je suppose qu'il vous fit jurer de ne révéler à personne votre rendez-vous avec le vieux baronnet.

— En effet. Il prétexta que cette mort était environnée de mystères, et que, si je parlais de ma lettre, on me soupçonnerait certainement. Il m'effraya pour obtenir mon silence.

— Évidemment. Cependant vous eûtes des doutes ? »

Mme Lyons hésita et baissa la tête.

« Je le connaissais, reprit-elle. Toutefois, s'il s'était conduit autrement à mon égard, jamais je ne l'aurais trahi.

— À mon avis, vous l'avez échappé belle, dit Sherlock Holmes. Vous le teniez en votre pouvoir, il le savait et vous vivez encore ! Pendant plusieurs mois, vous avez côtoyé un précipice… Maintenant, madame, il ne nous reste plus qu'à prendre congé de vous. Avant peu, vous entendrez parler de nous. »

Nous allâmes à la gare attendre l'arrivée du train de Londres. Sur le quai, Holmes me dit :

« Tout s'éclaircit et, peu à peu, les difficultés s'aplanissent autour de nous. Bientôt, je pourrai raconter d'une façon cohérente le crime le plus singulier et le plus sensationnel de notre époque. Ceux qui se livrent à l'étude de la criminalité se souviendront alors d'événements analogues survenus à Grodno, dans la Petite-Russie, en 1866. Il y a aussi les meurtres d'Anderson commis dans la Caroline du Nord… Mais cette affaire présente des particularités qui lui sont propres. Ainsi, à cette heure encore, la culpabilité de se Stapleton n'est pas matériellement établie. Seulement j'espère bien y être arrivé ce soir, avant de me mettre au lit. »

L'express de Londres pénétrait en gare. Un petit homme, trapu, musclé, sauta d'un wagon de première classe. Nous échangeâmes avec lui une poignée de main et je devinai, à la façon respectueuse dont Lestrade regarda mon compagnon, qu'il avait appris beaucoup de choses depuis le jour où nous avions « travaillé » ensemble pour la première fois. Je me souvenais du profond mépris avec lequel le praticien accueillit alors les raisonnements d'un théoricien tel que Sherlock Holmes.

« Un cas sérieux ? interrogea Lestrade.

— Le fait le plus extraordinaire qui se soit produit depuis nombre d'années, répondit Holmes. Nous avons devant nous deux heures avant de songer à nous mettre en route… Dînons ! Puis, mon cher Lestrade, vous chasserez le brouillard de Londres en aspirant à pleins poumons la fraîche brise vespérale de Dartmoor… Jamais venu dans ces parages ?… Non ?… Eh bien, je ne pense pas que vous oubliiez de longtemps votre première visite. »

XIV

LE CHIEN DES BASKERVILLE

Un des défauts de Sherlock Holmes — si l'on peut appeler cela un défaut — consistait en sa répugnance à communiquer ses projets à ceux qui devaient l'aider dans leur exécution. Il préférait attendre le dernier moment. J'attribue cette retenue, partie à son caractère impérieux qui le portait à dominer et à surprendre ses amis, et partie aussi à sa méfiance professionnelle, qui le poussait à ne négliger aucune précaution. Le résultat n'en était pas moins fort désagréable pour ceux qui l'assistaient dans ses entreprises. Pour mon compte, j'en ai souvent souffert, mais jamais autant que pendant la longue course en voiture que nous fîmes, ce soir-là, dans l'obscurité ;

Nous étions sur le point de tenter la suprême épreuve ; nous allions enfin donner notre dernier effort, et Holmes ne nous avait encore rien dit. À peine pouvais-je soupçonner ce qu'il comptait faire.

Je frémis par anticipation, lorsque le vent glacial qui nous frappait le visage et les sombres espaces qui s'étendaient de chaque côté de l'étroite route m'apprirent que nous retournions de nouveau sur la lande. Chaque tour de roue, chaque foulée des chevaux nous rapprochaient davantage de notre ultime aventure.

La présence du conducteur s'opposait à toute espèce de conversation intéressante, et nous ne parlâmes que de choses insignifiantes, alors que nos nerfs vibraient sous le coup de l'émotion et de l'attente.

Après cette longue contrainte, je me sentis soulagé à la vue de la maison de Frankland et en reconnaissant que nous nous dirigions vers le château.

Au lieu de nous arrêter à l'entrée principale, nous poussâmes jusqu'à la porte de l'avenue.

Là, Sherlock Holmes paya le cocher et lui ordonna de retrouver sur-le-champ à Coombe Tracey. Nous nous acheminâmes vers Merripit house.

« Êtes-vous armé, Lestrade ? » demanda mon ami.

Le petit détective sourit.

« Tant que j'aurai un pantalon, dit-il, j'y ferai coudre une poche-revolver, et aussi longtemps que j'aurai une poche-revolver, il se trouvera quelque chose dedans.

— Bien. Nous sommes également prêts pour toute éventualité, Watson et moi.

— Vous êtes peu communicatif, monsieur Holmes, reprit Lestrade. Qu'allons-nous faire ?

— Attendre.

— Vrai ! l'endroit ne me semble pas folâtre, fit le détective, en frissonnant à l'aspect des pentes sombres de la colline et de l'immense voile de brouillard qui recouvrait la grande fondrière de Grimpen. Je crois apercevoir devant nous les lumières d'une maison.

— C'est Merripit house, le terme de notre voyage, murmura Holmes. Je vous enjoins de marcher sur la pointe des pieds et de ne parler qu'à voix très basse. »

Nous suivîmes le sentier qui conduisait à la demeure des Stapleton ; mais, à deux cents mètres d'elle, Holmes fit halte.

« Cela suffit, dit-il. Ces rochers, à droite, nous serviront d'abri.

— C'est ici que nous devons attendre ? demanda Lestrade.

— Oui. Nous allons nous mettre en embuscade ici. Placez-vous dans ce creux, Lestrade. Vous, Watson, vous avez pénétré dans la maison, n'est-ce pas ? Pouvez-vous m'indiquer la situation des pièces ? Qu'y a-t-il derrière ces fenêtres grillées, de ce côté ?

— Les cuisines probablement.

— Et plus loin, celles qui sont si brillamment éclairées ?

— La salle à manger.

— Les stores sont levés. Vous connaissez mieux le terrain… Rampez sans bruit et voyez ce qui s'y passe… Mais au nom du ciel, que Stapleton ne se doute pas qu'on le surveille. »

Sur la pointe des pieds, je m'avançai dans le sentier et je parvins au petit mur qui entourait le verger.

À la faveur de cet abri, je me glissai jusqu'à un endroit d'où je pus apercevoir l'intérieur de la pièce.

Deux hommes étaient assis en face l'un de l'autre : sir Henry et Stapleton. Je distinguais nettement leur profil. Ils fumaient. Du café et des liqueurs se trouvaient devant eux, sur la table.

Stapleton parlait avec animation ; le baronnet semblait pâle et distrait. La longue promenade nocture qu'il devrait faire sur cette lande maudite assombrissait peut-être ses pensées.

Un instant, Stapleton se leva et sortit. Sir Henry remplit son verre, s'enfonça dans son fauteuil et souffla vers le plafond la fumée de son cigare.

J'entendis le grincement d'une porte et le craquement d'une chaussure sur le gravier.

Les pas suivaient l'allée qui borde le mur derrière lequel j'étais accroupi. Je risquai un œil et je vis le naturaliste s'arrêter à la porte d'un pavillon construit dans un coin du verger.

Une clef tourna dans la serrure et, comme Stapleton pénétrait dans le réduit, je perçus un bruit singulier, semblable au claquement d'une lanière de fouet.

Stapleton ne resta pas enfermé plus d'une minute. La clef tourna de nouveau ; il repassa devant moi et rentra dans la maison.

Quand il eut rejoint son hôte, je revins doucement auprès de mes compagnons auxquels je racontai ce dont j'avais été témoin.

« Vous dites donc, Watson, que la dame n'est pas là ? me demanda Holmes, lorsque j'eus terminé mon rapport.

— Non.

— Où peut-elle être, puisque sauf celles de la cuisine, toutes les autres fenêtres sont plongées dans l'obscurité ?

— Je l'ignore. »

J'ai dit qu'au-dessus de la grande fondrière de Grimpen s'étendait un voile de brouillard, épais et blanchâtre. Lentement, comme un mur mobile, bas, mais épais, il se rapprochait de nous. La lune l'éclairait, lui donnant, avec la cime des pics éloignés qui émergeaient de sa surface, l'aspect d'une gigantesque banquise.

Holmes se tourna de ce côté et laissa échapper quelques paroles d'impatience, arrachées sans doute par la marche lente — mais continue — du brouillard.

« Il va nous gagner, Watson, fit-il, en me le désignant d'un geste.

— Est-ce un contretemps fâcheux ?

— Très fâcheux… La seule chose au monde qui pût déranger mes combinaisons… Sir Henry ne tardera pas à partir maintenant !… Il est déjà dix heures… Notre succès — et même sa vie à lui — dépendent de sa sortie, avant que le brouillard ait atteint ce sentier. »

Au-dessus de nos têtes, la nuit était calme et sereine. Les étoiles scintillaient, pareilles à des clous d'or fixés sur la voûte céleste, et la lune baignait tout le paysage d'une lumière douce et incertaine.

Devant nous se détachait la masse sombre de la maison dont les toits dentelés, hérissés de cheminées, se profilaient sur un ciel teinté d'argent. De larges traînées lumineuses, partant des fenêtres du rez-de-chaussée, s'allongeaient sur le verger et jusque sur la lande. L'une d'elles s'éteignit subitement. Les domestiques venaient de quitter la cuisine.

Il ne resta plus que la lampe de la salle à manger où les deux hommes, le maître de céans aux pensées sanguinaires et le convive inconscient du danger qui le menaçait, continuaient à causer en fumant leur cigare.

De minute en minute, le voile opaque qui recouvrait la lande se rapprochait davantage de la demeure de Stapleton.

Déjà les légers flocons d'ouate, avant-coureurs de la brume, s'enroulaient autour du rayon de lumière projeté par la fenêtre illuminée. Le mur du verger le plus éloigné de nous devenait invisible et les arbres disparaissaient presque derrière un nuage de vapeurs blanches.

Bientôt des vagues de brouillard léchèrent les deux angles de la maison et se rejoignirent, la faisant ressembler à un vaisseau-fantôme qui voguerait sur une mer silencieuse.

Holmes crispa sa main sur le rocher qui nous cachait et frappa du pied dans un mouvement d'impatience.

« Si sir Henry n'est pas sorti avant un quart d'heure, dit-il, le sentier sera envahi à son tour. Dans une demi-heure, il nous sera impossible de distinguer notre main au bout de notre bras.

— Si nous nous retirions jusqu'à l'endroit où le terrain se relève ? insinuai-je.

— Oui, c'est préférable. »

À mesure que cette inondation de brouillard nous gagnait, nous fuyions devant elle. Maintenant six cents mètres environ nous séparaient de la maison. Et ce flot inexorable, dont la lune argentait la crête, nous repoussait toujours.

« Nous reculons trop, dit Holmes. Nous ne devons par courir la chance que le baronnet soit terrassé avant d'arriver jusqu'à nous. Restons où nous sommes, à tout prix. »

Mon ami se baissa et appliqua son oreille contre la terre.

« Merci, mon Dieu ! fit-il en se relevant… il me semble que je l'entends venir ! »

Un bruit de pas précipités rompit le silence de la lande.

Blottis au milieu des pierres, nous regardions avec insistance la muraille floconneuse qui nous barrait la vue de la maison.

Les pas devinrent de plus en plus distincts et, du brouillard, sortit, comme d'un rideau, l'homme que nous attendions.

Dès qu'il se retrouva dans une atmosphère plus claire, il regarda autour de lui, surpris de la limpidité de la nuit.

Rapidement, sir Henry descendit le sentier, passa tout près de l'endroit où nous étions tapis, et commença l'ascension de la colline qui se dressait derrière nous. Tout en marchant, il tournait à chaque instant la tête de côté et d'autre, comme un homme qui se sent mal à l'aise.

« Attention ! cria Holmes. Gare à vous ! je l'entends ! »

En même temps, je perçus le bruit sec d'un pistolet qu'on arme.

Il s'élevait du sein de cette mer de brume un bruit continu, semblable à un fouaillement. Les nuées ne se trouvaient plus qu'à cinquante mètres de nous et, tous trois, nous ne les perdions pas de vue, incertains de l'horreur qu'elles allaient nous vomir.

Mon coude touchait celui d'Holmes, et, à ce moment, je levai la tête vers lui. Il était pâle, mais exultant. Ses yeux étincelaient, à la pâle clarté de la lune. Soudain, ils devinrent fixes et ses lèvres s'entrouvrirent d'étonnement.

En même temps, Lestrade poussa un cri de terreur et se jeta la face contre terre.

Je sautai sur mes pieds. Ma main inerte se noua sur la crosse de mon revolver ; je sentis mon cerveau se paralyser devant l'effrayante apparition qui venait de surgir des profondeurs du brouillard.

C'était un chien ! un énorme chien noir, tel que les yeux des mortels n'en avaient jamais contemplé auparavant.

Sa gueule soufflait du feu ; ses prunelles luisaient comme des charbons ardents ; autour de ses babines et de ses crocs vacillaient des flammes.

Jamais les rêves les plus insensés d'un esprit en délire n'enfantèrent rien de plus sauvage, de plus terrifiant, de plus diabolique, que cette forme noire et cette face féroce qui s'étaient frayé un passage à travers le mur de brouillard.

Avec des bonds énormes, ce fantastique animal flairait la piste de notre ami, le serrant de près.

Cette apparition nous hypnotisait à tel point, qu'elle nous avait déjà dépassés, lorsque nous revînmes à nous.

Holmes et moi fîmes feu simultanément.

La bête hurla hideusement, ce qui nous prouva qu'au moins l'un de nous l'avait touchée. Cependant elle bondit en avant et continua sa course.

Sir Henry s'était retourné. Nous aperçûmes son visage décomposé et ses mains étendues en signe d'horreur devant cet être sans nom qui lui donnait la chasse.

Au cri de douleur du chien, toutes nos craintes s'évanouirent. Il était mortel, puisque vulnérable, et, si nous l'avions blessé, nous pouvions également le tuer.

Je n'ai jamais vu courir un homme avec la rapidité que Sherlock Holmes déploya cette nuit-là. Je suis réputé pour ma vitesse, mais il me devança avec autant de facilité que je dépassai moi-même le petit Lestrade.

Tandis que nous volions sur les traces du chien, nous entendîmes plusieurs cris répétés de sir Henry, ainsi que l'aboiement furieux de la bête. Je la vis s'élancer sur sa victime, la précipiter à terre et la saisir à la gorge. Holmes déchargea cinq fois son revolver dans les flancs du monstre. Dans un dernier hurlement d'agonie et après un dernier coup de dents lancé dans le vide, il roula sur le dos. Ses quatre pattes s'agitèrent convulsivement, puis il s'affaissa sur le côté, immobile.

Je m'avançai, tremblant encore, et j'appuyai le canon de mon revolver sur cette horrible tête. Inutile de presser la détente, le chien-géant était mort — et bien mort, cette fois !

Sir Henry s'était évanoui. Nous déchirâmes son col et Holmes murmura une prière d'action de grâces, en ne découvrant aucune trace de blessure. Dans quelques minutes, le baronnet serait revenu à lui.

Déjà notre jeune ami ouvrait ses yeux et essayait de se lever.

Lestrade lui desserra les dents et lui fit avaler quelques gouttes de cognac.

« Mon Dieu ! balbutia-t-il en tournant vers nous des yeux que la frayeur troublait encore. Qu'était-ce ? Au nom du ciel, dites-moi ce que c'était !

— Peu importe, puisqu'*il* est mort ! dit Holmes. Nous avons tué pour une bonne fois le revenant de la famille Baskerville. »

L'animal qui gisait à nos pieds avait des proportions qui le rendaient effrayant. Ce n'était ni un limier ni un dogue. Élancé, sauvage, aussi gros qu'une petite lionne, il était mâtiné de ces deux races. Même en ce moment, dans le repos de la mort, une flamme bleuâtre semblait suinter de son énorme gueule et un cercle de feu cernait ses yeux, petits, féroces.

« Je posai la main sur ce museau lumineux et, quand je retirai mes doigts, ils brillèrent dans les ténèbres.

— C'est du phosphore ! dis-je.

— Oui… une très curieuse préparation, répliqua Holmes, en flairant l'animal. Elle ne répand aucune odeur capable de nuire à l'odorat de la bête. Nous vous devons des excuses, sir Henry, pour vous avoir exposé à une semblable frayeur. Je croyais avoir affaire à un chien et non pas à une créature de cette sorte. Et puis le brouillard nous avait laissé peu de temps pour lui faire l'accueil que nous lui réservions.

— Vous m'avez sauvé la vie.

— Après l'avoir d'abord mise en péril. Vous sentez-vous assez fort pour vous tenir debout ?

— Versez-moi encore une gorgée de cognac et je serai prêt à tout… Là, merci !… Maintenant voulez-vous m'aider à me mettre sur pied… Qu'allez-vous faire ?

— Vous n'êtes pas en état de tenter cette nuit de nouvelles aventures. Attendez un moment et l'un de nous retournera avec vous au château. »

Sir Henry essaya de s'affermir sur ses jambes ; mais il était encore pâle comme un spectre et il tremblait de tous ses membres.

Nous le conduisîmes jusqu'à une roche sur laquelle il s'assit, tout frissonnant, la tête enfouie entre ses mains.

« Il faut que nous vous quittions, dit Holmes. Nous devons achever notre tâche et chaque minute a une importance capitale. Nous tenons notre crime, à cette heure ; il ne nous manque plus que le criminel. »

Et, tandis que nous nous hâtions dans le petit sentier, mon ami ajouta :

« Il y a mille à parier contre un que nous ne trouverons plus Stapleton chez lui. Les coups de revolver lui auront appris qu'il a perdu la partie.

— Nous étions assez loin de Merripit house, hasardai-je ; le brouillard aura étouffé le bruit des détonations.

« — Il suivait le chien pour l'exciter… vous pouvez en être certain… Non, non… il est déjà loin !… D'ailleurs nous fouillerons la maison pour nous en assurer. »

La porte d'entrée était ouverte. Nous nous ruâmes à l'intérieur, courant d'une chambre à l'autre, au grand étonnement d'un vieux domestique que nous rencontrâmes dans le corridor.

Seule, la salle à manger était restée éclairée. Holmes prit la lampe et explora jusqu'aux plus petits recoins. Nous ne découvrîmes aucune trace de Stapleton. Cependant, à l'étage supérieur, on avait fermé une porte à clef.

« Il y a quelqu'un ! s'écria Lestrade. J'ai entendu du bruit… Ouvrez !

Une plainte étouffée, un gémissement, partit de l'intérieur.

Holmes prit son élan et, d'un violent coup de pied appliqué à la hauteur de la serrure, fit voler la porte en éclats. Le revolver au poing, nous nous précipitâmes dans la pièce.

Nous ne vîmes rien qui ressemblât à l'affreux coquin que nous espérions y surprendre. Au contraire, nous nous arrêtâmes devant un objet si étrange, si inattendu, que nous en demeurâmes saisis pendant un moment.

Stapleton avait converti cette pièce en un petit musée. Dans des casiers vitrés, fixés au mur, cet être dangereux et complexe avait réuni ses collections de papillons et de phalènes.

Au centre, une poutre verticale soutenait l'armature de chêne vermoulu qui supportait les ardoises du toit. De cette poutre, pendait un corps si enveloppé, si emmailloté dans un drap qu'il nous fut impossible de reconnaître sur le moment si c'était celui d'un homme ou d'une femme.

Une première serviette enroulée autour du cou du pendu était fortement assujettie à la poutre par un clou. Une seconde enveloppait la partie inférieure du visage, laissant à découvert deux grands yeux noirs — pleins de surprise et de honte — qui nous regardaient avec angoisse.

Dans l'espace d'une seconde, nos eûmes tranché le bâillon, desserré les liens, et Mme Stapleton s'affaissait à nos pieds sur le parquet. Au moment où sa jolie tête retombait sur sa poitrine se distinguait sur la blancheur du cou le sillon rouge produit par une mèche de fouet.

« La brute ! cria Holmes… Vite, Lestrade, votre bouteille de cognac ! Asseyons-la dans un fauteuil… Elle s'est évanouie d'épuisement. »

La jeune femme entrouvrit les yeux.

« Est-il sauvé ? s'écria-t-elle, s'est-il échappé ?…

— Il ne peut nous échapper, madame, répondit froidement Sherlock Holmes.

— Non, non… pas mon mari… sir Henry ? Est-il sain et sauf ?

— Oui.

— Et le chien ?

— Mort. »

Mme Stapleton poussa un long soupir de satisfaction.

« Merci, mon Dieu, merci !… Oh ! le misérable !… Voyez dans quel état il m'a mise ! »

Elle releva ses manches et nous montra ses bras couverts d'ecchymoses.

« Mais cela n'est rien… rien ! reprit-elle, d'une voix entre-coupée de sanglots. C'est mon esprit et mon âme qu'il a torturés et souillés ! J'aurais tout supporté : les mauvais traitements, la solitude, ma vie brisée, tout, si j'avais pu conserver l'espoir qu'il m'aimait encore ! Aujourd'hui, mes illusions se sont envolées, et je sais que je n'ai été qu'un instrument entre ses mains.

— Vous n'éprouvez plus pour lui que du ressentiment, n'est-ce pas, madame ? demanda Holmes. Désignez-nous sa retraite. Vous l'avez aidé dans le mal, venez-nous en aide maintenant ; ce sera votre expiation.

— Il ne peut avoir dirigé ses pas que vers un seul endroit, répondit-elle. Au cœur même de la grande fondrière, il existe, sur un îlot de terre ferme, une ancienne mine d'étain. C'était là qu'il cachait son chien. Là, également, il s'était ménagé un refuge pour le cas où il aurait dû fuir précipitamment. Il y a couru certainement. »

Holmes prit la lampe et l'approcha de la fenêtre. Le brouillard en obscurcissait les vitres.

« Voyez, madame, dit-il. Je défie qui que ce soit de retrouver cette nuit son chemin à travers la grande fondrière de Grimpen. »

Mme Stapleton battit des mains ; ses lèvres se retroussèrent dans un rictus sinistre.

« Il peut y pénétrer, mais il n'en ressortira jamais ! s'écria-t-elle. Comment, par cette nuit épaisse, verrait-il les balises qui doivent le guider ?… Nous les avons plantées ensemble, lui et moi, pour marquer le seul chemin praticable… Ah ! s'il m'avait été permis de les arracher aujourd'hui, vous l'auriez à votre merci ! »

Il était évident que, pour commencer nos recherches, nous étions condamnés à attendre que le brouillard se fût dissipé. Nous confiâmes à Lestrade la garde de la maison et nous reprîmes, Holmes et moi, le chemin du château de Baskerville en compagnie du baronnet.

Impossible de taire plus longtemps à sir Henry l'histoire des Stapleton… Il supporta courageusement le coup que lui porta au cœur la vérité sur la femme qu'il avait aimée.

La secousse produite sur ses nerfs par les aventures de cette nuit déterminèrent une fièvre cérébrale. Le docteur Mortimer, accouru à son chevet, déclara qu'il ne faudrait rien moins qu'un long voyage autour du monde, pour rendre à sir Henry la vigueur et la santé qu'il possédait avant de devenir propriétaire de ce néfaste domaine.

J'arrive rapidement à la conclusion de cette singulière histoire, dans laquelle je me suis efforcé de faire partager au lecteur les angoisses et les vagues soupçons qui, pendant quelques jours, avaient troublé notre existence et qui venaient de se terminer d'une si tragique façon.

Le lendemain du drame de Merripit house, le brouillard se dissipa, et Mme Stapleton nous guida vers l'endroit où son mari et elle avaient tracé un chemin à travers la fondrière. Pendant le trajet, nous pûmes mesurer, à l'empressement qu'elle mettait à nous conduire sur les traces du naturaliste, combien cette femme avait souffert.

Elle resta sur une sorte de promontoire que la terre ferme jetait dans l'intérieur du marécage. À partir de ce point, de petites balises, plantées çà et là, indiquaient le sentier qui serpentait d'une touffe d'ajoncs à l'autre, au milieu de trous tapissés d'écume verdâtre et de flaques bourbeuses qui barraient la route aux étrangers. Des roseaux desséchés et des plantes aquatiques limoneuses exhalaient des odeurs fades de choses en décomposition ; une vapeur lourde, chargée de miasmes, nous montait au visage.

Au moindre faux pas, nous enfoncions jusqu'au-dessus du genou dans cette boue visqueuse, frissonnante, qui ondulait sous la pression de nos pieds jusqu'à plusieurs mètres de distance. Elle se collait à nos talons et, lorsque nous y tombions, on aurait dit qu'une main homicide nous tirait en bas, tellement était tenace l'étreinte qui nous enserrait.

Une seule fois, nous acquîmes la preuve que Stapleton nous avait devancés dans le sentier. Dans une touffe de joncs émergeant de la vase, il nous sembla distinguer quelque chose de noir.

Du sentier, Holmes sauta sur la touffe et s'enfonça jusqu'à la ceinture. Si nous n'avions pas été là pour le retirer, il n'aurait jamais plus foulé la terre ferme. Il tenait à la main une vieille bottine. À l'intérieur, on lisait cette adresse imprimée : « Meyer, Toronto ».

« Cela vaut bien un bain de boue, dit Sherlock. C'est la bottine volée à notre ami sir Henry.

— Stapleton l'aura jetée là dans sa fuite, fis-je.

— Certainement. Il l'avait conservée à la main, après s'en être servi pour mettre le chien sur la piste. Quand il a vu que tout était perdu, il s'est enfui de Merripit house, ayant toujours cette bottine, et il s'en est débarrassé ici. Cela nous montre qu'il a atteint, sain et sauf, ce point de la fondrière. »

Ce fut tout ce que nous découvrîmes de lui.

D'ailleurs, comment relever des traces de pas dans le marécage où cette surface de fange mobile reprenait son uniformité après le passage d'un homme ?

Parvenus sur un terrain plus solide formant une espèce d'île au milieu de la fondrière, nous poursuivîmes nos recherches avec un soin minutieux. Elles furent inutiles. Si la terre ne mentait pas, jamais Stapleton n'avait dû gagner cet endroit, malgré sa lutte désespérée contre le brouillard. Quelque part dans la grande fondrière de Grimpen, cet homme au cœur froid et cruel était enseveli, aspiré par la boue visqueuse.

Dans cette île surgie du milieu de la vase, nous trouvâmes de nombreuses traces de ses visites, ainsi que du séjour de son féroce allié. Une vieille roue et une brouette à demi remplie de décombres marquaient l'emplacement d'une mine abandonnée. Tout près de là, on retrouvait encore les vestiges des cabanes de mineurs, chassés sans doute par les exhalaisons pestilentielles du marais.

Dans l'une de ces cabanes, une niche à laquelle était fixée une chaîne, puis un amas d'os, indiquaient l'endroit où Stapleton attachait son chien. Un crâne auquel adhéraient encore des poils noirs gisait au milieu des débris.

« Un chien ! fit Holmes, en le retournant du pied. Par Dieu ! c'était un caniche ! Pauvre Mortimer, il ne reverra plus son favori !... Je doute qu'il reste ici des secrets que nous n'ayons pas pénétrés... Stapleton pouvait cacher son chien, mais il ne pouvait l'empêcher d'aboyer ! De là ces hurlements si terrifiants à entendre, même en plein jour. Enfermer la bête dans un des pavillons de Merripit house exposait le naturaliste aux plus grands risques et ce ne fut que le dernier jour, alors qu'il se croyait au terme de ses efforts, qu'il osa s'y décider... La pâte contenue dans cette boîte d'étain est sans doute la composition phosphorescente dont il enduisait son chien. Cette idée lui fut sûrement suggérée par l'histoire du chien des Baskerville et par le désir d'effrayer sir Charles jusqu'à le tuer. Est-il étonnant que ce pauvre diable de Selden ait couru, ait crié — ainsi que sir Henry et nous-mêmes — lorsqu'il vit bondir à sa poursuite, dans les ténèbres de la lande, une créature aussi étrange ?... Il faut admirer l'ingéniosité de l'invention. En effet, indépendamment de la possibilité de tuer sa victime, cela présentait l'avantage d'éloigner du monstre tous les paysans qui, le rencontrant sur la lande — cela est arrivé à plusieurs — auraient eu l'intention de l'examiner de trop près. Je l'ai dit à Londres, Watson, et je le répète ici à cette heure, nous n'avons jamais donné la chasse à un homme plus dangereux que celui qui gît là-bas. »

En prononçant ces dernières paroles, Holmes étendit la main vers le grand espace moucheté de vert qui représentait la fondrière de Grimpen et qui s'étendait au loin jusqu'aux pentes sombres de la lande.

XV
DÉTAILS RÉTROSPECTIFS

Un soir de novembre, âpre et brumeux, nous étions assis, Holmes et moi, au coin du feu qui pétillait gaiement dans la cheminée de notre salon de Baker street.

Depuis l'issue tragique de notre visite au château de Baskerville, mon ami s'était occupé de deux affaires de la plus haute importance. Dans la première, il avait dévoilé l'abominable conduite du colonel Upwood, lors du scandale des cartes à jouer au Nonpareil Club. Dans la seconde, au contraire, il avait démontré l'innocence de Mme Montpensier, accusée d'avoir assassiné sa belle-fille, Mlle Carère, jeune fille que l'on retrouva six mois plus tard à New York, vivante et mariée.

Le succès de ces dernières entreprises, si délicates et si importantes, avait mis Holmes en belle humeur ; je crus le moment venu de discuter les détails du mystère de Baskerville. J'avais patiemment attendu une occasion, car je savais qu'il n'aimait pas qu'on le troublât dans ses travaux, ni que son esprit, clair et méthodique, fût distrait de ses occupations présentes par un retour vers le passé.

Sir Henry et le docteur Mortimer, à la veille de partir pour le long voyage qui devait rendre au baronnet l'équilibre de ses nerfs rompu par les drames de la lande, se trouvaient de passage à Londres. Nos deux amis avaient passé l'après-midi avec nous et ce sujet de conversation était tout naturellement indiqué.

« En ce qui concerne l'homme qui se déguisait sous le nom de Stapleton, dit Holmes, la succession des événements était simple et compréhensible, bien qu'elle nous parût excessivement complexe, à nous qui n'avions, au début, aucune donnée sur le mobile de ses actions et qui ne pouvions connaître qu'une partie des faits. J'ai eu la bonne fortune de causer deux fois avec Mme Stapleton, et tous les points sont tellement élucidés que je crois être en mesure d'affirmer qu'il ne reste plus rien d'obscur dans cette affaire. Reportez-vous d'ailleurs, aux différentes notes de mon répertoire classées à la lettre B.

— Alors, demandai-je à Sherlock Holmes, expliquez-moi de mémoire comment vous êtes arrivé à dégager la vérité.

— Volontiers. Cependant je ne vous garantis pas de ne rien oublier. Une intense contention mentale produit le très curieux effet d'effacer le passé de notre esprit. Ainsi l'avocat, qui possède sa cause sur le bout du doigt et qui peut ergoter avec un témoin sur des détails infimes, s'aperçoit une ou deux semaines après sa plaidoirie, qu'il ne se souvient plus que de très peu de chose. De même, chacun des cas dont je m'occupe chasse le précédent, et Mlle Carère a remplacé dans ma mémoire sir Henry Baskerville. Demain, quelque nouveau problème soumis à mon appréciation chassera à son tour de mon souvenir la jeune Française et l'infâme colonel Upwood.

« Quant au chien des Baskerville, je suivrai de mon mieux l'ordre des événements ; si je viens à me tromper, vous me reprendrez.

« Mes enquêtes démontrent irréfutablement que la ressemblance entre le portrait d'Hugo et Stapleton n'était pas menteuse et que ce dernier appartenait bien à la race des Baskerville. Il était le fils du plus jeune frère de sir Charles, de ce Roger qui partit, à la suite de plusieurs scandales, pour l'Amérique du Sud, où, prétendait-on, il mourut célibataire. Il se maria, au contraire, et eut un enfant, ce misérable Stapleton auquel nous devons restituer le nom de son père.

« Là, ce descendant des Baskerville épousa Béryl Garcia, une des beautés de Costa-Rica, et pour fuir les conséquences d'un vol considérable commis au préjudice de l'État, il changea son nom en celui de Vandeleur, vint en Angleterre et ouvrit une école dans une petite localité du Yorkshire. La connaissance d'un pauvre précepteur, poitrinaire, faite sur le bateau qui amenait le naturaliste en Angleterre, l'avait décidé à se tourner vers l'enseignement et à mettre à profit le savoir de Fraser.

« Ainsi se nommait le précepteur. Mais Fraser succomba bientôt à la maladie qui le minait, et l'école, jusqu'alors en pleine prospérité, tomba peu à peu dans le discrédit. Stapleton se vit un beau jour forcé de mettre la clef sous la porte.

« Une fois encore, les Vandeleur abandonnèrent leur nom, et le naturaliste transporta dans le sud de l'Angleterre les restes de sa fortune, ses projets d'avenir et son goût pour l'entomologie. J'ai appris qu'au British Museum, il faisait autorité en la matière, et que le nom de Vandeleur était pour toujours attaché à une certaine phalène qu'il avait décrite le premier, lors de son séjour dans le Yorkshire.

« Arrivons maintenant à la seule partie de sa vie qui nous offre vraiment de l'intérêt. Stapleton avait pris ses informations et savait que deux existences seulement le séparaient de la possession du riche domaine de Baskerville.

« Je crois qu'à son arrivée dans le Devonshire, son plan était encore mal défini. Mais, dans le fait de présenter sa femme comme sa sœur, je trouve la preuve que, dès le début, il nourrissait déjà de mauvais desseins. Il avait l'intention manifeste de se servir d'elle comme d'un appât, quoiqu'il ne sût pas encore exactement de quelle façon il tendrait sa toile.

« Il convoitait le domaine et, pour en venir à ses fins, il était prêt à employer tous les moyens, à courir tous les risques. D'abord il s'installa dans le plus immédiat voisinage de la demeure de ses ancêtres ; puis il tâcha de conquérir l'amitié de sir Charles Baskerville et de ses autres voisins.

« Le baronnet lui-même se chargea de lui apprendre l'histoire du chien de la famille et prépara ainsi les voies de sa propre mort. Stapleton — je continuerai à l'appeler de ce nom — fut mis au courant, par Mortimer, de la maladie de cœur dont souffrait le vieux gentilhomme, qu'une émotion pouvait tuer. Sir Charles, acceptant comme véridique la lugubre légende, lui apparut également sous le jour d'un être superstitieux. Aussitôt, son esprit ingénieux lui suggéra le moyen de se débarrasser du baronnet. Malgré cela, il serait difficile de justifier une accusation de meurtre contre ce coquin.

« Cette idée une fois conçue, il commença à la mettre à exécution avec une incontestable finesse. Un criminel vulgaire se serait contenté de jouer purement et simplement du chien.

« L'artifice dont il usa pour donner à la bête un aspect diabolique fut un trait de génie de sa part. Il l'avait achetée à Londres chez Ross et Mangles, les grands marchands de Fulham street ; elle était la plus grosse et la plus féroce qu'ils eussent à vendre en ce moment. Il la conduisit à Grimpen par la ligne du chemin de fer du North Decon et fit à pied, sur la lande, une grande partie de la route, afin de ne pas attirer l'attention des gens du pays.

« Au cours de ses recherches entomologiques, il avait découvert le sentier qui conduisait au cœur de la grande fondrière ; il trouva la cachette sûre pour l'animal, et il l'enchaîna à une niche. Puis il attendit une occasion propice.

« Elle ne se présenta pas immédiatement. Impossible d'attirer, la nuit, le vieux gentilhomme hors de chez lui. Plusieurs fois, Stapleton rôda dans les environs, accompagné de son chien — mais sans succès. Ce fut pendant ces infructueuses tournées que des paysans aperçurent son terrible allié et que la légende du chien-démon reçut une nouvelle confirmation.

« Il avait espéré que sa femme le seconderait dans ses projets contre sir Charles, mais elle s'y refusa énergiquement. Elle ne voulait pas entraîner le vieux gentilhomme dans un commerce sentimental qui le livrerait sans défense à son ennemi. Les menaces et même les coups — je suis honteux de le dire — ne purent briser la résistance de la pauvre femme. Elle s'obstina à ne se mêler de rien, et Stapleton se trouva fort embarrassé.

« En s'éprenant d'une belle amitié pour ce drôle et en l'instituant le dispensateur de ses libéralités envers l'infortunée Laura Lyons, sir Charles lui fournit l'occasion qu'il recherchait depuis longtemps.

« Il se dit célibataire et exerça rapidement une influence considérable sur l'esprit de la fille de Frankland ; il la persuada qu'il l'épouserait, si elle parvenait à obtenir son divorce.

« Dès qu'il fut informé que, sur l'avis de Mortimer — avis qu'il appuya de tous ses efforts — sir Charles se disposait à quitter le château de Baskerville, il dressa promptement ses batteries. Il devait agir immédiatement, sous peine de voir sa victime lui échapper. Stapleton pressa donc Mme Lyons d'écrire la lettre pour laquelle elle suppliait le vieillard de lui accorder une entrevue, la veille de son départ pour Londres. Ensuite, à l'aide d'un argument spécieux, il la dissuada de se rendre à la grille de la lande. Sir Charles était à sa merci.

« Le soir, il revint de Coombe Tracey assez tôt pour aller chercher son chien, l'enduire de son infernale mixture et le conduire près de la porte, où, avec juste raison, il savait que sir Charles faisait le guet.

« Le chien, excité par son maître, sauta par-dessus la claire-voie, et poursuivit le malheureux baronnet, qui s'engagea en criant dans l'allée des Ifs. Pouvez-vous imaginez un spectacle plus saisissant que celui de cette énorme bête noire, à la gueule enflammée, aux yeux injectés de feu, bondissant, le long de cette sombre avenue, après ce vieillard inoffensif ! Au milieu de l'allée, la frayeur et son anévrisme terrassèrent sir Charles.

« L'animal galopait sur la bordure de gazon, tandis que le baronnet suivait la partie sablée, de telle sorte qu'on ne remarqua que les pas de l'homme. En le voyant immobile, le chien s'approcha probablement pour le flairer ; mais, le voyant mort, il fit demi-tour. C'est alors qu'il laissa sur le sol l'empreinte si judicieusement relevée par Mortimer. Stapleton le rappela et le reconduisit immédiatement au chenil de la grande fondrière de Grimpen. Le mystère demeura une énigme indéchiffrable pour la police, alarma toute la contrée et provoqua finalement la visite dont le docteur nous honora ici même, il y a quelques mois.

« Voilà pour la mort de sir Charles Baskerville.

« Comprenez-vous maintenant l'astuce infernale qui présidait à ces préparatifs ? Cependant, il serait absolument impossible de baser sur elle une accusation contre Stapleton. Son unique complice ne pouvait jamais le trahir, et le moyen employé était si grotesque, si inconcevable, que son efficacité en était accrue par cela même.

« Les deux femmes mêlées à l'affaire, Mmes Stapleton et Laura Lyons, conçurent bien quelques soupçons à l'encontre du naturaliste. Mme Stapleton n'ignorait pas ses sinistres desseins contre le vieillard ; elle connaissait aussi l'existence du chien.

« Mme Laura Lyons ne savait rien de tout cela ; mais la nouvelle de la mort de sir Charles l'avait d'autant plus impressionnée, qu'elle était survenue à l'heure précise d'un rendez-vous donné à l'instigation de Stapleton et non contremandé par elle. Comme l'une et l'autre vivaient sous la dépendance de ce dernier, il n'avait rien à redouter de leur part. Le succès couronna la première moitié de sa tâche ; il restait encore la seconde — de beaucoup la plus difficile.

« Il se peut que Stapleton ait ignoré l'existence de l'héritier canadien. En tout cas, il en entendit bientôt parler par le docteur Mortimer et, par lui, il apprit tous les détails de la prochaine arrivée de sir Henry Baskerville. Il s'arrêta d'abord à la pensée de tuer, à Londres, ce jeune étranger tombé du Canada, sans lui permettre d'atteindre le Devonshire.

« Depuis que sa femme avait refusé de l'aider à creuser la chausse-trape dans laquelle il espérait prendre sir Charles ? Stapleton se méfiait d'elle. Dans la crainte de la voir se soustraire à son influence, il n'osa pas la perdre de vue trop longtemps. Aussi l'emmena-t-il à Londres avec lui. Ils logèrent à Mexborough hotel, dans Craven street, l'un des établissements visités sur mon ordre par Cartwright pour rechercher un commencement de preuve.

« Il retint sa femme prisonnière dans sa chambre, tandis qu'affublé d'une fausse barbe, il suivait le docteur à Baker street, puis à la gare et enfin à Northumberland hotel.

« Mme Stapleton avait pressenti une partie des projets de son mari, mais elle en avait une telle peur — peur fondée sur sa brutalité et sur les mauvais procédés dont il l'abreuvait — qu'elle n'osa pas écrire à sir Henry pour le prévenir de dangers éventuels. Si sa lettre tombait entre les mains de Stapleton, sa propre existence serait compromise. Elle adopta l'expédient de découper dans un journal les mots composant le message et de déguiser son écriture sur l'adresse. La missive parvint au jeune baronnet et lui donna la première alarme.

« Pour lancer facilement le chien à la poursuite de sir Henry, il était essentiel que Stapleton se procurât un objet ayant appartenu au jeune homme. Avec une promptitude et une audace caractéristiques, il se mit en quête de cet objet, et nous ne pouvons douter que le valet d'étage ou la femme de chambre de l'hôtel n'aient été soudoyés par lui dans ce but. Par hasard, la première bottine remise était neuve et par conséquent sans utilité. Il la renvoya et en demanda une autre — une vieille. Cet incident, très instructif, me prouva immédiatement qu'il s'agissait d'un chien en chair et en os ; aucune autre supposition n'aurait expliqué ce besoin d'une bottine vieille et cette indifférence pour une neuve.

« Plus un détail est futile, ridicule, plus il mérite qu'on l'examine, et le point même qui semble compliquer une affaire est, quand on le considère attentivement, celui qui très probablement l'élucidera.

« Ensuite nous reçûmes, le lendemain matin, la visite de nos nouveaux amis, toujours espionnés par Stapleton dans son cab. Il savait où je demeurais, il me connaissait de vue ; j'en conclus que la carrière criminelle de Stapleton ne se bornait pas à cette seule tentative contre les Baskerville. En effet, pendant ces trois dernières années, on a commis dans l'ouest de l'Angleterre quatre vols qualifiés, tous restés impunis. Le dernier, datant du mois de mai, à Folkestone, a été surtout remarquable par le sang-froid avec lequel le voleur masqué a brûlé la cervelle du domestique qui venait de le surprendre. Je ne serais pas étonné que Stapleton augmentât ainsi ses ressources, de jour en jour plus minces, et que, depuis longtemps déjà, il méritât d'être classé parmi les coquins les plus audacieux et les plus résolus.

« Il nous a donné la mesure de sa décision le matin où il nous a glissé entre les doigts si heureusement — pour lui, — et le fait de me renvoyer mon propre nom par le cocher prouve son audace.

« Dès lors, il comprit que je l'avais démasqué à Londres et qu'il n'y avait rien à tenter dans cette ville. Il retourna à Dartmoor et attendit l'arrivée du baronnet.

— Un moment ! dis-je. Vous avez certainement décrit les événements dans leur ordre chronologique, mais il est un point que vous avez laissé dans l'ombre. Que devint le chien pendant le séjour de son maître à Londres ?

— Je m'en suis préoccupé, répondit Holmes ; ce détail avait son importance. Il est hors de doute que Stapleton ait eu un confident ; mais je suis non moins certain qu'il a toujours évité avec soin de lui donner barre sur lui en lui confiant tous ses projets.

« Un vieux domestique, nommé Anthony, vivait à Merripit house. Ses rapports avec Stapleton remontent à plusieurs années, à l'époque où la famille habitait le Yorkshire. Cet homme ne pouvait donc ignorer que son maître et sa maîtresse fussent mari et femme. Il a disparu du pays. Or Anthony n'est pas un nom aussi commun en Angleterre qu'Antonio en Espagne ou dans l'Amérique du Sud. De même que Mme Stapleton, il parlait couramment anglais, quoique avec un curieux grasseyement. Je l'ai aperçu plusieurs fois traversant la grande fondrière de Grimpen et suivant le chemin que Stapleton avait balisé. En l'absence de son maître, il prenait probablement soin du chien, sans soupçonner toutefois l'usage auquel on le destinait.

« Les Stapleton revinrent donc à Dartmoor, bientôt suivis par sir Henry et par vous.

« Un mot maintenant sur l'emploi de mon temps. Peut-être vous souvient-il qu'en examinant le papier sur lequel on avait collé les mots découpés dans le *Times*, je regardai attentivement le filigrane. Je tenais ce papier à quelques centimètres de mes yeux et je sentis un parfum à demi évaporé de jasmin blanc.

« Il existe soixante-quinze parfums qu'un expert en crime doit pouvoir distinguer les uns des autres, et bien souvent — j'en ai fait l'expérience — la solution rapide d'une affaire dépend de la subtilité de l'odorat. Le parfum me révéla la présence d'une femme, et déjà mes soupçons s'étaient tournés vers les Stapleton.

« Donc, avant même de partir pour le Devonshire, j'étais sûr de la présence d'un chien et j'avais flairé le criminel.

« Mon jeu consistait à surveiller Stapleton. Pour ne pas éveiller ses soupçons, je ne pouvais le faire qu'à la condition de ne pas être avec vous. Je trompai tout le monde, même vous, et, tandis qu'on me croyait toujours à Londres, je vins en secret à Dartmoor. Je ne supportai pas autant de privations qu'il vous plairait de le supposer ; d'ailleurs, pour bien conduire une enquête, on ne doit jamais s'arrêter à d'aussi menus détails.

« Le plus souvent, je demeurais à Coombe Tracey et je n'habitais la hutte de la lande que lorsque je jugeais nécessaire de me trouver sur le théâtre de l'action. Cartwright m'avait accompagné et, sous son déguisement de jeune campagnard, il me rendit de grands services. Grâce à lui, je ne manquai pas de nourriture ni de linge. Quand je surveillais Stapleton, Cartwright avait l'œil sur vous, de telle sorte que je tenais sous mes doigts toutes les touches du clavier.

« Je vous ai déjà dit que vos rapports, expédiés sur-le-champ de Baker street à Coombe Tracey, me parvenaient rapidement. Ils m'étaient fort utiles, et principalement celui qui contenait la biographie de Stapleton. Il me permit d'établir l'identité de l'homme et de la femme ; il affermit le terrain sous mes pieds.

« L'évasion du convict et ses relations avec les Barrymore embrouillèrent considérablement les choses, mais vous dégageâtes la lumière d'une façon très efficace, bien que mes observations personnelles m'eussent déjà imposé les mêmes conclusions.

« Le jour où vous découvrîtes ma présence sur la lande, j'étais au courant de tout, sans avoir toutefois la possibilité de déférer Stapleton au jury. Je vais plus loin : l'attentat dirigé contre sir Henry, la nuit où le malheureux convict trouva la mort, ne nous apporta pas la preuve concluante de la culpabilité du naturaliste.

« Il ne nous restait d'autre ressource que de le prendre sur le fait, les mains rouges de sang ; mais, pour cela, il fallait exposer sir Henry, seul, en apparence sans défense, comme un appât. Nous le fîmes, au prix de l'ébranlement des nerfs de notre client. Nous obligeâmes Stapleton à se découvrir. C'est ce qui le perdit.

« J'avoue que je me reproche d'avoir ainsi mis en péril la vie de sir Henry. Cela tint aux dispositions que j'avais prises. Mais comment prévoir la terrible et stupéfiante apparition de cette bête et le brouillard grâce auquel, à peine entrevue, elle se trouva sur nous. La santé de sir Henry paya la réussite de nos projets. La maladie sera heureusement de courte durée, puisque les médecins affirment qu'un voyage de quelques mois ramènera l'équilibre dans ses nerfs et l'oubli dans son cœur. Le baronnet aimait profondément et sincèrement Mme Stapleton, et la pensée qu'elle l'avait trompé est la chose qui l'a le plus douloureusement affecté dans cette sombre aventure.

« Quel rôle a joué Mme Stapleton ? Il est incontestable que, soit par l'amour, soit par la crainte — peut-être par ces deux sentiments — son mari exerçait sur elle une réelle influence. Sur son ordre, elle consentit à passer pour sa sœur ; mais toutefois cette influence cessa, dès qu'il essaya de la convertir en un instrument de meurtre. Elle avait tenté d'avertir sir Henry autant qu'elle pouvait le faire sans compromettre son mari.

« De son côté, Stapleton connut les tortures de la jalousie. Quand il vit le baronnet courtiser sa femme — quoique cela rentrât dans ses plans — il ne sut pas maîtriser un accès de colère ; ce fut une faute grave, qui dévoila toute la violence de son caractère, si habilement dissimulée jusqu'alors sous ses manières froides et compassées. En encourageant l'intimité des deux jeunes gens, il provoquait les fréquentes visites de sir Henry à Merripit house et préparait pour une heure quelconque l'opportunité qu'il désirait.

« Le jour de la crise, sa femme se retourna subitement contre lui. On avait vaguement parlé de la mort de Selden et Mme Stapleton avait découvert, dans le pavillon du verger, la présence du chien, ce même soir où sir Henry venait dîner chez eux.

« Elle accusa son mari de préméditer un crime. Une scène furieuse éclata, au cours de laquelle le naturaliste lui laissa entrevoir qu'elle avait une rivale. Sa fidélité se changea aussitôt en une haine féroce. Il comprit qu'elle le trahirait. Pour lui ôter toute possibilité de communiquer avec sir Henry, il l'enferma. Il espérait sans doute — ce qui se serait certainement produit —

que toute la contrée mettrait la mort du baronnet sur le compte du maléfice héréditaire, et qu'il amènerait sa femme à accepter le fait accompli et à se taire.

« En tout cas, j'estime qu'il se trompait et que, même sans notre intervention, son arrêt était irrévocablement prononcé. Une femme d'origine espagnole ne pardonne pas aussi facilement un semblable affront.

« Maintenant, mon cher Watson, je ne pourrais, sans recourir à mes notes, vous fournir plus de détails sur cette curieuse affaire. Je ne crois pas avoir rien oublié d'essentiel.

— Stapleton, demandai-je, n'espérait-il pas, avec son diable de chien, faire mourir sir Henry de peur, ainsi que cela était arrivé pour sir Charles ?

— Non ; la bête était sauvage, affamée. Cette apparition, si elle ne tuait pas le baronnet, avait pour but de paralyser sa résistance.

— Sans doute… Autre chose ! Si Stapleton avait été appelé à la succession de son parent, comment lui, l'héritier, aurait-il expliqué son séjour, sous un nom déguisé, dans le voisinage du domaine des Baskerville ? Comment aurait-il pu revendiquer cette fortune sans éveiller de soupçons ?

— La chose aurait été fort difficile, en vérité, et vous exigeriez de moi l'impossible, si vous me demandiez de résoudre ce problème. Je puis discuter le présent, le passé… mais je me déclare incapable de prédire la résolution qu'un homme prendra dans l'avenir… Mme Stapleton a entendu son mari discuter la question à plusieurs reprises. Il envisageait trois éventualités possibles. Dans la première, il revendiquerait cette fortune du fond de l'Amérique du Sud et, sans avoir à paraître en Angleterre, il serait envoyé en possession de cet héritage, sur la simple justification de son identité devant les autorités anglaises de là-bas. Dans la seconde, il se rendrait à Londres et y vivrait le temps nécessaire sous un habile déguisement. En troisième lieu, il se procurerait un complice, lequel, après la remise de toutes les preuves exigées par la loi, chausserait ses souliers moyennant une certaine commission. Par ce que nous savons de lui, nous sommes en mesure d'affirmer que Stapleton aurait tourné cette difficulté.

« Après ces quelques semaines de dur labeur, je crois, mon cher Watson, que nous pouvons nous octroyer un peu de distraction. Ce soir, j'ai une loge pour les *Huguenots*… Soyez prêt dans une demi-heure… Nous nous arrêterons en route pour dîner chez Marcini. »

TABLE DES MATIÈRES

IMPRIMÉ EN UNION EUROPÉENNE
le 18-07-2001
004/01 – Dépôt légal, Juillet 2001
N° d'impression : 8123